Denise

Lotus Land

3:00

Lotus Land

Monica Highland

McGRAW-HILL BOOK COMPANY

New York   St. Louis   San Francisco   Bogotá   Guatemala   Hamburg
Lisbon   Madrid   Mexico   Montreal   Panama   Paris   San Juan
São Paulo   Tokyo   Toronto

For kind permission to reprint copyrighted material, grateful acknowledgment is
made to the following sources:
Doubleday and Company, Inc., Publishers, for material from Homer, *The
Odyssey*, translated by Robert Fitzgerald. Copyright © 1961 by Robert Fitzgerald.
Harcourt Brace Jovanovich, Inc., and Faber and Faber, Publishers, for material
from "Burnt Norton" in *Four Quartets*, copyright 1943 by T. S. Eliot; renewed
1971 by Esme Valerie Eliot.
Alfred A. Knopf, Inc., Publishers, and George Allen & Unwin, Publishers, for
material from *A Hundred and Seventy Poems* (U.K. title *Chinese Poems*),
translated by Arthur Waley. Copyright 1919 and renewed 1947 by Arthur Waley.
New Directions Publishing Corp., Inc., for material from Ezra Pound, *The
Cantos of Ezra Pound*. Copyright 1934 by Ezra Pound.

First paperback edition, 1985
Published by arrangement with Coward-McCann, Inc.

1 2 3 4 5 6 7 8 9 D O H D O H 8 7 6 5

ISBN 0-07-028791-0

Library of Congress Cataloging in Publication Data

Highland, Monica.
Lotus land.
I. Title.
PS3558.I365L6   1985   813'.54   85-11347
ISBN 0-07-028791-0

For
   Clara
   Jordan
   Alexander
And the future

PROLOGUE

1881–1885

"Then I sent out two picked men and a runner
to learn what race of men that land sustained.
They fell in, soon enough, with Lotos Eaters,
who showed no will to do us harm, only
offering the sweet Lotos to our friends—
but those who ate this honeyed plant, the Lotos,
never cared to report, nor to return:
they longed to stay forever, browsing on
that native bloom, forgetful of their homeland."

The Odyssey
Book IX, lines 89–97
Translated by Robert Fitzgerald

SUNG could hardly believe that just three weeks ago, the home village had been as it always was. Only three weeks ago, he and his brothers and sisters were hunkered down—just as on every other evening he could remember—holding their bowls filled with rice, reaching with chopsticks into a common dish filled with red cabbage. The men had come in from the paddies, gossiping after a day's work; cousins and second cousins called to each other across the narrow streets, commenting on the crop, the recent rains, which would keep them for a few days from the extra work of irrigation, the careful opening and closing of the communal ditches.

Three doors down, his cousin Bin Tang told for the hundredth time of the wonderful day he had spent in the Big City, and how he had seen boats five times as tall as their own thatched village homes, anchored in the harbor, their decks swarming with round-eyed devils who claimed to have sailed these giant, floating pagodas thousands of *li* as far as the eye could see, and further, all the way to the Mountain of Gold. That mountain glittered under the sun during the day, and under the moon at night.

Bin Tang had told this incredible tale so many times now that the villagers had almost come to believe in its truth. For each time they questioned him, his story was the same. Yes, the pale-haired men spoke in barbarous tongues, but the masters whom they seemed to serve, living in the strange square houses built of brick on the small island of Shamein in the River of Pearl could speak, however imperfectly, the true language of the sons of Han. It was they, and especially one of the masters, over whose compound waved a strange banner of red and white stripes, holding a white-starred field of blue, who had spoken of the Golden Mountain. He told of riches to be had for the asking, of rice bowls which filled themselves magically at each day's end, of roast pig on every holiday, of vegetables, greener, juicier than even *their* own holiday fare. The *Yang Guektze*, the Foreign Devil, had said more.

He had hinted of women filled with lust, their hair like fine yellow silk, who yearned to close their legs upon the firm and sturdy manhood of the sons of Han. (The women of the village closed their ears at this part of the story or, if they were married, laughed coarsely and clucked with half-joking disdain. The men bandied earthy obscenities that failed to disguise entirely their secret yearning for this forbidden flesh. What if it were true? What if all of it were true?)

The Foreign Master, through his mouthpiece, promised to loan anyone willing to take advantage of his generosity the passage on his floating pagoda, across the seas to the Golden Mountain. They could pay him back later, out of the river of money that would flow into their hands as they helped the foreigners create a stronger magic! A Snorting Dragon that would coast on a canal made of iron, pulling behind it chariots for all who wished to ride, and wagons filled with rice—enough in one wagon to feed the home village for a year—magic plows that turned the soil without the use of a water buffalo, and machines that could stitch a man's jacket in an hour instead of a week, with only one threading of the needle. (Thus it was that the silken-haired, hot-blooded women of the Golden Mountain, not having to work, had nothing to attend to but the pleasures of their men.)

Bin Tang had gone to the Big City for the wedding of his first cousin An Kor. The wedding had lasted three days, and the men had drunk much *mao tai*. It had been at the end of the third day that Bin Tang and some of his cousins had caroused through the city streets, the wine giving them courage. They had joined a huge crowd of rapt young men on the banks of the Pearl River, listening to this Foreign Devil, whose tongue was as golden as the country he described.

Then, the devil spoke only to invite strong young men, gesturing expansively to the floating pagoda behind him. The pagoda would skim down the River Pearl, which would turn into the Great Water, deeper, bluer, wider, wider than any of them could ever see. And after that, the mountain.

The crowd stirred restively. One man, older, bolder than the rest, had called out, "Can we take our women and children, if we wish?"

An almost imperceptible frown crossed the face of the Foreign Devil, who then spoke rapidly to his Second Voice. "Not now," the answer came. "But later, if with your new wealth you want to send for them, they too can ride on the Great Pagoda."

As some of the younger men nervously stepped forward to offer themselves, Bin Tang and his cousins, both sobered and enchanted by the marvels they'd heard of, withdrew a little. . . .

And it was here that Bin Tang's narrative faltered. Here that the good-natured taunts of the village were called out, the part of the ritual that Sung liked best to hear.

"If you had gone, Bin Tang, you could *own* this village!" Sung's father might call out.

And Bin Tang might answer, "Are my ambitions so mean that this village would satisfy me?"

And Bin Yuen, the coarsest tongue in the compound, would grunt, with

10

gross insinuation, "Were you afraid to lose yourself in the Yellow Silk Forest?"

Bin Tang would say loyally, "What more could I ask for than my own old woman, who eats sour plums nine months out of every ten?" And Bin Tang's gap-toothed wife would grin complacently. It was true, she ate her weight in those salted, foul-tasting, dried plums, which were the ancient signal that a woman was carrying a new life. "What need have I for yellow silk, or even gold, when I have sons enough to buy me the best coffin in the province?"

Only Sung's cousin, Sung Jiug, of them all failed to enter into the bantering exchange. "What sort of credulous fools do you take us for?" he would sneer, when he could endure the folly no longer. "Can a pagoda float? Can a canal be made of iron? Can a dragon be harnessed?" And he would walk haughtily through the doorway into his tiny courtyard.

But Bin Tang would remain unperturbed. "It is true," he would say stubbornly. "Go see for yourself—if you have the stomach for it. Then return, and call me a liar."

Here Bin Tang knew he was safe. For he was the only one in anyone's memory who had ventured as far as the Big City. And no one else in the home village had either the wish, the means, the excuse, or the desire to go.

For the last precious second, Sung remembered the village, as it used to be: the two facing compounds—each containing a branch of the same large family, the walls earth-colored like the low houses themselves, each compound filled with busy life; daughters-in-law squabbling over one piece of crockery or other, grandmothers reciting stories of olden times, quoting proverbs to anyone who would listen, the old men pulling their sparse beards in well-earned content, the clean-swept courtyards themselves alive with chickens and ducks and a bad-tempered goose or two, a single cock strutting in display.

Beyond the twin compounds the paddies of the family extended in measured fertile crescents. Each son, as he grew up, knew and worked the land that would be his. Sung's father and his brothers worked hard but happily. Their own fathers had succeeded, after years of toil, in buying from their landlord, who had fallen on hard times—thanks to the gambling of his eldest son—a full hundred hectares.

The young boys, until their time came to work the land, fearlessly bullied the bad-tempered water buffalo, perched confidently on the broad back of each beast, driving them out at dawn, hitching them to plows or waterwheels or the communal threshing machine—whatever the season demanded—or, when they weren't needed, grazing them in the fallow paddies, swearing like men, wielding their switches, spending the long mornings and endless afternoons filling the hours with idle boasts and insults, and extravagant tales of what they would do when they became men.

"It is true," Bin Tang had said, for the last time, one week ago. "Go see for yourself—if you have the stomach for it. Then return, and call me a liar."

The men had been, as always, squatting in the common ground between the two compounds, enjoying the last light before they separated to go into their own homes and the lighting of the lamps.

11

It was Sung's own mother, calling out from the compound doorway, who shattered that life forever.

"Come quickly, my husband!"

Of course, Sung's father had not even looked up. He was a man of dignity, and would not answer unless addressed with the proper respect.

"What is it, woman?" he called negligently over his shoulder.

"A rat," she quavered. Sung sensed something in his mother's voice he'd never heard before. He would know later it was terror.

"And what am I to do about anything as insignificant as a rat?" Sung's father said jocularly. He was, after all, very fond of the mother of his sons.

"This is a dead rat," she said, "or almost dead. I heard it in the thatch. Then it fell just inches from where I stood, and could not run away, twitching on the earth."

Sung felt rather than heard the low, half-whispered chorus of *ai yahs* that rippled through the men of the village. Sung's father was not the first to move. It was his cousin, who never believed in anything, who noiselessly got to his feet and like a shadow disappeared behind the wall of the farther compound. The rest of that family quickly and silently withdrew, saying absolutely nothing, instead of the drawn-out garrulous goodbyes that usually marked the end of each evening meal.

It was not until the gate of the farther compound had been shut, and the bolt pulled through with a grim finality, that any of the men in Sung's own compound had moved so much as a finger.

"What is it, Father?" Sung asked.

But before he answered, his father, staring with unbelieving eyes at the locked gate, called out, "What sort of custom is this? Are we not all one family? Are we not all brothers and cousins?"

No answer came from behind the wall, and once again Sung repeated his question. "Father, what is it?"

"Nothing," Sung's father said. "We must hope that it is nothing. But many of the older ones have said it may be a sign of evil and sickness."

Calling to the other men, Sung's father said with the same boastfulness that the boys used with the buffalo, "Come, let us look upon this creature that has bewitched my wife and made *women* of our cousins across the way!"

The men of the compound hesitated. Sung's father smiled contemptuously and stepped across the threshold. While the men waited shamefaced in the dust, Sung's father came to the gateway of the compound holding the sick rat at arm's length in a pair of fire tongs. Flexing his work-hardened muscles, he flung the rodent as far as his strength allowed.

But the rat was not yet dead. Sung's uncles, cousins, father stood transfixed as the rat writhed convulsively in the fine dust, its tiny paws scratching frantically over its ears and eyes, breaking through the skin of its tender nose. Then, in a final agony, it turned and made a blind rush toward the group at the gate, who recoiled, drawing in their breath. Even then they had not the strength to move but stood frozen as the rat gave a high, shrill, batlike shriek, and fell, finally, limp in the dust.

12

"Come, my brothers," Sung's father said, after an endless moment. "*We* are not women. And besides, the evil lies *there,* dead, outside our walls. Let us ignore this foolish belief." He adopted the skeptical tone of his second cousin who had, for so many years, refused to believe in floating pagodas. "Have any of us *seen* the evil that comes from this omen?"

Resolutely, Sung's father strode back into the compound. Sung heard his voice, roughly comforting his mother. "Come now, old lady, the rat has gone. The remains of our dinner must be fed to the hogs!" And in a lower voice, which carried, nonetheless, outside to where the others stood, "Look sharp, Fu Ming, you must be brave, for the sake of our sons, if for nothing else."

It was this last that moved the men, against their will, into the compound that would become in the next days their prison, and their tomb.

But maybe it was nothing! Maybe Sung's father was right.

Each man went to his own hearth. Each called loudly for tea. More than a few reached furtively back into a secret cupboard where harsh rice wine was stored against occasions like births—and deaths.

The women scuttled in the evening round of chores, their faces drawn, too frightened to cry. Even the children, normally filled with noise and self-importance, stayed indoors this night, close to their parents, and the scant comfort to be received from the last charcoal embers left from the preparation of the evening meal.

Sung's father's cousin was the first to die. They were awakened by his gurgling screams that same night. Sung's father jolted upright, the padded comforter falling from his shoulders. But Sung's mother held fast to his arm. "Do not go. You can do nothing." Then, "For our sons, do not go."

They lay, the still-young couple, their four children sleeping close beside them, listening to the anguished shrieks grow louder, louder still, and then cease, only to be followed by the high, mourning wail of the dead man's wife. The tense silence broke then as one by one the women and children wailed in answer or whimpered in fear. The men said nothing only because they were men. It would be remembered, if anyone survived this, that they had faced their fate without fear.

In the cold dawn, the women of each household lit incense sticks and placed them in earthenware bowls before the scrolls of the household gods. The children were told to stay inside, and did.

Sung's father ventured forth and called out into the morning mists for the menfolk. "We must do our duty," he said. "We must bury our dead. We have no time to send to the temple, nor would the priests come. Perhaps when this is done, prayers may be said, and offerings made for their departed souls. But now we must get my cousin into the ground."

A younger man timidly ventured an opinion. "Would not prudence tell us to take the body outside the compound? We would wrap it in straw matting and bury it . . . later."

Sung's father lashed out. "Are we barbarians? Are we pigs, that we leave the bodies of our relatives to be gnawed by the half-wild dogs of the countryside?" Then he spoke more quietly. "We cannot do that. To leave

13

the body would be to pollute our own fields, and other people who might pass this way. No, we must bury him inside the walls."

Sung was not to see his great-uncle's body, nor the corpses of the two children which they found that morning. But he heard his father, head in his hands, shaking from the awful experience, whispering to his wife what he had seen.

"I could not believe that in so short a time a body could become so swollen and black. Had I not known he was my cousin, I would have thought him some abortion of the nether gods. He had no neck! His face had burst with pustules. Boils covered his body. The . . . infants burst as I touched them."

All that grief-filled day, under a light drizzle, the men of the compound dug a deep ditch along the northern wall. There was no need to ask its purpose. From time to time during the long afternoon, a young mother would approach, her eyes dry, her arms filled with what had once been her greatest joy. Even on that first day, when children sickened, their mothers, to spare themselves the unendurable affliction of watching them suffer, would snuff out their lives with their own hands.

The end of that day saw six of Sung's extended family in the common grave. And still no sound had been heard from the farther compound.

That evening's meal took place, for the first time in Sung's memory, within their own walls. Women watched from their doorways. No jokes tonight.

That night passed without incident. In next morning's dawn, as Sung's father and a few other men gathered after hastily drunk tea, they heard the ghastly shrieks again. But this time, after the moment's horror, they realized these screams came from the farther compound. The screams were followed by a babble of angry voices. Sung's father and his companions rushed to unbar their gate, in time to see the gate of the farther compound opened for an instant, just wide enough for the writhing body of a man to be thrust out.

"Ai yah!" the man screamed. "Is there no mercy?" Whatever else he wished to say was drowned in a gurgle of phlegm and blood. The man's neck was swollen larger than his head. He tore at it as he helplessly watched the gate slam shut and heard the bolt shot home.

He turned. They recognized him as Li Wu, their own distant cousin. Li Wu staggered in their direction—one step, then two.

"What madness is this," Sung's father murmured, "to turn men into animals? To cast out one's own flesh and blood?" The other men nodded in agreement, and Sung's father called out to the tottering figure lit by the early dawn, "Come, Li Wu, come."

A look of half-understanding came into the eyes of the doomed man, as if a last, dim sense of gratitude had entered his failing mind. But it was too late. In the next instant, he pitched forward, groveling in the dirt, struggling toward the open gate of the nearer compound. Then life left him as he breathed out in a last frothing moan, and he lay dead on the bare earth.

Sung's father automatically ran forward, even though he knew in his heart that he could do nothing. But anger rose, transforming him from the usually

14

calm man Sung had known to the voice of avenging justice. With the corpse of Li Wu at his feet, he raised his voice, quivering with indignation, in a shout that Sung would remember all his days.

"Is it for this that we have been born men? Are we not all brothers as the sages of old have told us? Does a man toil all his life for his family only to be cast out when he needs its comfort most?"

He paused, but no sound came from behind the cruelly shut gate.

"Have you no answer?" Sung's father shouted again. And when none came, he called out, "At least we can hope it is shame that keeps you silent." Then, for a moment, he lost all control, shouting obscenities, "Filthy pigs' abortions! Rotten turtle eggs! Dung of incestuous dogs!" He fought for calm. Trembling, he turned to the men behind him, saying, "Let us honor Li Wu with the company of our own dead."

Then in a last defiant roar, "Know this! Our gate stands open for all who suffer, for all who crave the solace of their kin, even as they perish."

The men moved forward to lift up Li Wu's contorted corpse. They gasped. Beneath the torn fabric of his trousers and jacket the flesh slipped under their hands like the skin of an overripe persimmon.

"Courage," Sung's father said, hoisting Li Wu's trunk. "Death from sickness is not to be sought after, but only cowards flee its scourge."

Li Wu's death was the first of seven that day; five in their own compound, two from the farther one. If there was any mercy in this sickness, it was that death came quickly. A sneeze, a feeling of one's bones dissolving, and almost before the death-terror could come the worst agony was over. Death was a swift release.

Indeed, it was the living who suffered most. But as if drawing courage from the bravery of Sung's father, the members of the nearer compound strove to maintain their sense of honor. Of those seventy-six souls only forty-three remained by the morning of the third day. More rodents had emerged from the thatched roofs; they were dispatched with hoes, even as they attacked the sick, and flung into a separate pit. The women of the compound imposed upon themselves an iron discipline; cooking, washing, and keeping their homes in perfect order, spending long hours instructing their children in the history of their family. It was their dearest hope that after this fierce onslaught some of their children would live, and remember.

Even their traditional pattern of mourning, perhaps the only time when women were permitted to lose control, had to be suppressed. It was Sung's mother who expressed it best, though she spoke rarely. "If we gave each of our loved ones the proper mourning, we wouldn't have the time left to cook the daily rice."

Though the gate of the farther compound was closed except when some poor creature was thrust forth, the life of Sung's family was in striking counterpoint to the day sounds of angry fighting, insults, the sudden high piercing wail of a wife bereaved—and at night, the drunken laughter, the click of dice, and groans that were an insult to the dead, the groans of a desperate, depraved lust.

On the morning of the fourth day, Sung's father called his sons to him.

15

"Take all the water buffalo, walk three *li* due north away from our village. Untether them, leave them free, then come home."

"But they will eat the rice, Father!"

"That is of no concern to us now. We must give life where we can."

When they returned, their father was dead. Their mother sat by him, restraining her grief. Sung's brothers died that night. He sat alone with his mother, her face etched sharply in the red light from the charcoal. She seemed calm, sure that he would live. "Always remember your family and your name. Never bring shame upon it. Know that you were born in the village of Yang Jou, fourteen *li* north of the T'ing River, which they say flows north of the River Pearl. They say we are three days west of the Big City. I do not know this, but they say it is true." She groped behind the worn images of the kitchen god and drew forth a packet of yellow papers. "Your father was head man of this compound. These papers say we own this land! Honor your father's memory and remember our name."

Even as she spoke, her eyes glazed. "Don't come near me," she said, and thrust the packet into his hand. "Leave me alone now, with your father."

Helpless, he went outside. The stench of death was everywhere. He looked for someone to talk to; the silence—the echoing silence—made him afraid to go to any other house.

As he stood, uncertain in the moonlight, the gate of the farther compound opened. Once again a man was flung forth ignominiously, followed by drunken shouts. "Go! Die the death of a liar!"

Sung recognized Bin Tang. He stood, swaying for an instant, and then sauntered, almost as if nothing were amiss, through the open gates and sat down in the dust next to Sung. His eyes glittered feverishly. "They say I'm sick over there. Well, youngster, I see you're alive. The stubborn ones live longer." He stared blankly at the little boy. "There was a floating pagoda," he said, "but in truth I was afraid to enter it."

If he had been afraid then, he was courageous in death. He swayed back, his legs uncrossed, his limbs relaxed in peace.

Sung dug his nails into skinny arms. Moving quickly, he went back into his own dwelling. He reached into a storage place for a length of cloth, emptied all the family's supplies—rice, tea, some garlic, and a few dried mushrooms—into this, and tied it up. He unwillingly approached the bodies of his parents, together even in death.

"I'm sorry," he said, and took the slim gold earrings that had been all of his mother's dowry from her ears, then went to the clothes chest, slipped on his father's best cloth shoes, shouldered into his best jacket. He looked around. There was nothing else to take. He closed his parents' eyes, and, moving silently, said farewell to his childhood and walked out of the compound.

He had one errand before he left. He walked nimbly across the paths of raised earth that marked off each rice paddy from the next; he was going to the farther compound, but not to the gate. In the old days, Sung had had a friend—someone to boast with on the water buffalo—a true cousin with the surname of Sung. In nights past, when they had been mischievous boys,

Sung had crossed over this same way. The cousins had whispered to each other through a chink in the eastern wall.

Sung found that chink, and scratched tentatively.

"Are you there, Sung Tsi?"

Astonishingly, Sung Tsi whispered back. "Is that you? They have said you are all dead."

"Do I look like a ghost?"

"You will be if they catch you. They say your family started this sickness."

Sung shrugged. "I'm going to the Big City. Will you come with me?"

"There is no Big City!"

"How is the sickness in your compound?"

"Many have died, but not all. Bin Tang was the only one today. The old ones pray for release. The others are too drunk to care."

"I'm going to the Big City," Sung said again, and his cousin's voice said, *"Wait!"*

In minutes, Sung Tsi was back. "My parents are dead," came his whisper. "You are my friend and cousin. Take this." A twist of paper found its way through the wall. "If I live, I will go with my aunt and uncle. They have lost their son and I will be the heir. This is half my family's fortune. My aunt and uncle will never know the difference."

Sung bent to pick it up, his fingers closing on the hardness of coins. "You are a friend."

A voice on the other side of the wall shouted, "What are you doing there?"

"Nothing, Uncle," Sung Tsi called out.

Sung hesitated, then set out across the paddy's borders to the high, raised road that led south to the River T'ing.

Her impression was one of dark against light, dark against light, as Magdalena Ortiz was hurled by her father past the flimsy walls, where shards of mud had fallen away and would not be replaced until the next rain, which, as he always said, might be never. She flew, in an eternal arc, the entire breadth of the hovel and landed standing up. She thought, with the humor that made him crazy even when she hadn't done anything wrong, that he couldn't keep this up for long; he'd destroy the house before he would make her tell.

Another blow, another trip across the shack. She fell this time on the dirt floor, and wisely decided not to get up. Her father stood over her and kicked her as hard as he could with his bare foot. She tried to protect her stomach, which, as she might have known, only maddened him further.

"Puta! Slut! Large, slovenly pig!" He turned to the woman weeping in the corner. "Do you know what you have raised here? You have raised the Whore of Sonoita!"

Of course, all her mother did was weep. Magdalena had thought often enough, and even told her mother when they had quarreled, that weeping was her only talent.

17

"Llorona," Magdalena had taunted. *"La Llorona!"* and her mother had wrung her hands and wept some more.

Now, Magdalena thought, surveying her mother wrapped like a mourner in her everlasting, worn, black shawl, now I give you a grief worthy of your tears.

Her father's last kick had opened the skin over her eye. She saw the hut through a mist of blood, her wailing *madre,* her father, finally with an excuse to act the brute he always was; those splintering walls, the light between them making the slats into the bars of a prison. She heaved herself up and held out a strong arm to keep her father at a safer distance.

"Enough," she said thickly. "I won't tell you who he is no matter how much you hit me."

He was too much of a coward to meet her direct defiance, and crossing the room with terrible cunning, he began to rain blows upon the cowering woman in the corner.

"Is that the only way you can show your manhood, Papa? Beating a helpless creature who is still stupid enough to love you? She is blameless in this."

"Just tell your father who it is," her mother moaned, rocking, sobbing. "Save us all this suffering."

Magdalena looked at her mother in contempt. Because it was her mother who, spying on her, had found out her secret; had timed the bloody rags that hadn't appeared for three months, had followed Magdalena out in the early dawn, when she had torn up her morning *quesadillas* and fed them to the few scrawny chickens her family could afford. And her mother had committed the betrayal; for all her wails, her cherished bruises, her sobbing in the night when her husband came home maddened with the cheapest *mescal* in Sonora; for all that, she had told her husband that Magdalena was with child.

Her father, his rage spent for the moment, stuck his thumbs in his belt and appraised his eldest daughter. He had to look up at her.

He decided once again to match himself against a person who wouldn't fight back. "Mindless crone," he snarled at his cringing wife. "*You* were the one who let her go away to work at the *ranchero!* My pesos were not enough for you. You thought I could not provide for this family!" His words rekindled his fury. Again he rained blows upon the unresisting old woman. "Do you see what happens now when the hens begin to crow?"

"Just tell him, Magdalena! Save me from this *cama de piedra,* this bed of stone. . . ."

That's it, Magdalena thought. Beds were not meant to be made of stone. She had a flashing memory of clean, whitewashed walls, cool linen sheets kicked aside, a man, his skin pale against hers, who had taught her something that would make her forever unfit for this hopeless village of Sonoita; he had shown her a man's tenderness to a woman.

"Whoever he is," her father gritted between his blackened teeth, unconsciously continuing her thought, "whoever it is, *I, I,* will make him marry you, you great ungainly slut! I will make him marry you, or I will kill him."

Blood from where he had opened her forehead dripped into her eyes. Heedless, she dashed it aside. "That is enough, *manoso,* coward! You turn

18

your head when you pass him in the street! You are afraid to say good morning to him. It is he who grants you your stinking living, though he knows you are too stupid even to herd the goats. It is he who keeps you in *mescal* and pesos to buy your diseased women, to insult a wife who never did you harm. Bantam! *Pajarito!*" she shouted, seeing him shrivel. "Bantam rooster! You could not kill him! You cannot reach—you could not reach to the top of his boots!"

They knew who it was then. As she had spoken, the realization of what she was telling them penetrated even their limited perceptions. She saw what she would remember as her father's final look of sincere and total disbelief; that she, Magdalena, "that great ungainly cow," could attract anyone, much less Señor John Frederick Smith, a *gringo* and the richest man in the world, a man who had the magic to draw wealth from the burning sand of the desert, which gave the villagers only prickly pear and a few stunted goats. John Frederick Smith, who owned all the land from here to Caborca, and for all they knew, beyond.

It had been a year since she had gone to work at the *ranchero*. She had started as a *cocinera*, kitchen maid, and even that had been heaven. She had tasted vegetables, and beef, and *buñuelos*. For the first time in her life she had learned there was food beyond *tortillas* and beans. She was, of course, not allowed to serve in the dining room, but one morning when Señora Smith had, screaming, banished her children from the house and locked herself up for her weekly bout of "headache," Magdalena had seen the children, sweating and pale, standing forlornly together in the dust, resigned to their unhappiness, and she had forgotten the rules. She tucked up her long skirt, stepped off the veranda where she had been removing tiny stones and gravel from tonight's *frijoles de olla,* and had gone down on her hands and knees in the dust.

While the children had stared goggle-eyed, she'd found ten little rocks of exactly the right size. "*Mira!* Look! I can hit this rock with this one!" She sat down on the veranda steps, flicking the rocks against each other with her fingernails, her skirt still rucked up about her sturdy, smooth legs. "If I hit this rock with *this* one," she said, speaking in Spanish, "then I can throw them on the back of my hand like *this!*"

The children, miraculously, laughed, and she laughed with them. John, her Juan, had told her later that he had seen it all from the upper veranda, that he had fallen in love then, not just with her statuesque, magnificent body, but with her other beauty. She had reached out to his children; she had given them kindness and laughter.

All she knew was the next day she was called in by the housekeeper, given a shirtwaist and a long cotton skirt, and told that from now on she would take care of the Señor's children. She hated the clothes, but she loved her job. Her life had changed. She had learned some English. She had been allowed, because the children had insisted, to take her meals with the family. She had inevitably taken the place of the children's mother, who could not stand the relentless harshness of the Sonoran climate. Magdalena had learned to love the children she cared for, and finally, their father.

"Do you know what your life will be now?" her own father said soberly.

19

"They say there will be a road through here soon. A road from nowhere to nowhere. You will live by that road. Our village alone," he said ironically, "is so poor we cannot afford a full-time whore. You will live by the lust of travelers, of scum, of bandits, and you will be lucky even to find that work. Your offspring's pale skin will be your continuing shame. You will starve, no doubt, but by the time you do, stupid girl, you will long for death."

He turned and left the shack.

From her mother, still huddled in a corner, came an altogether strange voice, the steady low-pitched voice of hard reason.

"It doesn't have to be that bad, *mija*. Come over here and sit by me."

Her mother unwound the shawl from her work-worn face and long gray hair.

"This is not the first time such a thing has happened in Sonoita, nor will it be the last. You can always marry Pedro Ramirez. Sleep with him tonight. Get him drunk! Get a little drunk yourself. Then tomorrow, say it was the drink, and his irresistible charm, that made you do it. And then," incredibly, she began to laugh, "that is when you start to cry."

Magdalena could scarcely believe her ears. "You, you are telling me—"

Her mother interrupted. "You are not a fool. Has it never occurred to you that you are taller, stronger, and of greater beauty than any of your brothers and sisters?"

Magdalena stared at this tiny woman smiling devilishly at her in the hut's gloom.

"Hasn't it occurred to you that you are taller, stronger, and of greater beauty than your father?"

"*Madre de Dios!* It is true that when I was younger, I," here she hesitated, "I felt I must belong . . . somewhere else."

Her mother laughed again, grimly. "Indeed, I was told I would live in a palace and never want for clothes or food . . ."

"What happened?"

"He searched for gold. He stayed here for a few days and told me he would be rich. I believed him! But if men are liars, they are also blind. The morning that man was gone I knew what I had to do. Your 'father' was the best of the worst in Sonoita. By midnight," again she spread her lips in a toothless grimace, "he was a family man."

"*Pobrecita,*" Magdalena said. "No wonder you cry." She thought for a minute. "What was he like, this man you say might have been my father? Where did he come from?"

"He was a liar like all the rest," her mother said with sad complacency. "He said he came from a City of Angels. All I know is for a few days I was with him there, in heaven."

Again, Magdalena could only stare. It was as if, all at once, the riddle of her life had been explained; why her "father" had always hated her, why she had always hated this place the others were content to call home, why she had gone to the bed of Señor Smith, not with a sense of strangeness, but with the brooding knowledge that it was the right thing to do.

Her mother was muttering, deep in her own dream. "The suffering comes later, *mija,* and it never stops. The rape of the wedding night, the brutal demands of a man who becomes more of a beast with each child you give him. The beatings, the sickness. Truly a woman's life is a bed of stone—"

"Cabrón!" Magdalena jumped to her feet. The word was for both of her fathers. She gazed inward, into the future. This town, if you could call it that, these six crumbling huts, the pig killed once a year for Christmas, the drunkenness, the babies who died every summer during the heat. She thought of poor Pedro, a born cuckold, who, even if he never realized what had been done to him, would be a laughingstock for the rest of his life. His skin was far darker than hers, and he was an ugly dog.

"Of course," her mother said craftily, "there is another way. You go to the *ranchero* and tell your *amigo* that if he does not help you, you will tell his wife, and the Franciscans who come through here once a year, and all the men who work for him. He will be shamed into. . . ."

Perhaps it was the *gringo* blood that coursed in Magdalena's veins, blood of a man she would never know, but whoever he was, he'd had the courage to, ah!, to go from nowhere to nowhere. Magdalena admired that.

In long afternoons, before and after love, John Frederick Smith had tried to explain to this great, glorious, simple girl where *he* had come from.

"The north!"

"What's that?" she would say sleepily, playing with the short golden hairs that grew in a triangle on his broad chest.

"There are trees," he would say, homesick, "green trees!"

"What are those?" she would say again, poking him to make him smile.

"They have tall buildings," he would say. "People live on top of each other. There is water, water as far as you can see. . . ."

And already her mother's daughter, Magdalena would dismiss him as a liar, but such a handsome one.

Even if what he said was not true, she knew there must be a better place to live than Sonoita. Even if she found nothing but death, it would be better than enduring the slow, lingering, living death of her mother.

"I would rather die than go to John Frederick, *mi madre,*" Magdalena said, "and maybe I will die. I'm leaving here. After I've been gone for a week, you may tell him I went off into the desert in order to spare him shame."

"You think any man is capable of shame?" her mother sneered.

"Ojalá que sí!" Magdalena said, and for some reason laughed. "I *hope* he suffers. Because I know I am going to."

"Do you want to die, my daughter?"

"No! I want to live. You can tell that pig, your husband, I have gone north to find my real father and to become very rich."

Her mother turned her face to the wall. "I shall say the prayer for the dead for you every night," she murmured. Then to herself, "Truly, life is a bed of—"

"I'm looking for a featherbed," Magdalena said, "with silk sheets! What do you think of that, *vieja!"*

Her mother didn't answer.

Impatiently, Magdalena looked around for anything she could take. She had her shirtwaist and skirt from the *ranchero,* and she had the clothes on her back. She had the sandals John Frederick had bought her when she began to eat meals with his household. She could not bring herself to take her mother's food—there was so little. She ate two stale *tortillas,* standing there, and a mouthful of cold beans. She tilted the *olla*—the earthenware jar that kept water miraculously cool and fresh in this land of burning sand—and drank it dry.

"You're really going to do this?" her mother asked.

"Cómo non? What else is there for me to do?"

Her mother considered, then reached inside the innermost folds of her ragged clothes and pulled out a knife.

Once more, Magdalena's mother had astonished her.

"I have kept it against bandits, against my husband, and against life itself. There is only so much one woman can bear." Again she gave that incongruous laugh. "Now you take it. You will need it more than I."

She made no move to embrace her daughter, but instead, holding the sharp tip of the blade, thrust the handle of the weapon upward toward her.

"Madre . . ." Magdalena said, but her mother turned her face to the wall.

"I will never see you again," she said.

There was no answer to that.

Magdalena twitched aside the ragged serape that served as their front door. For the last time she looked at Sonoita. Six huts, one *cantina,* two pigs that rooted listlessly, waiting for extinction.

The *ranchero* lay an hour's walk westward; she would not see its white-washed adobe walls again, or hold those children, or . . . .

The sun had an hour left in the sky, but the worst of the day's heat was gone. She began to walk across the desert. In twenty minutes, she could see nothing, *nothing.* Sonoita had dissolved in shimmering heat. She was in a world of cactus. Already she had the unwelcome company of two buzzards that wheeled slowly above her at a discreet distance. She broke off a piece of greasewood as the sun set and began to walk as a blind person might, sweeping the branch in front of her to discourage the *alacránes,* scorpions, and worse, the *cascabela,* the treacherous, undulating, sidewinding rattler.

"I'm not afraid," she said as the moon came up, and to her surprise, she wasn't. She had lived in the desert all her life. She knew how to endure out here, walking at night, finding meager shade for the day, taking both food and drink from the barrel cactus, or if she had to, the inhospitable prickly pear. She was strong! And with every step, she put the miserable shacks of Sonoita farther behind her.

Looking at the night sky, she found the seven bright stars of the Great Bear, the two lowest pointing to the fainter star that John Frederick had told her was the way "north." With her branch rhythmically sweeping a safe path in front of her, Magdalena kept her eyes on the heavens, and on that elusive star. She found herself believing there was a City of Angels.

"So this is Chicago, the Hub of the Middlewest," Clifford Creighton said to himself, but deliberately spoke aloud, almost drowned by the hubbub of the big, drafty, railroad station with a more motley mob of human beings than he'd ever dreamed existed.

What he'd expected, he didn't really know. Industry? Excitement? A chance for a young man to get ahead? But nothing from his boyhood in Baltimore had prepared him for this.

He had spoken only for his own ears, so he was surprised to hear a high, whining, nasal voice behind him say, "That's right, mister, this is Chicago, the Big Windy City."

He turned and saw a half-grown boy of thirteen, his face grimy, bifurcated between nose and mouth with the twin green streams that Clifford had already grown to expect since he'd left his gentle, sheltered home.

"Windy is right," Clifford Creighton said. "Wipe your nose, boy."

"What kind of talk is that?" the boy said, casually smearing an already crusted sleeve across the offending spot. "You talk funny."

Clifford Creighton shivered as a particularly cold blast swirled through the gray, gloomy reaches of the station. The hundreds of weary travelers, packed into this vast shed like animals, did absolutely nothing to mitigate the fierce cold. Clifford felt in his bones that he'd never be warm again.

"So do you," Clifford said, conscious of feeling utterly alien, the slightly slurred tones of his Baltimore accent sounding soft against the harsh twang of the boy facing him. "What's your name and where are you going?"

"My name's Roscoe. I'm not going anywhere. When we got here four years ago, Dad said this would be a fine town for a new beginning. A couple of weeks later, he got the pneumonia. Ma's home with the consumption and what's left of the kids. I come down here every day, carry a few suitcases, fetch a sandwich for a traveling man or two, divide what I get between Ma and me. I got to get out." He stopped his narrative to hack wrackingly, pathetically, into his sleeve. "While there's still time," the boy finished up.

"You don't make Chicago sound like the home of opportunity," Clifford said.

"Christ almighty! *Geez,* mister! Horses freeze solid and fall over dead in the street every day. I've seen people fight themselves senseless over a piece of bread." He eyed Clifford. "A real gent don't have a chance unless he brings his pile with him."

Roscoe's words worked on Clifford's already burgeoning loneliness, and as he looked at these strange, rough citizens—all of them foreign, whether they were "American" or not—his heart sank. He realized that all of them were there to *escape* from Chicago. With rising panic, he realized that he had spent almost all of his ready cash to get here. His hand automatically reached for his letter of credit. It represented his entire small patrimony, nothing anyone could call a "pile," and he knew, sickeningly, that it would do nothing more than pave the way to failure—in Chicago.

A disappearing train left vacancies in space and sound. In the vacuum, Clifford heard his own voice asking himself, as much as Roscoe, "What do I do now?"

The boy's answer was pat; a much-thought-about, yearned-for, concrete dream.

"I'd go to California. It don't cost much for a man with money. But

23

divvying up the way I do with Ma, saving up fourteen dollars is going to take me till I'm twenty. I'll be a dead man before that, mister. And who knows how much it'll cost in eight years? As soon as people get wise—"

But Clifford had heard only the first part of the boy's speech.

"Fourteen dollars! That wouldn't get you anywhere. Believe me, I know! I spent a lot more than that just to get here, and that's without a sleeper!"

But the boy was deep in his dream. The cold and his family apparently forgotten, he droned in a half-chant, "Two thousand miles! Two thousand miles across prairie and desert, all the way to the Promised Land. Two thousand miles for only twelve dollars." He opened his eyes. "Of course, it's fourteen now. That's what I mean, mister. I'll never save up enough. They keep raising the price on me, the bastards!"

Roscoe gave Clifford the twisted smile of a small child whose every illusion had been wrung out of him in cruel city slums. "Oh, the streets aren't paved with gold, but there's sunshine there right now. Sunshine, mister, can you believe it? There's oranges to eat when you can't get a job, and you can sleep on the beach when you can't get a room. But that'd be the worst. Because they say there's land and work almost for the asking. You don't need your pile to make it to California. All you need is fourteen bucks to get you there."

Clifford started as he felt a plucking on his sleeve. He drew his eyes away from the boy and saw a woman, a mother, holding a very sick child. She breathed illness, and in spite of himself, Clifford pulled back.

"A dime, mister," she whined. "Just a dime. A pickpocket stole all our money. I got to have a dime, just to feed the kid."

"Get lost, sweetheart! You and everybody else!" the kid snarled. "Tell your hard-luck story to the stockyard kings!"

She left, and Roscoe sniffed, giving Clifford that by-now-familiar cool, appraising stare.

"What'll it be—what'd you say your name was?"

"Clifford. Clifford Abercrombie Creighton."

"That's a classy mouthful, Clifford. So what'll it be? Shall I call you a cab? I'll call you a cab for a nickel."

All the worries of his twenty-one years crashed in on Clifford again. *What will it be? Where will I go? What can I do with my life? Where can I go?*

"I'd thought—" he began.

The boy interrupted him. "The fare's four dollars to the Palmer House, don't let him take you the long way. The Palmer House is ten dollars a night, that don't include breakfast. Don't eat in the dining room, it costs too much. Try for the free lunch in the bar down the street, but don't take your wallet, or it'll be your last meal. Don't drink the milk. I know a man who—"

"Why, that's fourteen dollars just for one day," Clifford interrupted him.

"You can add real quick," the boy sneered. "If the Palmer's too steep for you, you can try the Ritz. Ask for a room on the top floor. You'll have to sleep in your overcoat, but you'll save a few bucks."

Clifford didn't hear. Fourteen dollars, he said to himself. He could scarcely face the prospect of a day and night in this God-forsaken hole, and even after that day and night, what then? His imagination tried to carry him that far and failed. What job? What place to live? What possible chance for companionship? Two crazy images clashed in his travel-weary brain. Horses, pale blue and rigid, falling, skidding on icy pavements, and another picture, perhaps equally bizarre, of oranges on trees, each one a radiant, miniature sun . . . and himself, happy in the saddle, reaching up to pick a golden world.

"I'll *risk* it," he said, resolution flooding in, sweeping out his sense of confusion, of despair. "I'll *do* it. Where's the train, boy? Where do I get my ticket?"

"I'll take you there," Roscoe said. "I'll help you. For a nickel."

The scrawny youngster headed off like a shot. "Follow me," he called over his shoulder, and Clifford did, with difficulty, as Roscoe threaded his way through the shifting crowd to a ticket window distinguished from the others by a garish display of crudely printed posters: WHERE THE WESTERN MOUNTAINS MEET THE SEA! LOS ANGELES, PEARL OF THE PACIFIC! CALIFORNIA! LAND OF SUN AND OPPORTUNITY, and a last dazzling example of pictorial art showing a young man, a well-muscled adventurer, smiling—his regular teeth flashing under a luxuriant moustache—holding an enormous cornucopia of tropical fruit and glittering coins cascading into a golden pyramid beneath his expensively booted feet: CALIFORNIA! the legend read in bold-face sans-serif type, WHERE A MAN CAN MAKE HIS WAY!

In contrast to this glowing vision of success, the ticket seller directly beneath showed gray, wizened features, a straggly tobacco-stained moustache that failed to hide his irregular, blackened teeth, as he permitted himself a grudging half-smile at his potential customer.

Before Clifford could speak, the seller set him straight.

"If you're thinking of California, mister, you'd better step on it. Train's leaving in an hour, and the last car's filling fast."

"When's the next train after that?" Clifford asked, hoping to sound, if only to himself, like a prudent man who had his hands on all the ropes.

The ticket seller looked grim, vague.

"Next week, mebbee. Who knows what the charge'll be then?"

As Clifford hesitated, an immigrant family shouldered past him and up to the window.

"You still holding those tickets? Remember me? I'm Jenson. I had to sell my wife's silver candlesticks to do it, but I've raised the rest of the money!"

As Jenson stacked up enough coins to take a family of seven across the prairie, his wife—stocky and peasantlike—confirmed his statement by snarling an epithet at her spendthrift mate, then turned away to weep as the ticket seller scooped up the last of her dowry.

"Better hurry, Clifford," Roscoe said. "These Hunkies are going to fill up the train."

Clifford made a quick calculation. It would be the sensible thing to wait a week and think things over. But seven days at fourteen dollars a day? Wouldn't it be better, wouldn't it be more—*fun*—to spend that money in Los Angeles?

The muscled adventurer in the poster beamed down approvingly. Clifford squared his shoulders in half-conscious, self-mocking imitation as he stepped up to the ticket window.

"One," Clifford said, "for California."

"That's the spirit!" Roscoe said, as Clifford watched his money disappear.

The ticket seller handed him his piece of smudged cardboard.

"That all you got?" he said, nodding at Clifford's single scuffed Gladstone bag. "You'd better lay in your supplies. I *told* you, the train's leaving in an hour."

"Supplies?" Clifford asked.

The ticket seller permitted himself another tobacco-stained smile. "Thought this was a luxury Pullman, did you, son?"

Clifford felt his elbow being jiggled familiarly, and turning, saw a smiling redcap, who had appeared as if from nowhere.

"Call me Amos, suh," he cheerfully intoned. "I can square you away for California. What you needs is a little food, a lot of drink, and a blanket to wrap up in at night. I can get that for you in an hour."

"Would it be possible for you to reserve me a sleeping compartment? I'd be willing to pay a little extra."

Roscoe snickered; his nose loosened disastrously. The redcap ignored him and said reassuringly to Clifford, "The whole *car* is a sleeping compartment, mister! Now don't you think anything more about it. Go on over to the station bar, load up your belly on whatever they've got. Roscoe and me'll get your gear and meet you at the gate in forty minutes."

Not until he'd ordered a third beer did it occur to Clifford to wonder how it was that the redcap had known the boy's name.

Forty minutes and a bellyful later, Clifford arrived at the gate for the immigrant train to California. He was one of at least five hundred would-be California adventurers, each one more noisy, raucous, and odoriferous than the last. Clifford struggled to keep his feet in the crowd.

Then Roscoe darted through and, grabbing him unceremoniously by the arm, led him past nursing mothers, whining children, exasperated fathers, through the gate and there, God help him, was the train.

The ticket seller had told no lie when he'd said it was not a luxury Pullman.

Giving him no chance to protest or change his mind, Roscoe hustled Clifford down the long platform to the last car. Amos was waiting there for him.

"You're in luck," Amos said, forgetting for the moment his obsequious Southern manners, "I've got you a corner seat."

Clifford swung up the steps and into the train, followed by his two mentors. He had expected at worst a hard coach seat but what he saw—two roughhewn hard wooden benches that traveled the length of the car, facing inward, only to meet identical, long, wooden benches facing outward, where in a civilized train the aisle ought to have been—made him turn to his companions in dismay.

"Why, I—"

"There's your stuff," Roscoe said. "We got you a corner, and the window seat, away from the commode at the other end. They say things get pretty ripe in here, but you can stand on the back platform right out the door." Roscoe grinned devilishly into Clifford's stricken face. "Cheer up, mister! We got you the best seat on the train!"

Clifford gazed unbelievingly at the "best seat," a few square feet of hard wood bench marked out by two five-gallon jugs. He noticed, among those pushing in to fill up this present-day circle of Dante's Inferno, a cunning sharper looking to snatch that "best seat," and Clifford surprised himself, moved quickly, sat down in what was to be his corner for the next two thousand miles.

He gazed up in mute reproach at Roscoe and Amos.

"Knowing you was from Baltimore," the kid said smoothly, "we got you rye. 'Cause that's what they drink down there, ain't it?"

"That's right," Clifford said, surprised. "How'd you know that?"

"We got you ten gallons," Roscoe went on. "Save some for the other side of the Mississippi," he said, almost choking on his own witticism.

"What do I *eat*?" Clifford asked.

"They was out of almost everything," Roscoe said, making it sound as if the shortage of provisions was Clifford's fault and not his own, nor the store's. "But we was able to get you this ham. It's big! And one thing about ham, it lasts!"

As he spoke, he unrolled a matted khaki-colored old blanket, revealing one of the biggest hams Clifford had ever seen. Against the gray winter light, seeping through the streaked window of the car, the ham was a porcine summation of all the world's affliction.

"What do I sleep in—*on*?" Clifford asked helplessly.

Roscoe snapped the blanket. "Right here! The army's finest. Wrap yourself in this, and pray. If it was good enough for our Union boys, it ought to be good enough for you."

In Clifford's eyes, the matted cover looked indeed like a survivor of Gettysburg. A wounded survivor.

And suddenly it dawned on him. "This is *it*?" he asked incredulously. "This is what you bought me? This is what I'm taking? What about drinking water? Do they have it on the train? What about . . . bread?"

Roscoe looked up at the redcap. The redcap went into a dream. "Don't worry 'bout that! Res' your mind on where you goin'. Lordy, Lord! America's promised land. You can quench your thirst with oranges once you get there! You can live off the land, brother! You can live off the rich, green, rollin' land!"

The car had filled beyond its normal capacity. Just the other side of the jugs of rye, Clifford heard a child pleading for attention. "I'm sick, Ma, I'm going to be sick."

"In California," the exalted redcap continued, "a man can make his own way."

Clifford recognized the words from the poster.

With a dreadful lurch, the train began to move out.

"I'm going to throw up, Ma," the kid said, and he did.

"How much do I owe you?"

"How much you got?" Roscoe said innocently.

"Twenty dollars, ready cash . . ."

"Yo'ah a lucky man, suh," the redcap said, his accent shifting downward to total unintelligibility. "We done got yoah grub foah eighteen dollah. Caish on de barrelhaid."

Wordless, as if hypnotized, Clifford pulled out his wallet, counted out eighteen in cash.

Another lurch. The train began to move in earnest.

"Eat an orange for me," Roscoe said. He gave a last grimace, and he and his companion were gone.

Clifford settled back in a daze, only half aware of his traveling companions, the train, the acrid smell of his small neighbor's vomit.

Had he looked through the window, had he even cared to, he would have seen his two friendly "guides" in close conversation, dividing their take; he would have been unable to hear Roscoe's sneering, "Man! Was that an easy quickie!"

In the already fetid air of the crowded car, Clifford looked, unbelievingly, at the chaotic scene. If his Uncle Peter and Aunt Pauline, with all their Baltimore gentility, could see him now! In spite of himself, in spite of everything, he grinned. Just four nights ago he had dined with them, had spent the rest of the evening in their pretentious drawing room.

"You're sure you won't reconsider, Clifford?" his Uncle Peter had said, as if discharging a final obligation.

Clifford toyed with the thought of teasing them, but noticing his Aunt Pauline's increasing tenseness, her fingers tightly interwoven, he renounced that selfish pleasure.

"No, truly, Uncle Peter," he said, "I'm sure I've decided for the best." His aunt's fingers relaxed.

"To stay here would be asking too much, not only of me, but of you," he went on, interrupting the first words of his uncle's polite protest.

"I know that everything has happened very fast—"

But in truth it hadn't. Actually, he knew, as they did, that his father's suicide had marked the end of a long, indeed, irrevocable, series of events. His mother's death, following almost immediately on his own birth, had left his bereaved father with what he had always known was an almost insupportable burden. His father had always been kind, even devoted, but he lived in the memory of his beautiful dead wife and not in the growing interests of his son.

Clifford remembered the long nights of his childhood, spent in the rented rooms of a row house, his father working, alone, at chess problems, after tucking his son dutifully into bed. He could see now that his graduation from the University at Charlottesville, the Lawn and the Rotunda, which he had left only two weeks before, holding his freshly lettered degree, had been the signal his father had long awaited; an ironic reprieve, the license to take his own life—to tender it to his bride, still young and beautiful in death.

Clifford knew now that this had meant a final release for his father, an escape from lonely rooms at night, from a career which had long since ceased to interest him, and also a release from the family dinners—the first Sunday of each month—when his younger brother Peter, successful and rising in Baltimore society, married to the fashionable Pauline Harkness, had summoned them to interminable afternoon hours, long dinners after church, terrapin soup in the elaborate silver tureen, advancing through the baked clams, the standing roast, the sugary pudding, and then, without even a brandy for solace, the next three hours, spent in this very drawing room, as his cousins, chubby and untalented, stumbled through the *Minuet in G, Fur Elise,* and *In Hanging Gardens,* their first "crossed-hands" piece.

And over it all hung the heavy rebuke, the heavy unspoken rebuke. How kind Peter and Pauline were, how forbearing, for never putting into words their discomfort, their embarrassment, at having to entertain thus, to acknowledge, their poor, almost failed relations.

Clifford's father had at least left him no debts. Indeed, Clifford appreciated the fact that even now he had a letter of credit for two thousand dollars in the inner pocket of his waistcoat—a small figure, he knew, in the great world of eastern finance, but one that represented a thousand tiny deprivations on the part of his father—his father who had raised him, given him affection, seen him through the university, and said an honorable goodbye, his duties discharged.

Not so his Uncle Peter, whose offer of a lowly clerkship in his law firm had been tinged with condescension and contempt.

"After all, Clifford," his uncle had said, "I know my obligation. I wouldn't turn my back on anyone who bears the family name. Of course you have a long way to go, and you and your father's frivolous interest in the arts is probably not the best preparation to appear before the bar. But at least you can start out with *Coke on Littleton,*" he said, making the process sound as dry as dust—as Clifford suspected it would be.

"I want to be frank with you," his uncle continued. "You cannot expect a full partnership for years—perhaps never. My girls will inherit everything. Their husbands, if they marry—" here he paused to fix Clifford with a meaningful stare—"may be expected, rightfully, to take over the firm."

Clifford thought it over. He thought of *Coke on Littleton,* of days spent in tedious research, of evenings listening to *Für Elise.* He was seized by near panic and heard himself blurt out, "No, Uncle! No. I'd thought I might—I thought I might—go west, instead."

And when he saw his uncle sigh, he knew it had been a hollow offer.

"West?" Uncle Peter said, unable to conceal his relief.

"Yes, *west,*" Clifford had answered, and reaching into his imagination to grasp some name, "yes, west, to Chicago."

"Chicago!" his uncle exclaimed. "Why that's the beginning of the wilderness!"

"I hope so," Clifford had said, dryly. And, he thought now, grinning, if Chicago had not been quite the kind of wilderness his uncle had meant, he had certainly come into contact with the savages. In fact, he was going west with some.

He laughed out loud at this and found himself back in the present being

stared at. If he wasn't mistaken it was one of the Jenson kids, a boy of ten or
so, wearing overalls a few sizes too big for him, the legs loosely rolled above
the ankles, showing scuffed hand-me-down boots. But all this, in contrast to
the infamous Roscoe's costume, was of a fierce cleanliness.

The boy in turn saw something in Clifford that might have pleased his
mother. In spite of what struck the boy as strange, citified clothes—
Clifford's well-tailored suit of gray-blue traveling tweed, his six-button
lapeled waistcoat, his pinstripe shirt, his gray silk ascot tie knotted firmly
about his wing collar—the clean-shaven lean face above all this elegance
looked friendly and honest. Clifford's hair was a clean and ordinary blond,
his eyes brown. In the farmboy's view, Clifford's hands, long-fingered and
well-kept, looked strong but unused. His open face had taken its share of the
sun.

"My ma sent me," the boy shyly said, "to see if you might like to trade
some of your ham for some of our bread. It's homebaked," he added.

"I'll bet your name's Jenson."

"Gee, mister, how'd you know that?"

"Oh, I know a lot of things," Clifford smiled, teasing him gently, and then,
relenting, "I saw your dad getting the tickets in the station."

"Ma says Dad is a damn dreamy fool, and she's not much for swearing.
But Dad says it's going to be a whole new world. He's sick of the prairie and
all those rows of corn." The kid's eyes added an anxious silent question:
What do you think, mister?

"I don't like to take sides in a family argument," Clifford said diplomatically, "but I think I'm with your dad."

The confidence in his voice surprised him. He felt in his pocket for his
pearl-handled clasp knife, hitherto used largely as a masculine ornament, to
whittle amusing figures as he lounged away moonlit nights on the porches of
the now-forgotten Southern belles of Charlottesville. He unfolded the
knife's longer blade. He saw how inadequate it looked against the ham's
huge, solid bulk. But, he thought, those dreary Sunday dinners had not been
a total loss. He knew from his Uncle Peter the right way to carve a ham. He
cut through the fat, five inches down from the hock, starting the first cut, and
was immediately rewarded by seven broad smiles. Thus encouraged, he
continued slanting down with his second cut to finish the triangular piece and
carefully lifted out the moist, pink wedge.

"Gee, mister," the Jenson boy said, "that's neat!" He reached out his
hand and Clifford saw how clean his fingers were.

"Hold on," Clifford said. "That's just for starters. Now we get the first
real slice." And inserting the blade an inch beyond his second cut, he sliced
down through the meat until he felt the blade bite into bone.

"What's your name, son?" he asked as he pulled out an evenly cut slab of
ham that his Uncle Peter would have had to praise.

"You've just said it," the Jenson boy said, laughing.

"How's that?" Clifford asked.

"I'm Sunny, Sunny Jenson," the boy said. "My real name is Sven, but
that's hard for some folks to say, so I'm always called Sunny—not because

30

I'm a boy—that'd be Sonny, you know," and he spelled it out. "No, it's Sunny, like the sun."

"That's great," Clifford said, wondering if this could be an augury of the future, half laughing at himself as he thought this, but not rejecting the possibility.

Sunny held the ham wedges carefully between thumb and forefinger and threaded his way cautiously down the aisle where the Jenson family took up a good part of the center bench. Clifford was rewarded by the distant, dazzling smile of Mrs. Jenson, and in thirty seconds Sunny was back, carrying with him half a loaf of crusty homemade bread.

"Oh," Clifford protested, "this is far too much!"

"Ma says keep it, you look like you need it."

Clifford laughed, not knowing quite how to take that. He cut another slice of ham for himself, hacked at the heel of the bread, and bit into what would be the first of many memorable meals. In the crowded "free lunch" of the Station Bar, Clifford had stood among men three deep. In his natural shyness and excitement about the trip, he had contented himself with a hard-boiled egg and a limp pickle.

Now, rolling west, he found himself famished. He bit with relish into his crude repast. It was delicious and wonderfully salty. He looked doubtfully at the jugs beside him—one on the bench, one beneath the seat—taking up in their wicker-covered bulk as much room as another passenger. The redcap, in slapdash generosity, had provided one of the jugs with a battered tin cup, which sat rakishly on its neck next to Clifford like a dented top hat.

Removing it, Clifford grasped the tightly wedged bung, balancing the remains of his sandwich precariously on his lap. When he'd finally worked the bung free, he tilted the heavy jug very slightly forward and poured two fingers into the cup. He replaced the bung, took another bite of his sandwich, and tossed back the Baltimore rye with a silent toast: California!

The raw liquor scorched his throat. His eyes filled with tears. "Almighty God!" he breathed quietly.

He felt the warmth circling out from the vicinity of his solar plexus, finished his sandwich, and poured another shot. Relaxing for the first time in three days, he leaned back against the rough siding of the car. He looked for a moment at the wintry landscape, a few outlying farms, each one more doleful and deserted-looking than the last. Soon they became fewer, more widely spaced, and with great stretches of prairie between them.

He turned his attention to the interior of the car. There must have been a hundred people, twenty-five to a bench, and all the ragtag, cherished belongings each one of those hundred deemed necessary to start a new life. It was true. Clifford did have one of the four best locations in the car, and the other ninety-six passengers had already begun what would become an eleven-day game of musical benches. The grubby mother of the vomitous child on the other side of Clifford's rye had cleaned up the evidence of her child's sickness with a filthy rag, and prevailed on the person next to her to change places—whether in chagrin at her child's social error, or horror at Clifford's drinking habits, was hard to say. And so it was throughout the car.

A few hard-faced men had already pulled out decks of cards, oily from long use, and meeting each other's eyes, had begun to congregate at the far, less desirable end of the car, for what would be an increasingly rowdy, dangerously rancorous game of poker. The family men, scandalized for their wives and children, had begun their move, person by person, little by little, toward the end of the car that opened onto the rear platform, and the one spot of possible fresh air on all the train.

Each move brought with it an attendant shuffling of bundles, box lunches, bags, parcels, valises, postmanteaus, an occasional farm implement badly wrapped in burlap, with vocal accompaniment of "Oh!" "Excuse me!" "Watch that bag!" And sometimes, a shy introduction and an exchange of names.

The first day passed in the beneficent haze of Roscoe's rye. Clifford smiled on all. But inevitably the time came when he had to answer the call of nature. He was young and well-brought-up enough to be self-conscious as he picked his way to the other end of the car, apologizing to those he inconvenienced by his passage. A last maneuver through the poker game brought him to the crude toilet. Clifford opened the door and gasped. Already the stench seemed to him unbearable. People had relieved themselves with abandon, and only the vaguest idea of the location of the commode. A few—Clifford could hardly believe his eyes—had used their fingers as toilet paper and wiped their fingers on the walls. Now he fully understood Roscoe's and Amos' praise of his own location. And going back through the car with less politeness than on his first journey, he pulled aside the door to the rear platform. The air was smoke-filled, and dust and cinders from the engine flashed past. His nostrils drew in the smell of honest dirt. He relieved himself off the end of the train, watching with pleasure the golden airy chain his urine made before it hit the roadbed. If Aunt Pauline could see me now, he thought gleefully, and again laughed aloud.

That called for another drink! And another. He caught Mrs. Jenson's disapproving, maternal eye on him; he bowed to her, and sent along another slice of ham. The afternoon slid by, and early evening. They ate like lesser kings that night. Most of these immigrants were farmer folk and had set out on this mythical journey with all manner of biscuits, relishes, preserves, and lovingly packed boxes of cold fried chicken.

And still the train went on. The winter sun had long since disappeared, a waxing moon glittered down on endless, endless tracts of blue and silver snow. The prairie landscape was as strange and foreign as the moon. The hundred travelers in the car drew closer against the alien outside. Children cuddled to their mothers, voices hushed. Even the sharpers held down their action to give the babies time to get to sleep.

A conductor came through to light the lamps—three of them, hung from the ceiling, swaying erratically with the movements of the train, turning the car into an exotic kaleidoscope of light and shadow. Families reached for quilts, for blankets; mothers cradled children in their laps. A few unwrapped cumbersome mattresses and spread them in the aisles.

Clifford took off his ascot, unbuttoned his waistcoat, loosened the top button of his shirt, and let out his belt one discreet notch. He even, after a self-conscious glance about him, pulled off his boots and stowed them safely under his seat. That was about as far as he was prepared to go, since there were women in the car.

Others were not so fastidious. One burly farmer two benches over stripped down to his long johns. This did nothing to improve the heavy, humid, human smell that already lay in the car, a palpable miasma. Clifford sat straight up, head back, propped safely by the end of the car on one side and his trusty jugs on the other. Through half-closed eyes, sipping appreciatively from his cup, he watched, though he felt obscurely he shouldn't have, the communal process of undressing.

His eye was caught by a young woman sitting a little beyond the middle lantern. After what seemed to be a few minutes of hesitation, she shyly began to unbutton the high, tight collar of her shirtwaist which extended, in the fashion of the time, almost to the point of her plump little chin. She unbuttoned three buttons, then five. It was a tantalizing, endless process. Clifford watched transfixed, swaying to the movement of the car in his rye-induced trance, as the girl unbuttoned all the way down to her waist. And still she seemed to feel constricted! She raised one shoulder, then the other, then tentatively she allowed the garment to slip downward until her smooth white shoulders gleamed in the lantern light, and her low-cut camisole showed the firm, round swelling of her breasts.

God Almighty! Clifford poured himself another two fingers of rye.

He had never seen such an intimate display of womanhood. It was a revelation, and though he knew she was not deliberately provocative, he felt himself automatically responding—the nerve ends of his manhood tingling with an absolutely delicious combination of drunkenness and desire.

He watched the gentle rise and fall of her bosom, until his own flesh betrayed him in a way entirely unexpected. His eyes closed and he went to sleep.

He woke to a bleak dawn. The children who had been angelic visions the night before were howling for attention. His eyelids felt grainy, his head throbbed as he looked out over the snow-patched waste. This was only the second day! He lurched outside to relieve himself, and the merciless pitching of the car made him retch. His throat screamed for relief. A drink, please God, of cold, pure spring water.

He stumbled back inside. Several of the babies desperately needed changing. His dream girl of the night before had evidently caught a chill. Her blouse was buttoned up again; she was blowing her nose with a dejected air. God, he was thirsty! He straightened up, broke a chunk of bread off the remains of Mrs. Jenson's bread. The first bite was unbearably dry in his mouth, and almost without thinking, he poured himself a full cup of rye.

All that night Sung walked at a slow steady pace, each step taking him farther from the only world he had known. He moved mechanically, aware only of the numb sense of loss. Whenever he felt loneliness overcoming him, he remembered his mother's last words, drew new resolution from them and from the hard reality of his cousin's gift.

Before the moon had reached the western horizon, he recognized a small cluster of dwellings straddling the path—the village of Fu Yi, which had been, till then, the farthest reach of his travels. He remembered the day his father had taken him with him to speak to the village headman of the communal responsibility for maintaining the southward path. The headman's wife had treated him not like a child but as a grown man, placing a cup of tea before him. As he'd sat at the square table, listening to his elders politely exchanging courtesies before they discussed the practicalities of their problem, as he sipped the hot liquid noisily, he caught a shy glance of approval from his father, and after they had left—the two men agreeing on the work crews for the following week—his father had said to him, "You have behaved well, my son."

Now, as he slowed his steps, the guardian dogs of Fu Yi roused themselves and ran out barking. He half hoped to hear his presence challenged when he shouted at the dogs to drive them back, but he saw the disorder apparent even in the moonlight—gates ajar, doors ajar, and three figures lying dead in the first courtyard into which he looked.

No sounds of mourning reached his ears. Stepping back on the path, he continued his journey, wondering how far the deadly grip of the fatal disease extended. Was the whole world dead? Was he destined to walk forever alone?

Dawn found him at another village, the name of which he did not know. Here, too, the silence of death. But Sung was hungry. Gathering his courage, he went inside the compound and through the first open doorway. By now, the sight of an old woman and a child huddled lifeless held no fear for him. He crossed swiftly to the kitchen area. A few embers still smoldered in the charcoal stove.

Blowing the white ashes, he brought the coals alive and burning. He searched among the pitiful bits of kitchen crockery and found what he was looking for. Ordinarily, the women of his village had taken soup and other succulent dishes—the noonday meal—to their men in the paddies. But there were days when the fields to be worked lay so far from the home village that the men carried their own meal, a more primitive one—rice that cooked as they walked—in a portable charcoal brazier. Sung found tongs, transferred his fire, poured water still warm from the woman's last attempt at housewifery, and flung in a handful of his own rice. He nursed the fire for a few more moments, stored away some extra bits of charcoal, and set out again at a brisk pace. As long as he kept moving, the air against the stove would keep the coals alive. In an hour, he would have a meal.

By noon he had reached what he thought must be the River T'ing. In the time he had been walking he had not seen a living soul. He stopped, astonished. He had never seen so wide a stretch of water. As he stood, mesmerized, two figures appeared on the towpath of the farther bank. As Sung hesitated, wondering whether to call out to them, one of the men caught sight of him and shouted to his companion, "Look! A living ghost from the fields of death!"

Sung raised his hand to wave, starting to call out a denial, but with the high-pitched cry *"Ai yah!"* the men had already fled.

34

Sung fed his stove a lump of charcoal and considered. The river flowed at an exasperating slant, blocking his southward journey. He could see from the current it was too deep to cross. His road ended here. His mother had said to continue south until he found the eastern road. Once again he gauged the current, and making his best, his only, choice, he followed the towpath on his side—southeasterly, he guessed. He hoped for a crossing, and in less than an hour he saw the camel-back span of a gracefully arched stone bridge. Ordinarily, he might have gazed in amazement. Now, he matter-of-factly crossed it and continued on a road that finally turned due south.

He judged he had gone several *li* when, in the merciless blaze of midafternoon, he saw a village ahead of him and recognized the signs of normal life. The dogs ran out to greet him with snarls and barks. He could see men working in the outlying fields, and boys his own age tending the bad-tempered water buffalo. Nearing the village itself, he could hear the voices of the women calling back and forth as they went about their domestic tasks. His long journey had made him thirsty. The dogs snarled at his heels, but he went on and approached the open gate of the compound, calling out in the courteous phrase his father had taught him, "Greetings from my village across the river. I humbly crave permission to refresh myself, to take advantage of your generosity, to—"

The women stared at him in horror. The one said, "From beyond the river?" Another shouted, "Get back, son of a dog! Disease-bearing vermin!"

Sung heard a movement behind him and turned to see two young men, their faces twisted with loathing and fright. One of them picked up a clod of earth and threw it at him. It caught him squarely on the hip.

"Get away, run off, filthy turtle egg! Go north, across the river, and die."

It was not the pain but his father's strongest insult that stung Sung into rage. He bowed mockingly. "I desire a pot of tea," he hissed. "If it is not outside your gate in the time it takes water to boil, I will walk inside your compound and personally spit on each of your unmannerly first-born sons!"

A collective gasp answered him. Sung walked in the direction of the compound. "I thirst, *Lao Ma,* Old Mother," he said to the most ancient woman. "Might a stranger ask politely for a pot of tea?"

The second of the young men dropped the clod of earth he too had held. Sung could hear them muttering behind him. He stood quiet, idly swinging his stove to keep the coals alive. There was a scurrying in the compound, an extended, whispered conversation. Then the same old woman whom Sung had addressed tottered on bound feet and, beseeching the mercy of the gods in a tremulous voice, placed an earthenware teapot just outside the corner of the gate.

Forcing himself to swagger fearlessly, Sung picked up the pot, then returned to the exact center of the road. He put the spout to his mouth and sucked noisily. The hot liquid, mixed with indrawn air, cleared his dusty throat and warmed his stomach. As he took his second, gulping swallow, he felt the light sweat on his face and neck. With it came a delicious sense of fresh coolness as the air stirred against his skin.

Still savoring his power, he deliberately prolonged the time he needed to empty the pot. As he sucked in the last mouthful, a few leaves came with it. He chewed on them, tasting their bitterness, and with his tongue tucked the cud into his left cheek. Knowing that no one in the village would ever touch what he had held, he bowed again, holding the teapot within his two hands.

"I thank you for this gift of rare porcelain," he said. "I'll treasure it always, and piss in it every night!"

He had gone too far. Though the two young men dared not approach him, they renewed their attack, hurling clods of dirt at him and calling on the village dogs to set upon him.

Sung turned his back to them, and though he wished to run, as some of the missiles found their mark, he would not allow his attackers that satisfaction. Instead, he walked with dignity at a modest pace, and when one of the snapping dogs missed his heel, he turned and placed a well-aimed kick in the soft part of its throat. The animal retreated, howling, as the remainder of the pack withdrew to a safe distance.

With the fading curses of the village behind him, he continued on his southward journey, thinking that he had much to learn, things which his father, a man of honor, had not thought to teach him.

He was careful to give the next village he came to a wide berth by detouring across the lesser paths of its paddy terraces. Even the village following that, about three *li* farther on, he skirted. His anger had left him, and he realized the extent of his fatigue. In the shadow of a small clump of bamboo he put down his bundle after looking carefully about to make certain he was not observed.

Walking to the nearest, newly irrigated paddy, he filled his small cooking vessel and replenished it with rice. The last embers of the charcoal revived as he blew upon them and added two more pieces from his limited supply of fuel. As he waited for the rice to cook, his eye was caught by the sight of three tender new shoots thrusting up within the grove. Going over to them, he snapped them off carefully above the earth, broke them into smaller pieces, and thrust them in with the rice. As his meal cooked, he tried to estimate the distance he had traveled. He knew that soon he must come to the Eastern Road or else his mother had been mistaken. He refused to consider this possibility. Nor could he believe that Bin Tang, in the grip of death, would have lied to him.

Enjoying the feeling of the crisp bamboo shoots that he chewed together with the cooked rice, he felt his strength return. At the same time he was aware of his need for sleep, and since the sun was already low in the west, he feared that in the dark he might miss the road to the east. He decided to remain in the grove for the night. Going to the other side of the bamboo clump he relieved himself, and then returning to his bundle, he pillowed his head on his father's folded jacket and went into a fitful doze, his dreaming filled with images of the River of Pearl, the Floating Pagoda, the Mountain of Gold.

At the first light of dawn, eating the cold remnants of his evening meal as he walked, he started out again, due south. The few villages he passed stirred with normal life, and he felt he must have gone beyond the boundary of the black pestilence. Though he was observed curiously by the men going early to the fields and the boys driving out the buffalo, he felt no hostility from them. Indeed, one smiling, motherly woman called from her doorway, saying, "Are you lost, my son? You are young to be alone so far from home."

Her friendliness emboldened him to ask her for fresh tea, and he smiled to himself, thinking it was fortunate he had not carried out his threat.

By midmorning he came to what he knew instantly must be the Eastern Road. For the last *li* the pace of life had quickened. Larger buildings, no longer simply the dwellings of farmers, stood on either side. The Eastern Road was wide, wider than he could have ever imagined, but still it bore so many carts, wheelbarrows, herds of swine, that from time to time the air was filled with oaths and demands for passageway.

Sung faltered, then turned eastward. He had walked no more than two *li* when he heard the creaking wheels of a cart overtaking him. Turning his head he saw that it was pulled by an animal larger than a dog, smaller than a buffalo, with long, comical ears. A friendly faced man sitting on one shaft of the cart, flicking this animal from time to time with a whip, called out to him.

"I can see you have walked a great distance, *Siao di di,* Little Brother. Where are you going with such determination?"

"I look for the Big City and the River of Pearl."

"You have thirty *li* still to go."

Sung acknowledged this information with a single nod of his head, betraying with no outward sign the happiness that suffused his being. There *was* a Big City. If that was true, he might find there the Floating Pagoda.

"Put your bundle into the cart, and hop up onto the other shaft. I dare not stop this stubborn beast, for if I do, it will lay back its long ears and sing to the sky in a voice of brass!"

Sung did as he was told. At first he found it difficult to keep his balance, but then he settled to the jerky rhythm, saying *zia zia,* thank you, in syllables broken by the jerking of the cart.

"Where do you come from, *Siao di di,* Little Brother?"

Sung clamped his jaws shut, looking straight ahead.

"Never fear," the man said in friendly tones. "I too grew weary of drudging in the paddies of my father, driving out the stupid buffalo. There are other ways to live. I go now from town to town selling my goods. I see the world. Though I am not yet a man of great wealth, I control my own days. The time may come when I may wish for a wife and sons but if it does, I can purchase my own building and sell from there. I am a merchant," he said proudly. "No son of mine need dirty his hands in a landowner's mud. Meanwhile, in the bigger towns and the Big City, I can drink wine when I wish, served to me by a willow maiden, and then, if I wish. . . ." He broke off, with a wide grin. "But you are perhaps too young for that yet, Little Brother."

"I may be young, merchant," Sung said, answering the challenge, "but I can do a man's work."

To Sung's surprise, the merchant burst into laughter. "With seeds of such heat, you'll have many sons of your own."

Sung rode with the merchant that day and the next. When they stopped that night at an inn, Sung had his first taste of wine, and slept outside the door while the merchant laughed with a willing willow maiden.

Toward the end of the second day they reached the outskirts of the Big City. It was everything Bin Tang had said, and more.

Almost at once they were surrounded by beggars, eyeless women holding up babies with running sores and stumps where their limbs should have been. "Alms, master, alms to the starving poor who bring you good luck."

The merchant cleared a way through with his whip. "You must harden your heart, Little Brother, and not be deluded. These beggars have their own guild, and through threats of disease they extort money from those who fear them."

By now the streets were lined with every kind of shop, with teahouses and eating places, with merchants selling kites, pots, rare silk, adornments of jade and gold—more riches than Sung had ever dreamed existed.

The merchant's voice shattered his reverie. "I stop near here to replenish my merchandise. Wherè do you go now, Little Brother?"

"The River Pearl," Sung said, and then gathering his courage, "I have been told I can see upon it . . . floating pagodas."

As the merchant reined his donkey to a stop, that creature laid back its ears and gave a shriek unlike any sound Sung had ever heard. He leaped from the cart and snatched up his bundle.

"*Wait,* Little Brother! I understand now what you seek. But when you find it, it will be more like the Five-Storied Tower." He pointed to a hill a little beyond them, and Sung gasped at the sight of the biggest building he had ever seen, rising above the hill in five tiers, each marked with curving eaves of gleaming green tile.

"Follow this road. It will take you to the river, and the island of the foreign devils who own the great boats. Be careful to whom you speak along the way. Kwanjou, which the foreign devils call Canton, is not always safe for children alone."

"May the gods repay you for your kindness."

"I know you will prosper; for as you have said," the merchant added, laughing, "you can already do a man's work."

Sung dogtrotted down the street, keeping his eyes to the road, which was now paved with cobblestones, letting nothing distract him from his aim. He could never remember precisely how far he had gone, or how long it had taken him, but when he was stopped by a crush of shouting men, he was confronted by what he knew must be the River of Pearl, though its waters swirled past in silt-laden eddies the color of mud.

Suddenly it seemed so easy. There was the floating pagoda, looking, as the merchant had said, like the Five-Storied Tower; there was the crowd Bin Tang had spoken of, moving in eddies as did the river, stirred first by cowardice, then courage. Sung worked his way through the crowd until he could see, in front of the great ship, a table spread with papers, behind which sat two men whom he knew must be the foreign devils, their eyes round, their heads and faces covered with red fur.

While the others still hesitated, Sung stepped boldly forward. "I want to go to the Mountain of Gold," he said. "I will—"

The rest of his sentence was drowned out in the devils' roar of raucous laughter. "You are too small," one of them said in his barbarian accent. "Come back in five years. No, come back in ten!"

The men behind him, perhaps to cover their own fear, took up the cry. In a rage, Sung struck out at those closest to him, kicking and hitting with all the frustrated anger and sorrow of the past week.

"He has the temper of a scorpion," one peasant howled, holding his shin and hopping, and the crowd's laughter found a new focus in him.

The barbarians saw an advantage in this. One of them climbed on the table, and shouted out, "See? A mere child is willing to go, because he has heard of the wealth of the Golden Mountain."

He looked for the boy, to hold him up before the crowd as an example, but Sung had disappeared.

Sheltered between bales of silk and crates of tea, Sung used up every oath he had ever learned. He kicked the silk until his feet were sore. Reason returned when he had spent his anger. These foreign turtle eggs would not deny him. He settled down, safely hidden, to wait.

As he watched, he noted where the coolies were loading the great ship, chanting in pairs as they carried the bales and chests on their poles. As afternoon lengthened into night, he saw where the enlisted workers entered into the bowels of the ship. Sung began to see a pattern. Once they had signed, and the barbarian's chop had stamped the paper, they were given their first wages and encouraged to celebrate this new beginning at a teahouse just across from the ship. Sung could see that it was more than tea—poured liberally for them out of glass bottles—a strong wine that gave them the courage to walk with unsteady steps across the gangplank and vanish into that new life.

Sung waited, as a yellow moon rose over the river, turning it finally into pearl. Recruiting continued far into the sultry night. As a group of five drunken peasants emerged from the teahouse, Sung tensed himself. He willed himself invisible and fearlessly strode with the men across the gangplank. The gods smiled upon him. As soon as he reached the ship he went swiftly along the outer walkway to where the coolies were loading the last of the bales and crates.

Unnoticed, he stepped quickly inside, making sure there was no way he could be trapped, and waited patiently, another hour, until the coolies had finished their work. Only when they had gone did Sung climb up among the bales of silk, making a nest for himself among that soft firmness. He ran his roughened hands across it. "Truly, I am already rich," he told himself. "Not every man has a bed of silk."

His bundle yielded up two dumplings saved frugally from his last meal

39

with the merchant. With a full stomach and a mind at peace, he curled up, allowing himself to sink into a deep sleep. For the first time since terror had shattered his old world, he felt no fear. Even the sounds of the ship's cables being cast off, the pulsing life of the ship as it slowly slipped down the river failed to disturb his deep, regular breathing, the peaceful slumber of a ten-year-old boy.

She thought, as she slowly swirled up into consciousness, that she was still lying in the shade of the *barranca,* where she had fallen to her knees in exhaustion and pain. Then she thought, since she could see only gray in front of her eyes, that she might have died and was waiting in one of the anterooms of Purgatory—Heaven, if she was lucky—waiting for her Last Judgment. Then she thought of her mother's holy picture of the Pains of Hell—a woman with long hair, up to her waist in flames, and discarded *that* possibility. Because, whatever else had happened, there was no longer any pain.

She heard a voice—far from heavenly—that of a man, an old man, seemingly muttering to himself, "*Ai mamacita!* At least these *pendejo* rains have stopped."

She felt her shoulder jolted. "So tell me, *mija perdita,* orphan, are you dead, or are you alive? Or have you decided yet?"

"It would be hard to say," she heard her own voice reply.

"I have yet to hear the dead speak," the voice came to her, unimpressed.

With tremendous effort, she turned over. A room swung into view—low-ceilinged, walled with adobe.

She focused on a face, rough, weatherworn, grotesque, which was pushed down to within inches of her own.

"*Que feo esta,*" she said, forgetting her manners, "how ugly he is."

He regarded her for a moment. "Well, when it comes to that, you are no beauty."

She tried to raise herself on her elbow, then fell back. He laughed.

"Get away from me," she said weakly, "you smell like a goat."

"How should I not?" he snickered toothlessly. "I am a goatherd."

She closed her eyes. "Well, at least I'm not in Hell."

"Some people might argue that, my daughter." He laboriously made his way across the hut and built up his guttering fire into a tiny blaze. "I kept some of today's milk for you, in case you survived. Do you feel strong enough to drink it? There are those who say it has more nourishment than the Blood of Our Lord."

"This milk has hairs in it," she observed, when she had finished off the lukewarm mess.

"What are you, a queen?"

"My mother used to ask me that. . . ."

Then suddenly she was crying.

"I have to tell you it is all right," he said to her. "The baby is gone, perhaps you do not remember. I found you half-drowned, not just in the

40

waters of this rat-sucking flood, but in your own blood. I am used to delivering the mothers in my flock who have troubles when they drop, otherwise you would have been in Hell. . . . Come now, quiet down. Don't you hear what I'm telling you? Your trouble is over. You can go home."

"What was it?" she asked, almost inaudibly. "What would the baby have been?"

"A well-formed boy, with suspiciously light skin. Even considering the question of the *gringo* blood, I gave him the appropriate burial, under a *jalapeño* bush, which his *machismo* will continue to nourish for several more seasons."

She felt her stomach churn.

"If it had been a girl I would have put the tender corpse under the roots of my prickly pear—because, as they say, a woman is soft inside as the pulp of *la tuna,* but oh—" and he timed this rustic sally to duck out of the way as she feebly tried to strike out at him, "if you make a soft woman angry, she can be painful as the spines of the prickly pear itself."

"There," he said, satisfied, now that he had provoked her. "Have no fear, you will live."

He pulled up a rude milking stool, sat down by her pallet, and looked at her shrewdly. "I already said, that baby, *pobrecito,* was no *moreno*. What happened, did you get in trouble in San Diego? Wouldn't the shifty, stupid *bolillo* help you? Did he bring you out here and leave you where the road stopped? You can't have come all this way yourself. It's forty miles, it would have taken you at least a week."

While he was speaking, the girl drew herself up in the rough bed, her emaciated face showing a confused series of emotions, which he could not fathom.

"San Diego," she finally said. "One week! What a joke! Listen, you crazy old friend, I am not such a weakling that I would lose a baby or anything *else* in one week of walking. I come from the town of Sonoita!"

It was his turn to stare at her. "Is that far from here?" he asked politely. "I have never heard of it. Is it a small town?"

"Smaller than a fly dropping, and twice as unpleasant." But she was smiling broadly and shaking her head. "One week! I have been walking northward from it for a little over *two months!*"

"Liar!" he said.

"No! Why should I lie? I went three times through my fingers and toes, and the moon went twice through its cycle."

"But there is nothing down there! A man without water would die in two days."

"A man maybe," she said. "A woman born in the desert can live anywhere." She looked down to where her wristbones protruded cruelly in the firelight. "I will say this, however. There were those who thought me fat before I left."

"They say this is harsh land, where we are now," the goatherd said speculatively, "and it is true, *I* live here, but the Sonoran Desert—"

41

"What else could I do? It was not so difficult. I had little choice. I could only walk. I walked at night and slept in the day, in shade where I could find it, by greasewood or in a gully."

"A man dies without water very shortly."

"A woman has the sense to open a barrel cactus, or failing that, to scrape the spines from your vicious prickly pear."

"But the snakes? Weren't you afraid of the *cascabela?*"

"I was afraid all the time. There are more out there than you think, though what they can live on is hard to understand. The first one I saw was coiled and ready to strike. I stood in the moonlight until he changed his mind and went away. After the first week, I stopped sweeping my path clean and prayed to find the snakes. I would kill them, and eat them. They were beautiful in their own way."

"But the scorpions!"

"They aren't so beautiful. I *am* afraid of scorpions! I would pray only to see big ones. Because the small ones, as you know, are a ticket to Heaven."

"God was with you." The old man could no longer doubt her story.

"You are right," she said. "I have never looked at the heavens so much. And by the end of the third night, when I noticed I was still alive, I knew I was one of the lucky ones that God watches over." She smiled. "I used to try to tell my mother that, but she would never believe me."

He thought of the lost baby, but wisely kept his silence. It was not for him to judge the actions of a girl as brave as this.

"You are a *mujer de partes,*" he said thoughtfully. "Your mother would believe you now, I think."

"My mother would thank you for saving my life." She laughed. "My mother would say *I* do not have the manners to remember to thank you. But you must not think me ungrateful."

Thus reminded of his own manners, the goatherd got up and crossed to where *frijoles* simmered on his fire, along with a succulent leg of *cabrito,* baby goat. He broke it at its joint, giving her one piece, keeping the other, and swung the beanpot over to the floor between them.

She was ravenous, but she was prudent enough to eat slowly. After she had finished, she leaned back, closing her eyes, enjoying the security of warmth, safety, repletion.

Only then did the goatherd venture to remark, "You have told me where you came from, but not where you're going."

In the same dreamy tones in which she had told of speaking to the *cascabela,* she said, without opening her eyes, "I go north, until I reach the land of the *gringo.*" She opened her eyes and gave a devilish grin. "The land of the rich blond men!"

"Jezebel," he said, "Magdalen!"

"My mother knew that when I came from the womb. Magdalena is the name she gave me."

The goatherd cackled. "Well, *sinvergüenza,* your journey is almost ended."

The girl sat up and swung her legs to the floor.

"*Cuidado!* You do not want to start the bleeding, you great bony ox. I believed you when you told me of rattlesnakes and guardian angels. You believe me, now, when I say you are a week's walk west to San Diego, and two weeks' walk northwest to the City of Angels."

Her heart pulsed.

"The City of Angels? There *is* one?"

"I've never seen it. Some say it is extravagantly named. It is a dusty town, they say. I have been to San Diego many times. It is green, and is set beside more water than is seemly. People are rich in San Diego—"

"But the City of the Angels!"

"I have already told you," he said impatiently, "I know nothing about it, except that it is there!"

Gathering all her strength, Magdalena got up and lurched to the door of the hut. The stars were there in their glorious familiarity.

"I know English," she called over her shoulder to her rescuer, "I can speak their language." And to her mother, she added silently, "He wasn't lying, he didn't lie to you."

The first time Clifford had seen the white-capped mountains in the distance, he thought they must be a mirage. Either that, or the product of the rye-stimulated imagination. The sun caught the white peaks on the horizon, and it was hard to tell if they were real, or a bank of wildly farfetched clouds.

The train was climbing up, as it had been for the last few days, in the slow rise from the endless flat prairies, and was now cutting across that steep grade on a brief run to the Northwest. It was not until he heard Sunny Jenson call out, "Look, Ma! Look at them white mountains!" that Clifford was convinced of their reality. And then everyone in the car was moving over, to look at the fantastic, distant spectacle.

For a brief moment it was as if they were all together in delight and awe, as if that distant promise somehow justified their cramped days spent in stale air, and the cold nights huddled under blankets and overcoats by now stiffened with dirt and soot.

Then, as the engine rounded the turn, heading again straight west, the vision vanished. They were once again a group of disparate individuals and families who had had too many days of arbitrary contact. Though there had been no open conflict so far, the nerves of each "immigrant" had rubbed raw in a series of uniquely individual ways. Each card player, at the "bad" end of the car, was feeling the effects of the ongoing game. Each loser thought he had been cheated, each winner feared he would be robbed. A young couple, who had boarded the train as if it were a magic carpet to take them to the land of their blissful, if simpleminded, dreams, now scarcely spoke to each other, but stared through the long days in separate disillusionment. A nasty chest cold had spread through the car, especially affecting the children, and during the long nights, the drowsing restless car was filled with hacking coughs and fretful tears. There was not a mother aboard who did not accuse her husband of buying new life at the expense of their children. When each morning dawned with every child alive and only coughing, the women

43

subsided with exasperation and something close to regret. Their men hunched their shoulders, looked out the windows, and longed desperately for the consolation of The Game.

During the endless ride across the great American Prairie, what manners they had brought with them were rubbed thin. When they had stopped in the larger towns where food was available, the strongest men had crowded off, jostling ahead of the family groups without apology, leaving women and children far behind. Even the Jensons, who had withstood the rigors of the journey with remarkable equanimity and good humor, only added to the disharmony in the car. Because, who did they think they were!—accenting, as they did, the weaknesses, physical and moral, of the others?

Clifford heard one of the card players, working his way down to use the rear platform, after Sunny Jenson had cheerfully greeted him with a *Hi! Mister!*, saying under his breath, "If that little bastard says 'hi' to me once more, I'll break his fat neck."

Though Clifford sympathized with the gambler's point of view, he himself felt a sense of detachment, sitting there in his corner. He knew that some of his calm goodwill came from what he had begun to think of as his two best friends, his endless ham, his still half-filled jugs of rye. When he began to feel irritation at the endless bickering, the whining recriminations of the mothers, the truly menacing coughs of the miserable youngsters, Clifford tilted his jug and filled his cup. The ham gave him an endless, convenient thirst.

The morning after that first clean vision of the mountains, dawn found the train switchbacking up the lower slopes. For the first time in days they saw trees, full-grown trees, trees close together. Parts of the prairie had been in a dreary thaw; the snow in scabby patches had looked pocked, dirty gray. Here, in the lower reaches of the truly unbelievable mountains, fresh snowbanks, sometimes higher than the train, gleamed supernaturally white. Here and there they glimpsed flashes of clear mountain water cascading over glistening rocks, reflecting an intensely blue sky.

The train kept on. The passengers forgot their petty bickering. All of them, from the craftiest gambler to the most cretinous child, stared in an endless, beneficent trance at each new bright vista.

At about three o'clock in the afternoon of that day, the train slowed, then came to a complete halt. As questioning murmurs rose in the car, one of the conductors came through the farther door and called out, "It's nothing to worry about, folks. We stop here to take on fuel to build up pressure to get over the pass. And there's a snow slide ahead that we have to clear. Once we're started we won't be doing much more than a walking pace until we get to the summit. This is a good chance for anyone who wants to stretch his legs."

With one wild cry, most of the children, forgetting they were sick, scrambled for the exits, tumbled down into the shining carpets of clean snow. Within moments the bad boys were trying to kill each other with snowballs, which innocently covered potentially lethal rocks scavenged from the roadbed. Strangely enough the gamblers were self-conscious—they didn't need no leg-stretching, or fresh air! But one by one, with elaborately casual excuses, they got down out of the car. Standing then, with shy, solitary smiles, in snow up to their knees, they took deep delightful breaths, scooped great handfuls of snow, and of all things, washed their hands and faces.

Three wives, reaching a wordless agreement, got up and went out of the train. Clifford watched as they made their way carefully to an untouched slope, stood quietly conspiring for a few moments, then with girlish giggles that belied their status as wives and mothers, joined hands and let themselves fall back onto the cushion of snow, let go, and moved their arms in identical winglike motions. They very carefully got up and smiled as they looked back at the three angels they had created.

By now, Clifford was almost the only one left in the car. He filled his tin cup to the brim with rye, and stepping cautiously, so as not to spill a precious drop, he went down into the already beaten snow of the roadbed.

The cold crisp air caught at his lungs; he eagerly gulped it in. Together with a hefty swig from his mug, it lifted him with a delicious sense of elation. He bowed to the ladies and congratulated them on the perfection of their angels. He grunted amiably at the gamblers, and laughed out loud when he saw that the young woman who had been the object of his surreptitious lust was down on her hands and knees, screaming like a hoydenish tomboy, as she tried, unsuccessfully, to put huge gobs of wet snow down the neck of her little brother.

Clifford worked his way up past the other cars, answering an occasional greeting from anyone who spoke to him. It was wonderful to see—this whole small world on holiday.

At the tender behind the engine, he paused to watch the stokers shoveling on the new supply of anthracite. He looked up into the cab of the engine and exchanged waves with the engineer, who, leaning slumped against the window, was munching on a sandwich and taking sips from a tin cup of his own.

Clifford walked on ahead until he came to the crew of four men wielding snow shovels as they cleared away the slide across the tracks. "It ain't far around," one of them said, pausing in his work.

"I guess I'll just take a look," Clifford answered.

Regaining the track by the roadbed, he walked on, isolated in a white, magic world all his own. Taking another sip of rye he stepped out briskly, and before he realized how far he had come, he was only a few steps from the summit.

He covered the distance in a loping run and gasped as he saw the grandeur stretched before him.

The lower ranges glistened for miles ahead, granite outcroppings showing luminous purple against the sea of snow which, even as he had climbed, had begun to turn pink in the first glow of sunset.

Through the almost cloudless space before him, he could see ahead, beyond the snow. He saw the treeline and even farther; red, yellow, slate blue, bright orange, ocher.

It was too beautiful to be true, but there it lay, indescribable, undeniable, in front of him.

With something like reverence, Clifford scooped up, with his left hand, the pure crystals shining in the bank beside him. With an almost hieratic gesture, he let them fall from his hand into the still half-filled cup of rye, packing them down and watching them dissolve.

He lifted the cup to his lips, feeling the unaccustomed chill of the metal, and emptied it in one long, thrilling gulp. He toasted the future.

It would be the last fresh water he would taste until he reached the end of his journey.

At the first gong stroke of the morning call, Sung, in his dreams, saw the crimson sedan chair of a bridal procession passing through the home village preceded by the gaudily robed bearers of the gifts and dowry. With the second stroke, he found himself in the Big City by the River of Pearl. And now the procession had been changed into a funeral. The heavy coffin swung as it was carried by six bearers. And behind the protective screen of unbleached cotton, the chief mourners, all in white except for the red piping of their shoes, wailed extravagantly. The third stroke blended with the sound of a whistle, and he was leaving his silken bed in the hold of the ship, crawling forward to where the first of the Chinese workers looked at him with disbelief, and then adopted him with affection, sharing their meager food and shielding him on the rare occasions when the foreign devils made their inspections.

Not until the fourth stroke did he feel the biting teeth of the cold wind, and knew, as he stirred under his thin blanket, that he was in the foreign devils' railroad camp, close to a rocky shelf ten times as high as the Five-Storied Tower. Another day of long hours of extreme exertion rewarded by scant meals, and a few silver coins every week, was about to begin.

He rubbed his eyes. There was no need to get dressed. He folded his blanket, went behind a giant tree to relieve himself, and trotted briskly toward the chuck wagon, where already the weary, coughing, bleary-eyed coolies—clearing their throats and spitting—had begun to line up for the morning meal of *jook,* rice porridge, which the foreign devils expected them to work on until midday or even later, when they could look forward to a few scraps of salted meat or fish with their bowls of rice.

The fat cook, Ah Gee, grinned when Sung's turn came and said, *"Ai yah,* Wing On! You are even thinner today than yesterday, if such a thing can be possible," and before he filled the bowl with gruel, he—with a quick and careless motion undetected by the others—placed three or four scraps of fish and vegetable from last night's dinner in the bottom of Sung's bowl.

"You are kind," Sung said, after a slight pause.

He was still surprised, from time to time, to hear himself addressed by his new name. The original Wing On had been one of three dozen or more who had died in the nightmare crossing of the ocean. (Each person who had died had helped the others—the bodies were disposed of secretly at night, to keep the foreign devils from knowing that there were fewer mouths to feed—and when Wing On had died, they had given his papers to Sung, who by that time had become a mascot to them all.)

It was as Wing On, then, that Sung left the great ship and found, not a

46

mountain of gold, but a city as big as the one he had left, and a harbor that was almost a sea in itself. He had seen the Snorting Dragon—Bin Tang had not lied—had been crowded into a wooden box on wheels with scores of his countrymen. The dragon took them all on the iron canal as far as it could go, many, many *li*. When it stopped and the men got out, they could only laugh in disbelief at the trees, taller than any pagoda, and bigger near the ground than most of the buildings they had ever seen.

Great birds, wings stretching wider than a man could reach, circled above them. But where were the crops? Where were the rice paddies? "How could a man *live* here?" one of them asked, and later was to remember his ignorant words with bitterness. They were to learn, only too quickly, that the foreign devils had brought them here for just that reason: to build the iron canal for the dragon in this cursed place that was an impossible task for the weak foreign devil. What other people except true sons of Han could work as they did, during those weeks and months, through days of scorching heat, nights of chilling cold? What other people could work from before the sun came up until after it went down, and still have the courage to go on, day after day, month after month, even as they weakened, sickened, and died?

Every morning the foreign devils told them that before the big snows came, they had to get the dragon over those endless mountains. They told heartening stories of men just like them working ceaselessly toward them on the other side. They pointed to great pictures that showed where they "were," where they were "going," and they spoke gravely of what would happen if the snow came before they had "gotten through."

Sung didn't understand a word of this; no one else did either. By the end of the first week, no one cared about understanding. They understood enough to know the foreign devil was a liar.

The foreign devils had laughed at Sung when he presented his papers as Wing On. He was too small to wield the heavy, sharp picks with which the road crew hacked out the first rough path of the canal. He was too thin to hoist the great slabs of wood that had to be laid across this path. Though Sung tried valiantly, he could scarcely lift the heavy sledgehammer, much less bring it down accurately upon the blunt heads of the long sharp pieces of iron that held the shining metal strips on which the dragon traveled. And as for moving these, though he had worked with the gang who levered them into place upon the slabs of wood, his puny efforts were of no real use to the rest of the men.

Wing On ended up, working to the very limits of his endurance, as a runner, a messenger boy, and sometimes assistant cook. He staggered under huge loads of spikes that left his shoulders bruised and aching. He trotted out at midday to the exhausted workmen carrying, in true coolie fashion, stacks of covered dishes slung from either end of a flexible bamboo. And because of his speed and intensity, sometimes the foreign devil himself would use him to carry a message, and he began to learn a little of their strange, barbaric language.

At the end of the first week, when he took his place in line to collect his wages, he knew he had worked as hard as any of his countrymen. He heard from the front of the line a few weak protests, but they were drowned out by the loud barbaric voices.

"Here you go, Chink. This'll buy you a color-blind whore, and a quart of rotgut that'll make you think she's a slant-eyed beauty!"

The man in front of Sung held out his hand and numbly accepted the five small, thin silver coins that were his wages for eighty hours of back-breaking labor. Already, after only seven days, Sung had been around the devil long enough to know these coins were of little value.

When it was Sung's turn, he said to the paymaster, "Gold, please, mister!"

The two burly round-eyes looked at each other in disbelief and almost choked themselves laughing.

"Why, you runty piece of lizard shit! What makes you think—"

The man had the five coins ready, but Wing On's insolence had angered him. Any reference to gold enraged him, for he too had come to this land in search of gold and been as cruelly disillusioned as the rest of them.

He dropped three coins into the child's hand and deliberately put the other two into his own pocket. "Put that in your smart mouth and suck it! It's more than you deserve, you dirty little shit! We pay by weight here, and you're not even half a man!"

Sung stood with the coins in his hands, angrier than he had been since leaving the home village. But this time he knew there was nothing he could do except store up his wrath for the future.

That night the men were transported to another ramshackle camp which came to life once a week, where the foreign devil arranged for the coolies to spend their wages. Huge bonfires were set around a few ragged tents. White men with pushcarts sold the promised rotgut: "A whole quart for only a dime." In the firelight a few more foreign devils showed their teeth and shouted.

"What you Chinks need is music! Come on, Al! Give 'em somethin' to cheer up these yellow bellies! Play them somethin' good, Al. Sing!"

Al, who looked to Sung more like an animal than a man, pressed a box that hung on his chest and opened a mouth that could barely be seen in wads of reddish hair that stuck out all over his face. A sound came out more awful than when the merchant's stubborn beast had laid back its ears and raised his cry to the heavens.

> Let me tell you a tale, a good one I own
> Of a buckin' old bronc, a strawberry *rooan*! . . .

The sons of Han looked at each other in bewildered consternation. This was worse than anything that had happened to them so far.

"Come on, boys, drink up!" one of the pushcart salesmen yelled, and when they looked at him, he set them an example. He tilted up one of his own bottles and imprudently took a long swallow.

He gasped, his eyes watering, as he coughed out, smiling and nodding, trying to hold his voice steady. "That's the rawest skunk piss you'll find this side of the Rockies!"

48

> I was hangin' 'round *Town*
> Not earnin' a dime
> Bein' out of a *job*
> Just spendin' my *Time!*

There was nothing else to do. The sons of Han began to drink—to drown out the sound, to warm themselves against the night's biting cold, to forget that they had been cheated, to forget where they were.

"That's it, you stupid little slant-eyes. After the second bottle it begins to taste better. By the end of the night it gets up to dog shit!"

The Chinese, realizing that they were actually expected to sit down in front of a fire and rest, found their tongues loosening, and began to talk in phrases that in this short time had already become rusty in their throats.

"My old woman will call me a lying boaster when I return to the village and tell of this."

One man juggled his coins in his hand and watched as they took the fires' flickering light. "When *I* return, I shall have these made into ear pendants for the dowry of my eldest daughter. She is no beauty, but these should increase her value."

> When a fella steps up
> And he says I suppose
> You're a bronc-bustin' man
> From the look of your *clothes!*

"This work is not so hard," one man said, after he had drunk deeply. "At least it is better than getting the big-leg elephant disease."

Sung, who had remained in the shadows on the outskirts of the circle around the biggest fire, nodded his head in silent agreement. He could remember when old Sung Ya, in the farther compound, had begun to suffer, his left leg swelling until it grew larger than any tree in the village. He had become helpless, and before his death his grandchildren had had to wheel him about on a barrow when he needed to move, and had taken turns fanning the flies away from the gross appendage of their relative who had refused to die.

"They feed you here," another man said. "That is undeniable. They feed you better than on the big ship."

"Yes, that is true," a man who sat next to him responded immediately. "I have eaten worse in my home village"—he paused for effect—"during the last famine!"

Quiet laughter greeted the clown's sally, and in appreciation of this acknowledgment, the man tossed a coin into the air and beckoned to the seller of drinks.

The exchange was swiftly made.

> So he says, Come on boy,
> I'll give you a chanch!
> In his buckboard we jumps
> An' we rides to his *raynch!*

Sung watched the scene. With eyes unaffected by drink he took it all in: the huge fires, when they'd been told all week to be careful of fuel; the exhausted faces of his countrymen, softened now by the strong drink; and behind them, around them, smiling falsely, perhaps twenty foreign devils. He sensed, rather than saw, the steady movement of the pitifully small silver coins, moving *outward* from the work-calloused fingers of his countrymen into the hands of the devils who reminded him of the scavenging, half-wild dogs of his village.

He wanted to call out in warning, but already the voices rose, in louder, confused, slurred speech. And the barbarous noise of the singing donkey, the braying man blared on:

. . . In the morning we're *up*
And right after *chuck!*
We go out to see how
This old outlaw can *buck!*

And besides, he was only a boy.

After he realized what the devils were up to, he put his own coins into his shoe. Then, sadly, he watched his countrymen turn into beasts, remembering—though he tried not to—the noises of desperate pleasure that had come from the farther compound during the great sickness. He saw the faces of men he had worked with fill with vague, unsatisfied longings.

At a moment not long after, when Sung judged that perhaps each man had spent one coin, the music stopped. The flap of a tent suddenly was thrown back, and a huge foreign devil stepped out. He began to speak in a mixture of his own barbarous tongue and some strongly accented phrases that Sung understood, with difficulty.

"You watchee pretty girlie! You watchee go bang bang! Lookee lookee! Nookie nookie!"

As the men, still sitting, turned their astonished eyes toward him, he roughly beckoned to someone still inside the tent.

"Get your big tits out here, Martha!"

In the firelight there was a collective gasp.

"The first man gets in free," the devil said. "Get that, you yellow lizards? First man, free nookie nookie!"

Standing numbly in the firelight, a woman stared vacantly, appearing to see nothing. She was hideously deformed. Great white melons sagged to her waist, reminding Sung of Sung Ya's elephant sickness.

"Swing 'em around, Martha," the devil said negligently. "Give the Chinks a treat."

Again, the men around the fire gasped as the woman, with a look of purse-lipped concentration, made one of her melons go in one direction—and as that one was spinning, began to move the other.

"First one free," the devil sang out, "free nookie nookie!"

A man got up from his place in the firelight.

The devil moved toward him, taking him by the arm with one hand, kneading his crotch with the other. "Whooee! There's more there than I

50

thought." Then to the swaying woman, "You got a real treat coming, sweetheart!"

The man and the woman disappeared into the tent. In a moment, the sound of a woman's groans began to vibrate through the camp. The eyes of the waiting men began to glitter, and as if at a noiseless signal, three other unnoticed cones of cloth opened up, and more swollen women appeared.

The first tent opened, the first man staggered out. In answer to one great unasked question, he said, leering, "She has done things to me so filthy I cannot even—" He went back to his place and drank deep.

"Three coins, you little bastards! Thirty cents, you little fucks! It's a bargain!"

It was then, in the confused movement toward the tents, that Sung caught the flash of a silver coin lying in the dirt. He moved forward swiftly. He picked it up and looked around for its owner. Then he realized that he could never discover who had dropped it, and that whoever had would not realize its loss until the morning, if then.

For the rest of that drunken, lust-ridden night, Sung circled in the shadows with watchful eyes. The memory of his father would not allow him to steal from his countrymen, but whatever he found on the earth was not going to be stolen by the foreign devils.

He watched with contempt as the devils who sold the liquor sampled their own wares. When one of them, missing his pocket with his groping hand, dropped three coins, Sung scampered in, unnoticed, to pick them up.

> He can turn on a nickel
> And give you some change!

Next morning they brought the Chinese cook out to camp to fix breakfast. Sung was awake before the gong sounded. He watched as the men twitched with each new sound. Some of them vomited even where they lay.

"Come on, come on, get up, you bastards," a devil said. "This is your day off, your day of rest." He laughed unfeelingly.

This morning Sung was first in line. There was nobody with strength yet to get up and stand behind him.

The cook silently filled his bowl, watched as Sung ate, then filled it again.

"Do they always do this?" the boy asked.

"Every week the devil pays them, every week the devil robs them."

Before Sung could answer, the cook went on, "You must learn to swallow your anger, Little Brother, just as I have learned to swallow mine."

"But how can they save their wealth, then, to go back to the villages?"

The cook, shaking his head, could give him no answer.

Later that morning, wagons came to take the workmen back to their regular camp. Some men boasted weakly of their prowess with the barbarian women. Most sat in melancholy silence. As soon as they reached camp, Sung went to his bundle in the corner of the lean-to where he slept with a dozen others. He was alone.

He untied the sleeves of his father's jacket and took out the earthenware teapot. Carefully he slipped his shoes from his feet and counted the coins as

51

he dropped them one by one into the pot. To his original three he had added twenty more. He scooped up a handful of small stones and dropped them in, covering the coins, then retied the bundle. He permitted himself a scornful grin. If the devils thought they could cheat someone who had already cheated the Black Death, they were mistaken.

It was indeed as the cook had said. Each week the coolies labored, sweating, in the sun; at the end of each week, their pay fell through their fingers like so much quicksilver. Each week the men swore they would save their wages; but by the end of six days' hard labor, they were ready again to forget their plight, with drink and lust. Oblivion, for that brief time, was better than the truth. Each week they swore to forgo the deformed barbarian women, but just as the men had marshaled their defenses, the devils would bring in a crude novelty—a woman with a third eye, or one with a diamond winking from her navel, or a mermaid which they claimed to have caught off the deck of the floating pagoda.

The work was not going fast enough. They were slowed down by a stubborn outcrop of gray rock harder than the rest. The crew worked three days to lay one length of iron. Some of the men began to weaken. There were not yet the sudden deaths which were now a part of Sung's memories, but rather a slow, depressing loss of breath as they made their way higher into the mountains. Their coughing increased.

Now the threats of the foreign devil about the Great Winter began to be real to the men. Even in the day, even with the sun shining, an icy wind would cut through their thin clothing, making them shiver as they dripped with sweat. The men spit up great hunks of phlegm, some of it flecked with blood. One morning, one of them was too sick to go to work; he was gone from camp when the work crew returned that evening. No one wanted to ask what had happened.

Each Saturday night Sung kept his eyes open and added to his hoard. Each time he carried a meal to the crew he ate as much as he could before he got there.

One morning he woke with a feeling of heaviness in his chest. His skin was burning and he shivered as the wind cut through his shirt. He considered for a moment, then untied his bundle and put on his father's jacket, silently asking any spirit that might still be in there to protect him and make him well.

Taking his place in line, trying to breathe easily, he engaged the cook in conversation.

"The devil says the Great Winter is coming. Will it get much worse than this?"

"This weather is *nothing*, Little Brother."

As the cook spoke, his words formed clouds in the freezing air. He too was wearing a padded jacket this morning. (Most of the men, coming as they did from the Big City where it was never cold, had no such protection.)

Sung gulped down his *jook*. Wordless, the cook took his bowl from him and filled it with more. Appraisingly he looked the little boy over; his cheeks were dangerously flushed this morning. "I will tell the devil I need you to prepare the meals from now on'. This morning you can lie down by the cooking fire."

Once within the protection of the chuck wagon, Sung pestered the cook with questions.

"What *is* this Great Winter?"

"Cold," the cook said shortly.

"How will the work go when it is cold?"

"It will not."

"Where will everyone go?"

Silence from the cook. Then he said, "The devils will go to their warm dwellings with their fat wives and ugly children. I will go to the city by the sea. When the winter is gone, they will hire me again to be a cook."

The cook shrugged. "Some are already gone. Some will find their way back to the city by the sea. Many of our countrymen already live there."

"But they have no money," Sung said. "And how can they walk that far? Will the foreign devil take them there in wagons?"

"Are you a living question?" the cook snapped. "Did your parents teach you no manners? Am I to be punished for a kind deed by your unceasing voice?"

Sung lay all day, feverish but secure, within the safety of the wagon. Many unanswered questions remained in his mind, but he began to understand what the answers would be. Looking out of the wagon, he saw the bodies and faces of the work crew as they passed by to fill their bowls. Many were already as good as dead. The features of the others were gaunt. Some walked painfully, their legs straddled, and Sung had heard them grunt in pain as they tried to make water. Some said it was a disease that came from the melon-breasted females. Even without the great winter, Sung thought, most of them were doomed.

But he had not come all this way to die. I am a child, he thought. I have no one to protect me. From his shelf in the wagon he watched the cook, and calculated his chances.

"Do you have a large family?" Sung wheezed pathetically. "Do you have wives and children waiting for you in the City by the Sea?"

"Some wives, many children," the cook said matter-of-factly, not stopping the rhythm of his razor-sharp cleaver as he worked on the day's salt fish. "And they *don't* need another little brother."

Now it was Sung's turn to be silent.

The cook went on. "The City by the Sea is cold and often windy. It is an ugly place to live, and the ground shakes. But the Great Winter never comes there, and—as I have already told you—many sons of Han make their home in that place."

"How might one find this city?" Sung asked.

"*Jook* brain!" the cook snorted. "Have you not already come from there on the cursed dragon? All you have to do is follow the iron railing. You will pass many towns, but keep asking."

"Would the devils come after me?"

Again the cook snorted. "You're not important enough for them to waste

53

a sneeze on, much less their time and money. Your absence, Little Brother, would be a saving."

By the end of that day Sung's plans were made. The next morning he was up again, breathing lightly, but feeling better. He loitered around the office of the foreign devil, asking for errands, taking messages. He bided his time, and once, when he saw the office was empty, he fearlessly stepped inside, opened a desk drawer, and scooped out the coins he knew lay in the corner. He walked without haste back to his teapot. As he buried the coins in the gravel he saw, to his satisfaction, that two of the coins were gold.

Later that afternoon, the men lined up for their weekly pay. That night as always, the devils put on their debauch. The men, coughing, drank grimly. They no longer talked about earrings for their wives.

Sung collected sixteen coins, and quietly curled up in his jacket to sleep before the night was quite over.

He woke in the morning with the sound of the terrible gong in his ears, the hacking coughs and the resentful curses of the workers, but when he opened his eyes and sat up, he saw the morning sun glittering on a white world and he felt a great fear. The color of death had engulfed them all.

As the chuck wagon came into the desolate camp, Sung ran to meet it, shivering with more than the cold.

"Is this it, Ah Gee? The Great Winter? The Great Snow?"

"No, idiot!" the cook said, disgusted. "This is a spring shower, this is a heat wave. When the Great Snow comes, it will cover everything, this camp, the tracks, even the dragon itself, under its deadly blanket."

"I'm hungry," Sung said.

"Here, warm yourself."

That morning, Sung ate five bowls of *jook*. When they got back to the work camp, the cook, wordless, gave him a warm, greasy, paper-wrapped parcel.

While the rest of the men groaned and spat, Sung went for the last time into his lean-to. He sifted the coins from the gravel and put them at the bottom of the cache of rice that had come all the way from the home village. He knew that at this moment he was, except for the foreign devils, probably the richest man in the camp. He had his father's jacket for warmth, his teapot, and his next meal. What was there to be afraid of?

In broad daylight, his bundle slung over his shoulder, Sung walked out, westward, down the iron tracks.

The young woman stood on the sand of a small cove, looking out at the waves as they crested, foaming with a regular, gentle whoosh against the pale, glistening sand. The hills came down almost to the shore, covered with the softest, tenderest grass; she had stopped to feel it with her hands; it was green, the greenest thing she had ever seen. This endless water showed itself to her as blue, blue with purest white. Only in the past few days had she seen colors like these. It was a miracle; it was her reward.

The waves crested, broke, foamed in. She stepped a little closer, and the white bubbles covered her feet. How delicious! What a wonder! She looked around the deserted cove to be certain she was alone, for by now she met other travelers daily. There was no one, nothing but the benign hills and the inviting sea.

There was no need to take off her sandals—she had not worn them in months. Putting her bundle in a safe place, she walked in, still in her clothes, up to her knees, then her waist, feeling the gentle swells and the tug of the wet cloth around her legs. Yielding to an impulse, she took off her blouse, her skirt, everything. Her excuse to herself: They needed to be washed. She went along dutifully with this self-imposed charade, squeezing salt water through the coarse fabric, then stretching her skirt and blouse on a sunny rock, where the fresh air would complete the cleansing process.

Still the sea beckoned.

Cómo non? Before she had time to change her mind, she found herself almost skipping back into the surf, relishing the sense of sensuous freedom she felt as the water swirled between her thighs.

The waves were gentle, the blue water between them incredibly clear. Tiny golden fish darted about, unafraid of this new creature in their midst. Cautious, she stayed near the line of the breakers, kneeling down in the water to rinse her hair. To her amazement and chagrin a murkiness emanated from where she crouched, only to be mercifully sluiced away into the endless sea. Curiously, she rubbed a forearm, and as the film of dirt, sweat, and protective body oils came easily away, she marveled once more at her own strength—and since she was alone, her own beauty.

This was the first time she had ever known the luxury of a complete bath. In the squalor, filth, and poverty of her father's home, whatever water there was found its way into the inevitable pot of beans. Clothes were never laundered, and even after she had gone to work for the Señor John Frederick Smith, the scandalized kitchen help could only give her a galvanized tub half filled with water to bathe in, and then they made fun of her because she was so big she could fit only a third of herself in at a time.

She was not too big for this bathtub! She stayed in the water for what seemed to her an endless time, scrubbing at every part with her strong brown hands, and admiring the soft glow which the friction brought to the surface of her skin.

A frown fleetingly crossed her face. There *was* one other time she had been in water—when she had lost her baby in the flooded *barranca*. What a pathetic bag of bones she had been when the goatherd had found her.

But during the days he had given her shelter and food, her natural stamina had reasserted itself. Looking now at her body, she saw that her flirtation with motherhood had made the promising, somewhat angular figure of a girl into the near perfection of a voluptuous young woman.

Her breasts had grown during her pregnancy, and she cupped them now, feeling their resilient firmness as her nipples came erect. She felt a tingling that spread downward. She was pleased to see that her nipples had none of the—to her—distressing, blackish purple that some of the overworked mothers of Sonoita, her own among them, displayed. No, her own breasts were more like fresh fruit than exhausted flesh—her nipples bright fresh pink; for this, she imagined, she was in debt to the blond blood of her unknown father.

Now she let her hands stray downward, across the flat, smooth surface of her belly, and further, to that place which her mother said was the seat of all suffering, that place which Magdalena—despite her brush with death in the *barranca*—was convinced a kind Divinity had put there for the pleasure of women as well as men.

A wave of the incoming tide, a good deal stronger than the others, put an end to this line of thinking by tumbling her through the surf and up onto the sand.

"Pendejo," she swore at the ocean, shook her fist at it and ran back in, to free herself of the presumptuous grit, and to prove to herself that she was not afraid of this or *anything!* Only when she had satisfied herself on both counts did she walk dignified, glowing, her bounteous curves making her look like a golden goddess of the sea.

"Missee wanchee see pletty panty!"

From the balcony above, the mountainous white woman laughed coarsely. "Missee! That's good!"

"Plenty pletty panty!"

The woman who had spoken, and her two companions in trade, rocked with mirth, their great melons pressed against the iron railing, bulging, quivering.

He yelled up again, his thin shrill voice cutting through the boisterous cacophony of sounds that made up the Red Light district bordering San Francisco's Chinatown. It was three o'clock on a cloudy afternoon; most of the girls were taking a well-earned rest.

The kid yelled up again, grinning fiercely, dancing on bare feet as if the pavement were scorching him.

"Gottee watchee many many littee pletty panty!"

The obese whores gazed at each other, mystified.

"Huh?"

"What'd he say?"

"It's underwear, Lorraine."

"Well, why didn't he *say* so?"

"Christ almighty!"

The largest of the three women heaved in her chair like a sea lion and honked down, in a great, good-natured voice, at the little scrawny kid.

"No needee pantee, kid! That's what we *don't* need in our business!"

In a gesture of perhaps excessive coarseness, she spread her knees and showed him.

He resisted an impulse to flee from a sight that had frightened stronger men and yelled out, *"Race!"*

The women gazed at each other blankly.

"Race!"

Again, nothing.

The little kid reached into his pushcart, determined to demonstrate the

56

unique quality of his wares. He pulled out a pair of ample linen bloomers, edged with machine-made lace.

Again the women laughed. "I tell you, kid, we don't need 'em!"

The kid was stubborn. "Race! Rots of race makee snatchee plettie!"

The women weren't buying.

"Easy fuckee!" He screamed, "Easy pissee!"

And holding the bloomers wide he thrust his head up through the crotch and grinned in triumph.

"No klotch!" he shrieked in glee. "No klotch make easy fuckee! Rots of race make snatchee pletty!"

The women stared at each other. "Will you get a load of that, Lorraine! Crotchless underwear!" Their minds, so dull in most things, worked in unison, and quickly.

They thought of dressing up like wives, in pure white lace. They thought of covering their overworked parts with a curtain of chastity. They thought of the *gentility* of it all, followed by the sudden shock of exposure.

"I'll take a pair," the largest one boomed out. "No! I'll take two!"

"I'll take one!"

"Save one for me!"

The Chinese boy bargained fiercely, charging twice, three times, what he had bought his wares for. He jabbered incessantly, stuck his head repeatedly through the seamless crotches of his merchandise and made faces, knowing by now the value of laughter during any business transaction. He was shameless.

"Your price is too high!" Lorraine called down to him. "Too big!"

"You some twicee biggee radie! You pay twicee plice!"

Only when they offered to "take it out in trade," did his brassiness fail him.

"No!" he said.

For some reason, that made the women relent.

"The poor little kid. . . ."

"Christ, Lorraine, he's just a little kid. A little Chink kid."

They threw down handfuls of coins twisted in bills. He tightly wrapped his merchandise in compact rolls and threw them up.

"Catchee, missee!"

He carefully stashed his money and fell in behind his pushcart. Once out of their sight, he could allow himself to cough. It was time for him to leave this city. Even on summer days here the chilling fog cut through his bones, making him draw rasping breaths. But after his coughing fit passed, he managed a smile and went on. He would not have to spend another winter here. He had saved almost enough money to go to the City in the South where they said the days were sunlit the year around.

Clifford stirred into half-consciousness as the train hit the long trestle; the deep-toned, hypnotic clack had changed into a hollow roar. He heard this with no particular sense of anticipation. It had been in another life that he had stood alone, in the high pass, drinking the rye-flavored snow, looking over icy fields to the distant western sunset. In the days following, the squalor of the car had subdued all but that stupid kid, Sunny Jenson. Clifford rubbed his unshaven jowls. The hambone lay in his lap, greasy and gnawed-down; what flesh remained on it gleamed with a green, iridescent glaze. His remaining jug was less than a quarter full. He would have traded his letter of credit for a drink of cold, pure water, but the mere thought of such a miracle only emphasized the futility of his wish, and, resigned to endure with what he had, he tore off a dry, salty mouthful of the ancient meat, and, gagging, washed it down with rye.

The farther door of the car was flung open, as the roar of the trestle crossing subsided, to be replaced by the all-too-familiar clicking of the wheels.

"Well, folks," the conductor sang out, "we've just crossed over the Colorado River!"

A few faces turned dully toward him.

"Don't you know what that means?" Without waiting for a response, the conductor went on. "It means we've entered the Land of Promise, the land of oranges, gold, and sunshine!"

Clifford turned his bloodshot eyes and looked out. Surely, this was a mockery. As far as he could see, scrub-dotted stretches of barren earth lay between sterile, treeless mountains of chocolate-colored rock.

Up front, one of the women began to cry. The poker players swore softly; gamblers, they knew when they'd been had.

"We'll probably get to L.A. sometime tomorrow, if the track stays clear of sand." The conductor looked around once more at the gaunt faces and had the nerve to show his teeth. "Cheer up, folks! The worst is over."

The temperature hovered around eighty degrees. The windows wouldn't open. The fetid air was intolerable. The glare of the sun on the sand pained Clifford's eyes. He drained his cup once more—using it deliberately by now as an anesthetic—and lapsed back into merciful unconsciousness.

The young Chinaman trundled his covered cart up to the outskirts of the town of Bakersfield, near the bottom of the long valley through which he had passed during the last five weeks. He had learned that he could count on the curiosity of those who caught sight of him to ask what he so carefully concealed.

And so he walked down Main Street, headed south as always, his eyes glimpsing the range of mountains beyond that he knew by now were the only thing left between him and the City of the Angels.

This town, this Bakersfield, was larger than any he had entered for many days. A variety of stores that served the outlying ranches lined both sides of the street. Wagons and horsemen raised a cloud of choking dust as they vied for the right of way. Respectable matrons, in dresses of faded cotton, lifted their long skirts in a futile attempt at keeping them clean just one more day.

Sung had only to be sure that today wasn't Sunday.

He kept walking, slower now, wheeling his covered cart humbly down the side of the dirt thoroughfare. Then he began to whisper.

58

"It all right, missy. Soon we be through here. Sung take care of you, pletty gir. . . ."

Inevitably, a huge hog of a farmer, his red face streaming sweat in the harsh noon sun, couldn't resist the chance to bully a Chinaman perhaps an eighth his size.

"Hey Chinkee, we don't go for your kind around here!"

Sung kept his eyes on the cart. "It all right, missy. Sung take care of you. Find you nice law fish."

"We don't allow Chinamen on the streets of Bakersfield after dark, you little yellow bastard! You'd better make tracks, and fast!"

The farmer's bellows brought other men around them, eager for a chance to pick on a person who couldn't fight back, and this—kid—he couldn't have been more than thirteen—looked like the perfect victim.

A boy his own age, emboldened by the older farmers, sang out, "Ching Chong Chinaman, sitting on a fence," and only then did the "Chinaman" look up and speak to the farmers.

"This velly bad for young boy to see! Keep away prease! Velly bad! Young boy no can look!" And then, to the cart, "Keep quiet, no make noise. Young boy find out."

He kept his face stern and straight as perhaps eight sweat-soaked ranchers came his way, and followed behind him like water buffalo. Sung hunched his head over and quickened his pace ever so slightly. Now the words he whispered to his cart were different—some of the first words he had learned in English—"Cuntee Fuckee, Suckee, Loun' the Lurl," they thought they heard him say, and their faces turned several shades redder. Without meeting each other's eyes, they—attempting nonchalance—followed the Chinese kid and his covered cart. Their number, by now, had swelled to over a dozen.

"Hey kid," one of them finally said, "what you got in there?"

The boy ignored them, but went on whispering. Could he really be saying, "All right missy, fuckee suckee?!"

"Hey! Listen sharp when I talk to you, Chink!"

Only then did the boy turn around, frightened.

"I get out of town chop chop. I take . . . out of town, chop chop!"

"Take *what* out of town, God damn it! What have you got in the cart?"

By now, in fact, they had reached the southern outskirts. Sung looked carefully around. "No kiddee here, no radee?"

The men looked at each other in bewilderment. Then one of them said, "He means kids, don't he? And women?"

"I reckon," a young ranch hand said.

While they spoke, the Chinese boy and his cart had gone on. They had to trot to catch up.

"Hey, kid, what you got in the cart? Come on, you can tell us, we won't hurt you."

The boy looked furtive, then with an air of being hopelessly outnumbered said, with suddenly acquired clarity, "A mermaid, gentlemen."

Silence, except for the scuffing of nervous boots in sand.

59

"San Francisco radee fuck so much, she turn into fish. Is very sad. I take her over mountain to warm ocean. She swim away, be happy." He whispered consolingly into the cart, "All right, soon, missy, prenty fuckee suckee."

And then he walked off, due south.

It took the men close to an hour to persuade the kid to even consider letting them look. She lived in water in the cart, he said, and if she saw men looking at her, she would go mad with "rust." It took them awhile to figure out the boy was saying "lust" and by that time they would have given anything to see her. The boy was doubtful about the whole thing. He had watched her turn into half a fish, he said. She had given the last few men who touched her an awful disease, they'd turned into scaly monsters. She did like quarters though; they understood him to say that she pasted them on her bottom half where they made up a sort of skirt.

"Two beetee; one peekie," the boy said and it had to be a short peek, because he was pretty sure you could get sick just by looking.

"Too much rust," he said piteously, "too much fuckee suckee."

She was in there, all right, and when she saw them, she wiggled all over. Sometimes she reached out for them, and they leaped back. . . .

Some of them went home, rudely invading sugar bowls where the small change waited for this Sunday's collection box, because she wouldn't take dimes or nickels or pennies or—and this is what convinced them the kid was telling the truth—silver dollars, or paper money.

That night the wives of Bakersfield were ravished to a woman and asked by their men to do things they had never before considered or even heard of. One woman rushed out into the night from Mrs. Hunter's boardinghouse, shrieking "I can't take it anymore!" and vowed to devote herself from then on to good works, the American Indians, and literature. Others sank back into damp pillows and rewarded their drained husbands with contented smiles that promised a bright domestic future for those hardworking toilers in the dirt.

And a young Chinese boy pushed a cart, clinking with an overload of quarters, a little further down the Southern Road.

Early the next morning, cleaner than she'd ever been and certainly saltier, Magdalena put on her fresh clothes, twisted her long straight hair into a seemly bun, ate the very last of the goatherd's cured meat and cheese, and started out again, following the broad track northward from San Diego that soon swung away from the ocean, inland, and rose gradually into foothills that still, to Magdalena, looked magically green.

It seemed strange to be traveling where she was not alone. Every half hour or so she would be overtaken, by a carriage—a well-dressed *gringo* family on an outing—or a group of beautiful blond cowboys, each on his own beautiful horse, acting as if she were the first woman they'd ever seen in their lives, yipping at her, doubling back to take another look, but never turning ugly in their attentions.

Other groups, going south, seemed, in her imagination at least, to be more citified. Some wore dark suits. The men had grease in their hair, and the women wore broad-brimmed hats with feathers. Sometimes a man, even a family man, would salute her with a wave of the hand.

Early that afternoon, she saw a narrow cutoff and a row of weathered adobe arches. She had heard, since she was a child, that the priests of old times had come all through Mexico, even her wretched home Sonoita, and gone north, through California, founding "missions." She recognized that these ruined buildings must be what was left of one of those.

She needed to rest through the afternoon's heat, and the ruins provided shade. Only as she moved closer did she hear the welcome sounds of her own language, and turning a corner, saw an enormous and evidently happy family, spread out on rough serapes, eating a very substantial midday meal of *salsa, tortillas, frijoles de olla,* and the remains of an animal Magdalena recognized as an old friend, a plump, dark, roasted goat.

Some women sat up—most of the men were sleeping off the effects of this feast—and waving to Magdalena, motioned her over to sit down. They were overjoyed when she returned their greetings in Spanish.

"Ah, Señorita! Be our guest!" And then, with a trace of sternness, "Who allows you, young as you are, to go alone on El Camino Real?"

"I go with God," Magdalena said experimentally. "With Him watching over me, I am not afraid."

The matrons nodded. "Nevertheless," one of the older women said, "you should not put too much burden on His Grace. You should help him by being a little careful. There are *hombres sinvergüenza,* who would not scruple to take advantage."

Magdalena knew better than to argue. Besides, the smells of the feast had bewitched her. At home they had eaten like this perhaps once a year. "My sainted mother," she said demurely, "would have been happy to know . . ." It was not necessary to finish the sentence.

"Come, sit down, eat."

And she did, eating with extreme slowness, both for the sake of her manners, and to prolong the sensation—the fresh *tortillas,* the equally fresh *salsa* that crunched between her teeth, the beans which they served with fresh oregano, raw onion, and twists of lemon straight from the remains of the mission orchards. She could not believe such plenty. And to think that these were only the leftovers of their midday meal.

The matrons, for their part, watched the stranger closely. They noted with approval that her hair, under the dust of the day's journey, was clean and well combed; that her clothes were equally clean, and that her fingernails were spotless.

"Pedro!" called out one of the older women. "Bring the señorita a glass of wine!" And a half-grown boy, squatting near the men, hastily rose to obey.

"You are too kind," Magdalena said, taking the earthenware cup. She sipped carefully, only too conscious of the observant eyes of the older women. "It is very strong," she murmured, wishing she were all alone with a quart of it.

"Where do you go, señorita, and where have you come from?" the oldest woman among them asked sharply.

Magdalena was ready. *"Ai, abuela,* I have had a hard life—a bed of stone.

The good God in His wisdom took both my parents from me less than a month ago. They died in a . . . flood. My little brother died from the shock, in my arms. The head of the *ranchero,* where my father worked as a goatherd, tried, when I became an orphan, to take advantage of me. I had to steal away in the night, with only the clothes on my back. I go now to the City of the Angels, where, surely, a decent woman can find some work."

"Aiee, pobrecita!" the women said in chorus. "Oh, truly, life can be a tragedy, and the way of an honest woman is hard."

"A bed of stone," Magdalena agreed, keeping her eyes lowered, sipping again.

"Eh, Estrellita," the oldest woman there said to her neighbor, "this girl looks like a good one for your young Jaime. She's big enough to work·hard!"

"Anyone married to Jaime would have to work hard," another woman cackled.

Jaime's mother looked suspiciously at Magdalena, and then protectively over at her oldest son.

Magdalena, following her eyes, saw a young man, snoring, on his back, his belly quivering with each breath.

"My beloved mother told me, I could not begin to dream of marriage until I could present my husband with a suitable dowry."

This time the women exchanged a communication made up of glances and nods, rather than words.

After a pause, one of them spoke. "Have another *tortilla,* and perhaps some *cabrito.* It is hard to travel on an empty stomach."

"No, thank you," Magdalena managed. "I eat very little. My mother—"

"Where did you say you were going?" the oldest one interrupted.

"To the City of the Angels, to work. I . . . I speak some English, and I keep a house as clean as my soul."

"This branch of our family is traveling now, farther than Los Angeles. We're going to the mission of San Fernando for a wedding that will last three days. We had planned to go by way of San Gabriel, but—"

Here she stopped and looked at the five or six other older women, who nodded.

"—it would not be difficult to go by way of the City itself. And it would be pleasant to see the Plaza again, and to light a candle at the Church of Nuestra Señora. It is covered with gold leaf, did you know that? It is the richest church outside of the town of Tequila."

Magdalena nodded, pensively.

"My cousin has a cousin by marriage, who works at the big hotel there. It's possible he might find a place for a hardworking girl."

Magdalena cast about for the correct response, and found it. "God will repay you for helping an orphan," she said. "You must know what it is to be a suffering woman!"

The women, replete, well married, surrounded by husbands and children, whom they ruled with fists of iron, sighed gustily in agreement.

"Truly," one of them began, "life is a bed of stone."

The City of Los Angeles spread out from the Plaza. Running directly south, the chief business streets, Main and Spring, boasted three- and four-story buildings, pavement, and horsecars which ran at regular intervals. To the north and east, the more prosperous citizens had built frame houses in the prevailing gingerbread style, nostalgic echoes of their original American homes. These houses, tucked up on steep hills, each with its own wide veranda, gave their owners a gratifying view of the busy city below. Los Angeles was not beautiful, but it made money, and it attracted new residents, who made more money. Sometimes it seemed as if every other office on those two business streets belonged to a speculator in real estate. And already some of the more daring landowners with an eye to the future were building pretentious houses in the western plains that stretched from the little dusty town thirty or forty miles to the sea.

But still, the center was the Plaza. It, and the railroad tracks coming from the northeast, divided the city by color as well as money: the whites, safe in their frame houses up on the hill, the "Spanish" Mexicans clustered about the Plaza in one-story adobes, enclosing small, sometimes luxurious inner courtyards, and on the other side of the tracks an uncharted sea of black, brown, and yellow founding families of swarthy tint who had been pushed back by a relentless, impersonal tide of white. Indians—the original Chumash, blacks, and in ever-growing numbers, hordes of displaced, woman-less, Chinese men whose frustrations erupted regularly in stabbings, which went unreported by the papers and were ignored by the police. Nobody crossed the tracks; nobody went into Chinatown unless he had to.

Life, respectable life, started at the Plaza. The Church of Nuestra Señora La Reyna de Los Angeles clanged out the Angelus five times a day, and everyone, white or brown, stopped what they were doing for that minute and bowed their heads. Sunday afternoons saw concerts in the bandstand; Saturday evenings, the infinitely more exciting *paseo,* where all the beautiful Mexican women of the city strolled about the Plaza in one direction, and the handsome young men strolled in the other. After two hours of this, everyone went in to vespers, where, in flickering candlelight, notes might be exchanged, marriages made.

Various civic groups were always planting that wide dusty strip that lay between the bandstand and the church. The hardiest plants survived—sometimes—but the Plaza was also a thoroughfare, a place for young bloods to show off their horses, a natural turning place for carriages, buggies, surreys, all the vehicles that carried the population of the city. The northwest corner was perhaps the dustiest, the busiest, with vehicles of all kinds drawn up in ranks by the side and the front of the Pico House, a large, two-story hotel running a full city block—the biggest and best hotel in town.

The Chinese runner from the Pico House lounged negligently near the gate on the dusty platform where the passengers from this week's California immigrant train would come through. Already the ground trembled with its approach. A few relatives, obviously waiting to welcome their kin, began to clutch one another by the arm and to speak in the usual animated banalities.

The runner took note of them, for in some ways they made his job easier. Old Mr. Becker, his boss behind the front desk at the Pico House, had early taught him to ignore people being met by relatives, or couples with children, or—obviously—the poor.

It wasn't easy to tell rich from poor after an eleven-day train ride, but Mr. Becker said there were certain dependable things to watch for, and had taught the runner how to tell, from the cut and stitching, an expensive, tailor-made suit, however rumpled and soiled, from one bought off the rack. He was told as a general rule to stay away from women traveling alone. If they were the kind of women to put themselves in the hands of a Chinese stranger, chances were they would not be respectable. No, his job was to find prosperous, decent, unattached young men who could bear the rather sizable tariff of the Pico House. His job was necessary because passengers from this train were usually so confused that, as Mr. Becker had said, "Most of those poor Joes'll just be looking for a drink of good cold water, they're in no condition to tell a good hotel from a fleabag."

The runner examined the perfect crease in his own black, western-style trousers, the starched perfection of his shirt cuffs—Mr. Becker insisted that the staff dress in accordance with the standards of the hotel, and some of the maids added to their pocket money by doing up the laundry at night. As the train rumbled to a stop, the runner removed the snap-brim velour from his head and examined it meticulously for motes of dust. Few people wore hats anymore in Los Angeles, but he felt, and Mr. Becker agreed, that the somewhat excessive stuffiness of the headgear would counteract any initial distrust of the runner's distinctly Oriental appearance.

As the passengers, carrying assorted bundles of household goods and odd pieces of luggage, began jumping from the cars onto the platform, the runner saw that they were a particularly unpromising lot. Ignoring the larger family groups, he glanced at a pair of men and knew almost automatically that they were gamblers. The too-pointed toes of their shoes had been spit-polished at the last moment; honest men would not have thought to take the trouble. He began to wonder if he would have to go back alone. The thought did not worry him too much, because he had learned early from Mr. Becker that "no trade is better than bad trade." He was proud that during the six months he had been doing this, he had brought the hotel just one "bad apple."

The passengers, as always, had discovered the series of lemonade pushcarts that lined up to meet each immigrant train. Some of them, in tears, paid, drank, paid, and drank again. The runner, looking at this tableau with fastidious distaste, and with one last sweeping gaze along the platform, was turning to go when his eye was caught by the sight of a man alighting from the last car, which the runner had thought already empty of its passengers. Something about him, his entire bearing, the tilt of his head, the inexperienced way in which he carried his one bag, all these indicated to the runner that here was a product of gentle living, a good potential customer for the hotel.

He waited unobtrusively in the shade of a column to make certain this young man was not being met. The one thing that troubled the runner was the young gentleman's uncertain gait. If old Mr. Becker had taught him painstakingly how to recognize a man of breeding, he had needed only a few perfunctory lessons from Mr. Goldwater, who ran the hotel bar, in how to recognize a man who had drunk too much. But Mr. Goldwater had not stopped with that. He had made it clear that there were distinctions to be drawn between a gentleman who had drunk too much and a common drunk.

The young gentleman, despite his unkempt appearance, fell into the former category. His eyes were bloodshot, but his complexion was unmarred by broken veins. The surface soil of travel, the runner could see, covered the costume of a man who took proper pains with his appearance, and above it all—or, as Mr. Becker had once said, beneath it all—there was the solid evidence of his shoes, lusterless now, but clearly the hand-stitched product of a first-class bootmaker.

The runner made his decision and stepped forward.

"I beg your pardon, sir," he said in accented but perfectly clear English. "I have been sent to see if you would care to take a room at the Pico House."

"A house?" the gentleman said blankly. He swayed as he spoke. He was very drunk.

"The Pico House," the Chinese runner said a little pompously, "is number one hoterl in town."

The gentleman focused his eyes with difficulty. Again the runner could see ample evidence of breeding and good manners as the young man attempted, with maximum inefficiency, a half bow.

"How very kind," he muttered. "Would you be so good as to—"

He reeled and might have fallen had it not been for the runner's steadying grip.

"Almighty God," the young man managed, "all I want is a bed and a glass of water!"

"I wirl herlp you, sir," the young Chinese man said courteously, and keeping a firm but deferential hold on the young man's elbow, he skillfully picked up the bag with his free hand, and the strange couple, advancing with the careful measured pace of a wedding march, made their way through the reaches of the now almost deserted station to where the Pico House surrey waited.

It was only a short drive, no more than a few city blocks up the hill from the dusty station, across the equally dusty Plaza, already uncomfortably warm in the false summer which so often descends on Southern California in the so-called winter months, and into the crowded carriageway of the Pico House.

Even now, at a little past noon, when most of the town observed the civilized custom of the siesta, the Pico House lobby was alive with the animation characteristic of a growing society. The bar—Mr. Goldwater's separate concession—hummed busily, not with the raucous stupidities of men boorishly drinking away their lunch hour but with the low contented tones of businessmen who were confident that they were making money, even as they drank.

A fashionably dressed mixed party, the women in short-trained gowns, the men in morning dress, were greeted at the door of the restaurant by a smiling headwaiter, ready to guide them to their reserved table, and the wine steward smiled and bowed as he beckoned one of his underlings to bring out not one champagne bucket, or two, but three.

At the far end of the lobby, ranged attractively on plush-upholstered sofas, a bevy of young señoritas in the full Spanish dress of the day spread their skirts so that they overlapped each other, arranged their mantillas with long, self-conscious, beautiful fingers, and fluttered their fans wildly as they looked about at what to them was the den of the glamorous if dangerous *gringo*. They would wait here, sipping lemonade, until, with great ceremony, they would be taken across the Plaza in several carriages to the church for a family baptism. Only with much coaxing and pouting had they been allowed this treat, and sternly warned to speak to no strangers. But all the pouting and sulking became worth it when the doors of the Pico House were flung back and there, framed in the square of dazzling light, held up by a sinister *Chinito,* was the handsomest man any of them had ever seen!

"*Que bonito pelo*—what beautiful hair!" the youngest, Carmelita, whispered to her cousin. "It glows like the sun!"

"Yes, he is like a young god," Angelita agreed.

"*Es muy borracho,*" one of the older ones, Adelita, said sternly. "Just look, he can hardly stand up."

"Men are like that sometimes."

"The brutes!"

"Oh, I would like to touch that hair!"

"Carmelita!"

"Do you think he is like that . . . all over?"

Carmelita got a rap with her sister's fan for that one.

"You will never know, little one," Adelita said ominously, "and it's just as well. They say those men are even worse. . . ."

"Even worse than what?"

"Even worse, that's all."

"Just look at his feet."

They all did, then looked at each other, wide-eyed, above their suddenly motionless fans.

"But what does *that* mean?" Carmelita asked her cousin, after she had noted, along with the rest of them, that the disgracefully drunk and handsome *gringo* had feet that were shapely, but compared to those of her brother, for instance, of an astonishing length and breadth.

Her sister whispered gravely to Carmelita behind her fan.

"No!"

"It is what they say!"

It was too much for Carmelita. For the rest of that afternoon, all the way through the long baptism and family party that followed it with all its obligatory polite exchanges, she was troubled by impure thoughts.

Mr. Becker's first reactions were not quite as flattering as those of the sisters and cousins of the Dominguez family who were in town today. For an instant he thought that all his careful tutoring of the young Chinese runner had been in vain.

The tall blond traveler was so unsteady on his feet that he was in danger of falling without the support of his guide. But then, as the pair came a few steps closer to him across the lobby, Becker began to see what his protégé had seen, and smiled in wry approval.

Becker gave a brief nod to the runner, then opened the registration book. "Welcome to the Pico House, sir. I hope you had a pleasant trip to California."

For the first time the new guest's eyes came into focus, with a look of wild disbelief.

"Pleasant? *Pleasant?* Almighty God," he said. "Almighty God."

"If you would just sign here, sir."

The young man reached for the pen that Becker held out to him and missed it by a mile. He smiled disarmingly. With some effort, drawing heavily both on his Baltimore inheritance and his Charlottesville manners, he said, "Neither of us is such a fool as not to be aware that I am . . ." he hesitated, "well, let us say, pickled."

"There's no reason why you can't sign later," Mr. Becker said diplomatically. "What you need now is—" He broke off and snapped his fingers imperiously at one of the maids who'd been inventing small tasks—straightening the chairs, rearranging the flowers in the bouquets, flicking away imaginary dust from the highly polished surfaces of the mahogany tables that dotted the lobby—all this, while she listened and looked as curiously as the giggling girls in the corner at this new golden-haired stranger.

"You there! Take the gentleman up to 214. You know what he needs by now."

"A bed, a bed," the young man groaned, yearningly. "And water. Almighty God—"

"Clean him up," Becker said. "Take care of him."

The Chinese runner still carried his bag. Most of the traveler's weight fell, now, on the shoulders of the maid who supported him out of the lobby, down the hallway. They took the stairway slowly as the traveler muttered, every so often, "So kind. Everyone is very kind."

The runner and the maid worked as a practiced team, he opening the door and going forward quickly to turn down the bed.

Once the traveler was stretched upon it, they methodically stripped him of his clothes; she working from the top, he from the bottom. The boots were put immediately outside the door for shining, but not without another admiring inspection from the young Chinese. Perhaps a pair of boots like this would be the next thing he would buy for his own wardrobe.

The maid divested the traveler of his jacket, shirt, singlet. She carefully, in full view of the runner, went through every pocket, placing letters and money in a neat pile on the table beside the bed. The clothes were thrown into a corner; she would take everything down later to be washed. She permitted herself a discreet downward glance as the Chinese runner expertly shucked off the trousers and underclothing of the traveler.

The gentleman was snoring already, in deep, regular rhythm. The maid sat on the bed beside him. She poured a cup full of water from the earthenware pitcher that stood by every bedside in the Pico House. Holding the cup in one hand, she scooped up his head in the other, cradling him against the soft pillow of her breasts.

"*Que bonito pelo,*" she permitted herself to say, "he has hair like spun gold."

The Chinese runner, with a skeptical, knowing smile, stepped back into the shadows. He watched as the maid gently shook the traveler into sufficient consciousness for him to drink; he downed one cup, a second, a third, then settled back into peaceful sleep, his head safely nestled in the maid's starched bodice. It was time for her to let go, to get back to work. It was time for the boy to return to his duties.

Perhaps it was the inviting coolness of the room that held them thus—Maria Magdalena Ortiz, lately of the town of Sonoita; Sung Wing On, oldest son of the headman of the nearer compound of his home village; and Clifford Abercrombie Creighton, willing fugitive from the stifling restrictions of Baltimore society—in an unmeasured moment of time. Or perhaps it was the half-conscious realization that this was no casual conjunction of lives. They had traveled a long way to meet. Destiny had brought them to this room. Each was a fateful dreamer. Now that they were together, their lives would cross, and recross, in patterns of increasing complexity. Here, in the City of Angels, their lives might match, even surpass, their dreams.

BOOK I

1885

The Lotos blooms below the barren peak,
The Lotos blows by every winding creek;
All day the wind breathes low with mellower tone;
Thro' every hollow cave and alley lone
Round and round the spicy downs the yellow Lotos-dust is
blown.

TENNYSON, *The Lotos-Eaters*

$\mathcal{H}$E WAS awakened most unromantically by a dribble of water trickling into his right ear. He struggled for breath but was half choked by what felt like yards of starched linen and something most undeniably like—

He opened his eyes to dusky brown skin.

"Aye, *mi cábronito!* After thirty-six hours of drinking and peeing, you open at last your beautiful eyes."

He reached out a hand to steady himself and drew it back as if he'd been burned. It was more of that springy brown flesh. He became aware of his own nakedness and hastily tried to pull the sheet up around his neck.

White teeth flashed between full lips, and with a throaty laugh a heavily accented voice, warm and provocative, said, "It's too late now. I undress you already to make clean not only your filthy clothes but also you, my pretty young *gringo.*"

Clifford lay still, trying his best under the circumstances to look well bred. What happens next, he wondered. What did the circumstances warrant? What was he expected to do? He turned his head slightly away from that fleshy pillow. She as slightly adjusted her bosom to press against his left ear. He smiled; she smiled.

It was fair to say he'd never been in a situation like this before. He lay paralyzed by generations of Baltimore gentility. But even they weren't strong enough to inhibit the embarrassing protuberance under the sheet.

"You are as big as you are shy," she said, laughing. And carefully putting down her earthenware cup, she reached under the sheet and took him in a capable, voluptuous grip. He closed his eyes then, blotting out speculation as well as sight.

"Come now! You must help me with these buttons!"

Trembling, his fingers released that firm flesh from its confining linen bodice. He was lost, smothered in her warmth.

He thought dimly that as the male he must be the conqueror, but aside from his manly parts he was still tired, so tired. It seemed easiest to lie there, languid, as she left the bed just long enough to unfasten her petticoats and ruffled bloomers.

His mind tried to make connections. Did she look like a goddess? Venus rising from the half shell? No! Then he sighed and forgot everything.

As the bedsprings creaked she mounted and rode him with expert violence to a leaping climax.

He lay dazed, in ecstasy. She looked down and smiled.

"Next time it will last longer, *mijo*. Next time it will be for you *and* me."

He had only the foggiest notion of what she was talking about. How could it get better? It was the most amazing thing that had ever happened to him, but out of sheer politeness he heard himself say, "You are a wonderful teacher."

She laughed again and gave him a love pat that stung.

"We wait a little for the second lesson. Now perhaps we talk."

She slipped on a camisole and one of her petticoats, then strode lightly across the room to a tray of hot rolls and still steaming coffee that lay on a rustic wooden chest of drawers. She filled the two cups.

"I knew you would wake up this morning, *mijo*. Drink up, it's good for you. This we call *pan dulce*." She handed him a fresh roll crusted over with burnt sugar.

He sat up in bed and looked at her. She smiled and fell silent, seemingly content to watch him eat. His hunger overcame his self-consciousness. Like a child catered to by an indulgent mother, he greedily satisfied another appetite. But even as he did so he felt the first return of desire.

She prudently stepped back from the bed. "Not so fast. I tell you first we have to talk. I already know much about you, but you know nothing about me."

He was inundated by a flood of purely Presbyterian fears. Until this morning he had known nothing of the "physical side of love," except for its dangers. Had he been taken advantage of by a woman of the streets? Looking at the sudden collapse of the sheet, the statuesque beauty went on.

"You must not think I do this with every handsome stranger. I have waited a long time. Five months and three weeks I have been waiting for someone like you."

He cleared his throat experimentally, "My name is Clifford Creighton. May I have the honor of knowing yours?" He had never sounded more like the nephew of a banker; never had he felt manners to be so inadequate.

"I told you I know who you are," she said, her native temper flaring. "I know more about you than just this." She gestured contemptuously at his naked form. "You come all the way from the East. You don't have a wife or a *querida*. And you have a very big letter of credit."

Clifford's head jerked as he looked from the night table to the heavy wardrobe.

72

"*Cabrón!*" the girl said, her voice dripping scorn. "Do you think that I, Maria Magdalena Ortiz, would steal? Do you think I am a thief? Do you think I would be so stupid to stay here and tell you about it if I had?"

Hands on her hips, she addressed the ceiling. "Have I made the wrong choice after all this waiting? Have I given myself to an idiot?"

"I beg your pardon?"

"Is your brain as small as your member is large?"

For the first time Clifford seriously felt the need to assert himself. "Madame—" he began.

"Señorita," she insisted.

"As you wish," he responded, but she cut off whatever he was going to say by sitting down next to him on the bed and putting her hand reassuringly on his thigh.

"*Mira,* first of all, we must be friends. That has been my plan all along. Let me tell it to you now. I work hard here and I have a good character. I am a woman alone. I do not always want to work here and"—she snorted—"I don't want to be a wife and work myself into the grave. I too have come a long way to be here. *Comprende?*"

He thought perhaps that he did, sensing that she too had left something that she hadn't wanted to submit to.

"Yes," he said slowly. "I suppose I can understand. But how do I know I can trust you?"

She drew in a deep breath which—already—he suspected might be the signal for a tirade.

"Wait!" he said. "Suppose I even believed that I was the first one. Why would you pick *me*? I know that for all your kind words, I'm not rich, and I'm not *that* handsome."

"I have looked very carefully. Many rich men come here. But if they are rich, why should they help a Mexican girl? And the poor ones would be happy for *me* to make their living! There are two reasons I chose you. I loved another man. You will look like him when you are a little older. And you *do* have a picture of a woman in your papers. I know it is your mother."

Her grip tightened. "Even in a few months I know much about this city. Men come here every day. They don't want a hotel. It's too expensive. They don't, most of them, want bad girls. I try to tell you," she said. "You need a friend. I need some money. You give me the—" Her hand waved in the air as she searched for the word.

"Investment?" he said.

"For a small house. A little one. I know just the one."

"And then?" he asked.

"I have my own place. I have my own life. I make much money."

"And . . . ?"

"And then I pay you back and then I be your lifelong friend." She stopped and looked at him expectantly.

Everything had happened so fast that at first he felt unable to make any kind of adequate response. But then it was as if he heard from the other side of the continent the cautioning voice of his uncle condescendingly explaining to him the folly of such a commitment. Clifford felt automatic anger rising within him against the limiting, joyless past. Folly in Baltimore could be wisdom in Los Angeles, especially if what he had learned in this short span was any indication of the future.

The grip on his thigh communicated a double need. Money! Sex! Her face was just inches from his. He felt her delicious breath in the hollow of his neck. He thought about everything his uncle had told him of business and of partners.

"How much would we need?" he asked, knowing that if the sum were anything within reason he would agree. Who would turn down a partnership like this?

"Fifty-five dollars for a down payment"—the words were still new in her mouth—"and ten dollars for the first two months to get me started."

The ludicrousness of this petty sum staggered him, but he knew better than to betray that. He assumed his best imitation of his uncle's voice, "Those terms seem agreeable to me, and I suppose—"

He felt they should shake hands to bind the deal, but it was not his hand that she clasped.

"Oh my angel, my darling, my beautiful blond one! You are as strong as a bull and as kind as all the saints. You will never be sorry for this!"

A kaleidoscope of sensations . . . a tangle of arms and legs. She was naked in an instant, in his arms, all over him, biting, sighing, groaning, whispering. He had an instant's concern about their noisiness, his own astonished cries. His last coherent thought was that *this* excitement, *this* celebration of their joint venture, was nothing compared to the din of the morning traffic that had been rising from the streets of this burly city. He and Magdalena had already become part of all that.

Less than an hour later that same morning, Clifford, with all the outward appearance of a correct young Baltimorean, descended one branch of the double staircase that was the pride of the Pico House. The lobby still retained a deceptive early-morning coolness, its heavy drapes half-drawn against the oncoming heat of the day. Already the bartender was at his post, meticulously polishing glasses.

As Clifford took his first few tentative steps across the cool Spanish tiles, he became aware of a foreign-looking fellow half obscured by a shaded alcove. He stood as motionless as the great chunks of furniture that littered this pretentious tribute to the Colonial Spanish mode. But Clifford saw the glitter of his eyes as they alertly fixed upon him. The man was thin, no more than a boy, really, and dressed entirely in black.

Clifford moved forward; so did the stranger, discreetly.

"May I be of service, Mr. Clayton?"

"Creighton, I'm Clifford Creighton."

"Yes, I know," the boy replied with a tinge of impatience. "Crifford Clayton."

"Yes."

"Did you have a nice slreep?"

"I guess you could say that—yes."

"And now you have our fair city before you."

"Correct me if I'm mistaken," Clifford ventured, "but haven't we met?"

"Ah, indeed." The unctuousness of his words sounded wildly unsuitable to a boy of his age. "We encounter each other at railway station. I escort you to this hoterl. Now I am at your service."

Clifford tried to remember his arrival and failed miserably.

The boy stood before him, motionless, his head slightly lowered, in an attitude of mock submission.

"Yes," Clifford said. "Maybe you can help me. I need to get a feel for the city. I need to see the lie of the land."

"You take horsecar, maybe? End of town and back?" The boy made it sound dull beyond words. "*Or* you go to rivery stable, rent horse all day, see city, see nice countryside. I get you good price."

The phrase *beware of touts* flashed again through Clifford's mind. He dismissed it immediately. "Where?" he asked.

"We on Main Street right now, south side of Plraza. Cross Plraza, go north two blocks. Don't be afraid. Rivery stable on right. Say Sung sent you."

Clifford waved a response and pushed open the swinging doors. He was in the city. The heat hit him like a physical blow. Main Street, as the boy had euphemistically called it, was little more than a wide dirt track. Dust rose in clouds as carriages and wagons vied for the right of way. Red-eyed, unshaven men lounged in every doorway. He looked across the Plaza. It was nothing more than a parched vacant lot. A water tank stood unceremoniously in the middle; perhaps a hundred foreigners, Mexicans, milled around it.

Clifford took a breath and set out.

Once he had crossed the Plaza, the thin veneer of civilization dropped away. The street narrowed, the buildings diminished to a string of wooden shacks, scarcely higher than a tall man. Some of the doors here were open at the top; painted Mexican ladies lounged there and looked at him in frank invitation. There were Chinese here, too. He passed a butcher shop, its wares well past their prime, slabs of pork attracting flies, the glazed bodies of skinny chickens hanging next to festoons of bright red sausages.

Fresh as he was to this city, Clifford saw that these Chinese had little in common with Sung. It was not just their native dress. They were furtive, avoided meeting his eyes.

With great relief he saw ahead of him the sign reading McFarland Stables, and turned into the welcome gloom. Blinking, he called out and was waited upon by a red-haired, rawboned white man, close to his own age. "What can I do for you, mister?"

"I was told I might rent a horse for the day, to get the lie of the land. I was told, at the Pico House, that—"

"To say that Sung sent you. That kid's a real piss-cutter. He'll own his own bank by the time he's sixteen."

The man had already turned. "Come on out to the tack room. I'll show you what we got."

75

Clifford gaped at the heavy-horned Western saddles on their wooden stands. "I've never seen anything like those before," he said.

"You'd better get used to them if you're going to stay around here. You'll find they make easy riding."

For the first time since getting on the train in Chicago, Clifford's confidence wavered. He thought of venturing into "those streets," on a horse he didn't know, and in a saddle that looked like a rocking chair. Playing for time, he looked around the tack room. In the farthest corner, as if flung there carelessly, he caught sight of his possible salvation, an English saddle of a quality that even the dust could not obscure.

Strolling over to it, Clifford coolly asked, "Do you have a horse that matches this?"

McFarland snickered. "I've got a horse, but you wouldn't want to ride it. He came with the saddle, but I haven't been able to use him. When I put a *real* saddle on him he acts like a bronco, and no man around here is going to fork that sissy-looking, slippery piece of leather."

"I'll give him a try," Clifford said, hiding his elation.

"It's your funeral," McFarland replied. "And *you* saddle him up. He won't even take a real bit." He picked up the saddle and tossed it in Clifford's direction. "Maybe you'll change your mind when you see the horse."

The animal was a gaunt black stallion, standing hands taller than the Western ponies in the nearby stalls. It pricked its ears as they approached.

"He's an ugly devil, isn't he?" said McFarland.

Clifford grunted noncommittally. He could see the lines of a classic strain. The great beast's dish-shaped head in profile showed its Arab ancestry. Another foreigner in this strange land.

"If you want him you got him. A dollar for the day. That's half price, and I'll throw in a nosebag full of oats."

Clifford slipped the headstall over the great head and neck. He eased in the light bit, and noticed that the teeth showed a four-year-old. He had thought it a much older animal. Sidling in, he threw on the pad, settled the saddle. The big horse swung his head wide, then swooped down to nuzzle the nape of Clifford's neck.

"Looks like you two hit it off," McFarland said with a sudden change of tone. By this stage of his trip, Clifford had no trouble recognizing the false heartiness of a man eager to take advantage of a greenhorn. "Everything's spread out in this city. A man needs a horse to get around. I could give you a real bargain on that one. Most saddle horses around here go for twenty. I'd give you this one, with the saddle thrown in, for an even ten."

McFarland followed Clifford as he led his mount out of the stall, into the side alley.

"I'll think it over," Clifford said as he adjusted the stirrups.

The horse shifted. Clifford said, "Easy, boy." Then, to McFarland, "Does he have a name?"

"Not that I know of."

Clifford, his left foot in the stirrup, swung himself up and into the saddle. The horse trotted into traffic, under a tight rein. Clifford turned him south,

76

toward the Plaza and the center of the city. But he could feel the animal's reluctance to join the dust, the crush of vehicles, and decided to give him his head. The stallion doubled back past the stable, where McFarland still watched from the door.

"Ain't nothing out there, mister, but—"

The last thing Clifford heard was his derisive chuckle.

Within five minutes he had left the city limits behind him. He crossed a sandy stretch and a creek. His mount, as if instinctively, headed up a shallow valley. This was not Eastern countryside. Heavy brush covered both slopes, dry, spicy, aromatic. It was hot out here, burning hot, but not the heat he was used to. He took off his jacket and slung it across the horse's withers. The scorching breeze, curiously pleasant, ferociously dry, cooled his damp skin. A long-eared rabbit broke across the road ahead of him. He saw squirrels in profusion; they hardly bothered to stay out of his way. In a few moments, his horse started as a strange, awkward-looking, long-tailed bird ran ahead of him, making an ungodly clacking sound before it turned off into the brush.

He continued up the valley, conscious of his horse's springy gait, which confirmed him in his sense of its breeding. The whole day—his whole life—stretched before him. He reveled in his sense of freedom, of ease. As he felt the steady, firm movement of the great animal between his thighs, he thought back, almost unbelieving, to this morning's sensuous revelations. He remembered great, dusky breasts, caressing hands, the searching tongue, yielding lips.

Involuntarily, his legs tightened; his heels brushed the horse's flanks. His mount responded by breaking into an easy canter. The posting rhythm lulled him into a delicious reverie in which his memories of the morning, the movement of the beast beneath him, and the shimmering narrow hillsides fused in a timeless delight. An altogether un-Presbyterian thought crossed his mind. *Almighty God! Surely this is heaven on earth!*

He went on like that for what might have been an hour. When his mount showed signs of tiring, he slowed to a peaceful walk. It was so new, so wonderful. The country grew greener now, the hillsides steeper. Occasional sycamores dotted the lion-colored brush. He saw a line of amazing birds that looked like partridges, scooting along, the males helmeted with black crest feathers. There must have been thirty or forty of them, reluctant to fly, almost entirely unafraid.

He let the horse drift. He could tell by the sun that it was almost midday. His stomach reminded him that he'd had nothing to eat since this morning's *pan dulce*. He knew it might be the sensible thing to turn around. But the mountains ahead, the increasing lushness of the valley, drew him on.

The horse heard it before he did, and swiveling its ears forward, broke without warning into a gallop. Clifford almost lost his seat but recovered in time to rein down to a brisk canter, knowing that in spite of the horse's spirit, in his present condition he could not keep up such a pace for long. As he did this, he himself heard from a distance a sound he could scarcely give credence to—the high, clear call of a hunting horn.

The horse, automatically answering the call, swerved from the road onto a narrow trail that climbed the western slope. As they surged up, Clifford felt the tearing of this country's harsh underbrush pulling against the inadequate gabardine of his trousers. He ducked under the branches of a scrubby tree. Dust flying, stones skittering out from behind hooves, horse and rider made it to the crest.

A third blast from the horn greeted them, and Clifford, still unbelieving, found himself joining a group of galloping riders. He saw the leader of the hunt in classic pose, horn to his lips, the horn flashing golden under the sun. Then he heard behind him an English-accented voice calling out, "Well ridden, young man!"

But Clifford had no time even to look around, for he found himself having to use all his horsemanship to restrain the enthusiasm of the beast beneath him.

He came level with the hornsman, and looking ahead he saw the pack of hounds following the belling leader. Ahead of the leader he glimpsed the gray-yellow shape of the creature they were chasing. As it crossed a small open space, Clifford thought it looked more like a dog than a fox, but it ran fleetly, low to the ground. And in the next small clearing it seemed to turn its head almost impudently to look at its pursuers.

Then the animal turned abruptly, loping down the slope to the valley, the hounds after it. Close on the heels of the last hound came the hornsman, with Clifford on his livery stable reject just behind. The two of them by now were well ahead of the main body of the hunt and followed hell-for-leather, hooves slipping, forelegs braced against the steeper slopes as they skidded and scraped their way down.

Then, crossing the road that Clifford had recently left, they clambered madly up a trail on the valley's opposite slope. At the top, the trail widened. The leader of the hounds had actually gained on the creature. As if sensing this, it quickened its pace just before reaching a fork in the road.

Suddenly, a carriage came as if from nowhere and the quarry, slowing briefly in confusion, avoided the oncoming wheels and turned down the wider of the two roads. The driver of the carriage reined in as the hounds streamed by. Clifford and his new companion followed.

"My God!" the hornsman shouted. "We're going right down Colorado Street!"

Clifford could see buildings ahead on either side with an occasional carriage and wagon on the road.

"Old Rex is foundering," the hornsman called to him. "Look, sir, you must carry on." And he thrust his long dark whip into Clifford's impulsively outstretched hand.

"But I—" Clifford began, and then realized that his horse had already surged forward, leaving the hornsman behind.

Now Clifford saw that they were nearing a center of commerce. Women on wooden sidewalks stopped to watch aghast. And then he heard a voice from the street shouting, "Mad dog! Mad dog! Take cover!"

Merchants, pedestrians ran for entryways. Confusion reigned.

The creature, the hounds, and Clifford belted down the center of the busy thoroughfare as everyone scrambled aside. Just ahead, a heavy wagon moved into the right of way, and the winded quarry, panicked by this obstacle and all the shouting about it, made one last desperate choice and turned into the false security of a dark open doorway.

As Clifford dismounted from his heaving beast, he heard shouts from inside the building. The hounds bounded in between the legs and skirts of the fleeing occupants.

"Mad dog!" he heard shouted again.

"They're all mad dogs!"

"I beg your pardon," he courteously said, as he forced a passage through the doorway close behind the yelping pack.

He found himself in a large open space divided by counters. A frightened, angry-faced man, looking through a metal grill, yelled at him. "Call off your damned dogs! Don't you realize this is government property? This is a United States Post Office!"

"Indeed?" Clifford managed with a civil nod as he rushed forward and whipped off the dogs that were darting in, nipping at the creature at bay crouched under the far counter.

Then, unable to think of anything else to do, with a lucky twist of his wrist he curled the long whip under the counter and around the head of the snarling creature. He jerked it forward off balance. Then he leaped in and brought the heavy, leather-braided handle down on the furry skull between its ears. He felt the body go limp. And even as he dealt the second blow he saw the eyes beginning to glaze in death. Grabbing the animal's tail and whipping the hounds ahead of him, he made for the entry and emerged on the sun-drenched sidewalk.

The hounds still sounded in frenzy, answering the panicked shrieks and outraged cries of the citizenry. All this was compounded by the thud of hooves on packed earth as the main body of the hunt hurtled down Colorado Street and reined in immediately in front of the post office, the horses blowing hard, snorting, sidestepping into each other as their riders fought for control.

The first rider off his mount pushed his way toward Clifford with an air of authority, and called out, in that familiar English accent, "Calm yourselves, my friends! There is no mad dog. These are the hounds of the Valley Hunt, and our young friend here has served us all well by ridding our community of this marauding coyote."

As the noise of the crowd began to subside into murmurs of approval, the hornsman came up on his limping, heaving mount. Swinging down, he shouted to the hounds and they quieted under his voice.

The Englishman stepped forward as the master of the hounds maneuvered his pack down the boulevard. "We can at least exchange names, sir. I am Percy Logan-Fisher. Splendid job!" He was a tall, spare figure, obviously an outdoorsman, perhaps old enough to be Clifford's father. His deeply tanned face was in delightful contrast to his carefully trimmed moustache and Vandyke beard. His manners were those of a born aristocrat.

"My pleasure, sir. I am Clifford Creighton, recently of Baltimore."

"A delightful city in its own way," Logan-Fisher responded politely.

"Allow me to invite you to the collation we are holding to celebrate the end of the hunt."

"You are too kind," said Clifford.

"Not at all. We are greatly in your debt." Then, turning to the members of the hunt, Logan-Fisher addressed them with an expansive gesture. "This is Mr. Clifford Creighton, whose coolness has saved us from a possibly embarrassing incident."

"Hear, hear!" A voice came from the edge of the group of riders; others called out "Welcome!" and a general murmur of approval came from the shifting group. For the first time Clifford noticed that the Valley Hunt was made up almost equally of men and women.

"Back now to Shady Oaks, my friends!" Logan-Fisher announced.

Clifford's eyes scanned the group as the riders began wheeling their mounts toward their new goal. He saw—instinctively winnowing out the maids from the matrons—several bold and pretty faces, flushed from the morning's excitement, inspecting him with admiration. Only one girl, her silver-blond hair still in neat wings about her head after the morning's exertion, glanced at him and looked away indifferently.

But already Logan-Fisher commanded his attention. "Follow along with me, Creighton," he said, moving toward his own mount. "We won't press, for I can see your trusty friend is winded."

"I'm astonished he made it this far," Clifford answered, as he swung up into his English saddle. "He's been neglected at the livery."

"Ah, but he has the courage of the ancestry I can see in his forehead," said Logan-Fisher.

"I noticed that, too."

"He must come direct from the Barbary strain imported by Lady Blunt—a noble Barb."

"I plan to buy him," said Clifford with sudden decision in his voice. "And you have named him for me—Black Barb."

"Oh, bravo," Logan-Fisher responded. "Splendid!"

Shady Oaks was a substantial estate, the main residence built in the old Spanish colonial style, with white adobe walls more than two feet thick, and a roof of dark red tile. It fronted on a small lake of about three acres, the water an astonishingly deep blue under the cloudless sky. Servants' quarters and assorted outbuildings could be glimpsed through the grove of oaks that gave the *estancia* its name. From here there was no hint of the tawdry bustle of Los Angeles, or even the rural charm of that town which Clifford had learned from his host was named Pasadena.

Three sides of the house circled a courtyard where, sheltered by grape arbors and pepper trees from the midafternoon sun, the members of the Hunt now congregated. A long refectory table, covered with the finest Irish linen, was spread with the abundance of this land. Oranges in profusion. Clusters of grapes. Whole walnuts, which had been painstakingly shelled, then dipped repeatedly in a mixture of honey, fresh grape juice, and the finest sherry.

Clifford, straight from the rigors of an eastern winter and his purgatory on the train, gaped at dishes of fresh new peas, buttered summer squash, and salads of dewy lettuce. Added to these almost unimaginable delicacies were exotic "made dishes." Beatrice Logan-Fisher, elegant Englishwoman and gracious hostess who plainly enjoyed this unexpected visit from the mannerly young American, named them for him, her well-bred British voice tripping amusedly over the syllables: "These are *alcachofas,* you eat them a leaf at a time. And *frijoles de olla;* the servants tell me they make sound teeth—and these are alligator pears. . . ."

Just outside the circle of the courtyard a dressed animal stretched spread-eagled in front of low flames. "It will be ready in just a few minutes," Clifford's companion said, following his glance. *"Venado."*

"Venado? I beg your pardon?"

"Venison, Mr. Creighton, or," she continued, "we can offer you some well-cured ham."

Clifford's stomach rolled over. "Venison will be fine."

A few minutes later found him seated at one of several shaded tables with his attentive host. The repast was the finest he had ever tasted.

"At a later hour I can offer you something stronger," Logan-Fisher had said earlier. "For the sake of the ladies, bless them, we must be content now with champagne." A bottle, already half-emptied, stood in its own engraved bucket, glistening with cold.

"Ah," Clifford had said then, and repeated it now. "Ah, this is marvelous—magnificent."

Logan-Fisher chose to take his remark in its larger sense. "Beatrice and I have grown very fond of this place. My oldest brother, of course, came into the entailed family holdings—a dismally damp manorhouse in Devon—the private name for it is Scum-on-Moat. Sometimes I think *I'm* the lucky one."

As Logan-Fisher continued in this vein, Clifford gave himself up to pure enjoyment. Relaxed by the champagne, he gazed appreciatively at his fellow guests. How robust they were! How browned by the sun! Fragments of conversation came to him:

"Thank God for the rain last week. It freshened the new grove."

"What have you got there—limes?"

"My dear, I never feel more safe than when I'm in a sidesaddle, despite what the men may think."

"They're so blind about that kind of thing!"

A group of young ladies reclined in the shade, the full skirts of their riding habits spread about them with self-conscious grace.

A man's voice brayed out, loud among the delicate twitters. "I'm looking for a *new* woman! A woman who won't ride sidesaddle. A woman who admits she has legs!"

"Oh, Headsperth! Surely you're joking!"

There was a muted chorus of scandalized sighs and titters. One young girl clapped her hands over her ears and blushed deep red. Even the word "legs" provoked self-conscious embarrassment. Clifford felt that, in this respect, he might just as well be in Baltimore.

"Of course he's joking," said the only chunky maiden among them. "Headsperth *always* jokes."

Clifford looked at the object of their attention. He saw a florid young man, his elbow propped at an improbable angle in the cleft of one of the oaks. His debonair pretensions were undercut by an unfortunate plumpness. His chin was at best ill-defined, and as he turned to more easily speak to the ladies his posterior curves strained the seams of his riding breeches.

"That's Headsperth Bauer," Clifford's host murmured noncommittally. "His father's a banker. He himself writes verse."

"You don't say," Clifford remarked absently, his eyes resting on one of the group, the girl with silver-blond hair. She alone had not laughed, but still watched the would-be poet with keen attention. Then she felt Clifford's gaze upon her, looked up, and dropped her eyes.

"My niece, Victoria Landon—here from Australia," Logan-Fisher said, following Clifford's glance. "She visits us every two years."

"Ah," Clifford responded. He took another deep draft of champagne.

It had taken very little persuasion to make Clifford see how reasonable it was to accept the Logan-Fishers' invitation to stay over for the night.

"If not for *our* pleasure," Beatrice Logan-Fisher had said, "then—as Percy has pointed out—for that great black beast that brought you pell-mell amongst us to return with a decent rest."

By this time, Clifford had a stronger reason for putting off his return—the beautiful Victoria Landon. He knew it was madness, this thing that he had not yet so far even allowed his mind to put into words, but by the end of this day he had been emboldened by his string of triumphs: his morning with that Latin beauty, his first "business venture," his Barbary steed, his "heroism" in the hunt, and his gracious acceptance into this society typified by the Logan-Fishers—so elegant, so affluent, so kind.

The gentlemen lounged, now, over brandy. The other guests had long since departed. Percy, as if it had been the most natural thing in the world, had lent him dinner clothes. Their late supper, eaten on the south veranda where a refreshing breeze had teased at the curls of the ladies, had been taken *en famille,* just the four of them.

Miss Landon had spoken to him thus: "Have you been here long, Mr. Creighton?"

"Only a few days, Miss Landon."

"How interesting."

"And you, Miss Landon. Your uncle has told me that you make that long voyage pretty regularly."

"Yes, my parents feel that I should keep up the family ties. I'm afraid I don't altogether share their dedication to life in the outback—"

"And no wonder," her aunt had broken in. "The Australian outback is no place for an eighteen-year-old girl. My dear sister Eunice has never recognized the importance of—"

"Auntie!" Victoria said abruptly. "That reminds me, that in her last letter, Mummie. . . ."

And that had been the end of their exchange.

The ladies had retired shortly after supper. Percy, true to his earlier promise, had brought out decanters of brandy and port, together with some sharp and crumbly cheddar cheese.

Percy lit up a mild claro, puffed, exhaled, sighed with satisfaction as he leaned back. "I hope you won't think me too presumptuous, Clifford, if I ask straightaway just what you're planning on."

"Not at all, sir. I'd be happy to answer you, but the truth is I don't know yet. I can say I feel my future lies here."

"A young man like you could do well for himself."

"That is my hope, sir, and—" Clifford pushed on, unthinking. "Sir! Are your niece's affections engaged?"

"I beg your pardon?" Percy Logan-Fisher asked sharply.

"I know that may sound both presumptuous and precipitous, but I also know that my future will be influenced by your answer."

"I *say*," Logan-Fisher responded. "You come into this in the same way that you joined the hunt! But then," he went on, shrugging, "I must admit you didn't exactly disgrace yourself in that escapade."

"Don't misunderstand me. I . . . I want to marry Victoria." He stumbled on. "I can only assure you, sir, that if it seems I am moving too fast in this matter, I feel almost the same way myself. But what can I say, sir? The moment I saw her, I . . ."

"I say," Logan-Fisher repeated, and then fell silent. When he spoke again it was with considerably less warmth than before. "Notwithstanding, young man, the fact we know nothing at all about you, I'm afraid you may have picked up the wrong idea about my niece's situation. The girl is virtually penniless. Her mother married a missionary whose only purpose was to save souls. To use a hackneyed phrase, her face is her fortune, her only fortune. If she does marry, it must be to a man of considerable substance."

Clifford opened his mouth, but his host cut him off with a peremptory gesture. "And there is the matter of Headsperth Bauer. He, he *is* a man of substance. And, I believe, Victoria is taken with him."

Clifford drained his snifter. "As long as we're speaking frankly, sir—and, may I say, I'm glad we are—Headsperth Bauer is . . . ."

"An ass." Percy finished his sentence for him. "But that is not the issue at stake, young man. We know nothing *of* you—"

"Sir, you are speaking to a Creighton!" Even in his muddled state, after the sun and brandy, he sensed the inadequacy of this response. "My mother was a Cabot. And I am a graduate of the University of Virginia, and, *and*," his voice rose, "I have ridden with the Rose Tree Hunt out of Charlottesville."

"Be that as it may," Logan-Fisher said, after a judicious pause, "there is still the matter of property. My wife and I are settled on one thing. As long as Victoria is in our care, if she *does* marry, it must be to a man of property."

"Well, then. Perhaps you could advise me. Do you know of any property for sale?"

His host surveyed him for a long moment. Clifford waited uncomfortably in the silence that followed. Then Logan-Fisher jumped up from his chair and, with hand raised, approached his guest's chair. Clifford thought of the ride back to town, in the dark.

"By God, m'boy! If you aren't the thruster! Sometimes you Americans still astonish me."

The hand came down on Clifford's shoulder with a hearty clap. "Actually, I *do* know of land, some good land, already planted in walnuts and oranges. The owner overreached himself and is being forced to sell. Ten acres. A mile east of where we rode this morning. The house isn't much. But it's land. Good land." He paused. "By God, Clifford Creighton! You Americans!"

Clifford hoped that his smile didn't look as weak as he felt.

The next morning Clifford and Percy rode out Colorado Street to view the land. It was perfect, but as Percy had warned him, the house was little more than a summer cottage, suffering from neglect. The price, also as Percy had intimated, seemed to Clifford fantastically low. Percy took him to his own bank. Before the morning had ripened into noon, Clifford had his own account, had bargained with the hard-pressed owner, and put down a deposit. He gratefully accepted a light lunch and began the ride back into town measurably closer to the mythical being that Logan-Fisher had conjured up the night before—a man of substance.

Even Black Barb, after the night's rest and the solicitous care of the ranch hands, seemed to have gained new spirit, tossing his head as they rode back down the valley which, he had learned by now, was called the Arroyo Seco.

He arrived at the stable by sunset. His welcome was not cordial.

"I thought you were nothing but a common horse thief," McFarland sneered, as Clifford trotted into the gloom of the stable. "I guess you know now why I'm thinking of breaking that big galoot to pull his weight between the shafts."

Staying in the saddle, Clifford cut him short. "You won't have to go to that trouble," he said coolly. "I'm accepting your offer."

"What?"

"Ten dollars for the horse. Two dollars for two days rental." Clifford pulled out a roll of bills.

"Wait just a *minute!*"

"A deal is a deal. I believe you have that saying here in the West. Twelve dollars."

Before McFarland could answer, Clifford tugged at the reins and disappeared between the wagons and carriages of the dusty street.

After putting Barb into the care of the hotel stable, with orders as to care and feeding, Clifford made his way up the stairs of the Pico House. Suddenly he was exhausted. Too exhausted, even, to consider the wisdom of the decisions he'd made in the past thirty-six hours. More than anything else in the world he needed a wash and a nap.

It was not to be. Less than ten minutes after he lay down with a sigh, just as the noise of the streets had begun to fade, the door of his room silently opened. Magdalena came in, and, kneeling by his bed, touched his cheek, caressed his hair.

"You have been gone long, *mijo!*"

His soft, still Eastern-white skin flushed under her gaze. "I . . . met some people."

"You do not have to say anything." Her other hand trailed downward. "We are married in only one sense. We are business ventures."

"Partners."

"We are partners. And we will always be friends."

"Magdalena," he said, "I met a girl."

Her hands stopped their insistent kneading. She sat back on her haunches and sighed. "*No hay rosa sin espinas.* No rose without a thorn." Then she looked at him with a touch of real anger.

"In your eyes I may be a servant. Let me finish! A servant, or worse, a common *puta*. But I am neither of those. I know my destiny. You will not forget me. Some day you may even come to me for help."

"I would hate to think that I might ever hurt you."

Her mind worked visibly as she struggled to put together the sentence that would define their relationship.

"I have been careful with . . . I have been counting my dollars. *Ahora,* right now heartbreak is a luxury I can't afford." She looked at him with anxiety. "I will have the boardinghouse?"

"I am not a man to go back on my word."

"Oh, well! We *are* partners then!"

She slipped off her clothes and laid her brown body next to his. She began unbuttoning his shirt, her surprisingly soft hands resting on his bare skin. She laughed at the pattern her hands made over his heart.

"Brown and white, *rubio mio!* Not even in the city of the angels would the rest of them out there let us be more than—"

He kissed her. She was so ready for his kisses.

It was late that night when Magdalena arose noiselessly, put on her clothes, and padded on bare feet out the door, down the dark hall and the back stairs to the stuffy basement rooms that served as servants' quarters for the hotel staff.

She lay down upon her canvas cot and shed bitter tears. Her months in this city had been desperately lonely. The ease and wealth and love that she had hoped to find here seemed far away now—further even than when she had been rotting in Sonoita, because now there were no dreams. There was only the reality of menial work.

Six months and she had saved a little less than twelve dollars. Six months without a friend to talk to. And six months with no one to love. She knew it had been the wildest impulse, masquerading as reason, that had sent her into the arms of her beautiful blond one. Many men had come through this hotel richer than Clifford Creighton, but their hands were damp and their smiles cunning. They had been ready to bargain, but not for anything like real love. She had said no—until this morning.

Once again she had gambled. Once again she was wrong. But what she had said earlier that evening was right. At this point in her life she could not afford the luxury of heartbreak. And if this Clifford Creighton was not a complete *cabrón,* if he did not check out tomorrow morning without leaving a forwarding address, she would at least have a way out of this cursed hotel and the backbreaking labor that was turning her into an old woman before her time.

Her tears dried as her mind was racked by another set of worries. Once before she had received the seed of a blond lover. Once before she had carried a child. What if this time she was destined to become a mother? Would she find the strength to be able to take care of the little one and raise him without the protection of a father?

And yet what she said to Clifford was true. She valued freedom too much to submit to the disciplines of marriage, which in her memory meant the humiliation and poverty of that hovel in Sonoita.

But now was no time for hesitation! Tomorrow she would tell the major-domo that she was sick with a woman's pains and she would seize the opportunity to buy the house she'd been looking at. Perhaps tomorrow she would become a *mujer de partes.*

It was not to be. The house that she had pinned her hopes on had been sold. She stood on the sidewalk in front of it now, feeling that indeed the heavens no longer watched over her.

She hesitated as she walked back toward the Plaza. If the heavens had not smiled upon her perhaps it was because she had failed to ask them. Instead of returning in defeat to her tawdry room at the Pico House, she crossed the main square and entered the church of the Queen of the Angels.

There, in the beneficent twilight, surrounded by other women like herself, she prayed as simply and unselfishly as it was possible for her.

"Let me have a life of my own, and if I have a child let it not be a girl who must suffer like this, but a son who may be happy."

How long she stayed there she could not guess. But she knew as she left that whether her prayers were to be answered or not, a burden had been lifted from her shoulders. When she came once more into the brilliance of the Plaza at midday, she was able to greet the Chinese runner with something of her usual good humor.

"Que va, mijo? Where are you going?"

"I do my job. I go to the tlrain. You not work today, I see. And I see you not sick," Sung said, his eyes half-hidden beneath the rakish tilt of his fedora.

Magdalena decided to toss caution to the winds. "I was . . . I was trying to buy a house."

"The God of Wealth smiles on you now. You have found gold in your bed."

"Hold your tongue, *sinvergüenza!"* On the off-chance that he might know something, she said, "The house I wanted was already sold. You know the city. Do you know a place for sale that a woman like me could afford?"

"You mean plitty big house for you and rover?"

"No," she said after a pause. "I want a boardinghouse for workingmen. I want my own hotel."

"How much money you got?"

She told him the truth.

"You not buy much with that, missee."

She said nothing but gazed anxiously at him.

"Start small, end big, they say in my village."

With no further word the boy turned on his heel. She had no choice but to follow him. This time their steps didn't take them to the comparatively trim lawns of the northern part of town. Instead, Sung led the way south and east into a neighborhood where she'd never been.

Magdalena realized that he was taking her into Chinatown.

"Sung, I can't buy here. I need a place where white men can live."

He gave her a knowing sneer. "Many white men come here late at night. I know house on Clara Street. Clara Street not all Chinese."

He took Magdalena down rough paths where the dirt of the city had caked into half-dried mud. Magdalena's nostrils were assaulted by spices and human waste. Children played unattended in the filth.

They turned into Clara Street. The buildings here were a parody of what prosperous merchants had built on the north side of town, but she could see what her guide meant. This was a place between the forsaken, closed world of Chinatown and the inaccessible wealth of the white entrepreneurs. Her eye, already practiced in these matters, saw that here was a frontier. A man who would stay in a room on this street would be either on his way up—or on his way down.

Sung stepped determinedly now and paused at a run-down, two-story house a little bigger than the others. Whoever had built it had misjudged—it was too big, too grand for this street. The porch, though slanting, was capacious, large enough for boarders to rock and take their ease. The facade was marred by missing boards, and what was once painted white was now a disheartening, peeling gray. A FOR SALE sign, itself aging, hung askew behind a cracked window.

The tenant who opened the door was not in the least shocked that a Mexican girl and a Chinese boy wanted to buy the place. He went back to his grimy kitchen in his shirtsleeves, leaving the two of them to tour the house alone. Even Magdalena's strong heart faltered as she saw the work that would have to be done to make this into a house where decent men would stay.

Sung, seeing her hesitation, said, "But this house good wood. I know wood from the north. I get workmen cheap. They clean, whitewash. You sleep twenty men in here easy."

And responding to her astonished stare, he added, "Two, thlee men aloom."

"*Mucho trabajo*. I'll be more of a slave than before."

"No. No. You no be alone." His eyes looked at her appraisingly. "Many men do hard work. Many girls do housework. You be randlady."

"*Demasiado dinero*. Too much money. I don't have that."

"I get men cheap. I helrp you little bit."

Her frank brown eyes took him in for a long moment. "Why? Why should you help me?"

He laughed scornfully at her ignorance. "This is good for me too. I get cut from men, from girls, from you, from men I bring here I get plenty tip. I show them city—where to live, where to buy—I get more." He laughed in what she would grow to know as his characteristic, almost maniacal glee. "*You* work hard, missee. *I* get rich."

Magdalena drew in a long breath. The house was not quite what she'd had in mind but it would become her domain.

By five in the afternoon they had made a deal with the landlord, talked to tradesmen, and decided what would be required. She found Sung invaluable, both for his quick wit and for his practical sense of what needed to be done.

"You go see rover now," he cackled. "You crleverl girl, you see rover five minute. You make him give you money." As he laughed at his own vulgar joke, she realized that much of his accent was a deliberate affectation.

They agreed, when he had calmed down, to meet at the bank the following day.

"You walk home alone. I do more business here. No be aflraid. You learn how to walk down Clara Street alone."

She flared up. "I'm not afraid of rattlesnakes. Why should I be afraid of anything?"

He stood on the porch and watched her flounce fearlessly up the street. Then he scurried off.

Sung Wing On turned down streets few white men had ever seen. Here were gambling dens, the sweet smell of opium smoke; emaciated figures, their eyes glazed, standing openly in the street, smiling at voluptuous visions only their fevered eyes could see. Sung pushed past them contemptuously, turned into a dank alley where diseased women called to him, and came to what looked like a blank wall.

He knocked twice. The wall opened and let him in.

Now truly he was in another world. It was a measure of his enterprise as a businessman that he had found out about this place so young. The Chinese of Los Angeles, sensing early on that they would more than once fall victim to the prejudice of the round-eye, had built their business district in the only area open to them. Underground. A maze of dark tunnels sheltered scores of Chinese merchants, each keen on building his own mountain of gold.

"Sun Wing On, young bandit!" A voice drew Sung into a "store," a shallow alcove dug out of the dirt and braced by wooden beams. "How may I be of service to you?" This man was a broker of labor. He dealt in providing luckless men with long days of toil for only a few pennies a day.

Sung rapped out his requirements, stipulating that the wage be half the going price. They bargained then for an hour, unhurried, each knowing that it was necessary to go through every move of this delicate game, each knowing in the end that they would both be richer.

When it was over and the clicking of the abacus had finally ceased, the broker gave the young man a friendly cuff on the arm.

"Soon you will be wearing silks, my young master. I hope you will not forget those who have helped you. And how go the rest of your businesses? Have you sold any more 'priceless jade' to the Spanish señoritas? Do you still work in the barbarian hotel? Do you still get *cumshaw* from the stable, the laundry, the singsong girls, the restaurant, the shoeshine, the—"

His friendly voice followed Sung down the dark tunnel. A few rats leaped out of his way.

Emerging once more into the dust-laden twilight air, Sung became more furtive as he headed east toward the river that the Spaniards called Porciúncula. He threaded his way through the jetsam of a growing city. He stood still. His eyes scanned every inch of the horizon in every direction, then, protected by a camouflage of sumac, he slunk inside his second home, a six-foot length of thirty-inch pipe. He crouched motionless, enjoying it. This was his own, his fortress against the world. He lived at the Pico House; he laid up his treasures here.

At the far end of the pipe he stored his merchandise: "priceless jade," two "antique bronzes"—crude metal statues that were aged overnight by burial in dung—and one or two pieces of undisputed value he was keeping for his own future compound.

Here too was the old teapot that had been his first bank, but his supply of gold and silver coins had long since overflowed it. He knelt now before a rusty strongbox. Opening the heavy padlock he swung back the thick door and added his tips and commissions of the last week. Sung caressed the hoard with his eyes and held his mother's earrings in the palm of his hand.

His musings were interrupted by an impudent rat the size of a small terrier, which had blundered into the pipe. The rat stood up on its hind legs, challengingly, twitching its whiskered nose over yellow teeth. Making a fist around his memento of the home village, Sung struck out at the menacing rodent, once, twice, until it scuttled away.

Sung opened his fist and gazed again at the pathetically small earrings. This, only this, was all that remained of his family. He shivered. Though he was not superstitious, he could not help realizing that this was the third time this day he had caught sight of these omens of death: for there in the house on Clara Street, unnoticed by Magdalena, one of the same creatures had started out from under the loose boards of the front steps.

That night, in Room 306 of the Pico House, Magdalena Ortiz lay beside her spent lover. The money, her money, lay safe in the placket of her camisole. She too longed for sleep, but before she permitted herself this simple pleasure, she sent up a prayer to the Almighty, as brief as it was devout. "Thank you for sending me an angel!" And she smiled to think that her messenger from heaven had taken the form of a dandified, black-suited, ninety-pound, fourteen-year-old Chinese tout wearing a fedora instead of a halo.

The following week Clifford was busy. He made good on his agreement with Magdalena, sending her off, radiant, with more money than she'd ever had in her life, promising her that when the house was ready—sight unseen—he would be her first boarder. He rode out, almost every day, past the shallow creek that the citizens of this town were pleased to call a river, up the Arroyo to Pasadena, where he closed the deal on his own ten acres, and hired workers to make the shack on the property livable. His new foreman told him there were only a few weeks left of "winter" to prune back the walnuts, and since summer was coming soon, he'd better get the irrigation ditches clear. Clifford was happy to let them work at these projects, while he himself lent a hand in the shack, which became, under his hammering and painting, a clean and pleasant three-room cottage.

He preferred to start back to town in the early dusk after Barb had had a good rest. And each afternoon he would stop at Shady Oaks for a glass of sherry and some conversation with Percy Logan-Fisher, who was full of invaluable farming advice, and Beatrice, who daily pressed upon him a charming assortment of household goods. Clearly, Clifford's cottage had become, in her mind at least, a Pasadena Petit Trianon, a place to play at the simple life. Each afternoon Clifford avoided asking after Victoria, who, whether by accident or design, was absent from these twilight gatherings. Clifford decided to be prudent in his courtship—better not to press at all than to press too hard. At any rate he would see her at next Saturday's hunt.

And that morning came at last. For the first time since Clifford had been in Los Angeles, the city presented itself in an enchanting mantle of silvery mist. Gripped by a strong excitement that he strove mightily to keep in control, Clifford set out in the first glimmering of dawn. He wore rough clothes, which he had chosen with care. In his mind at least, he was every inch the dashing huntsman.

By this time Barb knew the way. In a little more than an hour Clifford approached the Logan-Fishers' *estancia*. He could hear the baying of the impatient hounds, the soft thud of horses' hoofs, kept in by their riders, and the high laughter of well-bred young women. His heart began to pound; he automatically stroked both of his cheeks to make sure that his shave had been close enough.

Then he rode in.

The courtyard was a joyous riot. Riders struggled to keep their horses in check, calling out to each other with jocular good humor. Mexican servants threaded their way with trepidation among the members of the hunt, thrusting up great steaming mugs of mulled wine.

"Logan-Fisher had the right idea today! This will certainly keep off the chill," someone remarked in a particularly fatuous tone, and though Clifford couldn't see the face of the speaker, he knew from his backside that it was Headsperth Bauer, his pudgy rival.

Clifford seized the wine; it added to the fire in his blood. He acknowledged greetings of people he was already beginning to know, but there was still no sign of the one for whom he waited.

"Percy! I don't like to keep the hounds in check!" And indeed, the hornsman was having a time of it.

"We lack only the Boulters, the Masseys, and . . . *my niece* . . . *Victoria*?"

The accented voice faltered. All eyes turned to follow Percy Logan-Fisher's gaze which was fixed, with horror and pity, on the slim figure of

Victoria, who, instead of her sedate riding habit, had chosen to appear this morning in a black Spanish hat with—my God!—a feather, a gaily embroidered Mexican shirt, seen until now only on servant girls on their days off. And this voluminous peasant garb was tucked into—a man's breeches. The sidesaddle was gone; slim legs *forked* her Appaloosa!

In the profound silence of scandalized Pasadena society, Victoria guided her mount up to Headsperth Bàuer. Clifford *felt* her shaking voice, as much as he heard it—a tremulous "I . . . I thought . . . you said you wanted to see a new woman. I heard you say it."

But Headsperth's jowl solidified into a disapproving knot. And at his other side, a chunky girl materialized out of the crowd. "What a charming joke, Victoria. But I'm afraid we can't wait for you to change."

As the girl's horse sidled away, Headsperth nudged his to follow her. His muttered, "Thank God for *you*, Belle," was clearly audible.

Glancing around, Clifford saw that, indeed, the women of all ages were draped in their full riding habits, firmly seated in their sidesaddles. And though Victoria herself looked to him more appealing and more appropriately garbed for this Western landscape, he had to admit to himself that this was the first time in his life he had seen a woman of *any* class riding astride. *Astride!* The very word, thought of in conjunction with the female form, sent a physical tremor through his loins.

Victoria's Appaloosa stood alone in an ever-widening circle. The hornsman took a deep breath, and at a signal from Logan-Fisher blew forcefully on his instrument. The hounds broke for it; the horses thundered after. The hunt was full on.

Victoria spurred her Appaloosa, but stayed close to the rear as they headed out into the chaparral that covered the low hills. Clifford followed her at a discreet distance. This time he held Black Barb with an iron hand. Before the hounds had taken their scent, Victoria veered off, riding hard up a barely discernible Indian trail, and Clifford followed, noticing, even in the stress of the moment, her perfect seat.

She rode then, and rode hard. Did she know she was being followed? Now there was no need to control Barb. Clifford knew the Arroyo began soon. Through the rage he felt on Victoria's behalf, and the exhilaration of the chase, Clifford felt another, stronger emotion: The cliffs were up ahead. If she didn't slow down soon, she would quite literally dash herself to bits.

They pounded into a clearing. They were by that time almost together, and the cliffs dead ahead. Victoria reined in her Appaloosa then, so forcefully that the beast reared and danced about.

"You damn fool—" Clifford began, but her voice cut him off.

"How dare you follow me! Go away, go away! And leave me alone!"

Almost frantic with emotion, Clifford reached for her reins. She struck out at him with her crop. But through this scuffle, the two horses had moved safely away from the edge. Both Clifford and Victoria, as well as their mounts, struggled for breath.

Then, with as much composure as he could muster, Clifford managed to remark, "I plan to walk for a while." He panted for a moment, then went on,

"Barb isn't used to this, I'm afraid. And though your Appaloosa is in better condition, I imagine both of them would benefit."

She sat frozen, watching him as he swung down.

"*Both* of them should walk, don't you think?" And he suited his action to the word. He could only hope that she wouldn't bolt again. After what seemed like forever, her feet, too, were on the ground. The breeches, if anything, looked more shocking, more provocative, than when she had been riding. He wondered where she had gotten them but had just enough sense not to ask.

They led their steeds conscientiously until they were cooled, and both of them kept their silence. He saw in Victoria a control perhaps as strong as his own, and was overwhelmed with compassion when he realized the direction of it; if he was struggling with his own desires, she was simply intent upon keeping from the final humiliation of tears.

He considered how best to break the silence, and decided that a steady blandness was the best weapon.

"Perhaps we might tether the horses, and rest a bit ourselves, Miss Landon? I've never ridden out this way. Will you help me to get my bearings?"

In silence they disposed of their mounts, and in moments they had sat down together in the shade of an enormous live oak. The Arroyo stretched before them in breathtaking beauty. Los Angeles was a rumpled spot on the far horizon; all the rest was Paradise. He waited, as peacefully as he could, for her to speak. Finally, she did.

"He said he wanted a new woman!" What might have been a tear sparkled in her eye, but refused to drop.

"Men like Headsperth Bauer—" But he decided not to take that tack. "And you *are* one," he said heartily, trying to sound harmless and, above all, friendly. "That was a remarkable piece of riding. And. . ."

She turned to look at him.

"And I could not but notice your remarkable seat."

"Mr. Creighton!" In unconscious parody of a woman outraged, she gripped her crop.

He shielded his head with his arms and went on. "You're exquisite! Splendid! And you even have. . . ." He blushed as he said it, and grinned at his own audacity, "Limbs! Legs!"

But she was intelligent enough to scent a "rescue."

"Don't pity *me!* Don't patronize me." She thrust her chin out in what he would come to recognize as a characteristic gesture.

"You'd better leave now," she told him icily. "Or there may be a scandal."

He could only laugh at that. "Are you joshing me, Miss Landon? A scandal after, after . . . dare I say it, this morning's 'breach'?"

"I hardly find that amusing, Mr. Creighton."

But he could tell that some part of her did.

"Victoria Landon, I can *save* you from scandal!"

"I'm sorry," the girl said primly, her hands crossed against her breeches.

"I'm afraid I don't take your meaning." She glanced down with maidenly reserve, and glanced rather wildly away.

"I am, after all, a man of property and a man of taste."

"And modesty to match" was her tart rejoinder.

"Tell me, Miss Landon, would you have used that crop on me?"

"My aim is as good as I want it to be," she said enigmatically.

He dared a full look at her now. As far as he could see, she had regained her composure, and was even enjoying the moment.

"Even the new women, Miss Landon," Clifford said, risking all, "generally refrain from whipping their husbands."

"How dare you!"

"Whether you know it or not, you're going to be my wife."

"In your dreams," she muttered, "perhaps."

"But I shall begin my courtship slowly," he grinned, ignoring her scorn. "I shall start by . . . ." He sat motionless and stared at her with all the openness he could muster. "I shall start by calling you Miss Victoria."

He essayed a bow from a sitting position. "May I ask, Miss Victoria," he said with mock gravity, "where ever did you get those stunning trousers?"

She rewarded him with lilting laughter and a few teasing flicks of her crop.

Magdalena looked down at the table. In the last month the young Chinese had been true to his word. Eight strapping hungry boarders—she had held the number down to that in spite of Sung's insistence that they could sleep twenty—sat up to the table with unconcealed eagerness.

"Estella Ramirez," called Magdalena regally. "The gentlemen are waiting for their meal."

"*Momentita, señora*," came the nasal voice from the kitchen and in a moment the swinging door was flung open by a sweating youngster carrying with great difficulty a veritable mountain of *tamales*.

"Don't let it get around, boys, that this here's the best bargain in the City of the Angels."

"Sure as Bob's your uncle."

"You got any of that . . . fresh sauce to go with 'em?"

"That sauce is too hot for me," spoke up the wimpiest of them.

"I made some up special for you. No chiles," she said. "But chiles are good for the stomach, you know."

"A couple more months here and you'll be lapping it up like it was no stronger than milk."

A contented silence broken only by gusty chewing fell over the table. Magdalena surveyed them all with satisfaction. Less than a month since she had left the Pico House, and already her own life was in order. It was not just that she could make her own living here, but that her tenants admired her. They had, of course, made the obligatory, expected late-night advances. With each refusal she had grown in stature in their eyes, and their respect for her was combined with genuine gratitude, since she had provided these lonely bachelors with something very like a home.

Sung had done his job well. Instead of the coarse workmen she had been prepared for, he had found boarders from middle-class downtown, from City Hall itself. Clerks, craftsmen, and a man who said, at least, that he was assistant to the mayor. Already she was close to making a profit; she could afford to provide her new family with a "sweet" for their Sunday afternoon suppers.

This week it would be *capirotada*. She laughed at their expressions of horror—*tortillas*, French bread, brown sugar, tomatoes, *onions*?—but could not fail to notice that in another fifteen minutes they had reduced the brown mountain to a few delicious crumbs.

The only person missing here was her beloved. His appearances at her table and in her bed had become less frequent of late, but perhaps that was a blessing in disguise. For when she did see him, he was a *toro*, a wild animal with her. She knew she could not possess him completely, but for the present at least they were happy together.

After the meal had ended she drifted into the kitchen to be sure that the cleaning was going well, and to order the next meal—a late-night snack of Mexican chocolate and *churros*. How she enjoyed having servants of her own! (Even if they were young and stupid.) She ordered a tub of hot water to be brought upstairs.

In her own room, which was small but clean, she shucked off her clothes and scrubbed her skin pink. She had become a fanatic for cleanliness and made sure to bathe every day. After growing up in the desert, she found this much water a miracle. The one luxury she had permitted herself (although she'd said it was for the boarders) was a new tub of outsized dimensions—large enough for a man, large enough for even her.

She dozed away the late afternoon, resting in sensuous *deshabille,* and by the time the first star was out, he had come to her, as she'd known he would.

First she made *him* bathe, sternly ordering the maids to take another full tub to the room of Señor Creighton. Then, after a seemly delay, she went to him.

They wasted no time on words. Her golden boy was no longer shy—far from it! She stepped too close to the tub, where he soaked away the day's exertions. He took hold of her strong arm. She tried, not too hard, to get away. But he tugged harder, and somehow, she was in there with him, petticoat and all.

"You hurt my clothes!"

His only answer was a laugh.

How could she resist him? It was true, he was not as romantic as she might have liked, but she had learned to distrust words without meaning. Clifford was her protector; he could do with her as he liked.

He pushed her back against the slanted backrest of the tub, sloshing her wet petticoats out and on to the floor, placing her strong legs out over either side of the tub. The soapy water acted in conjunction with the natural moistures of love. Their feverish coupling made sudsy waves. He steadied himself against his end of the tub, held on, first to her delicious thighs, then to her damp abundant curls. His rising passion made a tidal wave in the steaming water.

Then he was done. Perhaps four inches of water remained in the tub. Magdalena pulled herself up and stood on the wood floor beside him.

"*Qué lío,*" she scolded. "What a mess. I like water, *mijo,* but there can be too much of a good thing! What will I tell Estella!"

"You can say," he said, toweling off, "that this is the Anglo way. I practice swimming in here, an hour a day."

"What if it leaks through into the parlor?"

"Then I'll buy you another one."

What could she say?

"You are some *payaso,*" she said reprovingly.

"What's that?"

"A man from the circus, you know, someone funny."

"So that's how you speak to your business partner?"

He locked his arms under her shoulders and knees, lifted her onto the bed. "Now, stay there!"

"Until when?"

"Until . . . later. . . ."

Next morning, a considerably subdued Clifford made his way back up the Arroyo. His mind was almost completely inactive, but his instincts thrilled to the fresh morning. With no small amount of male pride he reflected that within two hours he would be keeping company with another beautiful woman.

But that was different, his Presbyterian upbringing assured him. That was Victoria, and Victoria was a lady. She had promised to ride with him to inspect what he hoped would be their first home.

Much had happened in the last month. His acreage had been tilled and weeded, his oranges were bearing magnificently. The "shack" gained in rustic style every day thanks to the ministrations of Beatrice, and the continuing work of himself and the boys.

He and Victoria had spoken little since the day when she appeared at the hunt in so provocative an outfit, but he thought that events might be shaping their future. For one thing, Headsperth Bauer had found himself another object for his affections—a rather large object in the person of Belle, the chunky, sensible girl who had had the grace to avoid entire social disaster the morning of the hunt.

None of the other Pasadena bachelors had seen fit to pay court to Victoria in the past weeks, and he counted on this. It was not that he wanted to win her by default, but that he thanked the small advantage that her gaffe had given him.

She was waiting for him, bright as the morning itself. After he'd paid his respects to Percy and Beatrice, the two of them were off. (He'd once again assured that splendid couple of the propriety of this excursion: It was not that Jed, Frank, Bud, and Otto were perfect chaperons, but that with them and all the other workers, he and Victoria would never be alone.)

Which of course was a blamed lie! They were furiously alone from the minute they rode out. Crossing the Arroyo, they rode due east, a few hundred yards north of Colorado Street; along the main *zanja*—irrigation ditch—of the town. It was cool and shady. Spreading pepper trees, like shimmering green lace, reached down with their branches to the surface of the water. They were in a cool, damp forest here. He led the way, once past the town, beside the "branch" that generously watered his own property. They kept silent as they entered the groves. The walnut trees were tall and majestic, the ground freshly raked. He was proud, but tried not to show it.

The "shack" stood on a very slight rise, almost hidden from view by its own grove of trees, tall and aromatic.

"Gum trees! Why didn't Auntie tell me you had gum trees?"

"I thought they were eucalyptus."

"No, those are gum trees! They come from home."

He thought that might be a good omen.

After they had tied the horses he led the way up the sloping path to the cottage.

"In some ways I'm of two minds about this place."

"What do you mean by that?" she asked.

"On the one hand," he said, "now that your aunt has helped me, it's so much more attractive and livable than it was."

She nodded.

He went on. "But it isn't really my idea of a house to live in permanently."

"I love it here," she said. "It reminds me of home."

By this time they were in the main room of the cottage. There were windows on three sides, a small infinity of panes set off by native dark wood. There was a good, if worn, rug on the floor, and Victoria could see her auntie's touch in the tied-back gingham curtains, a few assorted chairs, and a rustic sideboard, which she remembered, it seemed, from her earlier visits. Someone, Clifford or a worker, had jammed nasturtiums and Scotch broom into a clean jar.

She exclaimed over the kitchen arrangements: the scrubbed deal table, the sink of scoured soapstone, the icebox. Outside, she could see in the backyard the beginnings of a small kitchen garden, and forming a wavering border, a triple row of new geranium cuttings.

"Oh but this is absolutely charming! And you already have a garden!"

"I guess that's more José's planning than mine."

"But don't you find the rodents troublesome?"

"I . . . I . . . ."

"Back home, we always had trouble with wombats and roos."

"José put in those yellow flowers. He says marigolds keep off the bugs and squirrels."

He was excruciatingly conscious of her proximity, and it was with a real effort that he said, "Of course, in my limited experience, there's really nothing to dissuade a hungry ground squirrel."

"A shotgun would," she said decidedly.

"Well," he said, after an uneasy pause, "you've seen the place."

Turning away from the window she (accidentally?) brushed up against him, as she stepped back into the main room.

Desperately, Clifford searched his mind for something intelligent to say, but all he could think of was his relief at being out of the tiny dimensions of the kitchen, so that he could keep a safe, chivalric distance from this exquisite interloper.

But his relief was short-lived when he realized to his chagrin that he'd left open the door to his sleeping quarters. And before he could do anything to prevent her, she had gone through that door.

"Victoria, I—"

They almost collided as she hastily emerged.

"What a pleasant—" Her voice was an octave higher than usual.

"I *said* this was just a shack—"

Each spoke without waiting for the other to finish, their voices joining in a nervous fugue.

"In the outback, *our* family used to—"

"I could never ask a lady to—"

"Has my uncle told you? I'm going home on the eighteenth. Because my father says—"

"The eighteenth! But you—"

"And so," she brought out, standing erect, hand on her slim hip, "if you were sincere in what you said during our last conversation—"

He stared at her. "Last conversation?" As best he could recall their last conversation, it had concerned the merits of her aunt's trifle.

"On the cliffs," she said shrilly. "Our conversation on the *cliffs*."

"Oh."

"And so. *If* you were sincere, *if* you have something to ask me, I—" She faltered.

He couldn't look at her face. He stared instead at the hollow of her throat, at her delicately tanned skin, the infinitely touching pulse.

"Of course I was sincere," he managed. "But . . . Victoria. You must understand that I—" He began again. "Victoria. You could have anyone you want."

She laughed then. "I *have* given it some thought, Mr. Creighton. You may not be entirely what you seem. But," she paused, and smoothed the full skirt of her riding habit, "I too am an adventurer, in my own way."

"Miss Landon. Ummm. Would you do me the honor of . . . sharing my life?"

She took a deep breath. "Yes."

What began as a formal pledge, a chaste, respectful kiss to seal their betrothal, turned, before he became aware of what was happening, into a passionate embrace.

Her arms wound about his neck, her delicate breast burned into his rough shirt. Her smooth, flat belly pressed up against him.

He pulled away. "It's time to be getting back."

"Certainly, if that is your desire, Mr. Creighton." Her cheeks were flushed a deep rose. She gazed at him steadily.

"Uh, don't you think"—he groped for the right tone—"that since we're to be married, you might begin to call me Clifford?"

"Ever since that day," she said quietly, "to myself, I've called you Cliff."

His heart was too full for words.

Why, then, did that evening find him once again in Magdalena's arms? Because circumstances were such that there was no time to tell her. A tenant had refused to pay his rent; she had been forced to call the peace officer. What could he do but comfort her with love? The next night Clifford had felt a cold coming on, and she rubbed a salve redolent of Indian herbs upon his chest until one thing led to another. The next day it had been impossible to tell her, because of the intensity of the night before. And so it went on for three weeks.

By day he felt guilt; at night he didn't care. The wedding was coming on May first; after that, things would sort themselves out. As to how that would happen—well, he would let time take care of it.

The Logan-Fishers had been delighted about his engagement to Victoria, and had, in effect, taken every arrangement out of Clifford's hands. "We think of that girl as our own daughter," Percy had said on several occasions over his after-dinner port, and now he had this opportunity to demonstrate his affection. His magnanimity had been swift and imaginative.

"Now that you'll be my nephew, perhaps I can put something in your way. Bill Christy's wife has developed a distaste for this part of the country. I heard today that Christy will be heading east. A down payment of a hundred will take care of it, my bank will finance the rest. Not to worry. Christy will jump at it—he's spread himself too thin. He'd rather let a youngster like you take over than humiliate himself in front of his friends."

Clifford opened his mouth to speak, but Logan-Fisher had gone on. "And you'll be wanting to build, I'm sure. I—" His mouth twitched. "I've heard from Beatrice that early on you and, ah, my niece, spent a particularly pleasant morning where the Indian trail comes up out of the Arroyo. I'd be most happy if as a wedding present, Victoria's dowry, if you will, you'd allow me to deed over to you five acres along the bluff—together with the water rights—"

"You are too generous," Clifford responded, but Logan-Fisher overrode this remark.

"I chose that because, you'll find, it abuts the Christy acreage."

"I—"

"And, if you have nothing against this idea, Clifford, the way you can thank us is to allow us to make your wedding a bit more of a celebration than perhaps you had planned. I know, I know"—he raised a hand to cut off Clifford's rejoinder—"that you and my niece would have planned something more simple, but you must realize," he lowered his voice, "that Beatrice, as much as she loves the country hereabouts, has been blasted lonely. It would be a favor to her, dear boy, to let her plan a . . . give her something to do, you know."

Clifford could only nod. He had the strong feeling that he had lost all control of events—if, as a matter of fact, he had ever had any, and, on his next visit to Clara Street, he was sure of it.

Maria Magdalena Ortiz was an intelligent woman. At each point in time during the days that followed, she knew more about Clifford's marriage—his

98

wedding in fact—than he did. She heard from her boarders that the wealthy Englishman was inviting half of the city government to the Creighton wedding. Three of her own paying guests had been lucky enough to procure invitations.

Her own kitchen girls, Estella and Adelita, had heard from their cousins that more than two hundred people would be coming, including some of the old land-grant families. There was even a rumor that Doña Deogracia Ruiz de Ortega de Moreno de Arellanos de Mariné would be attending—the first time since her long period of mourning for her deceased husband, and one of the very few times she had deigned to appear in Anglo society, since she considered the new arrivals so hopelessly beneath her.

Magdalena knew what everyone would be wearing; she knew that two stalled oxen would be slaughtered in the traditional way. She knew which musicians would be playing, and how much spirits would be ordered. Even Sung Wing On knew all about it and had permitted himself a few remarks filled with innuendos.

She knew what to do in a case like this. Each time her beloved arranged his beautiful self in a way that implied "confession," she arranged her own countenance in an expression she had learned from her own mother. She thought of cream setting in a dish. She thought of sand brushed smooth by the wind. She cleansed her mind of all thought, and then embraced him.

Each man of substance, even in Sonoita, had two houses, the house with his wife, and his "Little House." If she could just keep him from blurting out the "truth" for the next month or so, she would have a good chance of keeping him forever. And (to tell the truth) it was not so hard, because her beloved, like all men, thought with his *berga*.

And so it was with considerable equanimity that Magdalena waited. She contented herself with her guests, and even when Clifford moved out his trunk with a shamefaced excuse, she had smiled, and told him not to work too hard at his new ranch.

Now, on the night of April 28, two days before Clifford's wedding, she was able to consider the future with guarded hope. It was after dinner on this pleasant night. Her guests lounged in the parlor, playing checkers. One read the *Gazette*, another perused his Bible. She sat back doing nothing, chatting politely to the mayor's clerk.

And then, a knock on the door.

Magdalena herself answered. She was well-enough known in the neighborhood by now that there was nothing to be afraid of. It was a hot night. A large yellow moon hung sullenly in the sky and tinted the street a thin, unhealthy, dingy, glittering gray.

"*Buenas noches,* señora," said a young woman about Magdalena's age, who cradled an infant in a *rebozo*. "They told us that we could find a room here."

Magdalena took in the little family group. The woman who had spoken could have been from Magdalena's own town. She was dressed plainly, in the Yaqui style. The darkness of her complexion and her fine cheekbones hid any trace of fatigue. Her husband in contrast showed incontrovertible signs of a long and trying journey. One keen glance revealed to Magdalena that here was not an Anglo of the kind who had been frequenting her rooms. His fine aristocratic features, his black hair, even the cut of his clothes, showed him to be comparatively well born and of Spanish descent. Why then was he with this woman of *Indio* blood?

All this took place in an instant, the instant before Magdalena said courteously, *"Lo siento,* I'm sorry. I have no rooms. All my rooms are taken."

"I knew this would happen," the man murmured in Spanish. "I should never have taken you away," he said to the woman. "I have ruined your life."

The woman ignored him and spoke directly to Magdalena using a dialect that she recognized.

"If they had told me a year ago what life had in store for me, I would have ended mine right then. Never has anyone known such suffering."

"I am sorry. I don't rent to families."

"He said he loved me. I believed him then and I even believe him now, but what is love in this world? When I found out I was carrying his child I prayed night and day. I prayed to everyone—all of the Fourteen Holy Helpers— Saint Katharine and Saint Eustace, Saint Dennis and Saint Barbara. Finally you can see," she gestured to the slumbering babe, "I had to pray to Saint Margaret for an easy childbirth. When he told his family, they tried to have me killed. That's when he took me away. He said the desert was too hard to cross, so we sailed out of Manzanillo. The captain took almost all our money," she sighed. "We were to start a new life, but now. . . ."

Her companion, who had been listening silently, shifted his weight and his knees buckled. Recovering himself, he mutterd with ancient good manners, "It is nothing. I beg your pardon. I just need some sleep."

Magdalena remembered with clarity those days with Señor John Frederick Smith, and the sorrows of her own mother. "I was mistaken. One of our rooms has just become vacant."

"Saint Christopher watch over us forever for bringing our travels to a safe and happy end."

"Come in then, at least for tonight, and keep the baby quiet. My other boarders need their sleep."

Magdalena showed them to Clifford's old room. The man had tottered on the staircase and steadied himself on the banister. In the room he collapsed on the bed. To Magdalena it looked to be more than exhaustion.

"I have the seasickness still upon me," he said politely.

The child stirred as the mother propped it on the pillows beside the man, its little brown fists pushing away the confining blanket as his mother loosened it.

The woman looked at Magdalena as the baby's whimpers grew more demanding. "Little Raoul will be quiet as soon as I have fed him. He too is tired."

The woman opened her bodice and lay down on her side to give her breast to the child. As the infant took the nipple greedily Magdalena turned her head—not for any reasons of delicacy, but because her own breast ached with feelings she could scarcely name. After three months of lovemaking with her *novio*, she was still no closer to being a mother. She knew she had lost more than her baby in that flooded *barranca*.

Magdalena always rose early on Saturdays. On weekdays she made it a habit to make the porridge herself and pour the steaming cups of coffee by her own hand. On Saturdays, she made pancakes and fresh fried eggs. Magdalena was surprised to turn and find the Indian woman standing next to her like a ghost.

"Tea," she said, "or a little broth. I need something to drink."

"Of course," said Magdalena, "but you and your husband may have breakfast with the rest of my guests."

"My throat," the woman moaned. "I need something for my throat. Saint Blaise protect me." She sneezed once and sat down next to the stove.

Magdalena prepared a cup of tea with honey and lemon which the woman took with a trembling hand. Then Magdalena continued with the breakfast, pouring buckwheat batter onto the hot griddle. As the woman turned to watch Magdalena, she sneezed again.

"I must go to little Raoul." And the woman staggered out of the kitchen.

When the family did not come down for breakfast Magdalena sent Estella up to the room, but she came back alone.

"The woman would not open the door," the servant girl reported. "I could hardly hear her when she said they need nothing."

By eleven, the boarders had finished lingering over their stacks of pancakes and homemade syrup. Now they waited their turns as great cauldrons of water were heated for their Saturday baths. They shaved with special care and laid out their best clothes in anticipation of their evening which might begin with a drink at the Pico House or Bella Union, after they had enjoyed their own meal at home which was part of their board. They engaged in bantering rivalry as they enlisted the help of the two servant girls in ironing, sewing on buttons, bringing fresh towels.

It was early afternoon when Sung Wing On stopped by as he always did, making the rounds of his various business enterprises. But today was different. The instant he stepped in the back door his carefully casual demeanor left him. He stiffened; his fists clenched. He gasped out something in Chinese; the blood drained from his face.

"You are the second ghost I see today," laughed Magdalena, in the midst of shelling a big bowl of peas. "Come in and sit down."

But he didn't move. He breathed with short inhalations trying to catch an indefinable scent. He held his head rigid, but his eyes scanned every corner of the room.

"What is it?" she said with some concern. "You look sick, *mijo*. I'll make you some tea like I did for the other one."

"Other one?"

"A family came last night. I gave them Clifford's room. He won't need it anymore," she said with false bravado.

Without saying another word Sung disappeared upstairs. When he came back, his young face was set in a grim mask. When he spoke it was with a fierce intensity that Magdalena had never heard before.

"Stay in kitchen. Do not say a word. You sit there. I come back."

And before Magdalena had a chance to say anything, the young Chinese was gone. She wasn't going anywhere, she thought to herself, she had to shell enough peas for a household of thirteen.

When he did come back it was with two sweating coolies and a steamer trunk. They tracked through her kitchen and up the back stairs without a word. Magdalena's hands began to sweat. What her mind had been denying since the night before suddenly became clear. The trunk bumped against each stair and she heard it land with a thump in front of Clifford's old room.

Her heart constricted by an unbearable dread, she raced up those same stairs. The workmen waited alone on the landing. She pushed open the door to Clifford's room and gasped at what she saw, and smelled.

"Get out! Get out!" Sung said in a desperate voice.

The room was filled with an indescribable smell of blood, vomit, and excrement. The curtains had been drawn. Magdalena closed and locked the door behind her. She had surprised Sung in an awful errand.

The trunk was open. The Spaniard lay half on the bed and half off while Sung tugged futilely at the body. Magdalena crossed the room and locked her strong arms under the corpse's shoulders. As they lifted him, black bile oozed from his lips onto her white blouse. She gagged. Together they folded him into the trunk. His skin burst under his fine cambric shirt. Sung closed the lid on the abomination.

Sung and Magdalena gazed, mute, deep into each other's eyes. Then Magdalena raced to the window, opened it, and retched. When she had regained control, she turned to see Sung waiting. Involuntarily she shuddered. Her angel had become a helper of the Devil. He hissed words at her that she could barely understand.

Magdalena looked over at the Indian girl. Only her head and neck were visible. Her neck was swollen dreadfully, and bleeding where she had clawed at it in hope of relief. In her mouth she bit a twisted end of sheet and Magdalena had a sudden memory of all the women in her village who had bitten down on *manta* to hold back the tortured cries of childbirth. Her glazed eyes met Magdalena's in silent entreaty, but as she moved forward to help, Sung thrust her back with all his might.

"You go now. Go down stair. Take bath. No say word." Then he said it again. "She die soon."

His little hand pinched the flesh of Magdalena's arm. "You no die. I no die. Everything be fine. I come back one hour for rady."

Sung opened the door, pushed the trunk out onto the landing, and she heard his voice barking orders in a tone of high arrogance.

He was true to his word. One hour later he was back with the empty trunk; one hour later the Indian girl was dead. It was only when they picked up that body bursting with suppuration that the baby began to cry.

High on the west side of the Arroyo the Logan-Fisher *estancia* bustled and seethed with every kind of activity. Under the oaks Mexican servants raked the dust into ornamental designs. The far end of the courtyard had been turned into an impromptu bandstand, its sheltering canopy already swathed in bunting and decorated by the flags of four nations—America for Clifford, England for the Logan-Fishers, Australia for the bride-elect, and Spain. This last had been suggested by Logan-Fisher in deference to the Señora Mariné and other prominent members of the Spanish land-grant aristocracy—the Picos, the Dominguezes, and the Estudillos. Logan-Fisher wanted this to be the wedding of the decade and such a thing wouldn't be possible without every facet of wealthy Los Angeles life.

Inside the *estancia,* in the cool afforded by foot-thick adobe walls, controlled chaos reigned. In the vast kitchen close to thirty young Mexican girls toiled at every possible culinary activity. Following the four-nation theme there were to be refreshments from each land. Besides the oxen and goat, Beatrice had searched her mind for something "typically Australian" and come up with lambs roasted whole. Servant girls gigglingly put together a trifle, sneaking sips from the sherry bottles. In a separate pantry, with the calm born of enormous tension, three downtown pastry cooks labored putting together a wedding cake, six-tiered and close to five feet high. And in the butler's pantry champagne and other wines carried up from the wine cellar chilled in great beds of cracked ice, crusted with wet sawdust, hauled in this morning from the vast icehouse on the edge of town.

In another wing of the *estancia,* Victoria stood on a dressmaker's table in her full wedding dress, exhorted every moment by her aunt to hold perfectly still while several young girls, their mouths stuffed full of straight pins, took last-minute tucks in the innumerable flounces of expensive English lace that made up the full skirt and train of her wedding dress. Victoria, almost at the end of her good humor, looked at her aunt and said, "I don't know how much more of this I can stand."

Her aunt responded in what by this time had become a favorite tradition of the Logan-Fishers. She disappeared into the adjacent den where Percy and Clifford were resting after lunch and reappeared almost instantly with an icy tumbler of champagne, which she handed up to her niece over the heads of the industrious Mexican girls as if paying homage to a mythic figure.

"Courage," she murmured. "It will be over soon."

The men by contrast presented a peaceful-seeming picture. They had no worries concerning their wedding attire. The rehearsal had taken place the night before and the happy couple had already spoken with the clergyman. All other wedding arrangements were being taken care of by the servants. There was nothing for the two men to do but sit back and enjoy the bottle of chilled champagne whence Victoria's glass had come.

"That's just like a woman," Logan-Fisher said to Cliff, "coming in and wrecking the balance of your serving. All we can do is open another bottle to even things up."

Cliff raised his glass in response and said, "I see you're experienced in handling such domestic matters. I can only hope that I can be as wise."

After the second bottle had been brought and opened, Cliff raised his glass and proposed a toast: "To my continuing luck."

Percy Logan-Fisher drank to it, but with some reservation. "You *have* been lucky, my boy."

"I don't know quite how to express this, sir, but when I was a youth in the

East there were times when I was without hope," Cliff said. The second bottle of champagne was beginning to tell. "It seemed as though life was nothing but unhappiness that I had to get through. But out here everything is different!"

Logan-Fisher looked at him. "In theory, my boy, I suppose you could say that!" He smiled a little sadly. "Certainly it looks different. But remembr what the first settlers called this place—The Land of Sudden Shakes. They were afraid when they came here, afraid even to go to sleep."

Clifford was too polite to contradict his benefactor.

"There's defeat and failure here too," continued Percy. "Don't forget that you got most of your own property from Christy. He came here full of hopes and dreams. Every year men lose everything to brush fires in the summer and floods in the winter. Irrigation fails and the groves dry up. . . ."

Percy went on, but Cliff scarcely listened as he sipped confidence with his champagne. He knew he was one of the lucky ones. None of that would happen to him.

Since there was no milk and no question of finding a wet nurse, Magdalena locked Estella in a back room with the baby and a sugar tit liberally laced with brandy. Though Magdalena told herself she wasn't afraid, she fortified herself by drinking about a quarter of a cup of the spirits. Her usually quick mind was almost paralyzed with terror. What happens next, she kept thinking. What do I do now? She knew the main thing was to keep calm. She knew the boarders were expecting their Saturday night dinner.

The other girl, Adelita, had the meal almost ready. How much did they know, Magdalena asked herself frantically. The stench of death was still in her nostrils. It seemed to her that it permeated every room of the house.

The ordinary events of the day went on. Adelita, grunting slightly from its weight, hauled a huge stew pot of *posole* onto the sideboard of the dining room. The relishes for this succulent dish were already there, together with a salad of hearty vegetables. Magdalena often teased her boarders that in this way—by filling their stomachs with good, wholesome food—she kept them from the corruptions of Saturday night.

But when she rang the dinner bell the response was not the usual boisterous rush down the stairs and into the dining room. Only three out of eight men appeared. Magdalena felt the dew of sweat on her upper lip and on the backs of her knees. She shivered.

"Fred says he's not coming down, Magdalena. And Jeff's been taking a nap since breakfast." The young man attempted a feeble smile. "Maybe those buckwheat cakes were a bit too much in this weather." And in a lower voice so he wouldn't hurt Magdalena's feelings he said to his neighbor, "Tom's been puking his guts out."

"But it can't be ptomaine," his neighbor responded. "Or else we'd all have it."

"Sit down," Magdalena said bravely. "Eat up, gentlemen. The *posole* is good for you. It settles the stomach." Even as she spoke she stole looks at her boarders, and she saw that their eyes shone feverishly; their necks were

104

swollen and had turned a dark ominous red. *"Dios mio,"* she prayed, "save us all."

It was then that time began to stop for her, or stretched out into the dreadful slowness that occurred only in her worst dreams. She saw in the slanting rays of the late afternoon sun that Sung had returned and was standing just inside the door of the dining room, looking at these men with awful knowledge. She watched, her hand at her throat, as one man tore desperately at his shirt collar, and then pitched forward, his face in his soup. Another man looked at her in horror, sure perhaps that he'd been poisoned, stood up, overturning his chair, and ran upstairs. He howled as he ran. The man who had collapsed into his bowl straightened convulsively, his poor tortured body bent back into a crescent shape, and fell heavily under the table. The servant girl came in from the kitchen. Her eyes widened with horror and she turned to run, but Sung moved wordlessly and pinned her in a viselike grip. Sung looked at Magdalena and she returned his gaze. If she had thought of the boy at all, she had not thought him capable of feeling. But looking into those eyes which others called inscrutable, she read agony.

By the next morning, Magdalena's clean and well-kept home had turned into a charnel house. Of the eight boarders three were dead. Sung had pulled them all into the upstairs room where the Mexican couple had died. The coolies with the unerring instinct of their kind, intuiting that this house had become a house of death, refused to come back. More than that, it seemed insane, hopeless, to repeatedly fold corpses into that steamer trunk when they were all living by now in the furthest circle of hell.

Sung and Magdalena had tried to keep this nightmare a secret from the servant girls, insisting that they stay downstairs in the kitchen or in the back room with the baby. Strong as she was, Magdalena felt her heart break when Estella, no more than twelve years old, came whimpering upstairs to her just after dawn.

"Señora, I am very sick. I've been throwing up, and look," she pulled up her simple homespun skirt to show Magdalena her thighs. Huge black growths pulsed in her groin. "What are these?" Then she broke down and began to cry for her mother.

Magdalena put the girl in her own bed and told her she would be fine. Then she left the room and began to cry herself. She knew from the terrible experience of the last endless night that the poor girl would probably be dead within a few hours. Magdalena wondered wearily why she was still alive and staggered down into the kitchen to make herself some *atole*. It was strange, but in her anguish she craved the simplest dishes from her youth.

"You idiot," she said to herself. "How can you be hungry?" She'd had neither sleep nor food the night before and she was ravenous.

As she sat in the kitchen with her head in her hands, she heard the door from the dining room silently open, looked up, and saw Sung standing there. How young he was, *pobrecito*. No more than fourteen and he would probably die too. He came and sat down.

"One more man sick upstair. No way get body out."

"What can I do?"

105

"You send letter to rover—"

She cut him off. "You know I can't do that," she laughed bitterly. "Even if he was still mine, I couldn't ask him. And you know, Sung, he's getting married today."

"And we going die today, if you don't send letter."

She tried to smile. "You're a very strong boy, and I'm strong too. Maybe we won't get sick."

He sneered at her. "No get sick. Sung no get sick, but round-eye kill us plenty, maybe."

Even as she tried to take in the import of what he was saying, the relative silence was broken by a long, gurgling scream. Fred, her star boarder, stood in the doorway, the telltale growths swelling his neck so that his head appeared grotesquely small above it.

"What have you done to me, you bitch, you slut?" he shouted. "How did you poison us? I'm dying, I'm dying!"

And with that he turned and ran toward the front door. Sung sprinted after him, but it was too late.

Outside there were a few peddlers, a milkman, and a family or two going to early Mass. The tormented man confronted each of these people in turn. They cringed away.

"She poisoned me. She poisoned me."

When he opened his mouth again, a great fountain of blood gushed from his lips. The people in the street drew back, horrified. One of them went off, presumably to find a policeman.

Sung, still in the doorway of the boardinghouse, stepped back into the shadows and slowly began to shut the door. But the people on the street had seen him. They whispered ominously among themselves.

Now Magdalena could see as well as Sung what might lie in store for them. There was great hatred of Chinese in this city and she was only a poor Mexican girl. If they didn't die from the disease, they might very well die at the hands of a mob.

Even though she fought against it with her last reserves of Mexican pride, it didn't take Sung long to convince her that they must send a message to Clifford.

"I go now to letter writer," he said. "I come back soon. No be afraid."

But she was afraid, more afraid than she'd ever been in her life, as a young boarder came into the kitchen and asked her piteously for a little cold water and then lay moaning on the parlor couch, as the little knot of passersby in front of the house began to swell and their mood turned dark with anger, and as a horse-drawn cart came to haul away the body in front of the house.

Less than an hour later, a vehicle from the coroner's office appeared. It was followed closely by a wagon in which rode a young man in an open shirt with the insignia of the Health Department on his arm. There were at least six policemen with him, and the wagon was filled with lumber.

Magdalena stood frozen, framed by the window in the front parlor. They won't come in here, she thought to herself fiercely, irrationally. I'll die first before I let them in.

But the little group had no intention of coming in. Rather, there appeared to be some argument about who was coming up on the porch at all.

After a few minutes the man in shirtsleeves came up, together with two policemen, each of whom carried an armload of wide lumber planks. Magdalena watched as if she were truly one of the damned in Hell as the man first nailed up a large red sign with skull and crossbones and the policeman began to hammer planks systematically across the parlor windows shutting out the light.

As they held up a plank across the front door Magdalena found her voice. "Wait! Don't do that! There's sick people in here. You've got to help."

The men stopped, thunderstruck. The man in shirtsleeves turned pale under his freckles. "Health Department," he finally managed. "We're from the Health Department. You're under strict quarantine here. Don't try to get out. You're under guard."

Magdalena understood perhaps half of his words. Her voice thickened through the purest desperation. She shouted out again, "There are dead people in here—three, maybe four. You must take them away."

The man said, "This is very serious." Realizing she was a foreigner he slowed his words. "You must not leave this house."

"I won't," she sobbed. "But you must help me."

"We'll leave a slat open in each window for light. And, for now, we'll guard the door. We'll get help to you soon."

The hammering went on for another hour and soon the first floor of the house was cast into deep gloom. Magdalena waited, trying to comfort the dying man, but no help came unless you thought of armed men stationed at every corner of the house as help.

She'd long since given up hope of seeing Sung again. He had promised to come back. She knew he was brave and not afraid of the disease. But she knew, because of his race, that he didn't like white men and was terrified of the police, and now the entire ground floor of the house was a prison. She had given herself up for lost and was praying on her knees in the parlor for a miracle when again she saw her saving angel. He was sauntering downstairs as if nothing had happened, but his dark suit and fedora were covered with twigs and leaves.

"Sung!"

"No worry, missee," he said sardonically.

And this time she could have sworn he used his fearsome English just to amuse her.

"This time I come by tlree."

Strange, that at the moment in her life which should have been the happiest, she felt nothing but bewilderment, that and the twin trickle of sweat from the back of her knees. To be the center of attention after all the feverish preparations, walking down the improvised aisle through the spacious courtyard, holding on to her Uncle Percy for support. . . . She caught snatches of conversation, whispers of admiration, and isolated from others, the clear, scornful voice of old Lavinia Bauer addressing her son: "You're an idiot, Headsperth! Your father always said so!" She supposed she would register that as a triumph, later. Now, she caught only isolated glimpses: her uncle, trembling as he gave her away, the minister looking at her questioningly, until she said "I do." Her Aunt Beatrice, under the shadow of her great picture hat, not crying at all, but looking supremely smug now that she had finally outwitted her pious sister, melting in the sands of the Australian outback: She had saved her niece from a life of devotion to the Aborigines.

Later, in the reception line, Victoria submitted to endless damp kisses, familiar pinches on the cheek, and continuous "well-wishes" from, it seemed, every substantial clan with a few notable exceptions—the Spanish land-grant families who held apart. The general feeling was that *they* stood in line for no one, that people stood in line for them.

After two hours of this, Victoria was ready to drop, but the festivities had only begun. She and Clifford had started the dancing, but her Aunt Beatrice had deftly removed her from the floor. Her reason was twofold; to bolster the wilting bride with a cold plate and a glass of champagne, and then to take her on a last series of introductions through what looked almost like an encampment. The land-grant families, through long experience with this sort of thing, had used the time when the rest of the party had been in line to stake out the best tables on the shady side of the courtyard. She was introduced to the Picos and the Dominguezes, and was then led to the most conspicuous of them all, the entourage of the recently widowed Señora Deogracia Ruiz de Ortega de Arellanos de Mariné, who, now that her elderly husband had died, controlled thousands of prime acres stretching from the edge of the San Gabriel Mission to the fertile vineyards of Cucamonga. As always, the Señora traveled in state. She sat stylishly gowned in black taffeta, sparkling with pounds of jet. Her tortoiseshell comb was a full foot high, and encrusted with—could they be *diamonds?* Even Victoria, new to the ways of Spanish California, could see that the lace mantilla that the comb supported was a good yard longer than custom demanded. The Señora's beautiful hands were weighted down with rings.

She was flanked by thirty or forty "close members" of the family. They too were dressed in costly black. And behind the Señora, safely under the protection of the largest oak, and further shaded by several large, fringed, pongee parasols, at least a half-dozen young nursemaids dressed in black cosseted one tot and one infant swathed to the point of suffocation in layers of expensive lace.

"How good of you to have brought your children," Victoria's aunt civilly remarked. "Can we do anything for their comfort?"

The Señora clutched at the intricately worked golden locket that rested against her bosom.

"What can we do against the will of God? I pray every day to Saint Joseph of Copertino that my beautiful babes not be taken from me! They are all that I have now that my husband has gone to his reward. My beautiful Maria Consuela Gloria Madonna, my beloved boy, Alessandro Luis Antonio, these flowers of Christ are the only things now which sweeten my life of suffering." The Señora fanned herself vigorously with her free hand. "God's will be done," she concluded.

Even Beatrice Logan-Fisher had no ready answer for that, and there was a barely perceptible pause until she smoothly responded, "What a lovely locket, Señora, and what an unusual design."

"It houses a relic of the True Cross," she replied, and bowed her head.

"Mmm," Beatrice Logan-Fisher said, and Victoria, somewhat to her alarm, found herself alone with this widow, scarcely older than she, who had already made herself into this surprising monument to Society and Religion.

"Ah, looking at you," the Señora declaimed, "I remember when I too was dressed in white! Be sure that you pray that your husband may be spared, so that you will not be left as I."

"Oh, I—"

"You Blide?!"

She turned, with some relief. There, totally out of place in this well-dressed crowd, was a Chinese coolie, barefoot and sweating.

"Yes, I am," she said. "What is it?"

"Retter. Clrifford Clayton." He waved a grubby folded paper in Victoria's direction.

The Señora grimaced in distaste and held up her fan.

Victoria scanned the crowd for her new husband. She saw him dancing with Mrs. Bauer on the far side of the floor.

"I will take the letter," Victoria said, holding out her hand. "You must excuse me, Señora."

"No for you, missee! This for *man!*"

Something about his secretive air made her seize the paper.

"No for *you!*"

And it was as much his consternation as the fact that the paper fell open, which made her read the first two words: *My Beloved* . . .

And after that, of course, she read on. *The very worst has happened. I am in trouble. Come to me now. Save me.*

She looked up and saw Clifford, in his morning suit, still waltzing.

She was overcome by a wave of nausea that almost felled her. She opened her mouth to speak, but couldn't. But she was conscious of the appraising gazes of both the coolie and the Señora, and she fought for control.

For a moment she debated. Should she simply walk out onto the floor, through the dancing couples, and hand him this . . . ? Her mind raced. Even if she had inadvertently given herself to a swine, she could not humiliate her aunt and uncle.

Then she caught sight of Cliff's face once again as he trundled the heavy-set Pasadena socialite about the floor to the strains of the sickeningly euphonic Strauss waltz. The banality of her situation overwhelmed her. She had been bought and sold as—she saw now—part of a business agreement between her husband and her uncle. She was to have been the good wife, the good mother, while down in that city she had never even seen, Clifford would keep. . . .

Clutching the note, she stepped onto the dance floor. She dodged one couple, then another, then was rudely bumped.

"There's the blushing bride," a coarse voice brayed.

She was within a foot of Clifford when in a dazzling series of turns he

109

waltzed out of her reach. And what would she say when she found him? A boot trod heavily on her train. She realized the futility of her position and returned breathless to the Señora's enclave, where the coolie still stood uncertainly.

An unexpected vision flew into her mind. The desolate little cottage with the roof of corrugated tin that her mother and father called home. The dusky aborigines and their countless kindnesses to her. The vast stretches of outback. Under that cloudless, luminous sky there had been no dishonesty, no treachery, no lies. A great sob welled up in her throat. Mother, she cried, what would you do? And she remembered with a little shudder of dreary apprehension that her mother had repeatedly told her, "You cannot run away from evil, dearest. It must be faced head on." She knew what she had to do.

"Would you follow me, please?" she said courteously to the coolie. "You have your horse in the stable, do you not?"

As he nodded she turned toward the house and went in the nearest door. The note dropped, unnoticed, into the dust. The coolie followed obediently. The Señora, after a moment's pause, gestured imperiously with her fan. "Pick that up," she said to a member of her retinue. "Put it aside for Señor Creighton."

Once inside the cool building, Victoria picked up her skirts and began to run. She sped down an almost-deserted wing and emerged from a back entrance close to the stable area. She heard the steady footfall of the coolie behind her. Over a hundred carriages impeded her way, but she pushed through, the delicate lace of her gown torn by rough wheels, dirtied by the dust.

"Saddle up Apple," she called to the man in charge of the stable. "And bring this man a fresh horse!"

"But—"

"Do it *now!*"

Then it was only moments until she was on her Appaloosa, her skirts tucked up anyhow, her hair beginning to loosen and stream down her neck. The coolie was already mounted.

"You take me there," she ordered. *"Fast!"*

Together they pounded at a hard gallop down the dirt road that led away from Shady Oaks.

The stableboys watched this apparition until the yards of tulle, lace, and the net of her veil floating behind her had disappeared. Wordless, they looked at each other and shrugged. It was not for them to question the ways of the new señora.

Only a few minutes later Clifford began to miss his bride. With a feeling of virtue he left the floor, congratulating himself on having danced with a full dozen wallflowers.

He took some champagne to cool himself and looked about for Victoria. None of the guests he had spoken to had seen her. But when he asked Beatrice Logan-Fisher, she had a clear, amusing memory of having left her with the Señora Mariné. He made his way, then, to the Mariné enclave. The Señora's eyes had been following his progress.

As he approached, she called out, "Ah, Señor Creighton, I believe we have something here of interest to you." She fanned herself and smiled charmingly. The she nodded to a retainer, who stepped forward, and with a bow, presented the soiled note.

Clifford unfolded it, read the contents.

"Almighty God," he whispered.

"How wise, Señor, to call upon your Creator." The Señora looked at him with opaque eyes. "Just before your beautiful bride read this note, we were discoursing on the efficacy of prayer."

It was a pale and shaken Clifford who sought out his uncle by marriage.

"Percy," he faltered. "I require the help of someone who is my best friend and whom I can trust totally."

Logan-Fisher rose to the occasion. "Whatever it is, my boy, I am at your service."

"I can't say right now what it is," Clifford said, looking him straight in the eye. "I am ashamed of it, but I can say that it concerns Victoria and I need you to ride with me into the city after her."

"Victoria?"

Clifford nodded.

"One moment with my wife," said Logan-Fisher. "I'll tell her that you and Victoria have left the party together. That way no one will notice our absence. The party should continue."

In a matter of minutes Logan-Fisher was riding with Clifford. The older man's jaw was set in a model of English expressionlessness. Clifford knew that Logan-Fisher's personal code would prohibit him from asking any questions—for the time being at least.

Victoria, hard on the heels of her Chinese guide, rode down the Arroyo and into a part of town she'd never known existed. The steel shoes of the horses slipped, skidding, and sparked as they turned into Clara Street. They had to rein in abruptly in the face of a hostile mob. Victoria could make out policemen, some other uniformed men, and armed guards. The center of all this was a two-story frame house with its windows boarded up. The police began to link elbows.

Her guide shied away, but Victoria was not to be stopped. She kicked Apple, crying out, "I'm coming through! Take care!"

By the time she'd gotten down the street to the house the policemen had almost encircled it, beginning to form a human cordon. The policemen nearest her looked up, dumbstruck by the vision of a young woman in her formal white gown, her veil held barely in place by a few last pins.

"I'm going in," she said to no one in particular.

"Look, lady, nobody's going in there!"

"Stand out of my way, sir. I don't want to hurt anyone!"

Victoria touched up Apple with the crop and hurtled directly at the blue-clad barrier.

"You're crazy, lady," one of them called as he fell back, knowing he was no equal to a determined woman on a plunging horse.

Apple responded to another touch of the crop by clattering up the wooden

111

stairs leading to the veranda. Victoria swung down, gathering her finery about her. Ignoring the large red quarantine sign on the door, Victoria pushed it open and went in.

A stench struck her nostrils. For the second time this day her stomach tightened and churned. Her eyes, unaccustomed to this sudden darkness, made out few details. She heard footsteps coming down the hall and a woman's Mexican-accented voice calling out, "Thank God you have brought help at—"

The Mexican girl spoke haltingly, "I know who you are."

"And I can guess who you may be, although we have not had the pleasure of an introduction. I am Victoria Landon." Here her voice hesitated. "Creighton."

The Mexican girl said with equal dignity, "I am Maria Magdalena Ortiz. This is my house. It has become a house of the dead. And now you are one of us."

"What makes you so certain of that?" she asked contemptuously. Victoria moved toward the parlor. "What is it, anyway? Diphtheria? Typhoid? Scarlet fever?"

"Quien sabe? How should I know? All I know is they're dying."

Victoria heard anguished sounds of a man coming from the parlor couch. She watched his final death agony. The man, his body bloated and black, took one last gurgling breath, shuddered and died.

"The plague," whispered Victoria.

"We are all dead."

For a moment Victoria appeared to acquiesce in this grim prediction. Then the training of her parents, and perhaps the influence of the Logan-Fishers, took hold. "Stuff and nonsense," she snapped. "I've never heard such poppycock in all my life. I have seen this disease before raging in Melbourne. Most die, it's true, but some don't."

"You're a liar."

"Get hold of yourself. There are things we must do. Are there other dead, and how many are ill?"

"Five are with God, if there is one."

"First, we must have the dead removed."

Magdalena threw up her arms. "I have asked for help I don't know how many times. These men are cowards. They won't come near the house. They won't listen."

"We will need fresh linens, disinfectants, food for the sick. I suppose your ice supply has melted. We will need that too."

Magdalena shrugged. "Talk is cheap."

Victoria paced to the door and went out on the porch. Blinking in the glaring sunlight, she announced to the apprehensive officers of the law, "Don't worry. I'm not leaving this house, but whoever is in charge should know that we need—"

But even before she had a chance to enumerate their requirements, two horsemen thrust their way through the milling crowd. They were held back by the human cordon. Victoria heard Cliff's desperate voice over the sound of the angry populace. "My wife! My wife!"

112

The muttering crowd fell silent. Victoria addressed herself only
uncle.

"Uncle Percy, how good of you to come. There are people here wh
your help. I understand there has been some reluctance among the
officers to take hold. But, for the sake of the sick, the dead have
removed. And in addition to that we will need—"

Victoria's voice carried out clearly as she repeated to her uncle t
requirements she had begun listing to Magdalena, adding a variety
medical supplies. She heard from inside the house one last request. "Th
is a nursing baby here. We need milk and a means to feed it."

Victoria relayed this last request, allowing her eyes to flick over for t
least moment in Clifford's direction.

"Victoria," Clifford shouted out, *"please!"*

"If you wish to be of service, you would do me a great kindness by
recovering Apple and giving her the care she deserves." Then, kicking her
train expertly, she turned on her heel and disappeared into the house,
slamming the door smartly behind her.

Glancing around, Clifford spotted Apple and began to move toward the
winded horse. What else was there to do? But Percy Logan-Fisher put out a
hand to restrain him.

"Hold on, old man. We've got to think this thing out a bit. We've a great
deal to do. But before we make any definite plans, we must have a clear
understanding of the situation *in toto.*"

With his hand still on Clifford's shoulder, he turned to the officer who
appeared to be in charge of the police cordon.

"Tell me, my good man," Logan-Fisher said, "just what is the nature of
the infection here?"

The young lieutenant moved closer to them, and spoke in a low, anxious
voice. "Nobody likes to say, sir. I don't think they want to tell us. All I know
is, I worked when diphtheria broke out, and the quarantine procedures
weren't anything like this. I've never seen them put planks on windows, and
I've *never* seen a human cordon. And they've sent out for more men. They
want to close off the whole block, or maybe more."

Though he'd done his best to keep his voice low, the crowd on the street
had pressed closer and took up the last of his phrases.

"They want to close off the whole block!"

"Well, what is it then?"

"Smallpox?"

"Holy Toledo! They say the man who came out of there turned black as a
nigger!"

"And they say a Chinaman stood right there in that door, grinning like a
demon of death!"

"It's the Chinks all right! They live like pigs! They eat garbage!"

"Why, in San Francisco—"

A sudden hush fell.

"Say, you don't think—?"

A woman began to cry.

A voice, loud with hatred and terror, yelled from the back, "Let's not

aste time talking! Let's burn the whole place down!"

Clifford stiffened. Logan-Fisher spoke urgently, and only to him.

"There's no time to waste. Get the horses out. Then I want you to get to City Hall. Do it instantly! I want you to tell Jordan Espey the situation that obtains here. We will need the provisions which my niece has asked for—"

"But how will I find him? And on a Sunday?"

"Never fear. He'll be there, in a situation like this."

"But you're the one who should go."

"Someone must stay here, old chap. I'm a bit winded from our ride."

Clifford looked at Logan-Fisher in surprise. The last thing he looked was tired. But it was not Clifford's place to question the older man.

"Whatever you say, sir."

Clifford would always remember the face of Percy Logan-Fisher as he stood erect and determined. "Good luck! Godspeed!" He uttered the words with an intensity of tone that Clifford would only understand later.

Logan-Fisher waited as casually as he could until Clifford was completely out of sight. Then he jumped nimbly onto the empty bed of the Health Department wagon. He had been an officer in the Coldstream Guards, and had fought in the Crimea. He knew that at a time like this, fear was the greatest enemy, and he addressed the crowd as if he were rallying his own troops.

"We all know there is danger here. But there will be no question of burning."

There were hostile murmurs, which he cut off with a commanding gesture.

"First of all, there are living beings in there. Second, burning might only spread the infection and threaten your own homes." He raised the pitch of his voice. "I need your help! The strongest men among you must form a gravedigging squad under the leadership of the health officers. And, ladies! If you would repair to your homes . . . we need all the linens and blankets you can spare."

As a ruffian took in a breath to protest, Logan-Fisher singled him out. "You, sir! I'm putting you in charge!"

Within a few minutes relative order was restored. Only then did Logan-Fisher set out to do what he had planned all along. He approached the young Health Department officer.

"It *is* the plague, is it not?"

The official nodded. "And it's quite impossible, sir, for us to dispose of the dead as casually as you suggested."

"I know that. My concern was to disperse a mob that was becoming ever more dangerous. You can use the men as you wish." His tone shifted. "Why haven't you removed the dead?"

The young man colored under the question.

"No one who goes in that house can come out, that's under the rules of the quarantine. And—don't you see? I'm very sorry, sir. No one in there has a chance. All we can do is wait."

Logan-Fisher fixed him with his steady gaze. "Have your men bring the wagon around the back. Have some canvas ready. Alert your men in the back. I'm going in."

The official hesitated. "Sir," he began.

Logan-Fisher interrupted, "I assure you I will take complete responsibility. Even if those living have only a few hours, we must do everything possible for them. And above all we must rid the premises of the dead. I myself will carry them to the wagon. No one else need touch them."

Logan-Fisher walked to the cordon. "Stand aside," he said.

"Nobody goes in there!"

The official nodded and shrugged his shoulders. Two policemen let go their hands just long enough for Percy Logan-Fisher to pass. He mounted the steps, turned and took one last look at the sunny street, and then went inside.

"Victoria," he called as he walked through the entry and down the hall.

They were in the kitchen—his niece, a Mexican girl, a Chinese youth, and a whimpering baby.

"Uncle Percy, you are a fool. A brave fool."

He rewarded her with a half-smile, but spoke to the Chinese. "You there, we have work to do."

The youth nodded and led him back to the parlor. Logan-Fisher took his silk handkerchief and tied it around the lower part of his face. Again and again, he had to stifle his gags during the next hour as they bumped the oozing bodies out of the house and into the cart.

At City Hall, Clifford found Jordan Espey just as Logan-Fisher had predicted. "No provisions will be necessary," said Espey, "and there's no need to worry the mayor about this. The important thing is to seal off the area. Frankly, the fewer people who know about this, the better. If we're lucky, those people will die quietly."

Clifford reached forward over the desk and pulled the man halfway out of his chair. He shook Espey until his teeth chattered, and flung him back down into his swivel chair.

"You listen to me, Buster," he raved. "My wife's in that house—" With a visible effort he got himself under control. "Look here, Espey, how do you think this is going to look? You can't shut up a thing like this. The eyes of the country are going to be on this city. How does the government handle an emergency?" He searched desperately for the key that would move this man to action. "Money," he said. "There's big money in the East. I've just come from Baltimore," he said frantically. "The talk there is all investments. Do you think they're going to put their money in a jerkwater town without a *responsible city government?*"

Espey looked up at him—a slow light of comprehension in his eyes.

Clifford assumed a demeanor he did not feel. "I'll work with you, Espey. I'm willing to work with you on this all the way. You call in the mayor. We'll put together a plan that people will be talking about for years. Now, as to the provisions . . ."

By the time the sun set that day, more than one transformation had taken place in the house on Clara Street. After the two men had removed the bodies, Logan-Fisher had stripped off his morning-suit, which was irrevoca-

115

bly stained with gore. He had called for boiling water and the strongest disinfectant, and—bare-chested—he and Sung had labored all the afternoon scrubbing the upstairs, throwing open windows to let in fresh light and air. The stench of corruption in the house was gradually replaced by the acrid but clean aroma of Jeyes Fluid.

All the dead were gone, the husband and wife, the five boarders, and the serving girl, Estella. The other one, a spindly thing no more than thirteen, little Adelita, was desperately ill. She had been placed in the servants' little screened porch off the kitchen. Health Department officials had brought cots and a small crib and dumped them unceremoniously on the porch. While the men did the unspeakable work, Magdalena and Victoria arranged the downstairs for the siege ahead. The crib was placed in a corner of the kitchen. The big dining room table was shoved to one side to be used for medicines and linen, and cots were set up for the men. Victoria and Magdalena would sleep in the sewing room. From the beginning, there was an unspoken agreement. The upstairs and the parlor were the province of the ill and the dead. Even now that they were cleansed, they were to be avoided if at all possible.

The women kept pots of water boiling in the kitchen; they had all had scorching baths. They sat now in the kitchen around the deal table, the soundly sleeping, half-drunk baby, and the four so far untouched by the scourge. Magdalena, her strong face lined from more than forty-eight hours without sleep. Sung, bereft of his natty suit, barefoot and in a pair of "round-eye" trousers much too big for him. Logan-Fisher, his tanned skin pale and dull. And Victoria, her elegant coiffeur done into a serviceable braid, her veil replaced by a kerchief, her wedding dress by the modest smock of a servant girl.

Their weary silence was interrupted by a shriek of unearthly suffering, and the sound of retching. They rose as one to aid the serving girl.

Adelita sat up in bed, her lips spilling vomit. Even as she finished, Sung had moved forward fearlessly, pulling the sheets from the bed, using them to swab up the discharge. Logan-Fisher swiftly took the soiled linen from Sung, carried it to the back door, and flung it in an improvised crate, already drenched in Jeyes Fluid. As Victoria brought clean linen and a new gown for Adelita, Magdalena adroitly twisted a section of the daily *Times*, lit it at the kitchen stove, waved the cleansing flame through the fetid air of the room. As Adelita lay back with a whimper, she was there with a damp cloth for the girl's forehead, and some sugar water with a spoonful of rum. This crisis passed, they reassembled around cups of strong tea.

Victoria repressed a sigh. Then, her reserve cracking under the inhuman pressure, she allowed herself to ask the unspeakable question: "Uncle, you know something of this disease. Do we . . . how long might we expect to stay in here?"

Logan-Fisher gave her a wan smile. "I won't lie to you, my dear. My understanding is that we must stay here a fortnight after the last recovery."

"But, uncle! Eight people have died in the last twenty-four hours, and in this house alone."

Logan-Fisher smiled again. "Quite right, my dear."

116

"Then . . ."

As the horror of it took over, she burst out, trying to make a sob into something resembling wit. "This isn't the wedding night I expected!"

"The Devil likes nothing better than a surprise," Magdalena said rashly, and Victoria spat out a bitter rejoinder.

"Nor was this quite the 'trouble' I had expected to find here, señorita!" Sneering, she turned to Logan-Fisher. "Can you imagine, uncle? This . . . *woman* had the ineffable good taste to send a *billet doux* to *my husband* on his wedding day!" Then, imperfectly attempting a Spanish accent, she recited, "My beloved! The very worst has happened! I am in trouble!"

A look of exhausted understanding crossed Logan-Fisher's face. "What a misinterpretation," he muttered.

Magdalena drew herself upright, eyes flashing. She grasped Sung's shoulder in a grip of iron. "What have you done?"

"Eeeek!" Sung gave a rodent-like shriek. "I go retter writer, he write Engrish retter. He sent best retter. Cost dollar extra. You got trouble? He say trouble. You want helrp? I give you helrp? So?" he said. "So?"

At this moment the baby began to cry. There was not the same timbre of terror attached to these screams. This was the plain gusty squawl of a baby who wouldn't be put off any longer by a sop of water and rum, the ungodly racket of a healthy baby in need of attention. Manlike, Logan-Fisher and Sung seemed not even to hear this sudden uproar. It was not their responsibility. The baby, a strong boy of about six months, pulled up in his crib, bouncing with rage, his swarthy, handsome little face twisted into an ill-tempered scowl. Victoria looked across at Magdalena, who sat with a menacing scowl of her own, her strong arms folded before her.

Victoria's impatience spilled over. "Señorita! I am the *bride* here! I am not the mother; I am certainly not the wet nurse. Since I have arrived in this house, besides contending with the horrors of an epidemic, I have changed this baby four times, and held it for a full twenty minutes. The Health Department has brought in bottles of fresh cow's milk. I can only say now, señorita, that it is your turn."

"Señora," said Magdalena, "may I say to *you* that though *I* am not the bride, I am not the mother. Your husband came to this town just a few months ago . . . and I assure you, this baby is no child of mine."

A flicker of relief crossed Victoria's aristocratic visage, but her words gave no clue to her feelings. "This is your house. The baby is in *your* charge, if I'm not mistaken."

By this time, they could hardly hear themselves speak. The men sat, hunched over. Sullenly, Magdalena rose to her feet, made her way across the kitchen, and gingerly picked up the infant. Miraculously, the baby ceased its cries, grasped Magdalena's ample breast in his greedy fists, and buried his damp face there.

In the golden quiet broken only by his uneven gasps, Victoria looked over at Magdalena and allowed herself a tight smile. "In Australia, where my parents have seen sickness of this kind, they often said that those who lived were the ones who had something to live for. . . ."

The baby reached up and pulled on Magdalena's lip. In the laughter that followed this they noticed that Logan-Fisher had slumped forward.

With great effort he pulled himself to his feet. "It would be best," he said, "if I retired upstairs."

Three weeks later, a cool sun rose over Clara Street, a street that had suffered a nightmare and had finally, tentatively, awakened. Magdalena's house had not been the only one stricken. Thirty-nine deaths had taxed the organizational powers of the city government. The whole city had waited with bated breath as the infection had spread, and then diminished. Through Clifford's influence at City Hall, and the cool action of Jordan Espey, the worst had failed to materialize.

Those past three weeks had been the most trying in Clifford Creighton's life. Not only had he been at the head of the committees set up to deal with the epidemic, thus entailing an infinity of major and minor decisions, but in his personal life he had found himself the bearer of the most painful news that he could imagine when he rode up the Arroyo on Black Barb, carrying to Beatrice Logan-Fisher the announcement of her husband's death. For once he had felt no desire to hasten up the road that had seemed to lead to an enchanted life. For he knew that if it had not been for his own folly, Percy Logan-Fisher, his benefactor and friend, would still be with them.

The anguish of the announcement to Beatrice and the subsequent mourning were prolonged by the forced suspension of a memorial service. Beatrice said that she wished to wait until the quarantine was lifted so that Victoria could be present. But of course there was always the nagging anxiety that she herself would not survive the ordeal, that the memorial service would be for two instead of one.

During the past three weeks he thought he had caught occasional glimpses of his bride as she would pass ghostlike by the partially boarded windows of the house. God forgive him, he had caught occasional glimpses of Magdalena as well.

In the long hours alone at night when he lay awake drenched with sweat and gripped by apprehensions, he had tried to trace the true source of his chagrin. Was it guilt pure and simple, a breach of the morality his father had taught him? Was it a baser emotion? Pure animal fear that he had lost one of them, both of them? Or was it simply anger and shame at letting himself be found out?

But through it all he was tormented by a stronger sorrow—the idea of having betrayed a woman so straight that on her wedding day she had set out to confront her rival. A woman so courageous that she had not flinched even in the face of almost certain death. As Clifford searched his own mind he was not sure he would have shown the same headstrong bravery. And out of this admiration, even awe, were sown the seeds of an even greater affection and tenderness. If he were lucky enough to get her back, perhaps he would have the chance . . . but it was out of his hands now.

He joined the waiting crowd, who still hung back a little from the police cordon, still staunch in their officialdom. There was a wagon loaded with sandwiches and hot coffee which was dispensed by half a dozen Sisters of Mercy. There were relatives barely able to believe that their loved ones had survived. A few cynical newsmen hung about in ill-fitting suits asking inane questions of anyone they could collar. Inside the cordon, a squadron of smartly turned-out members of the Health Department made a last-minute door-to-door check. At each house they left, with some little ceremony they ripped down the quarantine sign.

Finally, just as it seemed the crowd outside the cordon could no longer stand the suspense, they were interrupted by the clop of hoofs which signaled the arrival of the mayor, in an expansive mood. The newsmen converged upon him, and he, with careful informality, obliged them with a few words.

"I hope you gentlemen of the press will let the whole world know that our growing city has come through a potentially disastrous situation with flying colors."

He warmed to the smattering of applause. "You know it's not easy to face up to a thing like this. It takes courage and a level head—not only from the city government itself, but also from the private sector. We owe much to my deputy, Jordan Espey, Monroe Kirkbride of Public Sanitation, and a gentleman only recently come among us, a man who has worked ceaselessly—Mr. Clifford Abercrombie Creighton. . . ."

But by this time the crowd had shifted its attention. At an unseen signal from the Health Department, the human cordon loosened and became instead individual men in blue uniforms. A ragged cheer went up as first one door on Clara Street opened, then another. As the pale survivors of an awful siege emerged, the crowd surged forward to meet them. There were embraces, and some tears.

And still, Clifford waited.

Inside the house, the little group had come together in the kitchen for their last goodbyes. During these days of trial they had come to know one another well.

Victoria would never forget the last hours before her uncle's death. Percy Logan-Fisher had sat upright in an easy chair. "Stand back, Victoria. Come no nearer."

Without hesitating she rushed forward and took his hand in her own. "Oh, Uncle Percy. . . ."

Toward the end, between violent spasms, he gave Victoria messages of love for his wife, and then, "I ask you not to judge Clifford harshly." His hand tightened on her own as she glanced away. "Look at me. Who can judge the true motives of men? There is none of us without his secret weakness." Though his very behavior seemed to belie these words, Victoria could only believe in his sincerity.

"Now you must leave me," he rasped.

"No, Uncle!"

"Victoria, I cannot allow you to see me at the end. Please be good enough to send Sung in here to me."

And Sung, in his turn, would carry with him for all of his life the vision of this blond girl as brave as she was beautiful, as she controlled her grief and asked him with courtesy to attend her uncle at his death.

It was only a matter of minutes before the muffled sounds of agony began. Victoria broke down then and sobbed, and she could not refuse Magdalena's comforting arms.

Hours later Sung emerged. And after he had washed himself he spoke with all the conviction he could command to comfort both women. "He was a good, good man. But we all must think of living. Many die, but some live. And I tell you we will live."

The boy had been right. Though twelve had died, including all eight boarders, Sung, Magdalena, and Victoria had survived. Even little Adelita had miraculously recovered, and in the last few days had gained strength enough to take her turn with baby Raoul, who had stubbornly attached himself to Magdalena and shouted vociferously when he was parted from her arms.

Now Sung stood in the back doorway. He was dressed in his freshly pressed black suit, his fedora tipped rakishly over his left eye.

"Goodbye, dear ladies. I wish you wellr."

"Sung, you have been splendid in every way. You must know that if there is anything I can do in the years to come, I shall be at your service." Victoria clasped his hand.

He allowed himself a smile, then nodded to Magdalena. "We talk soon." And then he was gone.

The two women gazed at each other and in that gaze was a multitude of feelings.

"I can see what he sees in you," said Magdalena.

"May I return the compliment?" Victoria gravely responded.

"I have something to live for," said Magdalena as she jounced the gurgling baby Raoul on her hip. "And you have given me that."

"Was he going to give you up?"

"To be honest, I don't know. . . ."

Clifford could wait no longer. Apprehension, guilt, fear, anticipation colored his shifting thoughts. He walked more and more slowly the closer he came to the house on Clara Street. He finally stopped, unable to advance and equally unable to retreat.

He saw the door open and his wife come out onto the veranda. To him she appeared more beautiful and desirable than ever before.

Even as he looked at her—still paralyzed by his emotions—he saw Magdalena, with an infant in her arms, step out and take her place beside his wife. He saw them embrace. As Victoria walked down the steps, little Adelita came to stand by Magdalena's side. Magdalena, holding the baby and giving support to Adelita, guided them to the sunny end of the porch where they sat down in a wicker glider.

Victoria turned back one last time and waved. Starting down the path from the house to the street, she glanced about her briefly and then raised her face to the sun.

"Victoria!" Clifford rushed forward, ready to take her in his arms.

But when he was within a few feet of her, she fended him off, her right arm stiffly outstretched. "Wait a minute, Clifford Creighton," she said sternly. "There may be time for that later."

"Oh, Victoria, what can I say?"

"I don't care to hear what you have to say at the moment. I have a few things to say to you myself."

"I—"

"First," she said, cutting him off, "you can't expect anyone to live in this kind of house, much less a woman of Magdalena's quality. You just can't shirk your responsibility! You have to make sure that Magdalena and the baby have a decent place to live. Second, after you do that, *you're never going to see her again."*

"Does this mean you'll give me another chance?"

Her eyes narrowed. She could see that he had also suffered, perhaps as much, in his own male way, as she and Magdalena.

"Cliff, if you do the things I ask, I will never talk about any of this again. And *I* am a woman of my word."

She saw the relief soften the lines of his face, but before he could respond, Victoria said, as casually as if she were suggesting an ordinary afternoon's excursion, "I would love to stretch my legs, and if Apple and Black Barb are near enough, I would very much enjoy a canter."

She said little during their walk to McFarland Stables and even less on the ride out of town. Clifford respected her silence; for he too was lost in his own thoughts, recalling Percy Logan-Fisher's words to him before their wedding day.

How swiftly Logan-Fisher's predictions had come true. Clifford *had* been lucky, but his luck had run out. He could see that he had allowed himself to drift aimlessly in the currents of life, controlled largely by his own passions.

Clifford looked over at his wife, riding with easy dignity beside him. With his glance again came the realization of what he had come close to losing. And she had given him a second chance! He became aware of a new sense of determination and direction in his life. He would never run this kind of risk again. He would do everything in his power to build her the life she deserved.

By now they had cleared the outskirts of the city and started up the Arroyo. He felt that he was leaving behind him not only the city but his old life of indecision.

"Well, that's that," Victoria said, turning her head, as if she had been reading his very thoughts. She smiled. "Barb is a fine mount, but he's no match for Apple. I'll race you and I'll win."

She spurred Apple. Clifford caught his breath. The sheer style of it! Black Barb, without urging, took up the chase. Clifford saw her ahead, her hair streaming out behind. He knew that this was more than just a casual pursuit, that it would end only with the consummation of their marriage.

BOOK II

1895

They rested there, escaped awhile
  From cares that wear the life away,
To eat the lotus of the Nile
  And drink the poppies of Cathay,—
To fling their loads of custom down,
  Like drift-weed, on the sand-slopes brown,
And in the sea-waves drown the restless pack
Of duties, claims, and needs that barked upon their track.

WHITTIER, *The Tent on the Beach*

*D*URING the past ten years, Los Angeles had attracted more Eastern money and business. The city limits stretched out tentacles, especially to the south and west. Now small communities, often no more than a fruit stand and a few dwellings, dotted the rural roads that meandered through acres of bean fields, occasional orchards, all the way to the Pacific.

As more of the central area was taken up with business buildings, the new citizens—adventurers, young men with an idea and a buck, and Midwestern families set on making their way and escaping hard winters—sought refuge from their hot and dusty workplaces and made their homes on Bunker Hill, in Westlake Park, sometimes as far away as five miles from the Plaza.

Pasadena, on the other hand, had changed first from a winter to an all-year resort and then to a solidly founded and somewhat stratified society. The Valley Hunt Club, as Pasadena's oldest institution, reflected this metamorphosis. In 1885, it had been a group of rough-and-tumble riders that had gathered for Sunday excursions. But with the influx of "hotel people" and the threat of "foreigners," the Pasadenans had turned their club into a bastion of gentility. Riding became less important than who you were, how you were connected, and what kind of house you had. And with the building of an actual clubhouse, teas, formal dinners, and bridge became the acceptable activities for these Englishmen, the early families, and the few newcomers who had proven themselves.

Clifford Creighton was one of the latter. His rise had been at once both circumspect and spectacular. Though he was not a man much given to introspection, he could see that his marriage had been doubly blessed. Not only had he loved Victoria with all his heart, but that beautiful object of his affections had needed only money and a good husband to put her in the very forefront of the new society.

He had become the good husband and the money had come to them

125

miraculously. In the ten years that Pasadena had developed into a thriving, prosperous residential resort, he had been a part of it. From his first lucky acquisition, he had sensed, accurately, the movement of growth. Simply by buying and selling the golden property of Southern California, Cliff had, by the time he was thirty-one years old, increased his wealth in effortlessly geometric progressions.

By this point in his life, Clifford was secure enough in his fortune—made up as it was of that most enduring commodity, the earth itself—that he had recently, secretly, embarked on a series of minor financial speculations: refrigerated railway cars, which, if they succeeded, would triple the value of his citrus crops and extend their market; the new motor cars, which seemed adapted to the great distances of the West and the sprawling nature of the city; the local oil supply, which, if the motor cars "went," would be necessary as fuel. He made it a practice to speak to no one of these matters, since it was better to be thought of as a conservative developer of land, who took no risks. And he relished, as well, that image of himself as a man whose wealth mounted up by mysterious means.

But his transformation into a very rich man would not have been possible without what some of his business associates referred to inelegantly as a "stake." Again, circumstances had conspired almost literally to thrust the money into his hands.

His first year of marriage to Victoria had been idyllic. They had spent long summer days in their rustic cottage. They had indulged in lazy but invigorating morning rides, galloping along the trail beside the *zanja,* returning to intimate meals that seemed more like picnics. Their evenings were illuminated by the kind of lovemaking that Clifford had scarcely even dared to dream of. She was all and more than any man could ever want.

And if sometimes he allowed himself to wonder what would have happened if Headsperth Bauer had approved of that apparition of a "new woman" on the misty morning of that fabled hunt, if he even allowed himself to consider that it might be Headsperth's body that she might be clasping at this very moment, he banished these nagging doubts from his mind. Actions blotted out thoughts.

Their honeymoon was brought to an abrupt halt by the great inevitabilities of humankind. Victoria discovered she was with child and at almost the same time her Aunt Beatrice, who had never truly recovered from the shock of Percy Logan-Fisher's death, began to weaken so visibly that the young couple, remembering everything that they owed her, set up housekeeping in the northern wing of Shady Oaks. Here they could keep a watchful eye on Beatrice, and Victoria could give her aunt as much care, sympathy, and comfort as she deserved. But life had lost all meaning for Beatrice, and though she put up a brave show of taking interest in the ordinary course of experience, it was not long until she joined her husband.

When Beatrice Logan-Fisher's will was read it revealed that, after providing pensions for every member of the staff, the remainder was left to her niece without any conditions attached. And with the birth of Ruth Anne Creighton, Clifford sold his cottage and grove, making a real killing. Though they were a young family, blessed with a fortune and an estate, they felt a certain uneasiness. Shady Oaks held too many bittersweet memories. It was Victoria who suggested that Clifford build them a house entirely their own on the bluff where Cliff had vowed to make her his wife. And Clifford had set about constructing a mansion that would have been the envy of his stuffy Baltimore uncle.

The newly named San Rafael Road ran below the ridge. From it, a long, curving driveway led up the slope to a circular promontory which overlooked the Arroyo and the town beyond. The structure itself was three stories and considerably wider than it was tall. The face that it presented to the spacious grounds was calculated to offer a facade of almost blatant wealth. Clifford envisioned nothing less than a castle and with the aid of tons of quarried rock trained in from Nevada, he constructed not merely a home but a monument. But once an awed visitor was lucky enough to gain entrance to this edifice, he could not help but realize the influence that Creighton's lovely wife exerted upon him. The entry hall was as vast and crepuscular as a great cathedral. The wide staircase that ascended the full three stories might have led to a monstrous choirloft above. And on either side of this inhibiting vestibule a library as big as a small auditorium and a drawing room furnished in exquisite formal taste reinforced this demonstration of unending wealth. Beyond these public rooms sheer beauty and lightness of spirit took over. The entire eastern portion of the house had been inset with countless windows both to take advantage of the beneficent early morning light and the breathtaking view of the lush Arroyo, which spread beneath them like their own private park, and the burgeoning city that formed the southern boundaries of their view. The ground floor on this side was little more than a series of French windows almost always open to the pure air, and a wide, formal terrace done in the Italianate manner. Below a roughly landscaped hill, another terrace and a third shelf of land left room for at least two tennis courts.

Clifford had always considered it one of his luckiest strokes that in looking over a piece of property adjoining the newly built Afro-American Methodist church on Lincoln Avenue he had, largely out of curiosity, looked at a bulletin board and read, "Young couple newly arrived from Atlanta seeks work of any kind." At Ruth's birth, Pansy Priest had gone to Shady Oaks to help Victoria. And as Clifford became more involved with his various enterprises, Porter Priest, Pansy's husband, had made himself useful in looking after the local property and conducting the day-to-day details of the construction of the new mansion. By the time it was completed, the Priests had become invaluable to the Creightons, and rooms had been built off the northern wing for the Priests and their own growing family.

Today the sounds of children's laughter filled the house and spilled out onto the upper terrace where Clifford Creighton was doing his best to hang a birthday *piñata,* gaily decorated with pink, green, and yellow tissue paper and heavy with candies and small favors. This bit of Hispanic whimsy had been Victoria's idea. As a young wife and mother, she was in constant and pleasant competition with other Pasadena matrons to think up new diversions for their children. But Clifford was darned if he could see what was so special about a gaudy papier-mâché stork filled with candy that would doubtless be bad for the children's teeth. Some of his irritation must have communicated itself to Porter Priest, who suggested tactfully, as he often did, "I'll take care of this, sir. May I suggest that you refresh yourself with a cool glass of champagne? Some is chilling for the parents of our guests in the pergola by the bluff."

Clifford made his way to the far end of the upper terrace, across a lawn, and to a little open-air structure that overlooked the Arroyo. He sent a cork flying and poured himself a glass. Turning to the house, Cliff looked with pride at the structure that his rising fortune and Victoria's taste had created. The landscaping, though promising botanical wonders, still needed a few years to attain maturity. But the rose garden, perhaps Victoria's favorite, flourished in abundant color.

The young trees that they had planted had already begun to provide some skimpy shade against the summer sun. A *copa de ora* vine covered the arbor leading back to the stables. Today, the lower terrace was set with round tables covered in fine linen. The best English chinaware, heavy pieces of sterling silver, and crystal goblets sparkled.

What a pity, he thought, that Percy and Beatrice had not lived to see their wedding present turned into the most beautiful estate in Pasadena.

A quick glance at his watch showed him that the party was about to begin. He smoothed back the hair over his temples and shot his cuffs. Although he thought of himself as a modest man, he could not resist a twinge of contentment verging on a disgraceful complacency. The last ten years sat lightly on him. If anything, he felt stronger, more sure of himself, and almost as youthful as when he had first come to California.

As the French doors were flung open perhaps fifty children, in their best pinafores and Little Lord Fauntleroy suits, skipped and ran, laughing and shouting, to where the *piñata* hung. The parents and other notable guests followed and stood in a loose circle about the prancing children.

And there she was! Victoria. His Victoria. She was more beautiful than when they first met. Motherhood had not taken away her girlish attraction. Her white lace garden dress, which would have meant disaster for a woman who showed her age, only enhanced Victoria's peach complexion, slim waist, and elegant and lively bearing. She wore her silver-blond hair in the romantic style of the Gibson girl but she had daringly decorated this coiffeur with a spray of wildflowers.

Victoria supervised the ritual of the *piñata*. One at a time each child was blindfolded, guided this way and that, and given a stick to take a whack at the dancing target. As each child thrashed out, the other youngsters screamed with delight when Porter Priest pulled on a rope that always brought the *piñata* just out of reach.

Ruth, the birthday girl, was a stout child of nine, who lacked, unfortunately, both her mother's good looks and her father's good nature. Her parents, however, were tolerant of any flaws in their first-born. If there had been the hurly-burly of family competition between brothers and sisters, this chunky, opinionated youngster might have appeared to them as something less than charming. But as it was, they saw her through a cloud of love. Though there had been some concern that Ruth had no little brothers or sisters, Victoria's physician had assured her repeatedly that she was young and healthy, and there was no cause for real concern.

"My turn, my turn!" Ruth shouted, her statement not so much a plea as a demand.

"My dear," her mother said, "a good hostess—"

But when she saw Ruth's face cloud over with the threat of noisy tears, her mother changed tactics.

"I don't think Alessandro has had a chance yet," Victoria said, and nodding, she called across the crowd, "Señora Mariné, would you permit your handsome son to share in this ceremony? I know he is too grown-up for it, but I hear that his father would never say no to a child's request."

Ruth stared blank-faced at the dashing fourteen-year-old who lounged self-consciously within that invisible but impregnable circle of the Señora's dignity and position.

"You are too gracious, though my son may not be expert in these peasant pastimes. Try your luck, *luz de mis ojos*." She tapped him coquettishly on his shoulder with her folded fan.

Alessandro, not quite suppressing a smirk of satisfaction at becoming the center of attention, bowed to his mother. "As you wish, Mama. I will try not to dishonor our family." And he walked with a slight swagger to Victoria, allowing his eyes to be covered by the blindfold.

"Mama, may I?" It was little Maria, Señora Mariné's younger child, one year older than Ruth, but pale and forlorn in contrast to Ruth's bumptiousness. Maria Mariné's tiny Spanish face was already set in an expression of the resignation that comes from constant denial.

"No! No! No!" the Señora said. "It is not ladylike. It is not of our class. And it does not do for you to get out in the sun."

Sadly Maria watched her older brother, who had feigned indifference to the younger children's awkward attempts, but who had measured carefully the height to which Priest had jerked the *piñata*. Alessandro flailed out accurately on his first attempt and the *piñata* burst with a loud crash, releasing all its contents to the delighted shrieks of the children and the applause of the adults. The next instant all the proper, neatly dressed youngsters were scrambling in fierce competition as if their lives depended on the size of their booty.

Only Ruth hung back, looking with awe and admiration at the young Spaniard, who casually removed his blindfold with one hand and smoothed his barely discernible moustache with the other.

"Oh, Alessandro, you're so strong," she murmured.

"*Es nada*," he shrugged, but it was evident that in this one thing, at least, he and the little girl were in complete agreement.

Slightly put off by the reversion of their well-brought-up children to savagery, the watching adults, amid much laughter and many pleasantries, left their offspring to the care of the servants and repaired to the terrace below for their just reward. Alessandro, after a moment's hesitation, followed the adults, leaving Ruth to stare after him with wistful eyes.

Once on the terrace, the various couples helped themselves to champagne and to hot and cold hors d'oeuvres which Pansy Priest passed graciously and efficiently. The guests formed casual circles, some seated at the more formal tables, others circulating from group to group or resting on pretty little benches which overlooked the enchanting view below. This gathering, taken as a whole, represented the full flower of Pasadena gentry. They were young, prosperous; they observed the traditions of the past, but fixed their eyes on the possibilities of the future.

Perhaps the only exception was Headsperth Bauer. During the last decade his serious poetic attempts had withered even as his self-esteem ripened. Some said there was little enough cause for that. He had sold while others had bought. He had planted groves of apples, which were perhaps the only fruit unsuited to this spectacularly mild climate. He had predicted the rapid decline of rail power and motor transportation, backing his perverse vision by building a "Cycle Way," a raised trestle which was to stretch all the way from Pasadena to Los Angeles. He foresaw a future solely devoted to the bicycle. It was one of his most exasperating but endearing qualities that when no one, absolutely no one, agreed with what his prophecies and assessments might bring, it daunted him not one whit.

He and his wife Belle had been married almost as long as Clifford and Victoria. Their union had not been rewarded with children; he forgave her for that, as he forgave her for the many times when she had, in her feminine weakness, been misguided enough to question his judgment.

Belle, never handsome, had grown a little plainer over the years, but she still rode hard, and livened every group by her robust good humor. In her unpretentious way she showed two faces to the world. In the company of her husband, she seemed resigned to her lot, obedient, even a little dull, but as one of the members of the circle remarked, "You know, when you get Belle alone, she's *funny*, and twenty times as smart as that great lummox she puts up with."

The lummox stood now, in his characteristic pose, leaning on one elbow against the pergola, enraptured at his handiwork: the beginnings of the Cycle Way itself which staggered higgledy-piggledy down the Arroyo, awkward on its wooden supports, an ungainly cousin to the newfangled roller coaster. "There," he remarked to his wife, "you see the wave of the future."

"Yes, dear."

The few who heard this were too fond of Belle to mention that the Cycle Way had so far not been completed for lack of funds, and it was doubtful now if it would ever be. And while no one liked to admit it, there was not a person in this coterie who had not been the recipient of Headsperth's own style of kindness—an introduction to his father's banking connections, a sympathetic word at the failure of an investment, or an occasional poem marking a birthday or a felicitous recovery.

The conversation shifted to how the members of the Valley Hunt Club could best celebrate their next anniversary.

"We should really hunt in full fig again," Roger Boulter nostalgically remembered. "It's been three years, hasn't it, since we've done anything like that?"

"The reason it's *been* three years," Harriet Wembley-Spencer said tartly, "is that the noblest game we took then was a helpless cow!"

"It almost broke our treasury to settle with that unappreciative farmer. . . ."

There was a chorus of quiet chuckles. "Of course never again can we hope to match Clifford's performance when he brought the coyote to earth in the post office."

Headsperth was annoyed by their frivolous chatter. "Won't you people ever get over your obsession with horseflesh?" He waited for a response, and when none was forthcoming, he said, with heavy sarcasm, "If you must ride, there's always a chariot race."

The exuberance that comes with champagne made this seem like the one good idea which poor Headsperth Bauer had ever had.

"A chariot race. Do you mean a Roman chariot race?"

"Ben-Hur and all that?"

"Horses crashing about a rough track?"

"Crashing is right," Clifford muttered.

"I say, that's a bit dangerous, isn't it?" Harriet Wembley-Spencer queried.

"Look here," Roger Boulter said, "would we be required to dress up in actual Roman togas?"

"Well, it would be a chariot race," Headsperth said with mild disdain.

"Where would we get the chariots?"

"Do you think we could use wagons?"

"No, *chariots!* We'll form a committee; we'll build them to scale."

"But where will we put this thing on? We can't use Colorado Street anymore."

"May I suggest"—and all heads turned at the sound of the familiar voice and heavy accent—"several acres of my own land, here, at the bottom of the Arroyo? I know my husband, *que Dios lo cuida*, would have been a fierce contender in this race of yours." The Señora, for all her careful cultivation of eccentricity, was a canny businesswoman, and she knew these Anglos were soon to be at the very center of power.

And perhaps it was for much the same motive that Clifford Creighton, who had been watching these exchanges with a grim look of disbelief, came forward, bowed to the Señora, and took in the rest with his glance.

"I can't say that this seems to me to be a particularly sensible enterprise. In fact, it sounds downright foolhardy. I wouldn't ride in it myself. But," he raised his voice against the few low jeers, "Señora, if you are generous enough to lend your land, the very least I can do as a builder is to construct bleachers, and grade the slope into a relatively safe track."

"Family life has turned Creighton into a stick-in-the-mud," Headsperth Bauer bellowed. "This sounds like adventure! And I'm for it!"

"Headsperth," Belle murmured, but he turned his broad back to her and folded his arms.

Alessandro stepped forward, touching his upper lip. "With your permission, beloved Mama, I too should like to take part in this excitement, for the honor of our family. It is not so far, I think, from the brave tradition of our ancestors, the *conquistadores."*

"Ah, to do that, my angel, is to flirt with death. But no man of the Mariné blood has avoided that opportunity!"

"Truly, Señora," Clifford remonstrated, "do you think this is altogether wise? This will be something more than just a horse race. A true Roman chariot requires four horses. They'll be going at a full gallop. Even a grown man—"

The Señora haughtily flicked the fringe of her embroidered shawl. "Ah, Señor Creighton, you are too timid."

Several of the younger members of the group exchanged glances. Victoria, observing this, drew herself up but said nothing.

Then Belle cut through the social strain and spoke up in a clear voice. "Tell me, Victoria, what *do* you do to get such splendid results with your roses?"

And the afternoon drifted away, like so many others, to the clink of champagne glasses, the ebb and flow of easy laughter, and the sound of the children's merriment drifting down from the upper terrace.

Not until the last guests had gone did Victoria allow herself to ask her husband, in carefully neutral tones, "Do you really mean you're not going to race? You're one of the few men who can control a four-in-hand."

"You know very well, Victoria, that to race any wheeled vehicle is risky. It's a job for a professional. It's a circus act."

Victoria set her jaw and did not reply. What, she asked herself, had happened to Clifford? If he was like this at the age of thirty-one, what might she expect in another twenty years? And in the years between?

In the light landaulet which carried Belle and Headsperth across the Arroyo, another domestic exchange took place.

"Headsperth, dear, you haven't ridden in a good many years. How could you have volunteered to do that? You know you can't—"

"Belle, dear, I appreciate your concern, but a man must live up to his image. I would hate anyone to say that I had shirked or evaded . . . that I was a coward." Headsperth sighed. "Besides, it will never happen anyway! It's simply another one of their schemes that will never get off the ground."

By 1895, Chinatown had grown rapidly. Despite anti-Chinese riots in Pasadena and other outbreaks of hostility from the whites, the ramshackle, wooden doorways and basement apartments held more than shifty-eyed men, singsong girls, and aromatic herbs. There was already great wealth here, but it was hidden.

Sung Wing On was one of those who had prospered. At twenty-four, he was little known north of Temple Street, where the round-eyes pursued their interests, but within the undrawn borders that marked off Chinatown itself, Sung was one of the three Responsible Men to whom you applied if you were in trouble. Sung could settle a dispute between shop owners with fair judgment. He could find jobs for people of every skill, and took only minimal *cumshaw*. He could bring over male relatives from China as straight laborers. If it were a woman or an old one, from time to time—and at greater expense—he'd arrange to smuggle in these loved ones as stowaways, contraband. Had not the fearless Young Master been a stowaway himself? And there were rumors, well-founded ones, that human cargo was not the only contraband Sung smuggled. And so, the troubled inhabitants of this beleaguered community did not hesitate to ask the advice and the services of this mysteriously successful man. Sung, this youngest of "the three Big Ones," was the most approachable, perhaps because he was an orphan and had no family obligations of his own.

It was characteristic of the Chinese in general and Sung in particular that the Jade Tree, Sung Wing On's opulent studio of Oriental art, was almost invisible from the crowded, noisy street. No sign graced its entrance; indeed, there scarcely *was* an entrance. And once inside the courtyard, only a few two-by-fours and a wheelbarrow gave any clue of habitation. Nervous round-eyes—only the wealthiest, brought here by Sung's agents—invariably thought they had been swindled at best when they had been brought this far; and at worst, that they had been trapped for ransom or were to be sold into the white slave trade.

But if the nervous wealthy could stay their fears and go one courtyard further, they found themselves in an emporium both vast and dim, which held great ivory carvings, pigskin chests, cabinets of curios, and enormous inlaid screens.

It was a rare customer who saw further than this room, who had proven not only his own riches but his esthetic sense, and was allowed into the upper reaches of this outwardly deceptive treasure house. Above the downstairs showrooms, Sung maintained his private apartments, and it was here that his own sensual nature, the voluptuous love of beauty that made him a natural connoisseur of his own country's rich artistic heritage, was allowed full play.

The entry hall was graced by a huge carved Buddha, more than six feet tall. (Some malicious neighbors said that a temple in Northern Siam was still looking for the one it had "lost.") A gold-leaf and red-lacquer carved archway led into the main room, where the walls were hung with rare Sung Dynasty scrolls. A series of straight-back, heavily carved, teakwood "courtiers' chairs," designed for maximum dignity and discomfort, were arranged in a perfect semicircle around the one Western piece of furniture in the room, an immense businessman's desk—the desk of a tycoon—kept perfectly clean except for the elegant brush and ink of a practiced calligrapher. On one side of the desk a locked display case of dazzling precious jewels, on the other a series of teapoys, where servants, during the course of any business discussion, unobtrusively laid dishes marked by their succulence and rarity. And at the back, half hidden from view by a beaded curtain— which, it was said, had cost the entire population of Lu Sing the virginity of its marriageable maidens—the sleeping apartments of the mysterious Sung Wing On, which no one ever saw.

The young man of whom everyone spoke in hushed tones sat now, toward the end of a business interview. An elderly Chinese couple, the T'ings, sat side by side, their heads respectfully bent forward in thanks to what they felt was a magician, who had performed the miracle of bringing over not one but two of their young male grandchildren. They could look forward now, without fear, to their old age, and—provided Sung could find at least one of the grandsons a wife—the continuation of their ancestral line.

"Young Master," old Mr. T'ing said, "we can never repay you for what you have done for us. It is not good to live alone in this strange country; and across the sea, the armies of warlords make life a thing of peril and uncertainty. By bringing to us our descendants, you have taken away our loneliness and given new life to another generation."

Sung nodded and said, "I know the conditions in the Middle Kingdom. And I know, too, what it is to be alone."

The older man fumbled for his purse. "No amount of money would be sufficient. Even as it is, we cannot offer you much. But what we can give, we give with gratitude from our—"

Sung raised his hand. "Please say no more, Old Father. It would offend the spirit of *my* father were I to accept payment for bringing together two strands of a family." (Sung did not feel it necessary to say that he had already picked up two sizable commissions from this transaction, on both shores of the Pacific. Also, unbeknownst to the burly grandsons, they had both brought packets of rough-cut gems in the hems of "new" trousers which they'd been issued aboard ship.)

"A thousand thanks, Young Master," old Mr. T'ing said, leaning his head even farther forward. "May the gods reward you with long life and many grandchildren of your own."

Mrs. T'ing, who had remained silent, ventured to raise her head at this. She glanced shyly at the young man before her. "You can't have grandchildren without a wife!"

Her husband was scandalized. "Quiet, Old Woman!"

"I can only speak what any woman knows is the truth. Even as magic a person as the Young Master needs a wife to have a son."

Sung smiled. "You are right, Old Mother. I think of it often. But," here he hesitated, "the woman I want, no one could find for me."

The old woman, emboldened by his frankness in speaking to her, said, "In my home village it was often said, 'A man who waits for a wife worthy of him has no descendants.' Since you have no mother or grandmother to tell you these simple truths, allow me to speak this woman's wisdom. Take your second wife first, and the wait for your first wife will not seem so long."

Sung felt his ears burning.

Mr. T'ing spoke in a low voice. "My garrulous wife, for once, is right." Raising his head, he swept the room with his gaze. "Forgive my temerity, but permit me to ask, of what ultimate worth is all this, if you do not use it to magnify your family name?"

"I . . . I only specialize in transporting wives," Sung said in some confusion. "I would not know how to go about finding one."

"There is a matchmaker here whose integrity is beyond question. He is expensive, but he does not deal in lazy brides, or barren ones, or women unfit to look upon. He has been enough corrupted by Western ways that he consults the wishes of the groom. I can give you his name."

"I know his name," Sung blurted. In fact, for many nights he'd considered this very move, but he had been held back by the impossible extravagance of the feminine image which had haunted him.

In spite of the deference with which he was received, Sung experienced a trace of embarrassment when, the next afternoon, he found himself a sheepish customer of Chinatown's most illustrious matchmaker. Though there could be no doubt of the reason for Sung's presence (and he knew in addition that old Mr. T'ing had certainly been in touch with this entrepreneur of love), still Sung felt reluctant to express his wishes. With exquisite tact the matchmaker endeavored to put him at his ease, serving him jasmine-flavored tea and sweet cakes.

"Every man of substance must have a wife, the better to reflect his qualities," the matchmaker purred. "Although you are a man of virility and youth, it is never too soon to begin that family which shall magnify your position in the community. You may be assured, sir, that future generations will thank you for this trivial-seeming errand which you have put off until today."

For once the glib Sung had nothing to say, but the matchmaker went on, scarcely pausing for breath.

"The young woman who shall become mother of your children is lucky indeed. And I know of many women who are different as far as their superficial characteristics, their singing voices, their skill at *pi-ba,* their ability to recite whilst you are at rest from a tiring day of business affairs. But let me assure you, honored sir, that all of the women with whom I am acquainted share certain more basic qualities in common. Obedience. Discipline. Respect for the household gods. And loyalty to the family above all else. Also I have made sure, in the most delicate possible way, to verify with their mothers that the bones in their hips are both widely placed and pliable."

The matchmaker paused and fixed Sung with an earnest gaze. "I have done everything in my power, sir, to insure that these industrious young women will provide you with descendants enough to," here he permitted himself a smile, "provide you with your own small army."

Sung took a deep breath and began to speak, but the matchmaker went on.

"Of course, Esteemed Pillar, a man of your wide knowledge and experience knows that a girl with these attributes and accomplishments does not, cannot, come cheap. These pure women have been raised as carefully as prize peonies in the greenhouse of the Emperor by families whose blood, though of simple stock, is utterly without taint. These girls must be packaged, as no one knows better than yourself, as carefully as rare porcelain transported for miles over the dangerous roads of our Middle Kingdom, smuggled on board ship at great expense, and then, last but not least, spirited through the customs of the infamous round-eye officials. All this, sir, I am prepared to do for you, so that your mind, already burdened by the cares of your many enterprises, should not have to be troubled by the intricate little worries associated with this kind of transaction."

Again Sung opened his mouth, but the matchmaker was nearing his well-rehearsed conclusion.

"Not until that glad day, sir, when the seed of Sung Wing On shall be deposited, after appropriate ceremonies, into the willing receptacle which shall carry on his name unto generations untold, shall you, after a reasonable down payment of course, have even to consider this subject again."

The matchmaker reached into a battered drawer of his cluttered desk, pulled out a roll of tissue-thin paper, spat importantly into his cake of dry ink, brandished his brush in preparation for his very finest calligraphy, and said, "Now, sir, if I could have a description of the wife you require."

Sung Wing On, who had dressed for this occasion in Chinese robes of gray silk with a red and gold dragon snapping angrily across his slender chest, looked out the fly-specked window of the matchmaker's tiny office into the dust and teeming excitement of the Los Angeles streets.

"I want her to be small, smaller than I, but very strong. I want her not to be silent. I want a girl of courage with a mouth that talks back. I want her to have skill on a horse. She should ride faster than the wind. And," here he turned to look at the matchmaker who had made an ugly blot in the midst of his last character, "if you are the matchmaker you say you are, you will bring me a woman with eyes the color of forged steel and hair which changes in the sunlight from silver to gold."

The matchmaker put down his brush and closed his teeth with a click. Now it was his turn to be speechless.

Out in the street on his way home from the matchmaker's, Sung wondered what might really come of his impetuous visit. He had surprised himself almost as much as the matchmaker when he had voiced his true desires in respect to the woman he wished to marry. Tiredly, his mind began to grapple with what it might mean. Perhaps there had been a reason why he had chosen to remain alone for so many years.

He decided not to pursue this and tried to force his mind instead on his masterly negotiations with regard to the down payment and the ultimate price that he was to pay for the bride: Sung had skillfully insisted, despite all the subtle wiles used by the matchmaker after he had recovered his aplomb, upon a minimal down payment and the rest of the exorbitant price to be paid in a lump sum at the delivery of the bride-elect. Sung comforted himself that in reality he was not out much money, because he knew and the matchmaker knew that this outrageous, even preposterous match would never come about.

Sung sighed. He was a hard-headed businessman. Why had he allowed himself this lapse in dignity? He knew his name would be bandied about, the butt of those licentious jokes that his countrymen so loved, in every gambling den, teahouse, and even brothel in this city for weeks to come. He sighed. A deeper, sadder knowledge told him why he had done it. Perhaps simply by putting this apparition into words he might consign it to the air, get it once and for all out of his body—expel that fearless blond goddess who had for ten years so persistently haunted his dreams.

"Honorable Cousin Sung, do you not recognize and speak to your cousin in the street?"

It took Sung a few moments to fix his eyes on the speaker and recognize with a combination of distaste and relief Yun-ling, a distant cousin from the farther compound of his own home village.

During the last few years he had found it both useful and profitable to arrange for the entry of some of his own surviving relatives. When he had first received those initial supplicating letters, both whining and obsequious in tone, asking for passage, papers, jobs in the Mountain of Gold, he had been consumed with rage. These were the people who in their heartless carousings had literally locked their doors against one half of the family, leaving them to die. At the same time he could not help but be flattered by this evidence of his fame that had spread far enough to reach that small village so many *li* from the city on the River of Pearl.

He had imported one cousin for the memory of Bin Tang, who had seen the vision but lacked the courage to act on it; then a second in honor of Sung Tsi, who had passed his own pitiful inheritance through the chinks of that wall and perished terribly only a few days later. And then, a third cousin, in salute to his own father, who had taught him never to turn his back on his family.

The entire home village now numbered only eight. There were some days that Sung had regretted his deeds, for he knew that his relatives traded on his position, but he also realized they were necessary to his own well-being, providing as they did links to the past. They above all others knew how far he had come, how far he had risen. And they did, in the end, give him the kind of loyalty that only a blood relationship commanded.

"Honorable Cousin, your unworthy relatives have traced your footsteps all this day and the last."

"What is it this time?" Sung asked with a sigh of impatience.

"We want nothing. We request only the honor of an audience with you."

Sung looked skeptical. He'd heard these words before and wondered what favor was going to be asked of him. "I am very busy."

"Tonight, an hour after the evening meal, might we have the good fortune and favor to find you in your office?"

"I pursue my business affairs every evening after dinner as everyone knows," said Sung a trifle sententiously. "I do not waste my time in singsong houses or playing fan-tan."

This crushing speech did not have its usual withering effect. The cousin, sweating visibly under the sun's rays, rewarded him unexpectedly with the most brilliant of smiles.

"Until tonight, Gracious Benefactor," and with that he was gone.

Sung had changed into his serviceable work clothes of lightweight wool. He planned to work late that night on the accounts of his various businesses.

137

They numbered, by this time, almost a dozen, both legal and illegal. The art store, opulent as it appeared, was only a convenient front for other enterprises, more lucrative, more mundane, which brought Sung his real income. Each of these businesses had two separate sets of books. One of them, for the government, was kept in the imaginative, "honest" manner of a hardworking illiterate Chinese peasant; the other set, for only his eyes, contained entirely different sets of figures, meticulous in the extreme and set out in an elaborate code that only he could understand.

With his customary discipline Sung set to work. His primary pleasure as an esthetic young man was to literally watch the acquisition of his wealth in this manner. He had worked two or three hours when it occurred to him to speculate upon the whereabouts of his shiftless cousin. It was not that it mattered—Sung would be working at any rate until the early morning hours—but he was conscious of rising exasperation, knowing that a demand was to be made of him.

It was nearly ten when he heard the tentative knock. Whatever vague notions he may have had, had in no way prepared him for the almost incredible spectacle that presented itself.

The cousin who had spoken to him on the street, together with his other two imported cousins, bowed formally after they had entered the room. Behind their bent bodies, Sung saw a human figure, shrouded in coarse red silk of the tenth quality: a girl-figure to be exact.

"Honorable Cousin," Yun-ling, the obvious spokesman of the delegation, said as they came to a standing position, once again hiding the doll-like figure from view, "it has not escaped the attention of your family on either side of the great waters that what our generous benefactor, who has preceded us to the Mountain of Gold, needs most is a wife. You work too hard, Beloved Cousin." Here he gestured expansively. "These are the hours when a man should console himself with the tender ministrations of a wife. Yet here you are as you are every night over those books which, it is true, increase your wealth and the wealth of the village. But I tell you, Cousin, for your own good, it is my duty to remind you of this, since I surpass you in years if not in substance. You cannot go on in this solitary life you have chosen. You will die a young man with no sons to carry your name."

Was Sung mistaken, or did he hear his other two shiftless cousins snicker slightly under their breath?

Yun-ling snapped his fingers. "Hey," he said, not unkindly, "little one, come forward. Let him get a look at you."

Sung heard the rough shiver of silk and the barely perceptible tinkle of concealed bells as the girl pattered forward, keeping her face behind its veils averted.

"Honorable Cousin, here you have another cousin, but distant enough for decency's sake. She is a poor wretch from our compound. She was left an orphan during the great sickness. Even a girl child was precious to us at that time. She is not worthy of you, Young Master, but please accept her for the sake of your village, your family, and your cousins, who hold you in such high esteem."

Sung stared transfixed at this diminutive red and gold package. "How, by the Buddha, did you get her across?"

All three cousins allowed themselves satisfied chuckles.

"It was not easy and it was not cheap. We had to keep her passage unknown from the one man in Chinatown who knows everything. She was smuggled in a fine tea chest. She has been here for a week already. We have been fattening her up, for you."

"I don't want a wife," Sung blurted. "This gift does not please me."

The little figure under its veils began to tremble. He heard musical whimpers of the most pathetic nature.

Yun-ling seemed unconcerned and went on blithely. "You are hard, Cousin, too hard. It is just as I said. Work has aged you before your time."

With that he signaled to the other two men who had so far remained silent.

"It is against every custom as we all know," he said, "but a new land makes new ways. Yun-lei," he said, "reveal our unworthy gift and the Young Master's heart will be softened."

Yun-lei stepped forward and, with a broad and greasy grin, lifted with two stubby paws the corners of the heavy veil.

Looking out from beneath black hair parted in the middle and decorated with inferior pink jade ornaments, two dark eyes, both beseeching and at the same time curious, fixed themselves intently upon Sung. She had begun to cry at his curt rejection. The tears still glistened on cheeks smooth and fresh as a peach tree's first blossoms. Her mouth had been painted in to make her look older than her years. Her lips, wide and vulnerable, quivered as she tried to smile. Sung saw with immense compassion that her ears had been only recently pierced. They carried plain gold loops which were a farm girl's only dowry.

"But this is just a child," he said roughly to cover his emotions. "She's not old enough to make any man a wife."

Yun-ling looked censoriously at his young cousin. "How quickly you forget the ways of our village. This girl is fast approaching her fifteenth year. Were we at home she might already be a mother. And it is over a year since she first experienced the flowers of womanhood."

Sung felt himself blush. He had forgotten the directness of the ways of the home village.

"By what name are you called, Little One?" Sung asked, his voice soft to not frighten her any further.

"She is called Lin," said Yun-ling. "Does this mean that you are pleased, Young Master? May we go ahead with plans for the wedding? There are many in your debt who long to repay you. Your nuptials shall be such as only the richest in our province could afford."

Sung, still looking at the girl child's expectant face, thought, as he always did, as a businessman. Perhaps it was true that this was a gift of gratitude. It was far more likely that this female was designed to chain him forever to his impoverished home village and its grasping inhabitants. Yet his sympathy had been touched. There was also the fact that on this very same day he had invested a substantial sum to procure the kind of woman he had desired

139

since those desperate days ten years before. Sung smiled bitterly. Dreams were one thing, but he knew what the round-eye thought of the Chinese. He knew that the chances of the matchmaker bringing him a woman with hair the color of gold was the same as finding a grain of rice in the River Pearl. Better to take what life offered. There was a saying in the home village that all women were the same in the dark. He could still close his eyes and dream.

He nodded his head and said curtly, "I'll take her" and was rewarded with the least tremor of a delicate crimson smile.

Raoul watched his foster mother with unutterable disgust. Magdalena was on her hands and knees, her skirts rucked up around her strong thighs, scrubbing as she did each and every morning the bleached bare planks of her kitchen floor. He waited, slouching in the doorway, until his mother worked herself into a corner, painfully straightened up, and sat down to a cup of tea which she had placed on a side table earlier as a modest reward. He cracked his knuckles to get her attention, then, with deliberate insolence, walked across the still damp surface, dragging his mud-caked boots.

"Raoul, don't do that! Don't you see what you've done? I just finished with this floor."

He answered her by saying nothing, and grinning slyly. Already at ten he was becoming a handful. He needed a father's strong hand. Magdalena's boarders, over the years, thinking to ingratiate themselves with her, had showered the boy with attention, only to destroy his trust by thoughtless discipline, unnecessarily raised voices, or—when they had found themselves wives—leaving the boardinghouse, and leaving him without another "father."

The likable tot had turned into a sullen child. He preferred to stay in his room all day, only to run in the streets at night, when he knew she would worry. He ate to excess, knowing it would displease her, and bathed only when she threatened to take the switch to him. Now he stood at the stove and ladled himself a generous portion of the *frijoles de olla* that simmered continuously on the back plate. As he smeared the beans on a tortilla he either by accident or design let a dollop of the syrupy mixture sizzle down on the stove.

"Raoul! Please don't do that! You clean that up right now!"

But he could be deaf when he wanted, and he went out the back door, without hearing her, letting the screen door slam behind him.

Sighing, Magdalena went back down on her knees, tracing his steps with a soapy cloth. Where had he found mud, anyway, in this city, and at this time of year?

That boy, he breaks a mother's heart, she thought. It had been a mixed blessing that she had been allowed to adopt the orphan. As a baby he had been a comfort, so she would not be lonely. But now he was growing up to be as bad as the worst man in Sonoita. He was a *brujo,* a demon, a sorcerer.

Of course, she knew it wasn't easy for him. Because of where they lived now, he was almost the only Mexican boy in his school. She knew they made fun of him there because of his accent. (He, in turn, made fun of *her* heavier one.) Everything, she often thought, would have been easier if they had been able to stay on Clara Street. If the boy was a mixed blessing, so was this handsome, yellow, three-story house on Carroll Street on the edge of the Bunker Hill district. Clifford had been more than generous with this gift, but it had been left to her to find out the disadvantages of increased material wealth.

Sung had helped in those early days. He had filled every room in the substantial mansion with a boarder. She kept house now for an even dozen, not including Raoul and the servant girls. That was twelve rooms to clean each day, twelve beds to make, close to fifty meals each day, three hundred and fifty meals a week. . . .

She knew that part of her burden was of her own making. Her standards were high, not only in her choice of boarders, but in the quality of service she provided. On the one hand she took pride in the fact that there was a waiting list. Young men on the way up in the city government knew that hers was the best place to save money and live comfortably, as well as to make contacts with Bud Thompson, Robert E. "Bob" O'Shea, and Jordan Espey, who over the years had become her star boarders. While she admired Espey and knew his theoretical usefulness, the other side was that he expected all the niceties: clean linen, fresh napkins with every meal. Her profits were often eaten up in extra purchases and extra work.

After ten years, even Magdalena, strong as she was, had to recognize that being a self-made woman wasn't much fun. She thought nostalgically more than once of the easy give and take on Clara Street; even at the Pico House, life had had variety, color; the future still held promise. . . .

That night, at dinner, Raoul had still not come home. She moved competently about the well-appointed dining room. Her boarders had all, at one time or another, implored her to sit down and eat with them, but the years of her Mexican upbringing, her continual exasperation with her servant girls, and the feeling that she herself was no more than a servant to these city officials, conspired to keep her upright and on the move. Her girls brought the steaming dishes from the butler's pantry to the sideboard, but it was she who kept her boarders' plates continually filled. Tonight the dinner was chicken and dumplings.

Jordan Espey, presiding at the head of the table, was full of news. Leaning conspiratorially into the table, he fairly clucked with excitement.

"I never would have seen it if I hadn't been in the mayor's office. He had me in there on the carpet! There'd been a civic improvement delegation down there again, and he wants *me* to do something about it! I *told* him, there isn't any money for that sort of thing. But then his secretary brought in this enormous sheaf of papers. *Well!* He tried to cover it with his hand, but if you think I've worked in City Hall for twenty years without learning to read upside down, and if he thinks I'm still so green that I don't recognize the forms for a forced land sale. . . ."

"Land? What kind of land?"

"Who went broke this time?"

"What are they going to do with it, Espey?"

"A secret auction. Of course they can't do that legally. But I heard his secretary place the newspaper announcements for the eighteenth. And I know for a fact the real auction is on the seventeenth."

"Where is it, anyway?"

"About ten miles due west."

"That's nothing but bean fields."

"And there's another tract further south."

Most of the men had begun to chuckle. "You can't even grow beans *there,* Espey."

Espey was adamant. "Everyone knows land is the best investment you can make out here, boys. It's five fifty-acre parcels at ten dollars an acre. That's the floor bid. All I can tell you is, I'm sending my broker out there. . . ."

But even as he spoke, the conversation at the other end of the table had turned to another subject.

Later that evening when the meal had been cleared, Magdalena sought out Bud Thompson, the most likable of her recent boarders, if one of the most naïve. She made him sit down with her in the porch swing, took his hand, and in her most confiding manner, said, "I need to ask your advice, Mr. Thompson. Is it true, what Mr. Espey said, about the land?"

"As far as I know. I've never known Espey to be wrong yet."

"Do you . . . do *you* plan to buy?"

"Shucks, no. I don't have that kind of money."

"I had a friend once who became a rich man by buying land."

"But it's hard times now. And that land is so far out it will take years for the city to catch up with it. You'd have to say goodbye to your money for years."

Magdalena's breast heaved. "Sometimes, to gain, you must take a risk. Mr. Thompson, we have known each other for almost a year now. I am going to ask you a favor." For a moment she let her hand rest on his knee.

He gazed at her with frank admiration. He, along with half her boarders at any given time, was more than a little in love with this handsome, hard-working, elusive Señora.

"Anything you want, ma'am. You know that."

"I have saved a few dollars. But I do not think that I can buy property here. I am a Mexican, and a woman." She searched delicately for words that would not hurt his feelings. "I do not think they know you so well yet at the mayor's office. Would you take my banknotes, go to that auction, buy a tract of land, and later, in a month or so, deed it over to me as a gift?"

"You'd trust me to do that?" She could see his face in the light of the streetlamp. In spite of herself she was distracted by the sheen of his blond hair, the glitter of his strong white teeth. It was the curse of her nature that she found herself attracted always to the same man, even if he carried different names. But this sweet boy was much too young for her.

"Of course I trust you—why should I not? I can recognize an honest man."

"I'll do it, ma'am." He paused and said shyly, "I only wish I could buy it for you myself."

142

For a fraction of a second she allowed herself the luxury of what might have been, ten years ago. What might have been, had it not been for her position in this limited society, her duty to her boarders to keep up appearances, her duty to Raoul, to give him at least (whether he appreciated it or not) a mother who was upright and chaste. She sighed, for lost romance, for pleasure renounced, and gave that nice knee a last pat, more businesslike than loving.

"*Bueno.* I go to the bank, I give you the money, you buy the property, maybe in a few years I don't work so hard."

Later that night as she brushed out her long hair, her thoughts returned to the matter of the land. Jordan Espey had been truly excited, and she knew he was not a stupid man. Her brief caress of Mr. Thompson had reminded her strongly of those other days with Clifford. If anyone could judge the value of this acreage and take advantage of it, it was her former lover. Though she might at times feel his generous gift to her of this house was a greater burden than she had expected, still, she realized she had done nothing to repay either him or his young wife for what they had done for her. Now she was in possession of some private knowledge, which might in some measure make up for everything she had received.

If she did communicate with him, this would be the first time in ten years. She heard a door slam downstairs and knew that Raoul had returned. She tightened her dressing gown about her with a sigh and got up to quiet him before he woke the whole house. But her last thought, as she turned to the inevitable unpleasant scene with her son, was that she would send a messenger to Clifford Creighton the first thing in the morning.

For a full two weeks the elders of the Pure Heart Benevolent Association, which took in roughly half of the influential citizenry of prosperous Chinatown, had been in an absolute fever of preparations for the coming wedding of their youngest, most powerful member, Sung Wing On. As soon as it had been discovered that the feckless cousins, those seedy poor relations who were Sung's continual embarrassment, had actually taken the initiative and brought over a bride, all of Sung's colleagues, rivals, and compatriots had banded together and adroitly taken over the arrangements from Yun-ling. A wedding like this was an important matter. It had political implications, and for the farsighted businessmen of Chinatown it meant the beginning of a powerful new dynasty.

In tearooms and gambling dens the wedding had been discussed. Chinatown was split into three Benevolent Associations. The five first families distributed their membership among these three. The most important of the Benevolent Associations, or Tongs, as some people persisted in calling them, was the Pure Heart, to which Sung, naturally, belonged.

After some anxious discussion, it was decided to restrict the wedding party to the several hundred members—and their families—who belonged to the Pure Heart, and limit the invitations outside it only to the officers of the Golden Dragon and the Purple Mountain, the other two associations that vied for power with the Pure Heart. This in itself was considered a triumph of diplomacy, since communications among the three associations in the last four months had been limited to the ghostly whisper of a cleaver hurtling down dark alleys, and the muted thunk as it embedded itself in the skull of some unimportant underling.

The main meeting hall of the Pure Heart Benevolent Association was given a new coat of paint; rough trestle tables set up inside, quantities of red paper bought, and penmen put to work, inscribing good luck, long life, and fertility symbols.

Almost as soon as Sung had had the thought *I am to be married,* festivities were out of his hands and beyond him. All he could ask was that the traditions of the home village that he remembered be observed as far as this was practical.

He had not laid eyes on his wife-to-be since that first night, as was proper. She was safely in the keeping of the few women here in Chinatown; they, presumably, were instructing her in all the ways they knew to please a man. Because she was without family there could be no question of exchanging lavish family gifts or bargaining over the wife's dowry. But Sung, conscious of his own munificence, had sent to the old women seventy bolts of red and gold silk, with instructions that some of it be made into a bridal costume, some for sleeping garments, gifts for the women attending her, a set of sheets for the bridal night and draperies for above the bed, and most elegant of all—in his mind at least—that twenty-five of these bolts be set aside as part of the dowry of the sponsors' own girl children. Even as he did this, and combed through his inventory of jewels to select pieces for this delicate child bride, he was aware that he acted not only on behalf of his side of the family but for hers as well.

Sung heard indirectly in the week before the wedding that one of the few sedan chairs in the city was being refurbished, lacquered in red and gold to convey the bride through the streets to the site of the ceremony. And to complete her wedding costume, he had hired the best Oriental craftsmen in all of California to create the traditional ornamental headdress of red silk hung with golden tassels and embroidered elaborately with peaches. A decorative fringe, worth a small fortune in itself, made up of tiny seed pearls, small pieces of jade, and leaves hammered from twenty-four-carat gold, was fashioned to tinkle at the slightest motion.

At noon on the wedding day, Sung, dressed in a robe of plum-colored silk and a black silk jacket, his head covered with the traditional cap, a red knot at the top, went to the door of his office and found waiting for him a crowd of young bachelors. In the home village they might have been his cronies, here they were his social inferiors. However, they kept up a steady stream of those remarks that were required in a situation like this, managing to be both bawdy and respectful.

Sung tried to think; tried to remember his father, his mother, what it meant to have a family, to start a family, but it was all a blur, and he found himself emotionally detached from it, thinking only—quite aware of his own superficiality—that this would be the biggest banquet, the most elaborate celebration that Chinatown had ever seen.

When he arrived at the portals of the Pure Heart Benevolent Association the room was already packed and spectators stood three deep outside.

"Long life to the Young Master and many sons!"

"May you have as many sons as there are grains of sand on the beach!"

"May your name be remembered unto four generations."

He did not acknowledge these greetings. He thought ludicrously that he was taller, that he weighed more, as he strode, the focus of all eyes, into the center of the room. Here he was formally greeted by the President of the Pure Heart, who led him to the platform on which were placed two formal chairs of red lacquer and gold leaf carving. Sung bowed stiffly to the nervous delegations from the Golden Dragon and the Purple Mountain. Any further thoughts were wiped from his mind as he heard the sound of gongs, strings of firecrackers, and the shouts of the bearers calling to the crowd to make way for the bride.

He quickly seated himself, holding erect and composed, his hands concealed mandarin fashion in the voluminous sleeves of his gown.

Then there was a flurry in the doorway as the gong still sounded and the final string of firecrackers sputtered out. Six sweating bearers, clad in coarse red jackets, carried the bridal chair though the doors and lowered it to the floor. They were followed by the attending women, who, giggling in their self-importance, broke the red-paper seal on the door and led out the tiny red-clad figure of the girl bride, her face hidden behind a veil. A heavy sigh breathed through the hall as so many men remembered the felicitousness of old days and realized that this kind of consummation would never be for them. And perhaps it was the breath of so many lonely men that swayed against the delicate beads of her headdress sending an almost imperceptible celestial music to Sung's ears. For so many years he had not had a heart. To live, to survive what he had been through, he could not allow himself to feel. Now as he, under half-closed lids, watched as this delicate creature was helped toward the chair with faltering steps, his chest swelled and ached. He grieved that his parents were not here to see this; he yearned for his children who had not yet been born.

As in a dream he saw the Buddhist priest. As in a dream he heard the prayers and smelled the incense. As in a dream he watched the wine poured into the delicate cup. He drank his two-thirds—to drink more would mean he would be a tyrant, to drink less would mean he would be henpecked for the rest of his life—set the cup down on a little table, and with ceremony lifted the veil of his bride. She sat motionless, her eyes almost shut, her head tilted modestly downward. Lifting the cup, he placed it in her hands and whispered, "We will have a long life and a happy one." Though he knew he should keep his features immobile he gave her the hint of an encouraging smile as she briefly looked up, met his eyes for a fleeting instant, and drained the cup before she once again lowered her eyes.

Then the ritual teasing began. Lin, he was happy to see, knew that she, for the present, should neither eat nor respond in any way to the taunting remarks.

"If you don't eat, you'll have no strength for what lies ahead."

"If your husband is as good in his marriage bed as he is in his business dealings, you will find yourself the mother of triplets before the night is over."

"I have heard it said that his rod is as strong as the giant pendulum which strikes the hour in the five-story temple which we all remember from the olden times."

"He is small in stature," said an older man who could afford this sally, "but remember the bite of the tiny mosquito, how it stings, how you remember it for days."

"Sung has not seen a woman since he has come to this city. Watch out, Little One, now that he has come out from behind his desk you will see nothing but the ceiling for the next six months. So you'd better eat now! You won't get another chance in a hurry!"

"And you, be sure to eat the curried lobster, Master Sung."

As if in response to this remark the doors were flung open and at least forty waiters brought in trays of dozens of oysters, clams, and sea urchins—a sly wedding gift from the Golden Dragon and Purple Mountain associations, implying as it did that the potency of the membership of the Pure Heart might need a boost. This gambit was taken in good part and shouts of laughter filled the hall.

And a voice called out, "After eating these the population of Chinatown should double nine months from tonight." Again the sadness underneath the bawdy confidence. This was an empty boast. Most of the men here would go home to lonely beds.

Sung gazed at the stranger beside him and was choked suddenly and unexpectedly by lust. She was his! His to do with as he pleased. As if divining his thoughts, she risked a glance at him and her cheeks flushed red. Sung knew that this banquet, this vast celebration, would go on for at least three days. He also knew that after only a matter of three or four hours he would be alone with this untouched precious girl, naked between silk sheets.

Following the mountains of oysters and lobster curry came great platters of every manner of seafood delicacy. Squid, octopus, shark's fin, more sea urchins, steamed whole fish, shrimp—all were brought in relentless succession and put before the guests. The President of the Association, with great éclat, severed the head of the dorado with his chopsticks and placed it on Sung's porcelain plate. Knowing what was expected of him, Sung lifted it between his ornamental ivory chopsticks and, after cracking the bone to the brain, sucked out the delectable contents, smacking his lips as good manners dictated. And then with exclamations of delight he crunched the eyeballs appreciatively.

Still steadfastly Lin refused every morsel that was put on her plate, until at last, after two solid hours of feasting, the waiters brought each guest the tiny obligatory bowl of white rice. Then Sung for the first time—but certainly not the last—allowed himself to be stern with his bride.

"As your husband I request that you take some nourishment."

Sung lifted some long slender noodles from his plate onto hers, saying, "These are for our long life. You must eat them."

146

Lin, her eyes flicking toward him in gratitude, for the first time took up her chopsticks in her delicate clawlike hand. Gracefully she lifted them to her mouth. Her chopsticks moved like lightning as she pushed these delicious lengths into her mouth.

"And now," said Sung, "you must eat some of the rice. You must remember in our village the rice bowl must be empty. To leave any grains behind is to lose so many years." Sung spooned a little sauce from a perfectly cooked duck onto her rice to flavor it. With the appearance of great reluctance she began to eat.

The nearby guests, up to now engrossed in satisfying their own appetites, dazed as they were after drinking toast after toast of warm rice wine, noticed the movement of the bride's chopsticks. And once again with great gusto, the ceremony of teasing was renewed.

"Ah, she's already taking the seed of the future!"

"And it is stained red!"

"A thousand grains, a thousand sons. Refill the little girl's bowl!"

"Fill it indeed!"

Amidst the chorus of shrill cackles, Sung stole a look at his beautiful bride and decided that both of them had observed the conventions long enough. He gazed around at the rest of the crowd. Although the noodles and the rice had already made their appearance, the hundreds of wedding guests he could see from his place on the dais were still feasting on delicacies that were rarely seen even among the rich in Chinatown: eight jewel rice pudding, almond junket, and orange soup with Yuan-hsiao. This together with the whiskey which had been added at the height of the festivities assailed Sung with a faint wave of nausea. The evening had turned gross and in the glazed eyes of the mostly male guests he was reminded uncomfortably of the wild nights he had spent in the railroad camps as an orphan youth.

"Respected wife," he said shortly, "we are leaving now."

Again he read in her shy look a question which she was too polite or too unsure to ask. It was too early to leave, but he stood up, and his hosts, covering their discomfiture, swung into the next phase of this elaborate wedding feast.

Most of the women, but only a handful of men, stood up with the couple. The bride was again bundled into her sedan chair and, with much joking, whisked out the door. Sung and his bachelors followed at a slower pace to give the bride time to get ready.

It was late afternoon. The sun beat mercilessly into the dusty streets. According to the custom of ancient times the men stopped at several drinking houses on their way. Sung confined himself to an abstemious glass of rice wine at each stop and countered their bawdy remarks absently. He was ready for this to be over.

After what seemed like an eternity they arrived at Sung's apartment. The women stood giggling outside the beaded curtain. Now that it was close to the time, a hush fell on the men. Sung saw in their eyes, again, that loneliness and envy. He knew most of them would never in their lives attain to the good fortune that was in his hands now. Then one strong hand pushed him inside the beaded barrier. As he stood blinking in the semidark, he heard a great rustle behind him. They were, again according to an ancient custom, sealing up the door with red paper on which symbols in gold of long life and fertility had been painted.

And then they were gone. In the silence, Sung sensed the little girl's presence, almost lost in his great carved, lacquered bed. He saw that the old women had placed a tray of tea cakes and a flask of rice wine on one of the small tables. With careful nonchalance he skirted the canopied bed, poured himself the wine, hoping that it would warm him. He knew that he should change into his sleeping garments, but he wasn't sure where he should go.

The old women had prepared some warm, perfumed water, and self-consciously, his back to her, one layer at a time, he removed his wedding attire, sluiced off his nervous sweat, and put on a loose satin robe especially sewn for this night.

Then—what else could he do? He approached the bed. His side had been turned down, and he slipped between the new red silk sheets. Again, he was almost painfully aware of the tiny figure beside him, although the sheets were pulled up just past her nose. Only her beautiful almond eyes, her pale forehead, and her carefully coiffed hair were visible.

He lay back to compose himself against the Western-style pillows. Honored Father, he thought, can you see me now? Have I fulfilled your wishes? I have taken a wife from our own home village. . . . He was assailed by a vision of his father, utterly honest, utterly brave. He had lived in poverty, but his character had been pure gold. Sung, and only Sung, knew that the abundant wealth with which he was surrounded was for the most part a sham. The priceless antiques below were, many of them, no more than three weeks old, copper and brass aged overnight. Much of his jade was agate. Unlike his father's, Sung's ways were not always honest. A man from the Middle Kingdom could not be honest in this land. And Sung knew also that the respect that he was accorded by the people of Chinatown was based on fear and need as much as true esteem. Father, he thought. . . .

A thin, piping sound broke through his reverie.

"Have I displeased you, Young Master?"

They were the first words he had heard Lin speak.

Startled, he looked over at her. To his great chagrin, he saw that her cheeks were streaked with tears.

"I am too ugly. They all told me I was too ugly. And too small. They told me I was too small."

"But you are a gift from the village," he said politely. "And a very pretty one."

"They wouldn't send their own daughters," Lin sobbed. "They sent me because I was an orphan. They said I would die on the great ship, and that it wouldn't matter. They said you had cheated death, and that you were a witch. They said you would throw me in the streets. They said you had fourteen ears! They said. . . ."

And as though the terrible days of the great sickness had happened only yesterday he was consumed with rage at the poltroons from the other side of his village. How cruel they were, how petty, how stupid. And he took some comfort from the fact that although he had not the honor of his own father, he was more of a man than the rest of the farther compound.

He reached under the covers and took her hand. She trembled like the leaves of the willow.

"I don't know what to do," she whimpered. "The old grandmothers said that I must wait for the sea serpent. What does that mean?"

Sung had an inkling. He felt that sea serpent uncoiling even as she spoke. But—though he would never admit it to any man and especially to her—he was as inexperienced as she. Except for the blond demon who came to him in his dreams, he had never lain with a woman. The only women a young Chinese could touch were plentiful in Chinatown, but they were the women of the watermelon breasts and the vile disease.

Sung allowed his hand to travel up her arm and slip inside the upper portion of her silken garments. Her breasts were smooth, soft, small, and incredibly fresh, not much bigger than the succulent lichee. His sea serpent had assumed truly mythic proportions. Lin's tears had dried by now, her whimpers were no longer brokenhearted. His serpent knew exactly where to go, into the grotto of the black pearl.

When, after a few minutes, it was over, their previous embarrassment overcame them both again. He felt dampness, and saw a darker shade of red against the sheets.

"Did I hurt you?" he said anxiously.

"Your serpent was so very big!" But she didn't sound too hurt.

"Respected Wife," he muttered, arranging his gown around him, "it is my wish that you should take some nourishment."

He, still self-conscious, crossed the room, and returned with wine and cakes. She was sitting up against the pillows. Her hair had come undone and spilled in lustrous waves across the sheets. Incredibly, his sea serpent stirred again. As he watched this delicate creature munching on *dim sum* with what turned out to be a hearty appetite, he laughed out loud.

Magdalena sat on her back porch, peeling apples. Ay, she thought to herself. A woman's work is never done. Why didn't I listen when the other women told me? She gazed across the porch at Adelita, who had turned from an energetic girl into a stout, phlegmatic spinster. Though she had survived the plague, life was all over for her: She lived only for the next meal, and she was only twenty-four.

That is what is in store for me, Magdalena thought glumly. There is no love in my life. No men to warm my bed. Only work, everlasting work. She thought of Señor Thompson and his errand, and for the hundredth time that day she bitterly regretted her decision. *Madre de Dios!* How could I have been so stupid! How could I have given him all my money! What if he runs away with it? Then I will be poor again, as poor as when I was a child, with nothing but work and an ungrateful son to fill my old age.

Some of her worries were assuaged, however, when she heard the creaky latch on the wrought-iron gate shut in front, and footsteps, which she already recognized as Thompson's, coming through the side yard. The stricken look on his face brought back all her fears. At a nod of her head, Adelita got up and left the two of them alone. Whatever it was, she thought, at least he had come back.

"Miz Ortiz, I don't know how to tell you this." His round boyish face was flushed. Had he not been a grown man, she would have thought he was about to cry.

"I went out there like you said. I put in your bid. I beat out Espey with no trouble. But there was someone else there, in a big black automobile. There were two of them, one man to make the bids, another one in the car, and there were curtains pulled down. I . . . I feel so bad about it! They doubled our bid! There wasn't a damn thing I could do." He managed a rueful smile. "The mayor looked like he was gonna have a stroke."

She opened her mouth to reply but Thompson sat down beside her. "Aw, ma'am, Magdalena, don't feel bad. You wouldn't have wanted it anyway. It isn't good farmland! They can't grow a damn thing on it. And you wouldn't want to live out there because it smells like a saloon on the weekend. The ground's mushy with oil. And who needs that?"

He held up a boot to show it to her, and she had to smile. He had ruined a pair of boots for her.

He handed her the envelope with her money, clumsily excused himself, and disappeared into the kitchen, banging the screen door.

Alone again, she sighed; a combination of resignation and relief. She was no richer, but she was no poorer. And the land was one less burden she would have to carry.

She returned to her homely chore. Rich or not, she had a dozen men to feed. But she had scarcely reestablished the rhythm when the screen door slammed again. She looked up to see Mr. Thompson, looking sheepish.

"Miz Ortiz? Excuse me for bothering you, I know you're busy. But I . . . I . . . may I sit down?"

Without waiting for a reply he lowered himself awkwardly onto the steps beside her.

"Miz Ortiz?"

She looked across at him.

"You, you mean all the world to me."

She had nothing to say to that.

"When you asked me last night to buy that land, well, well, it meant all the world to me."

She smiled politely.

"When I, well, I failed you, see? So what I mean to say is . . . well, I know you have that foster son."

Her smile became a little more strained.

"You took him in, and you didn't even have a husband. That was mighty white of you."

"Hmm."

"What I mean to say is, I'm a poor man. But I admire you, Miz Ortiz. I admire you more than I can say. You're a good woman. So what I want . . . what I want is . . ."

She wondered momentarily if he wanted an extension on his rent. But he awkwardly fished in his pocket and brought out a small tissue-wrapped object.

"This belonged to my mother," he said. "She told me to give it to my wife but it looks like I'm not the marrying kind. I think she'd want for you to have it."

The package lay lightly in her hand. The paper rustled as she stripped several layers of tissue, yellowish with age. It was a cameo brooch, a woman in profile, the background a deep amber, the woman intricately carved. She recognized it as authentic, a good piece. It lay peaceful in her hand, the last of the sun's rays glittering on its intricate gold setting.

"Understand, ma'am, this doesn't bind you to anything. I'd be obliged if you'd think of this as just a pledge of friendship. And I'd like you to wear it—for me."

He watched as she pinned it on her ample bosom. "I wish I had more to give you. Because. . . ."

But his courage had clearly left him. He got up and went back in through the kitchen.

Magdalena returned to peeling her apples. There was one man on earth who prized her. It might not be much. But it put her back to work with a smile.

Little less than a month after the wedding, Sung sat at his desk working late into the night. Not for the first time he considered the possibility of separating his office and his living quarters. His new wife had become a serious impediment to his work; she disturbed him in a way he had not foreseen. It took but a glimpse of her delicate limbs or a flash of her seductive scent in his nostrils and he forgot all about the dual systems of his accounts or the figure he cut in the community. She had but to walk in front of his desk or to replace the maid in bringing him his pot of tea to have him grasp her by the arm and push her firmly through that beaded curtain and once again down into the softness of that silken bed. Several times in the last week she had even weakly protested, saying it might be too much, implying that it might even be bad for his health. But he was as a man hypnotized, having kept himself so long from this exquisite pleasure and having now the undisputed right to indulge in it at his whim. He could not help himself. From time to time—usually during the first five minutes after completion—he would think, I must be a man of moderation. I must learn control. I must keep to the middle way. But an hour or so later Lin would catch his eye and business would take second place.

Tonight he vowed to himself he would work for at least an hour more, he would work for at least forty-five minutes. He heard a knock on the door downstairs, heard two sets of footsteps on the stairs, and as his servant announced a caller he thought once again that he should separate his home and office. More than once they had been disturbed in the very act of love.

The intruder tonight proved to be a messenger sent by the matchmaker.

"Honored sir, my master humbly craves your presence at his place of business."

"I will be happy to see him," Sung replied, "tomorrow at his place of business."

"Honored sir," the messenger said, "my master says it is a matter of some urgency. It is a matter best not discussed before the eyes of others." He lowered his voice and gazed significantly at the beaded curtain and what lay beyond. "My master says this is a piece of business best concluded when only the two of you are present, and he urges," here the messenger shuddered slightly, "he requests most urgently that you come now."

"Certainly," Sung said, "if it is a matter of such pressing importance."

He stood swiftly, crossed to the beads, and spoke in a low voice to Lin. "I am called out tonight on business. You may go to sleep without me."

As they made their way through the streets already shut up for the night, Sung considered the best way to conclude these unfinished negotiations. He would ask for his entire down payment back, but after several hours would settle for half.

The light was still on in the matchmaker's office. He opened the door furtively, dismissed the messenger, and pulled Sung inside. Sung seated himself, his hands in his lap, and waited to be offered tea. He heard scuffling from the back room and then a tremendous crash. He looked inquiringly at the matchmaker and then at the back wall. Another crash and the flimsy partition shook.

"Young Master," the matchmaker bleated, "this is a happy day for you."

There was silence from the back room, but it was an ominous one.

"It is not for nothing that I am called the miracle worker of love. You've asked me for the impossible and this time I have astonished even myself. I have searched in the mountains and the great plains to the east, sending out messages to the other members of our guild—"

Bang. Bang. Bang. The door to the back room echoed and shook.

The matchmaker took a deep breath and gazed fixedly at Sung's shoes. "There are those," he said rapidly, "who believe that our world, instead of being held up by the giant turtle, is a glistening, mysterious, two-sided mirror. Imagine on the one side, Young Master, the Middle Kingdom. But on the other," he raised his voice to a shout, "on the other side an enigmatic world of green fields! Fertile valleys! Great kings and queens! But *many hardships!* This woman of character came from far, far away. She, even as you, courageously crossed a great ocean. She fought goblins, dragons, and men who would try her virtue."

Here the matchmaker crossed the room and flattened himself against the flimsy partition.

"This empress of benevolence made her way as in a chariot drawn by silken threads . . ."

"You can keep the down payment."

". . . to a far country."

Sung made for the door.

"Wait!" The matchmaker held onto him with a desperate grasp.

"This place we are now, Young Master, this Mountain of Gold, is but a dream of the Buddha. We are, so to say, in the shadow between the two mirrors."

Unwillingly, Sung's mind throbbed for an instant with a vision of the far northern camps, his starving countrymen, his awareness of being out of time and space.

The matchmaker sensed his hesitance and rushed on. "She came, this golden goddess, to a far region of *this* country—Tex-as. A place of fierce storms and blowing sands much like the uncharted, uncivilized region beyond our own Great Wall."

The matchmaker stepped to the door and gingerly unbolted it, as if he were opening the cage of a tiger.

Bang! Whoosh!

The first thing Sung saw was her truly ferocious scowl. Her eyes, if she had them, were hidden under thick blond brows. Her forehead was hidden under a frizzle of white-blond hair. She wore a man's blue work shirt of rough cotton, the cuffs rolled up to show grubby hands, the nails bitten down to the nub. She shook her fist at the matchmaker and stamped her feet, her heavy boots shaking the office. She wore men's pants, and pants over *them* made of leather with a fringe. She stank of animals.

"Here she is, Honored Sir. A woman with hair the color of gold and silver. She is audacious. She came all the way in a boxcar from Tex-as. I am told she injured severely any man who tried to touch her."

Sung sensed with an emotion much closer to terror than lust that she had fixed him with an appraising stare. Her brows lifted just enough to reveal eyes of piercing blue.

She swaggered across the room, punched Sung in the chest, looked back at the matchmaker, and said, "Wosbon?"

The matchmaker bowed and smiled. "Yes," he said.

"Yippee!" she shrieked, locked her arms around Sung, and began covering him with loud kisses. She backed off and held him at arm's length. Grinning, she raised both index fingers to the corners of her eyes and lifted them in imitation of his own. "Funny! You funny!" She laughed, and Sung thought that her tones echoed the desirous honk of the female water buffaloes of the home village when they came into heat.

They were exactly the same height. Her hands, though small, were as strong as any man's.

"Wosbon!" she said and gave him a wide grin of pure insanity. "Me Katarina! Me wife!" She frowned, her brows beetling. "Me good girl! Me wife! Good girl! Good!" She turned to the matchmaker. "Sign paper now!"

Sung made for the door. The matchmaker desperately raised his voice. "You have given your word, Young Master! I have found what you asked for." The matchmaker pointed at a grubby paper pinned to her chest. There, written in rough Chinese characters, she was certified as strong, pure, fourteen years old, and a good cook.

153

"She is strange," the matchmaker conceded. "I have never seen one like her. She comes from the other side of the world. She too is a stranger to the Mountain of Gold. In Tex-as she was a cook for many men. She will not be idle."

The girl glanced back and forth, her brow knit in concentration. When she saw them look at the paper on her chest, she grinned wildly and pounded her sternum.

"I Slovak girl. Come from Košice. Work! Work! Work!" she said in bad English. "Work like dynamite!" Her voice rasped like an ungreased wagon wheel. Her eyes shone with maniacal happiness. "Sign paper! Go to bed! Ha, ha, ha, ha." She clapped Sung on the back. "Wosbon!"

He blinked and regained his balance.

The matchmaker shrugged. "She is everything you asked for. You have already married your second wife first. Now try your first wife second."

"This is not what I expected," Sung said.

Again the matchmaker shrugged. "Life is rarely what one expects, especially in this country." He motioned to the back room. "You can spend the night with her here. We can bargain on price in the morning."

The girl, seeing them look toward the back room, stamped her feet and held out one arm.

"Wife! Wife! Wife! Sign paper first!"

The matchmaker reached into a desk and pulled out the first paper he found. It was a receipted bill from the Sam Sing Butcher Shop for a week's supply of fresh pork. "Just write something down, I beg of you." He held out a brush.

Sung hesitated.

"In the name of the Buddha," the matchmaker pleaded, "just make a character. Don't ruin my business. I give her to you free."

Sung heard her beside him breathing heavily. A vestige of honor made him sign his own name and he winced as her shriek pierced his ears. She grabbed the brush from his hand and painted a bold black X across the receipt. Then Sung felt his ribs crack beneath her determined embrace.

"Name! Name!" she screamed.

The matchmaker whispered, "Sung. Sung Wing On."

"Love!" she shouted. "Love good! Katarina love Sung Wing On!" She hauled him into the back and slammed the door. "Ha, ha, ha, ha," she shouted. "Wife now!"

Once they were alone, she circled the bare room, then swaggered over and nudged him in the ribs. "Damn cute!" she said.

Sung, afraid to look at her, glanced desperately around the tiny cubicle, which was furnished only with a camp cot and an unpainted table on which stood a washbasin and a jug of water. As his eyes returned to her he thought to himself that she was certainly no Victoria Creighton. And searching for something to say he blurted out, "In Tex-as, you ride horse?"

Her brow furrowed with effort to understand, then her face lit up. "You tell 'um, cowboy. Whoopee!" Putting her hands on imaginary reins, jutting her haunches out at an improbable inhuman angle, she began to gallop around the room, which shook with every step.

"Yippee yi yo kai yai!" She reined in next to him, grinning madly, her eyes alight with wild happiness, her hair standing almost on end, blazing whitely around her face. She looked at him with unutterable triumph. Then she grabbed him in her grubby paws, leaned forward, and bit him fiercely on the neck.

"Aie-yah!"

She threw her head back and laughed. "Damn cute! Wife now!" she said, pushing him toward the bed. In a fit of crazy abandon she began to discard her layers of clothes. They whirled around the room in clouds of dust.

Stark naked, she stood in front of him and whacked herself on her firm rump. She began once again to gallop around the room, this time whinnying like a mare in heat.

Dumbstruck, he took a good look at her. To his astonishment, his sea serpent responded as he gazed at the milky-white muscled flesh, her dainty pink-tipped breasts, the hair around her grotto which shone in the lamplight like skeins of golden silk.

Her voice lowered as she pranced over to him with a seductive sidestep.

"You good cowboy," she whispered gutturally. "Ride my horse."

Suddenly her tongue was in his cheek. Then down his throat. Son of the Buddha! Was this how they did it! She did not wait for him to ride. Her brown hands ripped his trousers from him and flung them across the room. With her strong white teeth she gripped the frog fasteners that held the shirt together, ripped them off, spat them out on the floor. Soon he was as naked as she was. She wrestled him to the floor; he lay there stunned while she rode him, her eyes rolled up into her head. She pulled handfuls of shining frizzy hair out of her scalp, beat his flanks, and shouted, "Ride 'um, cowboy!"

He thought with horror of the matchmaker in the adjoining room and remembered prurient tales that bachelors had told of the peepholes into this very room. If those tales were true . . .

The slight diminishment that he experienced at these chilling thoughts had the salubrious side effect of delaying his final spasm, and then delaying it some more. He felt as though he were locked in time, prisoner of an insane night demon. His sea serpent began to sting and burn like the peppers from Szechwan Province. Sweat formed on the glistening brow of this witch and fell upon him like a tropical rain.

"Aieee!" she began to groan, and after what seemed like an eternity, shuddered all over, and fell across his supine body. But she had inflamed him in such a way that he had only begun.

"Sorcerer," he muttered in his native dialect, stood her up against the wall, looked into her face. "Foreign devil," he snarled. "Ugh." He turned her face to the wall and rammed her from behind.

"Aieee!"

She threw back her head like the strange beast with the long ears that Sung remembered from his journey to the City of the Five-Storied Tower. She brayed like that beast in great gulps and gaspings.

"Ee-on! Ee-on!"

But she was stronger than he was and threw him back. He came at her again and bit into her neck as hard as she had bitten him earlier—a primitive grip he had seen among dogs long ago in his home village—tasting the salt of her body, the dirt from her long journey between his teeth, and breathing her rank animal smell deeply into his nostrils. He pinned her against the wall, again locked in an eternity of pleasure that was just this side of pain.

She beat against the partition. Again Sung thought of possible observers. Again this postponed his inevitable conclusion.

But she was as hard to hold on to as a jellyfish. She wrenched her neck from his teeth and as adroitly dislodged his sea serpent. The girl elbowed him in the solar plexus, whirled around, and pushed against him with all her strength. He flew a good ten feet and smacked up against the opposite wall. She came at him, snorting. It was her turn to pin him by his shoulders within her strong arms. He reached down, taking her under the knees and slammed her to him, her feet off the floor. She kicked wildly, which only added to his pleasure and her feigned anger at being no longer in control. He slipped his hands under her buttocks, and thrusting out from the wall, he carried her back to the cot.

Now he was a bull, enraged. He held her motionless, and, thirsting, teeth bared, he saw in those clouds of blond frizzy hair *all the women,* the foreign women, who had frightened him so much. Now he would have his revenge and revenge was sweet.

She was quieting a little. Her shouts had deepened to groans and weakened now to sighs and whispers. She was begging him for something. To stop? To go on? He couldn't know and didn't care. He knew only that he was on the trail of the blond woman who had come to him at night in his dreams. Was it Victoria Creighton? Or was it . . . ?

But these vagrant thoughts were interrupted by the action of his sea serpent which now seemed to have its own life, growing in tingling intensity until, reaching a point of almost unbearable sensation, finally burst forth in a series of spasms as it rode the soft warm waves of her inner seas.

He lay motionless against her soft breast, closer for a few moments, it seemed to him, to death than life. But after a time he was brought back to this world by her husky voice.

"Me good wife. We do this more. Huh, cowboy?"

When, after hours of battle, the sea serpent had crested the waves four more times, Sung wondered numbly if he could go home. But it was not to be. Not until dawn did she release him and fall into something deeper than sleep.

Sung staggered about the room, gathered up his clothes, and put them on as best he could. Lifting the shabby, thin blanket that had long since been kicked from the cot, he took a last glance at the clean line of her back and the lovely white melons of her buttocks before gently covering her nakedness.

Holding his jacket together across his slim chest with one shaking hand, he let himself into the matchmaker's anteroom with the other.

The matchmaker was behind his desk, his face pale. All traces of his former aplomb had left him. Several other bachelors stood up against the far wall, looking both sheepish and envious. Sung guessed that the stories about the peepholes had been true, but he was beyond caring.

The matchmaker seemed unable to speak. Sung wiped his brow with his wrist and looked down at the mingled blood and sweat which he saw there. He took a deep breath and composed a sentence: "I have further need of your services, matchmaker. Find a house of modest means within two blocks of my home. Let it be furnished and let there be rooms for many children."

"Many, many children," the matchmaker said in reverential tones.

Sung groped for another sentence.

"I do not find it convenient at this time to bring my second wife into my household. I have learned that the Tex-ans have their own ways."

He saw two of the bachelors exchange knowing glances, and gripping his jacket tighter about him, he left the matchmaker's office with as much dignity as he could summon.

He turned into the public bathhouse. Was it his imagination, or did the owner's greeting carry a tone of lascivious envy? He soaked for an hour in scalding perfumed waters and sent a messenger home for a fresh change of clothing. After a dozen cups of tea and a bowl of *jook* he felt that he might be able to return to his first wife.

Lin was already dressed and had busied herself with some needlework. Sitting quietly in a pretty little alcove which she had taken over as her own, her greeting betrayed not a hint of concern or displeasure. As he sat down across from her, she rose and went to the sideboard, where she poured a cup of strong green tea. She placed it before him with a bow, saying nothing. He thanked her and sipped from it noisily. It became clear to him not only that she was waiting for him to speak first, but that some word had already reached her about his night's adventures.

"Lin, there are some things I must tell you about this Land of the Golden Mountain. It is fitting that a husband should keep nothing from his wife. This land"—he found himself hesitating over his choice of words—"is a land of great abundance. A man has many opportunities here." Again he hesitated under her clear gaze, which he could not interpret. "When a man reaches my age," he began . . . "Respected Wife, I know that family means everything to you. In our home village, from time to time . . ." He fell silent.

Her voice was so low he had to strain to hear it.

"I have not pleased my illustrious husband." Her voice was as soft as a brook on smooth stones.

He paused and thought before answering. If she knew that he had indeed taken a second wife, she must know at least some of the circumstances surrounding the event.

"It is not true that you have not pleased me. In fact, only the great

pleasure that I have learned from you has made such a thing a possibility."
For a moment he looked at her with concern. "You are as delicate as a bowl
of rare porcelain. I have thought sometimes in the last days that the lust of an
older man might be too much for a child of your years. If I *were* to take a
concubine . . ."

Again the clear gaze. He had no idea what she thought.

"I will be your first wife?" she queried.

"Always and forever," he reassured her.

For the first time her full lips, which she had begun to tint the color of a
pink peony, curled over pearl teeth in the barest hint of a sneer.

"I am told your other little girl's house will have room for children. As
first wife, I require for your own honor a bigger house."

"Certainly."

She permitted herself a slight smile.

"If you honor me thus, you may take as many inferior wives as you wish."

"I do not see anything like that in the future," he said.

"The future is inscrutable."

He acknowledged the justice of this with a nod.

She went on. "But one thing I can tell you of the future is this. As soon as
a suitable house for your *first* wife is found you may begin to furnish one of
the children's rooms."

Her eyes dropped modestly to the needlework that lay in her lap. She was
no more than a child herself, but she had been embroidering the ceremonial
infant garb of the wealthy which they, as peasants, had glimpsed from afar in
the old home village.

Recognizing what it was, Sung could find nothing to say.

Even after he had settled his small family in what he supposed must be
called a "box," immediately facing on the dirt oval track that had been
hastily constructed for what he considered this absurd event, Cliff felt his old
irritation rising. Once presented with this scene, he had thought that Victoria
and Ruth would at last have perceived the folly of this tasteless extrava-
ganza. Instead, there they were clutching the splintery wooden rail, commenting with eager enthusiasm on the confused scene before them.

"Look, Mother!" Ruth exclaimed, pointing with her right arm fully
extended. "Isn't that Alessandro Mariné, over there in the yellow robe by
the pink chariot?"

And Victoria, instead of rebuking her daughter for this abandoned gesture,
answered with equal enthusiasm, "I do believe you're right, darling. And
isn't that Roger Boulter just beyond him? Don't they look manly in their
classic costumes?"

Clifford snorted. Alessandro Mariné's skinny thighs shone a sickly blue-
gray in the bright sun, and Roger Boulter's inch-wide purple ribbons
wrapped round his brow set off an incipient bald spot.

What was wrong with his women that they couldn't see the reality of the
thing?

Shielding his eyes against the sun, Clifford took in all the trappings of this crackbrained event. He preferred to admire the scene before him for its property values. And he was pleased with the agreement that he had reached with the Señora. Just what use this splendid field below the abruptly rising San Gabriel Mountains ultimately would be put to, he was not certain. This property was still part of the vast Mariné holdings, but the fact that she had lent it for this occasion, the fact that he had installed these "improvements," meant that it would probably become part of Pasadena's public lands. And once the Señora had realized the advantages of this prestige and public favor, she could be led to see the profits to be gained by disposing of other unused parts of the original land grant. He was glad that he had entered into this temporary partnership with her.

But for the moment that was the only thing he was glad about. As Victoria and Ruth continued their enthusiastic comments, he looked with a horseman's eye at the semi-chaos that ruled in the center of the track, where eight chariots—rented finally from a second-rate circus—were being hitched up to their matched teams under the supervision of their inexperienced drivers. Luckily, a few of the circus handlers had come with the equipment. Otherwise, he thought, they would never have been able to get the first heat started.

Even so, he felt that he alone appreciated the devastating parody of horsemanship displayed as the first three chariots took part in the opening heat. The professional handlers had problems in holding the teams—one of grays, one of whites, and one of roans—at the starting line. But at last they were off and he was happy to see that Alessandro Mariné fell safely behind the uncontrollable bolting of the other two teams, which swung wide and almost crashed on the first turn. Had Alessandro been a real horseman, he could have gathered his team together and taken the lead on the rail. But Cliff was relieved when Alessandro made no move to take advantage of this opening. Cliff could see that the boy was frightened, and felt a grudging admiration for him.

Finally the team of grays pulled ahead of the whites. Though Victoria and especially Ruth were disappointed by Alessandro's elimination, Cliff, to his surprise, heard himself speak in the boy's defense.

"Look," he said, "he was the one driver who showed judgment and sense. They're all three lucky to be alive."

"Oh, Daddy," Ruth exclaimed in a despairing tone. And she and her mother exchanged a confidential feminine glance of there-he-goes-again.

"Really, dear," Victoria said in an elaborately conversational tone. "I'm afraid I still can't understand why you aren't there with the other racers. When I think of what a superior horseman you are—"

"I've told you already, Victoria, what my feelings are about this," snapped Clifford. Then in an effort to maintain family harmony he continued, "Besides, I wouldn't be caught dead in a toga."

"Well, Headsperth's doing it."

"Well, Victoria, Headsperth *would*."

During the next two hours of the elimination heats, Cliff had time to wonder if Victoria had simply been teasing him or if she could possibly still have some lingering interest in Headsperth. It couldn't be, he thought. But he acknowledged that there was no accounting for what went on in the heads of women.

By this time, Headsperth, having won two heats, was the popular favorite. Clifford watched him strutting back and forth, answering greetings from the crowd. He looked like a stuffed sausage in his gladiator costume. Belle, in contrast, was pale and tense in the third box up from the Creightons'. She was the only other person present, so far as Cliff could tell, who understood the danger here.

At last it was time for the final race, which pitted Headsperth Bauer against Eddie Nash.

Three chariots were no longer in running condition, and it was sheer good fortune that no horse had been seriously hurt. The bleachers at the far turn had been battered more than once, and Clifford congratulated himself that he'd had the foresight to build the protective bar with extra strength.

Headsperth's chariot, decorated with a lion's head, was pulled by a well-matched team of chestnuts, more subdued now than they were in the first heats. Nash's—most improbably—sported the almost nude figure of a trapeze artiste; his team of blacks seemed less winded than those of his opponent. Nash had contented himself with a simple toga—doubtless one of his household's second-best sheets, run up by his dutiful wife on her sewing machine, its border decorated by fylfots. He wore strapped sandals and a ribbon of turquoise blue. It was evident that sartorially Headsperth felt he had already won the race.

With ceremony, Headsperth climbed into the chariot; it trembled under his considerable weight. The crowd cheered; he rewarded them with a wave. His gilded cardboard breastplate caught the sun. The leather fringes of his short skirt hung raggedly halfway about his knees. Some wretch, possibly Headsperth himself, had been busy with the scissors. His head was decorated with an impossible crest. From this distance it looked like painted broom straws. This "headdress" was securely fastened under the chin, disappearing into folds of fat.

What does she see in him? What did she ever see in him? The leather fringe swayed as the chestnuts nervously sidestepped their way toward the starting line. The crowd cheered again, and with one free, chunky arm Headsperth saluted them. Clifford had to admit that there was something about him people liked.

At the wave of the starting flag, Headsperth, deep in his impersonation of a courageous gladiator, had the foolhardy impulse to flash his whip over the seemingly tired chestnuts, as unnecessary a gesture as anyone could think of. The crowd shouted and clapped at this showmanship.

For the second time today, Headsperth had drawn the outside. Nash, had he been a better horseman, would have held the advantage, but if it were possible he appeared more mindless even than Headsperth. Clifford had seen in the earlier heats Nash's tendency to take the turns wide, or rather, to let the turns take care of themselves.

As they approached the first turn, Clifford could see that Headsperth was determined to take the lead, instead of waiting for the back stretch where he could have done so easily. But Nash, because he simply didn't know what he was doing, allowed his wildly galloping blacks to swing wide on the curve. At the last possible moment Headsperth appeared to see that if he passed he would foul, and brutally reined in his chestnuts.

On the far straightaway Nash was well on the outside, and this time Headsperth tried to take his chariot through on the rail. But again there was too little space for him, and through the clouds of dust, Clifford saw him struggle to control his nearly frantic team.

The two chariots passed in front of them. The crowd shrieked wildly at what it took to be splendid horsemanship, when it was actually nothing but a couple of fools mishandling the reins. Clifford, because he was not cheering, was able to take it all in: Pasadena society gone mad. The frilly white parasols had been discarded, bankers and lawyers, mothers and grandmothers, well-brought-up children howled like banshees, jumped up and down like chimps. He regretted to see that his wife and daughter were howling and jumping like the rest of them. And again he saw Belle, who knew horses, her face a mask of terror, her hands still gripped around the railing, her body perfectly still in the storm of excitement around her.

Now as the two chariots careened into the second and final lap, Headsperth, overcome with confidence, again flourished his whip over the heads of his horses, actually flicking the pole horse on the ear. Eddie Nash and his team were well on the wide turn. To Cliff's horror, he saw that Headsperth's last gesture had so enraged the chestnuts that in spite of their tired state they fought out of control, tossing their heads as the pole horse whinnied. They closed fast on Eddie's team as the blacks bore in for their turn, their driver making no effort to guide them.

Cliff watched, powerless, as the gap between the chariots narrowed, leading to an inevitable crash. He heard himself shouting, "No! No, Headsperth, pull them out!" But even as he heard his own warning cry, he knew that it was useless.

The chestnuts cut in front of the blacks just on the turn and Headsperth's skidding chariot fouled Eddie's off-wheel. A snapping noise followed the sharp crack as the cheap wood of Headsperth's chariot splintered and, shards flying, broke to bits. The chestnuts came up and over the blacks and all eight horses were down kicking and screaming.

Cliff vaulted the rail of their box and headed up the track. He saw Headsperth thrown forward as if diving into the dirt. For a moment his body hung almost straight in the air. The leather fringe of his gladiator skirt fell away from his pale pink, plump thighs, revealing the snowy white, amply cut seat of his drawers.

After the first shock had sobered the shouting crowd, gasps and screams came from the spectators. Cliff saw hoofs flashing over Headsperth's body as it crumpled in the dust. Eddie Nash slumped almost unnoticed in his chariot, which had escaped serious harm. Headsperth was the one in real danger; Clifford knew sickeningly that for his foolishness Headsperth Bauer faced almost certain death.

161

Cliff went in under the flying hoofs, crouching close to the dirt. As he reached out to grab Headsperth, Clifford heard a young voice shouting, "Easy there, you brute. Easy!" and knew that someone was helping him, beating the nearest horse back. Cliff pulled the unconscious horseman free of the wreck with as much decorum as he could in the circumstances. He arranged the leather fringe decently over the dust-stained expanse of Headsperth's drawers. Looking up, Cliff saw that it was young Alessandro Mariné who had fended off the fear-crazed horse and had it back on its legs, clubbing it with his fist between the eyes, driving it off. The other horses, still down, bit and kicked and screamed.

Now the circus grooms, who had had to run almost the whole length of the track, were there, and with Alessandro's and Cliff's help they freed the frantic horses of the snarled harness, heading them away from the wreckage.

Eddie Nash pulled himself up slowly and stepped down from the back of his chariot, holding his side. Headsperth still lay motionless, but Cliff could see that he was breathing. An ugly bruise swelled on his forehead.

The crowd began to close in and suddenly Victoria was there saying, "Oh, Cliff, Cliff!"

And Belle was kneeling beside Headsperth. He stirred now, opening his eyes, and as they focused he said: "My God, Cliff! What the hell happened?"

"You're all right, Headsperth. Just knocked out. You always were a wild one with the reins."

A doctor, whom no one recognized, had pushed his way through the crowd. After a quick examination, he suspected at least one broken rib for Eddie Nash and a slight concussion for Headsperth.

Now that there was no further possibility of real danger, all of Clifford's early irritation and recent horror changed into a kind of uncontrolled hilarity. In a flash he saw the spindly, callow, aristocratic Alessandro in an unfair fight with a steed four times his size—the chunky Headsperth, poor unfortunate clown, diving ungracefully into bare earth. And all of the cream of his Pasadena peers, who had so suavely made fun of his earlier misgivings, reduced to a pack of bleating, blithering, ignoble savages. Savoring that most exhilarating tonic—the sure knowledge of having been right with the equally sure knowledge that everyone knew it now—he gazed for the first time with a measure of charity on this scene and felt his mouth stretch into a wide and amiable grin.

Victoria, who had been kneeling next to Belle above the wretch who had once been the object of her own affections, straightened up now with a slight enigmatic sigh and placed her hands in the small of her back. She took a deep breath and her eyes met her husband's. If Clifford read those eyes like a book, it was not with a sense of easy familiarity, but as a man might take down a masterpiece, and reading the words again find better, truer, even funnier meanings. *If you dare say I told you so,* she flashed at him, but he made his smile wider and more harmless, his eyes as vacant as a good-natured babe's.

162

Then it was his turn to be surrounded, heaped with praise, lauded for his bravery. He accepted every compliment with exemplary modesty, conscious every moment of Victoria's intelligent gaze flashing him the message that soon they would be alone.

Seeing Alessandro Mariné standing behind Victoria with Ruth beside him looking up in admiration, Cliff said, "I certainly want to thank you for your help, young man. You took your life in your hands—"

Ruth's high voice piped out, "Oh, Alessandro, you are so brave! I shall never forget what I have seen today."

Perhaps as much in response to this childish praise as to Cliff's admiration, Alessandro made a deep, ceremonial bow. When he straightened, his young face was pale. "But, Señor Creighton, *you* have been wounded."

Cliff, looking down, saw that his left trouser leg had been slashed from the knee down and was drenched in blood. It was only then that Cliff felt the smarting pain and knew that it was he who had sustained the greatest injury, cut by a thrashing hoof.

From that moment on, the day reached perfection and stayed there. Clifford savored every minute of it. Allowing himself to be helped by no one but Victoria, he leaned heavily on her delicious form and limped bravely to an improvised first-aid station, where he sank back into a sling chair. As his wound was cleansed and bandaged he accepted several swills of the best brandy with liberal lashings of champagne. These, together with a judicious administration of laudanum, enclosed him in a haze of happiness and he declared himself not only able to attend tonight's club gala but even, in fact, to dance.

At home, in the early evening, he allowed himself the pleasures of a sybarite. He was bathed by the beautiful Victoria and his body tingled. Under the twin embraces of the Santa Ana breeze and his wife's smiling kisses as they fell into what some poet called the cosmic dance, he found himself assailed again by internal mirth, thinking of those classic tales wherein the ladies of ancient Rome had been inflamed by the sight of bloody gladiators. After their last tremors, he gazed at her, giddy. She laughed out loud. Had their thoughts been running parallel? It was part of the fun that they would leave the question unanswered.

He thought he might need another drink to get him to the club. They feasted alone in the twilight on caviar, thin-sliced venison, and champagne. When they made a fashionably late entrance to rounds of "hear-hear," "jolly good," and "stout man," he made good on his promise to dance, and knew what it was to be the prince of the evening.

All around him he heard comments on the day and questions about the future.

"Bauer was a damn fool."

"Belle was a brick."

"We certainly can't risk another chariot race."

"What about a team game?"

"Soccer?"

163

"Polo?"

"What about a parade? That way the women and children can participate."

"How about a flower show?"

"What the masses really enjoy is football."

"Oh, really, Herbert. . . ."

But none of it concerned Cliff. He waltzed on clouds of love and self-esteem. Victoria finally had to be firm, and bundled him before midnight into the motor.

After another session of love, Clifford marveled at how the familiar could be repeatedly novel with Victoria. His wife fell into a deep slumber, but still Cliff could not sleep. He opened the French doors that led to the bedroom balcony and stood gazing at the city, where an occasional light still gleamed. His eyes swept the crest of the San Gabriel Mountains. He felt in total balance and harmony with his world. Whatever doubts he had had during the last ten years concerning Victoria's motives for marrying him—was it that she didn't want to return to Australia? Was she heartbroken by Headsperth's change of affection?—drifted away from him now.

As if this were not enough, this morning he had settled two debts. Having heard that his old friend Sung—his personal benefactor when he had first come to this city and Victoria's personal protector during the great plague—had undergone the dubious good fortune to be married twice in a month, he had settled a large tract of land from his recent acquisition upon him. At the same time, in acknowledgment of everything that he owed to Magdalena Ortiz for making possible the purchase of five fifty-acre parcels of potentially valuable property at an unprecedented bargain price, he had deeded over an equal number of acres to her.

BOOK III

1906

They wove the lotus band to deck
And fan with pensile wreath each neck;
And every guest, to shade his head,
Three little fragrant chaplets spread:
And one was of the Egyptian leaf,
The rest were roses, fair and brief:
While from a golden vase profound,
To all on flowery beds around,
A Hebe, of celestial shape,
Pour'd the rich droppings of the grape!

Anacreon, *Ode 70*
Translated by Thomas Moore

SAN RAFAÊL DRIVE: The very air above this shaded lane was of a different quality than the commoner ether that circulated above the greater Los Angeles area. Residents of Pasadena were wont to say that this velvety quality, this silken atmosphere, came from the paradisal profusion of carefully cultivated vines and plants and from the purple-blossomed jacarandas that canopied the streets and entwined their branches overhead. Others, less fortunate, suggested that the greenhouse effect, the green tint of the air, existed because San Rafael Drive stank of money.

The newly developing Southern California consciousness—Pasadena had become the Biarritz of the American West—allowed itself baronial pretensions. Here, on the western rim of the Arroyo, a man's home literally was his castle. Barely visible behind thick walls and wrought-iron gates, stones were piled upon stones in the manner of the edifices high above the tumbling waters of the Middle Rhine. Turrets, escarpments, buttresses, all attested to the extraordinary wealth of these madcap entrepreneurs.

On Sundays, when the middle classes took their excursions, peering through ornate gates for a wistful look at a better life, they were apt to search in particular for a glimpse of the Creighton mansion, but it was set a quarter of a mile up a long winding drive and hidden by a jungle of semitropical plants.

Had they been able, this Sunday morning, to travel that neatly raked gravel drive, they would have found an unseemly domestic altercation, quite out of tune with the surroundings.

Mr. Priest, his usual dignity shattered, his *café-au-lait* complexion beaded with sweat, had become the victim of an animal passion. The object of his lust was a Scripps-Booth roadster, bright yellow in tone. What might have been sedate daffodil had been relentlessly burnished until it rivaled the sun. Priest hovered over the car like an attentive lover, polishing its windscreen until it resembled air itself.

167

"Will you hurry it *up*, Priest? I don't have all day!" Ruth Anne Creighton, now twenty, impatiently paced in front of the guard entry, where her parents watched with a mixture of amusement and apprehension. Her heels crunching on the gravel made Priest wince, but still he could not relinquish his beloved machine to the usurper.

Ruth tapped her foot menacingly. It was a fleshy foot, encased in the best gray kid, the top two buttons left undone. She was bothered, when nervous, by swelling ankles. Ruth was clothed this morning in an attractive Liberty dress, the newest, most fashionable print, but her father, watching in disapproval from the topmost marble step, had to admit to himself that these new, imported floral fabrics, as lovely as they looked on most young people of the day, did not really suit his daughter. The frills attendant upon this style made what he considered to be her handsome features just the tiniest bit coarse.

And, he thought with a twinge of exasperation, her behavior today was as flibbertigibbet as the dress, the car, and her forthcoming excursion.

"Priest, *please!* If you don't hurry, I'm going to be late!"

"Now, dear, a little patience. A lady never loses control."

"Oh, Mother! You don't understand! This is a *very important* rally! And they especially asked for Poopsy."

Clifford heard himself grunt. *Poopsy.* He fixed his wife with a glance full of reproach. What had he done, where had he gone wrong? How had fate and his family conspired to give him a daughter as tall as he was, and with *no common sense?*

"Horses have names," he remarked rhetorically to his wife. "Black Barb and Apple. Those were real names. Machines don't have names. They don't eat hay, Victoria. They don't answer to names. So there's no reason they should have names."

His daughter flung him a petulant look and stuck out her lower lip. "You don't know anything about it." She looked to Victoria for confirmation. "Does he, Mother?"

Victoria neatly avoided this, as she did any family unpleasantness, by calling into the cavernous entry hall, "Mrs. Priest? Would you mind bringing Ruth's duster? I'm afraid she really will be late."

Mrs. Priest emerged with the utmost ceremony, carrying that garment across outstretched arms.

Ruth, docile at last, came to the foot of the stairs to be swathed, first in an ankle-length, cream-colored car coat, then in a wide picture hat, draped with what seemed like yards of cream-colored veil. Long cream-colored driving gloves, and Ruth was ready.

Priest gave a final swat of his chamois to an already spotless fender and stepped back with a sigh. With a series of girlish squeaks, Ruth settled herself behind the wheel.

"Remember," Clifford felt impelled to remind her, "just keep your mind on driving. A car isn't like a horse, after all. It doesn't have an intelligence of its own—"

But Ruth had already, with Priest's assistance at the crank, started up the Scripps-Booth, and with a ferocious burst of gravel was already chugging down the drive, Priest jogtrotting in front to open the gate.

Clifford Creighton looked sourly after his daughter. He was dressed this morning in impeccable country tweeds, and his years of good living rested lightly upon him. His looks, which he had always felt were "too boyish for business," had been changed only in the last year or two by patches of silver just over his ears. Victoria pronounced them distinguished, and he secretly agreed. Clifford still rode the bridle paths of the Arroyo early every morning, and these pleasant excursions kept him fit, tanned, and slim. He and Victoria were often seen down at the club on the weekends, vigorously "addressing the ball."

Victoria! She seemed to have reversed the aging process. While most women, no matter how well kept, began to show the effects of the years by their late thirties, Victoria had, if anything, grown more beautiful. Exercise, fresh air, the best care, and perhaps the fact that she'd had but the one child, all had combined to sculpt her beauty. She had grown from an enticing girl to a magnificent woman. At times, Clifford dared to believe it was because she had been extraordinarily happy.

Feeling all this, and still in love with his wife, he was nevertheless unable to keep his mind from returning to its original source of irritation: his daughter and that automobile.

Again, he heard himself saying, "Machines don't have names, Victoria, you know that."

"Yes, dear, you're absolutely right. But she does love it, and she's still a child in many ways. Besides, it's more than a car. It gives her independence. And it's good for a woman to have that."

She moved closer and put an arm around his waist. "You've always said that, Cliff."

Clifford grunted.

If in later years people thought of California as orange groves and snowcaps, for those who lived there early in the century along the ancient trails first traveled by Franciscans, California and El Camino Real formed an endless, eternal, lion-colored field of dry rye grass, beautiful in its own way, but as harsh, as monochromatic as Midwestern prairie.

Many of the old Spanish land grants had been carved from this raw land, and the adobes of the first great families rose, each one a separate surprise in the midst of a savage nowhere. If the homes of Anglos were castles, the early Spaniards had built fortresses. With thick walls for protection from commoners and nature, they shut themselves away from the rest of the world. They had lost much in recent years, but no one could take from them either their *estancias* or their names.

Though some aficionados felt that the Estudillos' gray-walled establishment at the base of Mount Rubidoux was the crowning example of the original land-grant architecture, rivaled perhaps by the Dominguez *rancho* standing to the south of the city, the true *cognoscenti* in these matters knew that nothing really compared with the sprawling Mariné adobe close to the San Gabriel Mission.

The original two courtyards, surrounded by cool *salas,* protected from both heat and cold by three-foot-thick walls of native clay bricks, remained at the center of this stronghold. Through the generations, this heart of the Mariné family had been adorned with art works imported from Mexico and Spain, as well as artifacts preserved from the Gabriellano Indians. The dark, heavy, mission-constructed furniture—sideboards, chests, pewlike benches, *priedieus*—blended with weathered roughhewn beams that imposed a regular pattern upon the plastered ceiling. Later generations would soften the bleak, uncomfortable angularity of the benches and chairs with a profusion of cushions hand-embroidered by unmarried daughters, who were enabled thus to pass their time in a manner both decorative and useful. For it was one of the oddities of many of these land-grant families that though the men never failed in their conjugal duties to the family, sons were scarce and daughters embarrassingly plentiful.

As the Mariné family had grown, courtyard after courtyard had been added, encircling the original enclosures. To find the true center of the *estancia* now took a good quarter of an hour and had been compared by more than one eastern visitor to the royal maze at Hampton Court.

Fifty years ago one of the Mariné girls had turned her unrealized passion to horticulture. She had sent for cuttings and seeds from the most famous botanical gardens of the world. From the royal gardens of Portugal she had received rare herbs and flowering bushes. One entire inner courtyard had not been tiled at all but strewn with a carefully artless assortment of wildflowers that had come to them from the castle of distant cousins in Málaga, who had collected these seeds from the hills of the Holy Land. From Soochow, fabled Oriental city of gardens, she had been able to obtain a cutting of the wisteria vine from the Garden of the Careless Husband. Although that unfortunate had lost his garden in one night of gambling, the Mariné wisteria, over the years, had flourished, spreading out from the original courtyard, and now, supported by trellises, provided in spring a lavender canopy that stretched over a full two acres. Every outside wall was covered to a thickness of at least six inches by brilliant and thorny vermilion bougainvillea.

The true inheritors of the Mariné family numbered the Señora herself, and her two children—Alessandro, now twenty-five, sole male descendant, and Maria, twenty-two, dutiful and melancholy younger sister. Her association with the real world had so far been confined to daily midmorning Mass and the making of novenas in which she prayed for either a husband or a vocation that would satisfy both her mother's stringent requirements and her own romantic vision.

Though they preserved the original courtyards almost as a museum, only a few months after the death of her beloved husband the Señora had packed up the best pieces of art and the most opulent pieces of furniture and moved

170

her tiny family to the southwest corner of the *estancia*. When pressed by gossips and visitors as to why she had made this unprecedented move, she answered with bowed head. She wished to be at a place in the house where she could be within sight of the Mission. But the more prosaic truth was that at the time of her beloved husband's demise, the Señora, while affecting the ways of a much older woman, had been a mere girl. She knew the conditions of her marriage very well. She knew that in return for great wealth and the most illustrious of all Spanish names, she must give up the excitements and diversions of the outside world. It was also true that the Mission Road ran directly in front of this wing of the *estancia*. If she could no longer participate, there was no law, either of God or of man, which kept her from at least watching some of that life she had given up.

And so it was that on this Sunday in spring, after having spent the previous week in rigorous Lenten devotions, the Mariné family, somewhat lightheaded from the strict fasting on which the Señora insisted, sat on the balcony, refreshing themselves with heavily cinnamoned coffee, and gazed with disbelief at the noisy, raucous, colorful pageant unfolding beneath their incredulous eyes.

"It is a scandal!" the Señora snapped, furiously beating her fan against the dust-thickened air. "I shall speak to Father Clement immediately."

"I believe, Mama," her son opined, putting a careful finger to his moustache, "that you will find that it is Father Clement who is in part responsible. He is the one who has let out this ground. You know how devoted he is to the idea of a school for the orphaned poor of the parish."

"Just what *is* this dreadful display?" his mother asked in withering tones.

"I believe they call it a car rally, Mama."

Part of Mission Road had been roped off and made into a rough enclosure. There was no track here, only a chaos of ruts and ridges. A few hastily constructed booths, draped with bunting, had been set up to sell lemonade, and next to this stood a platform which served as the judges' stand. Father Clement's acolytes offered glasses of the Mission's own harsh, sour vintage at a higher rate than in the town's poshest restaurants, but it was all for charity. Except for the Marinés, there were few spectators, because the purpose of this event was limited to the pleasure of its participants.

Fifty devotees of the cult of the motorcar had assembled here today. Ruth was not the only car-loving resident of Pasadena. Some of the others had come from as far away as Long Beach, and one dashing young couple, members of the Victoria Club, had made the hazardous journey from Riverside.

After considerable confusion, the cars were arranged in a rough circle where, with maximum gunning of motors and an occasional toot of a klaxon, they chugged endlessly about, careful not to exceed the posted limit which had been tacked up on every available wall, booth, and tree: NO FASTER THAN 10 M.P.H.

The vehicles themselves were decorated in a variety of styles, some sprigged with paper flowers, others trailing colored streamers. The Riverside couple had mounted crossed flags on their radiator, the Union Jack and the Stars and Stripes, which flapped in unison. Large red, white, and blue rosettes adorned their dusters, and the backseat held a mountain of red, white, and blue balloons.

Among these black, maroon, and dark-green vehicles, Poopsy shone like a golden planet. The eyes of the judges followed this bit of insouciant yellow as it made its jaunty circuit, and the other drivers could not forgo sidelong glances at this sunny rival, whether out of envy or disapproval it was hard to say. But the Señora had no doubts.

"I have never seen such a brazen breach of taste. A car of that color during Lent! And look, is it not a girl driving it?"

"Mama, I would never do that," said Maria, with a touch of longing in her voice.

"By the veil of the Virgin, see that you don't! You must remember that *we* have different ways of doing things."

"But, Mama, surely I'm not mistaken," ventured Alessandro. "Isn't that the little Creighton girl driving the yellow roadster?"

The Señora, leaning forward, looked through her lorgnette, and when she next spoke it was in a different tone.

"You must remember, Alessandro, not to judge these new families too harshly. It is not their fault if they lack the guidance of our Holy Mother Church, and Ruth has always been a nice girl, as well brought up as she could be under the circumstances. The Creighton family is a new family, but it would not be too much to say that they are part of the gentry. And is it not true, my son—and correct me if I'm wrong—that part of our lands abut the Creighton holdings?"

Alessandro nodded, not taking his eyes from the intrepid girl below.

"I think," the Señora remarked, not missing a beat of her fan, "that the spirit of this Lenten season would not be profaned if we allowed ourselves a treat this afternoon." Here she turned to her daughter, who with equal but more forlorn attention, was also engrossed in the rally. "Maria, my precious, you have been alone too much in the last weeks. I think we might enliven the rest of this afternoon by bringing you a little company."

Maria looked at her mother with stricken eyes, but the Señora had returned her attention to her son.

"Alessandro, after Señorita Creighton has finished with her exercise, please ask her to join us for afternoon *almuerzo*."

It was then that Alessandro astonished his mother and sister as he never had before and perhaps never would again. He had been standing in self-conscious perfection, clothed in creamy linen, but his motionless attentiveness was transformed in an instant as he let out a yell which the Señora could only associate with the vulgar *charros* of the day. In the blink of an eye he had leaped onto the rail of the balcony and, after balancing briefly, jumped two stories to the earth below. It was the sheerest of coincidences that at that moment the driver of the yellow roadster looked up and saw his short but graceful flight.

It was all so gloriously exciting. She had made this trip all the way out here in a little less than two hours. And when in the traffic on Atlantic Boulevard she had stopped to give Poopsy a much-needed drink of water, the absolutely darlingest young man had pulled over his bicycle, alighted from it, and hoisted the water can for her. A charming young girl like her, he had said, shouldn't worry her pretty little head about such things. But she had shown him!

What fun it was to leave that impudent young man in his Arrow collar, who looked as though he could have come from a Leyendecker poster, standing in a cloud of dust. *Her* dust! No one would ever know how much fun it was to ride about on wheels. Mummy and Daddy were such sticks. They only saw what she looked like, but they didn't know how she felt. She knew she wasn't pretty enough for her mother's standards, but when she got behind the wheel she stopped being Daddy's Little Ruthie and Mummy's Dear Girl.

The rally seemed to her like being in Heaven, because finally here under the bright sun she was with people who didn't expect her to sit in a drawing room or make conversation. People would never tell her tactfully that she was "short-waisted" or "big-boned." Here she was the driver of Poopsy. And Poopsy was tiny and sunshiny and bright. Driving around the circle she felt a wave of happiness as pure as champagne. She waved gaily at the drivers opposite and tooted her klaxon.

She heard and then saw what happened next. "Oh, my God, he'll kill himself!" A few women screamed. Slamming on her brakes to avoid hitting a car that had screeched to a halt in front of her, she followed everyone's eyes to the balcony of the venerable Mariné adobe. There, teetering precariously on the carved balustrade of the second-story balcony, she saw—*Oh, my God!*—and her gasps were added to the others.

A slim figure lay crumpled for an instant on the baked earth. Even as she considered whether she should jump from her car to render aid, the figure sprang up, gave itself a shake, and loped—incredibly—in her direction. And then, as if a vision from Heaven itself, the face that she had loved all of her life appeared miraculously, just inches away, coated now with a bewitching veil of masculine sweat and a fine drift of dust.

Alessandro Luis Antonio de Ortega de Moreno de Arrellanos de Mariné y Ruiz smiled at her, his teeth beneath his moustache as blinding as the sun.

"Señorita Creighton," he said, his voice slurred by his beautiful accent, "my mother sends me to respectfully request that you join us *para merendar.*"

"I—I," Ruth breathed, but through her enchantment came the sound of twenty-five car horns. "I—"

"Get a move on, sister. We aren't here to watch you flirt with lover boy."

Alessandro had always been a man of action and before her delighted and astonished eyes, he silenced their insolent honks by grasping Poopsy's door and vaulting easily into the passenger seat.

"How I love your dashing car," he murmured, again in the accent that brought up gooseflesh all over her body.

Ruth heard herself giggle. "Won't you join me in a spin?"
He threw his fine head back and laughed.

In a back room of a sleazy Mexican bar on North Spring Street a group of dispirited Mexican men gambled away their week's earnings. The men crouched in a sweaty circle, money changing hands, drinking tequila and mescal, encouraging their favorites and cursing when they lost. Two roosters fought to a bloody conclusion. In the twinkling of an eye one cock lay dead in a pool of blood.

Raoul slouched about, wordlessly collecting on his bets. The men paid up grudgingly. He was not one of them in his tailor-made suit and patent-leather shoes. It would be fair to say their contempt was mutual. He hated their Indian ways, torn and coarse manta shirts, their horny feet in scuffed, worn-down *huaraches*.

"Chinga tu madre!" he heard one of them mutter under his breath and he returned the insult with an arrogant sneer.

"Hey, Raoul," one of the band muttered, "how come you always know which cock will win?"

The reply came easily to his lips. "Because I am a winner, *cábron*, and you . . ." He let the insult lie there.

The truth was he always knew which cock would win, because he bribed the owners to find out. He did little more than break even in these games, but the pleasure of appearing to win was worth the investment.

"If you know so much, Raoul, perhaps you can tell us who your father is."

A subdued snigger rose from the assembled men and Raoul's victory turned to ashes in his mouth. He pocketed the damp dollar bills and turned on his heel. It wasn't the first time he'd heard these insults and it would not be the last. It was a tired ritual and by now no one was more tired of it than he. Ever since he could remember, Magdalena had assured him that although his real mother was a humble Indian, his father had been a true aristocrat. But this was only a woman's babble. His parents' papers had disappeared in the confusion surrounding the great epidemic, and Magdalena, that stupid cow, could not even remember what town they had come from.

Raoul knew it would be futile to challenge his tormentors. He had no skill with the knife, and even less skill with those muttered incantations with which the Indian peon communicated. His language, his thoughts were white. His skin was as brown as theirs.

Alone on the deserted city street in the blinding afternoon sun he thought of what he might do now. But contemptuous as he was of the companions he had just left, he had to admit to himself that they formed the only circle that would admit him. There was no other place to go except the back room of La Tortuga or home to his mother and her *gringo* boarders.

He began the long walk up Bunker Hill. He passed mothers and fathers shepherding their children home from church. He saw little girls standing on their front lawns twirling hoops on sticks, fathers in their shirtsleeves lazily playing catch with their sons. This calm, this contentment, this happiness, was something he perceived, but was denied. This was the world of his

174

childhood, where his mother was worse than a servant, and those pretty children, once their parents were indoors, would call him spic and greaser.

His feet slowed almost to a halt as he approached the big yellow house on Carroll Street. Without going past the wrought-iron gates he knew by looking down at his expensive gold watch exactly what would be going on. The "boys," as his mother called them, would have just finished Sunday dinner. Something heavy and bland and greasy. Chicken and dumplings that made him want to puke. The "boys," some of them balding by now, their faces pink with repletion, would be rearing back in their chairs, their white linen napkins spotted with gravy.

"Magdalena, that was some dinner. If I were a gopher, I'd go for you."

"Miz Ortiz, if you could kiss as well as you cook. . . ."

In his mind's eye, with an emotional revulsion that amounted almost to physical nausea, he saw Adelita in the kitchen lining up little white dishes on the linoleum sideboard, dolloping in chunks of bread pudding.

Ah, *Dios,* if he had a knife he would kill them all.

Brutally, he thrust open the gate.

The lawn which he crushed beneath his boots was overly watered and lined with a double row of false-genteel petunias. The house itself was newly painted a brave buttercup yellow—as if paint could change a boarding house.

He pushed noisily through the front door and paused at the parlor. Everything that Raoul most detested could be summed up in this room. The arms of the horsehair sofa and matching loveseat were fussily protected by embroidered anti-maccassars. A heavy oak whatnot filled the greater part of the wall, its various recesses ornamented by pieces of gaudily hand-painted china, silver-gilt trinkets, porcelain shepherds in sentimental poses, and a pair of praying hands. A circle of cane chairs lined the walls as a grim reminder that this room was not meant now—and never was—for a family, but served merely as a way station for a series of faceless transients. Raoul sneered for the thousandth time at the sky-blue rug which yielded up an unlikely harvest of bright pink cabbage roses and sighed as he trod on the amateurish rag rug—his mother had clumsily braided it with her own hands—that served as a runner between this room and the next.

He went into the dining room where the boarders had indeed just finished their chicken and dumplings.

"Hey Raoul!" Thompson grinned foolishly. "We missed you for lunch, partner, and it was a good one. I just told your mother. . . ."

Raoul took in a breath, gazed across the bald pates, and fixed his mother with an accusing eye. By now there was no need to ask it aloud. They had had this argument so many times.

Why do you go on doing this? You don't have to do this. Why do you debase yourself this way?

And across the dining room his mother stood by the sideboard, her hands behind her back in the servile position that he hated, wordlessly and clearly answering him: *You tell me what else to do and I'll do it, mijo.*

Just as he had in the back room of *La Tortuga,* but with even more rage if that were possible, he turned on his heel and stamped away, out the front

175

door again and down the street. There was only one place for Mexicans in this town and that was the Plaza. He would have a dozen beers and the sun would be down. It would be time for the one amusement the Mexican community was allowed here in Los Angeles—the *paseo*.

Magdalena watched him go with a feeling of pain that was made no easier to bear by the fact that she understood much of his frustration and confusion. She had expected when she had come into land money, oil money, that her life would certainly change for the better. Clifford Creighton's gift of "worthless bean fields" had already put thousands of dollars into her savings accounts. She knew nothing counted so much in this society as money—and land.

She could still remember that night a little more than ten years before, when she and her handsome young boarder, Bud Thompson, had driven out in a hired landaulet to see the acreage that Thompson had been unable to buy and "Old Man Creighton" had then given her for a present. The twilight had been warm and lush; the deserted marshes had stretched in front of them like the landscape of another world. Bud's face had puckered boyishly in the dusk. "Gosh, Miz Ortiz, I don't know what you're going to be able to do with it." But she had already picked up a great handful of the viscous scum which formed across the land. The vision of her old lover grazed her memory. He was giving her something of value, she knew it. "There is money here, Mr. Thompson. Here, smell!" Impishly she pushed the pungent mess up at him. Instinctively he grasped her wrist. What happened *then* had been as much a salute to her old lover as to the young boy who had made her happy that night, and for a few years after. That *brea,* that tar, had brought her a fortune.

But, money or not, she was Mexican, an unmarried woman with an unexplainable child, and—embarrassingly—illiterate. It was true that she numbered among her friends some of the most powerful and influential people in the city. Over the past twenty years there were few city employees who had not spent their days between university and marriage in the big yellow house on Carroll Street. But when they got married they melted into another world.

Not until after she had come into her money did Magdalena realize that she had never met any of their wives. She had asked one couple after another to dinner and had been put off by what she recognized now were genteel excuses. She had enrolled Raoul in a "better" school, and he'd come home bleeding. Finally she'd decided to give a gala, late-night supper and invite all the boarders she had known over the years and their wives.

She had engaged the musicians from the Pico House on their night off, and remembering the tastes of the Anglo guests from the hotel, she had planned a sumptuous buffet—everything from poached salmon to petits fours. She had spent a small fortune on a new dress—dull red silk, liberally sewn with beads of jet.

Perhaps a third of those invited had come, and all but five were male. They stood in tight, nervous groups and spoke in whispers. The five wives, dressed in ecru, beige, and gray, were pressed forward, one by one, by their husbands, their resentment barely veiled by thin, pale smiles. Some of the men enjoyed themselves, remembering old times; the women grew more remote. Ironically, it was Jordan Espey, usually so correct, who turned the evening into pure disaster.

"Who would have thought, Magdalena, when the corpses were stacked up like cordwood around you, that you could ever pull off an evening like this?" He turned to explain to the horrified women. "Few of you young ladies remember when we had a plague epidemic right in this town. Magdalena was the heroine, and Clifford Creighton the hero! Why, he came into my office . . ."

Magdalena had wanted to say, *It's not what you think, and besides, it was twenty years ago!* But she had already lost her tongue with these women. She had been totally unable to respond to their few remarks about tennis, the women's club, the literary society, and the exclusive private schools their children attended. And what *could* she say? Tennis? She had walked twelve hundred miles. The Women's Club? Her club was made up of admiring men. The blessings of children? Already her son lived to break her heart. No! She was bigger than these women, in body and soul.

And so she had laughed heartily, and pounded the backs of her old friends, and hitched up her skirts for a lively polka. She had drunk too much champagne, defiantly ignored her young son's contemptuous eyes, and not until the last guest had left did she break down in sobs.

She had not received one return invitation. It was not so bad for her. Within the limits of her own world, she was treated with respect. She had power, respect, and very considerable wealth. She had fashioned her own life, and she was proud of it. But her son had been a victim. What could he answer when they called him a bastard, an orphan, a greaser? The best they said was that his mother was the mistress of Clifford Creighton; the worst, that she pleasured all the men who had ever spent the night under her roof.

Her heart ached for Raoul, because she knew there was nothing she could do for him.

First it started with a single tear. Then Maria's chest began to heave—she couldn't control herself any more. It was so unfair. "I never get to go anywhere! I never get to do anything! Nobody ever comes here, and nothing, *nothing* will ever happen to me!"

The Señora wielded her fan but with less conviction than usual. "Calm yourself, my precious. Remember, you are a Mariné."

A muffled sound came from the sobbing girl.

"What was that?"

"A prisoner has more freedom than I do." Then she looked up. "I am so lonely, Mama."

The Señora rapidly went over the afternoon's events in her mind. Certainly things had not turned out quite as she had planned. Full of admiration for Alessandro, the two of them had watched as he and the Señorita Creighton had circled in that quaint "rally." Full of pride and excitement, they had watched as the yellow roadster garnered one of several prizes. The Señora had snapped her fingers for trays of chocolate and *churros,* and the servants had scurried about in a flurry, putting all in readiness.

177

Then she and Maria had watched as Alessandro slipped behind the steering wheel and, with Ruth clutching at her voluminous veils, zoomed off to the east, away from the adobe. For over two hours they had awaited its return. The chocolate had crusted over and was taken away. And still the two women sat alone.

The Señora was of two minds about all this. The longer her son spent with the Creighton girl, the better. Still, she sympathized with her daughter. It was true, they were virtual prisoners out here. And with so few sons in the old land-grant families, she was at a loss as to how and when this charming child might be married into a suitable family.

"We're no better off than the servants," Maria sobbed. "At least they have the *paseo!*"

"The *paseo!*" her mother exclaimed. "That is not for persons like us, except perhaps for fiestas and on special Holy Days."

"But Father Clement says that many girls of good character go there!"

"Of good character, perhaps, but not of good lineage."

Something in her mother's voice—a longing that mirrored her own—gave Maria the courage to go on. "It's for families, Father Clement says. And everyone's in a state of grace, because they've just come from Mass. The girls are always with a chaperone. And all they do is walk—the girls circle in one direction, the boys in another. So what could possibly happen?"

There's more than one way of walking, the Señora thought.

A silence hung between them in the fast-falling dusk. Maria sat apathetically, dabbing at her nose with a lace handkerchief. Her mother knew she had said all she was going to say.

"I don't know what your dear, sainted father would say about this," Señora Mariné said suddenly, "but put on your best pink dress, and *compose yourself.* I can have Bernardo bring out the Hispano-Suiza." She smiled wryly. "If your brother can spend the afternoon motoring, so can we."

Her daughter looked up at her incredulously. "You mean, Mama, we will truly go to the Plaza?"

The Señora frowned. "One circle only. Then we will go to the church and begin a novena for your father."

Maria weighed nine days of prayer against one round of fun. But she would gladly recite ten thousand litanies to get out of this house for only one hour.

"The pink dress, Mama," she said calmly. "And shall I bring my parasol?"

"The Chinese ivory fan," her mother said decidedly. "The fan works better at night."

On every Sunday night, for as long as anyone could remember, every Latino had spent the twilight hours at the *paseo*. Everyone, *everyone* took this walk, aunts and uncles and children and babies, all dressed in their Sunday best. And it was part of the ritual that the families with unmarried daughters walked in one direction, and the families with unmarried sons in the other. The girls were always strictly chaperoned, the boys walked together in rowdy groups—but their families, too, were not far behind. The older members exchanged greetings ceremoniously each time they passed. The young men and women tried to look anywhere but at each other.

There had been talk of building a bandstand in the middle of the Plaza, but as yet the hard-packed earth had been marked off only by a few cobblestoned paths that nobody used, since all the traffic was at the periphery. Sometimes musicians played; tonight, so far, the center stood deserted. (And, by common consent, although some curious Anglo guests at the Pico House peered from their second-story windows, the whites had deserted the normally busy square and left the Latinos to their "primitive" amusements.)

The Señora had Bernardo park the Hispano-Suiza behind the Plaza church. They walked through the churchyard lit up with a few candles, and almost before they knew it, they were swept up into the heady excitement of the *paseo*.

Instinctively, the Señora knew which way to head, and behaving in a way that Maria had never believed her mother was capable of, began almost to serve as a model to her daughter, coyly half-covering her face, appearing to look in no direction, tossing her still jet-black curls in such a way that her still-slender posterior seemed to be directly involved with that bewitching movement.

But all this was lost on Maria. Still dazed by the fact that she had been allowed to leave the confines of the family adobe, she gawked about her, tripping from time to time on the uneven surface of the cobblestones, bumping into this or that venerable paterfamilias struggling to keep his own womenfolk in line. Her attention was captivated by the members of the other slowly moving circle, wherein she saw more handsome young men than she had ever dreamed existed in the world.

"Maria, please! You will disgrace us! You must behave like a young woman here, not a clumsy little girl."

Even as she spoke, the Señora caught the eye of a black-suited heavyset man who was walking alone, and just as he came abreast of her, tossed her head arrogantly, as if he were the last person in the world she would ever consider.

"But, Mama!"

"Keep your eyes down. The boys will have no use for you if you look at them!"

"But I want to see everything!"

"Just peep! Use your fan. Like this."

A handsome young Lothario gazed significantly at Maria. Maria unfolded her ivory fan, lowered her eyes with a great sweep of her lashes, and, just as he passed, looked up at him with the startled, soulful look of a dove.

"What an angel!"—a disembodied murmur that was lost in the crowd.

"Mama, did you hear what he said?"

"Certainly, but you must pretend to be deaf."

By this time they had made almost the full circle of the Plaza and were approaching the Queen of the Angels. As she thought of the novena, Maria's heart sank. Still, the last fifteen minutes had been worth it all. Then, miraculously, the Señora kept on walking. The stocky man in the black suit once again fixed her with a look of stifled passion.

"Obviously a man of rare sensibility," the Señora whispered approvingly.

"Mama!"

"It does no harm to look, little one. It is only a game." She lowered her voice. "For this one night, we are away from our duties to the family. And besides, no one knows who we are."

Though the Señora spoke with confidence, she was mistaken. Already the rumor was traveling through both circles that a member of the landed gentry was among them.

But the rumors had not yet reached Raoul.

He swaggered in the company of three unsavory companions, taking all the liberties allowed a rowdy bachelor. He teased the prim chaperones—"Why are you wasting your time with that little girl? Come away with *me* and show me the wisdom of a fully ripened woman!" He pulled the braids of poor but honest shopgirls. "When you earn your dowry, I will be yours forever!" If he found girls unprotected by a male relative, he made remarks that brought blushes to their cheeks. "Those are some pink flowers you have on your balcony!" And if a fat mother became too upset with his inciting remarks, he darted into the other circle just after she had passed, and planted a pinch where it would do the most good. He knew that while he could not go too far, he was safe in his bad behavior. Despite his mother's reputation, he was certainly the richest young man here tonight. Though they might be outraged by his behavior, and even his name, still he would be a very good catch for any of these plump young pullets.

"Hey, Raoul! Look at that soft fat one! Once you started to bounce on that, you wouldn't get any sleep for a month."

"She's hotter than the *chile serrano,* I bet. What do you think, Raoul?"

But Raoul's eyes had gone past the smoldering eyes and breasts of the flashy, sullen bad girl and had fastened on the pale pink flounces of the one behind her.

She was young, still a child perhaps. Her baby fat had barely given way to firm, budding young breasts. She practiced none of the wiles of the other girls here. Her hair had not been frizzed into feverish tendrils about her face. Rather, it was decorated with girlish ribbons. Her face was pale, while the cheeks of every other girl here, if not painted with rouge, had at least been mercilessly chafed. And her dress, pale pink cotton, looked more suitable for Easter Mass than Sunday night at the *paseo.*

"Who's that girl?" he asked casually of his *compadres.*

But characteristically, they were winking and leering at the statuesque *mamacita* of a certain age who slithered shamelessly along beside the girl.

"The older they get the better they get!" one brash boy said to the woman in black silk. And for a moment Raoul was distracted. The woman must have been at least forty, but her figure was slender, her eyes knowing.

Then he recognized the real attraction of this strange pair. They were rich! The rustle he had heard as the older woman passed had come from real silk.

"Who were they?" he repeated casually. But his companions shrugged.

Some ragtag musicians, a *conjunto norteño* that looked as if it had seen better days, went to the center of the Plaza. The accordionist wheezed through a few scales, the player of the guitar disconsolately attempted to tune his instrument string by string. The bass player sighed impatiently as he sounded an occasional low note.

The next time Raoul passed the girl in pink with her svelte chaperone, he did the inconceivable, leaving his gaping companions, and fell into step with the equally stunned women.

"Señora," he said respectfully, "your sister graces our Plaza. She is exquisite. Although I have not seen her here before, may I be bold enough to exchange a few words with her?"

The Señora gazed at this upstart with maximum hauteur. "In the first place, niño, you speak of my daughter—"

"No!" Raoul expostulated. "That cannot be true." By this time he had maneuvered himself into a position so that he spoke to the Señora over the head of the little girl in pink, who regarded him from under her ribbons with not altogether girlish innocence. "You are much too young to have a—"

"And in the second place, why should she speak to you? Get back where you belong!"

Raoul dropped out of sight as if obeying her command. But instead of rejoining his oafish companions he made straight for the musicians, who were apathetically killing time, hoping against hope that someone would buy a song before they would have to begin giving their music away.

Raoul rummaged in both pockets and came up with crumpled paper money, all this night's gambling winnings.

"Do you see this?" he imperiously demanded. "All this is yours if you do what I say."

"Mama, why did you send him away?" asked Maria.

"Because it wasn't proper. He was a very improper young man."

"How did you meet Papa?"

And after a pause the Señora responded evasively. "When you're older. There's a time for these things." The Señora was saved from further explanations by Maria's excited cry.

"Look, here he comes!"

"Maria! A lady never betrays surprise."

Once again, Raoul fell into step with the girl and her mother. A soft and sentimental melody began to waft over the Plaza, the well-known strains of "Los Dolores de mi Madre," "My Mother's Sorrow," and then segued into "Que Linda mi Madre." As the Señora gazed rigidly ahead, Raoul queried gently, "Do you like the music? They are playing it for you. I have asked them to play every song they know about beautiful mothers."

The Señora snapped her fan shut and spoke with theatrical scorn. "*I* was not brought up to speak to strangers."

"But, Señora," he said confidently, "after we have this dance, we will no longer be strangers."

For an instant the Señora allowed herself to glance into the center of the Plaza where a few couples already waltzed to "Amor de Madre."

"I cannot," she said. "My duties as a mother forbid it, because my little girl would be left alone."

Raoul seriously considered this predicament. "In that case," he said in disappointed tones, "I will have to dance with your daughter."

He flashed a smile of gleaming white teeth. "Do not worry, Señora, I will protect her as if she was my own."

Maria blinked at her mother. The Señora, seeing herself outwitted in an ancient game, nodded.

"You have my permission."

With exaggerated respect, Raoul, holding Maria's arm as if she was a precious china doll, escorted her to the center of the Plaza where the others were dancing. Holding her at arm's length he began a slow waltz. And in that instant, the *conjunto*, wreathed in conspiratorial grins, took up the bouncing strains of "Jésusita en Chihuahua." Raoul grasped the girl firmly—arms outstretched, *cachete a cachete,* his cheek pressed against hers, his chest pressed against her yielding breast. And then they were galloping across the Plaza, as bachelors from every quarter raised their voices in excited yips.

"Cachete y ella! Hold her close!"

The mothers looked on in dismay and the Señora herself moved forward to put an end to things, when she felt the grip of thick fingers on her upper arm.

"I have you now, my beauty, and I will never let you go."

The Señora smelled brilliantine as she found herself whirled into the dance. Ah, it had been such a long time since she had danced like this, or had been held in strong arms.

They danced the steps of the polka. Everyone from as far south as Hermosillo, as far north as Santa Barbara, knew this simple but exciting dance. The Indians had learned it from their Spanish masters and had added their own vitality, energy, and lust. The Franciscan fathers called it the "Dance of the Devil," but everyone knew it was the dance of exuberance and love.

"Claude," a woman said from an upper balcony at the Pico House, "come over here. You'll never believe what they're doing now."

"Umph," her husband said. He was deep in a financial journal.

And the woman alone looked wistfully down. Perhaps a thousand people had moved in the space of five minutes from order into chaos, dancing, stealing kisses, holding each other and refusing to dance, while the musicians played as if their lives depended on it. Mexican men threw their wide-brimmed hats into the air and shouted.

"Claude, really . . ." but then it was over. And in the settling dust, people began rather sheepishly, she thought, to take up their original pattern.

"What is your name?" Raoul said to the girl, his arms locked about her waist now.

"Please," she said, "I'm frightened. Let me go. My name is Maria."

"But what's your family name? Who are you? Where do you come from?"

And then the Señora was there, her face flushed with a mixture of pleasure, anger and anxiety.

"Unhand my daughter. The dance is over."

"Wait," Raoul protested. "Wait!" But even as he spoke they disappeared into the crowd. "I did it for you, Maria! I did this all for you!" he called out to the vanishing pink figure.

182

The music started again, more softly. He stood foolishly alone, conscious of the amused stares of the people about him. One old woman was looking at him with some sympathy, however. And with no real hope Raoul addressed his question to her.

"Who were they, *abuela?* Do you know?"

She cackled. "I do know, poor boy. I know more than they think. The old one is now the Señora Deogracia Ruiz de Ortega de Moreno de Arellanos de Mariné of San Gabriel, but *I* knew her before she climbed so high."

From the beginning, the house on Marchessault Street had not been a center of peace. But by now, eleven years after the first passionate encounter of Sung and Katarina, it was barely controlled bedlam. At twenty-five, Katarina had blessed Sung's name with eight descendants—three boys and five girls. Katarina was of sturdy stock, the people of Chinatown said, her hips were wide, very wide. Although she would not touch the salted plum, the merchants knew that for years to come in order to be in favor with the household they would have to keep a ready supply of sauerkraut prepared in the Slovak manner with a liberal sprinkling of paprika and caraway seeds.

Katarina's children created a human rainbow reflecting the variety of their mixed inheritance. And almost every nine months merchants and old grandmothers would buy into pools betting on sex, skin color, and hair—frizzy like the wild woman, straight black like a true son of Han, or some strain between the Middle Kingdom and that strange, big land, Tex-as.

Over the years Sung Wing On, remembering the richest landowners outside the home village, had tried with all the honor of which he was capable to divide his time equally between his two wives: "He who has no favorite will never find a cleaver in his belly." But sometimes, pondering this ancient wisdom, he wondered half-humorously if the cleaver might not offer him an honorable way out. Merchants often made him the butt of good-humored jokes despite his wealth and power, and pointing to his silver hairs never missed an opportunity to remind him that he would be an old man at the age of forty.

Tonight, Sunday, as every second Sunday, he would spend with Katarina. Walking from his office, he decided to take the long way around to Katarina's, telling himself that the exercise would do him good. In his effort to treat his wives equally, he had set both Lin and Katarina up on the same block, on the same street, in almost identical houses. In theory this worked well enough. The buckling sidewalks of Marchessault Street became a playground for the children of both families. They ran in and out of each other's houses without constraint. The women, however, had failed to hit it off. Walking around the block to avoid passing Lin's house, Sung grimaced at the thought of the two or three meetings that had occurred over the last eleven years, meetings that had been filled with tears, screams, and recriminations. It was Katarina who made the more noise, but Lin who made it harder for him in the long run.

With weary steps Sung approached the house of his cowgirl wife. He pushed his way through the clutter—balls, wagons, a torn kite—and walked up the steps of the porch from which he could already hear the great din.

"Daddy! Daddy! Daddy! Daddy! Daddy!"

It was two or more of his children shouting at him. He oofed as one of them, running to hug him, butted him in the stomach. Again and again he had lectured Katarina on the proper deportment of a son or daughter of Han. Katarina had laughed in his face. There were times when he could think only of the round-eye expression: His wife was a few bricks short of a load.

He allowed himself to be pulled into the kitchen where Katarina was fixing dinner. The cowboys of Tex-as must have had stomachs of iron. He was sure she was the worst cook in the New World. She boiled eggs. She mashed potatoes. She boiled beef for a long time, with no seasonings but onion and cabbage. His hopes had risen once, early on, when Katarina had come home with five pounds of black Cantonese dried mushrooms. He had returned that night with visions of snow peas stir-fried with those delectable fungi, only to find himself confronted by a ghastly black gruel. She had boiled a year's supply of mushrooms in a huge cauldron all day. What could he do but eat it? No wonder his hair was turning silver. His tongue still shrank at the memory.

Tonight it was mashed potatoes in won-ton papers. She called them *Pee Roh Hee!* And a side dish of carrots, boiled. She was fond of saying that she had eaten nothing but carrots in the old country, and that carrots were what made her "walk like 'lectric," giving her energy that even Sung could barely equal and never surpass.

"Wosbon!" She flung down her cleaver, expertly flipping it so that it quivered erect in the chopping block.

She slithered across the kitchen in worn-down bedroom slippers and threw her arms around him, almost picking him up off the ground. One of the children—he had trouble remembering all the outlandish names—seized this opportunity and picked up the cleaver, threatening the younger children, who raised a theatrical howl. From what he could see, it looked as if they were fighting over the carrots—could such a thing be possible?

"These babies drive me crazy, wosbon! Do something! I'm gonna kill them! I use dynamite!"

It was one of her favorite expressions, and in fact she had named her favorite daughter Dynamite. Katarina was forever trying to find words—find expression—for the explosive quality that was so much a part of her makeup.

"Daddy, he's gonna hit me!"

"You hit me first, caca brain!"

"Where's the hammer? I'll hit you with a hammer! Remember last time?"

Sung remembered. He had come home tired from a day's work and found a middle son stretched out as if dead on the living-room floor, with several of his brothers and sisters sobbing around him. As the boy had been hunched over his first-grade reader, one of his brothers had grabbed a hammer and, creeping up behind him, playfully knocked him unconscious.

Sung closed his eyes and muttered a prayer to the Goddess of Mercy. When he opened them, the chopping block had fallen on its side with an awful thud, and carrot slices rolled busily to every corner of the room. The eldest daughter held the cleaver up out of reach, while two boys fought each other for the privilege of who would get to fight her next. At least that's what Sung thought was going on. One of the boys kicked little Dyna right in the face and she sat down on the floor and began to sob.

Katarina, who had been noisily kissing him all this time, instantly heard the tone of real distress. She flung Sung from her, ran to her eldest daughter, grabbed the cleaver and began to whirl it, clearing children from the room the way priests in the home village had exorcised evil spirits. Then she picked up the sobbing child and held her in her lap.

"Big dumb bad boys, I kill 'em for you, honey! Ah, ah, ah, don't cry, I'm going to kill 'em, don't worry."

She expertly felt for broken bones. "Daddy ride you piggyback? Play Texas cow pony?"

"Nooooo!"

"Mommy play peekaboo?"

"Nooo!"

But, still holding the child, Katarina reached down to the kitchen floor and scooped up two carrot slices. Jouncing Dyna on one knee, she began to chant, "Look at Mommy! Mommy have glasses? Look at Mommy's new glasses!"

She'd already squeezed a carrot slice in under each brow, like two monocles, so that instead of eyes the orange and yellow aureole of carrot presented itself. The tot began instantly to laugh, and so did Sung. This was Katarina's favorite diversion, and in fact there was something almost magically entertaining about it. Many nights before, after, and even during their sexual encounters, she had slipped carrot slices in under her silver brows, turning herself into an insanely provocative, beneficent witch.

"Dyna do it!" And she decorated her now laughing daughter in a similar manner.

Sung smiled. Never in his wildest dreams could he have imagined himself the father of such a family, and now Dyna was holding out her chubby arms, her carrots forgotten along with her tears.

"Daddy play piggyback! Ride 'em cowboy!" And Sung, as he did on every one of these evenings, let out a whinny and cantered over to the two of them, carefully set the child on his shoulders and took a gentle trot around the house, from disordered room to disordered room, ignoring the entreaties of the other children who wanted rides, and giving Katarina a chance to gather up the "dinner" from the kitchen floor and boil it up into the mush she loved so well.

That night when the children had been swatted off to bed, Sung sought the courage for which he was so well known in the community.

"Katarina, two nights ago when I came to this house the door was locked from the inside," Sung ventured. "You should not do that to your husband."

Katarina ground her teeth. "Thursday, Friday, Saturday night you spend with that woman! I no take that. I beat you up."

And before he could answer, she rushed off in the direction of her broom which she kept for just that purpose.

"No," Sung said, attempting a voice of sweet reason. "That is not true, darlring. One night I spend with Lin, one night I spend at the Tong, one night I was . . . gambling."

Katarina sneered and pounded the business end of the broom on the floor. "You liar. I send the boys down to look for you. You in bed with her, again."

Her insolence infuriated him even though, or especially because, she was right. Concealing his hands in his silken sleeves, he hissed at her in disdain.

"I am master in my house, worthless woman. I give you the food for your table. My money buys clothes for you and the children." Here he smiled ironically. "You as wife keep clean house, teach children honor and obedience, and," he flushed darkly, "be ready for your husband's emblaces."

They knew each other well enough so that he could almost see her mind work. She had two choices now. The first, which all the gods knew she had done often enough in the past, was to begin to beat him around the head and shoulders with her broom, driving him out to the sidewalk with Slovak curses. The second, which he took a particular delight in seeing, was that she would strive to put together a rational thought. He flattered himself that it was because she desired him. She leaned on the broom and gazed at him fixedly.

"You good man," she grated. "Very wise. Very fair. You sleep with wife—one, two, one, two." He saw her knuckles tighten on the broom as she strove for self-control. "I no like to sleep alone," she said, smiling falsely. She dropped her broom with a clatter and, placing her cheek on folded hands, screwed her eyes shut.

"Where is Sung? Where is Wosbon? No Wosbon, no nookey-nookey-nookey!" She opened her eyes to see what effect this speech had had on him.

Though secretly pleased with her performance and what it promised, Sung gave no indication of this. Instead, he followed up his advantage by saying, "I am the husband. I sleep where I want to sleep. Tonight I sleep here—not because you say so, because I say so. First I go say goodnight to number one wife and children."

"Ten minutes."

"You do not tell your master what to do."

"Fifteen minutes."

"If I find door locked, you buy train ticket for Tex-as."

If Katarina's house had been nothing but bright lights and noises, Lin's house was immaculate, dimly lit, almost oppressively silent, and redolent of incense. Over the years, each time Katarina had exacted a present from Sung—an excursion on the red car to the ocean, one to a livery stable where she might spend the afternoon in the saddle—Lin had demanded an "equal" gift in the form of lacquer bowls and bolts of silk. After eleven years of marriage, Sung thought, the house of his number one wife held more valuables than his own store.

Lin had raised her eight children with the discipline of a warlord without ever pitching her voice above a whisper. In truth, Sung was glad he had two wives to choose from; the nights on the pillow with Lin were the equivalent of Katarina's meals. A few perfunctory minutes while she looked into the middle distance. Sometimes he felt that she had been married too soon, and that their firstborn, George, their eldest son whom Sung valued more than life itself, had so inflicted her with pain that she had developed a permanent distrust for that connection between a man and a woman which should bring only pleasure. Or perhaps, in her quiet way, she was punishing him for having taken a second wife.

On the other hand, Lin did everything a good Chinese wife should to honor her husband. In particular he knew that three or four nights a week he could look forward to dinners fit for the emperor himself. Often on Katarina's nights he would stop by Lin's home "just for a few minutes," knowing she would offer him the middle part of a crab finely spiced, just a snack, but he would end up staying for sixteen courses. Dazed both with food and the boundless respect he was accorded in this house, he would drift into oblivion.

Tonight Lin greeted him with her customary deep bow. "Again you honor me, my husband. My happiness knows no limits."

Behind her stood the older children. At a signal from George they bowed low. They were dressed in identical silk pajamas.

"Honored father—"

But Lin would not allow George to continue, or the other children to speak. She held up a pale, bejeweled hand and imperiously pointed in the direction of the sleeping quarters.

"Do not disturb your father. He has worked long and hard for all of us today and he needs his rest."

For the second time in one evening, Sung asserted himself. "Eldest son," he queried, "you are doing well with your lessons?"

George smiled widely, pleased to be singled out.

"I do my best to honor the household. In American school I got picked for the team and I play left field for the baseball. My teacher, Miss Bruinslot, gives me all A's! In Chinese school I learned three new characters last week."

"Another night I will look at your calligraphy."

Again Lin flicked her fingers and the children were gone.

Before Sung could open his mouth to speak, a servant had brought in a tray with a flagon of warm rice wine and tiny morsels of iced sea urchin.

"This is all the worthless servant could find, although I sent him to the market at three this morning."

Against his will Sung took a bite or two and downed two quick cups of rice wine.

Ah, delicious.

"I cannot—"

"Esteemed husband," Lin said firmly, "for many months I have pondered what I will say to you tonight."

Sung quickly drank another glass of wine. "Yes?" he said cautiously.

187

"In the home village, we left as poor peasant orphans, you and I. And even now, though it is because of you and you alone that the people of our village have rice in their mouths, the illustrious name of Sung Wing On is not sufficiently respected. There is only one way to make those ignorant, ungrateful cousins on the other side of the great water understand the magnificent heights to which, through your brilliant talents, you have risen."

"Ah, yes," said Sung. He sensed a silken trap. "And how is that?" he asked.

"To hear of your greatness is not enough for those ignorant ones, but to see your eldest son carried always in a sedan chair of gold, your unworthy wife the recipient of your boundless generosity . . ."

"You want to go back," Sung said in astonishment. "You want to go back to the home village."

"You are right, husband. Your sons should see what they came from. They should see you are a man of respect both here and there—"

"Out of the question."

In a pretty gesture of humility, Lin sank gracefully to her knees before him.

"When I was young," she began, the tears already gathering in her almond eyes, "they made me eat bitterness. They made me sweep the earthen floors and empty the human refuse. Now I would return with all our children and your wealth." Her tiny hands twitched convulsively. "And repay them with honeyed words and lavish gifts."

The contrast between Lin's posture before him and Katarina's recent behavior inclined him to grant Lin's request, but also reminded him that he had little time left if he were to maintain the careful balance that he had striven for all these years. Quickly he calculated the expense. It was minimal in proportion to the wealth he had amassed. And he allowed himself the fleeting vision of Lin clad in expensive silks, traveling with all their children, each in his own sedan chair. What pleasant and conclusive revenge. And . . . for at least a year he would have the rampant freedom of the savage and uncomplicated pleasures offered by his second wife.

"It pleases me to grant your request," he said suddenly, and glanced at his watch.

"The train leaves for San Francisco tomorrow," his wife said smoothly. "I have already purchased the tickets."

"But, but," he stammered, "even though I have been pleased to grant your request, and even if you could make suitable preparations within that time, the press of business would prohibit my accompanying you on such short notice."

"I would never presume to inconvenience my husband in any way," Lin whispered. "I have obtained tickets only for the children and myself. Were you to go with us to the city to the north you would be deprived, for several evenings, of the comforts of your other home."

Sung felt a surge of pure animal rage. So that was it! This trip would do him honor, she had told the truth in that. But in doing him this honor, it was *she* who planned to deprive him of the fruits of her gender. His male vanity was offended, and his anger rose.

"In that case then," he said stiffly, "I must content myself with escorting you to the station. *If* I can spare time from the demands of my many enterprises and my other family obligations."

He stood up just a trifle unsteadily and went out, the murmured thanks of Lin still in his ears.

On the street, after he had gone only half a block, he saw striding down the center, walking in her own words "like 'lectric," Katarina, broom in hand, her wild blond hair flying out in every direction. When she saw him she dropped her weapon, ran to him, skirts and petticoats flying, and knocked his breath out with an enthusiastic hug.

"You come home," she breathed into his ear, and bit his neck. "Tonight I no have to fight for you."

Sung was conscious that more than one pair of eyes must be watching this undignified scene, but, he thought philosophically, it was not every man in Los Angeles who had two women fight over his favors.

"Let go, woman," he said, but without conviction.

"Come home," she breathed, and bit him again. "I give you horseback ride."

They had held up Sunday dinner for a full hour and the only two things that had kept Cliff from really losing his temper were their tradition of Sunday-night formality and the second bottle of champagne. Even so, he could not keep from giving some vent to his annoyance.

"I always said no good would come from letting her have that car." He took another sip from his glass. "Poopsy!" he snorted.

"Now, dear," Victoria said soothingly.

"I know you think I'm old-fashioned, but still some standards have to be kept up. Ruth is a girl, after all."

"Now, dear, when I was her age I was already her mother."

"Umph!" Clifford responded.

Whatever else he might have planned to say was cut off by Ruth's breathless, excited entrance into the drawing room. In one hand she held her trophy and with the other she struggled with the knot of her motoring veil.

"Oh, Mother," she sighed.

Although Victoria heard the new intonation of her daughter's voice, Cliff was beyond any such sensitivity.

"Ruth," he said, "do you know what time it is? Do you know what day it is? For your information this is Sunday and we've been waiting over an hour." His tone of paternal authority was slightly undermined by the champagne's effervescence.

Victoria, seeing a chance to save not only her husband's dignity but also to smooth over this potentially volatile scene, said, "Don't fret, Ruth, it's just that your father was worried, as any good father would be. You *are* late, but we can see that it's because you've had a wonderful outing. Before you tell

189

us about it, why don't you run upstairs and change? I'm sure Pansy is ready to help you and when we're seated at dinner you can tell us all about it." As she said this she patted Clifford on the arm.

"Oh, Mother," Ruth sighed again, and turned and left the room, trailing her loosened veil behind her like a train.

Pansy Priest had already laid out Ruth's best Sunday dinner dress of a pale yellow dotted swiss.

"There's some warm water here with scent for you to sponge off, Miss Ruth. You won't have time to take a proper bath. Your daddy is fit to be tied. You are *late!*"

"I know, Pansy, but—"

"Don't give me no buts, young lady. You know how your daddy gets. And my spinach soufflé is toughening up like shoe leather."

"Oh, Pansy." Dreamily Ruth disrobed, dreamily she moved the sopping sponge across her substantial but attractive upper body.

"You been mesmerized, or what?" Pansy asked sternly. "Just what is your excuse for staying out so late? You better think of one right now, 'cause it's dollars to doughnuts that's going to be your dinner conversation tonight."

"Pansy, do you think it's possible to fall in love at first sight?"

"Sweet Jesus! What makes you ask that, honey?"

Ruth took a deep breath.

"Pansy, you'll absolutely never believe what happened. I was out there at the rally and it was just like every other rally. I mean it was wonderful, every rally is wonderful. But this one was out by the Mission. You know, the Mission in San Gabriel? I never knew they were so picturesque. You know, Pansy, there's an enormously rich heritage there. I never knew that we Californians had such an enormously rich heritage. So I was driving around in a circle. You know, how at a rally you drive around in a circle? And they were about to give the prizes, but they hadn't given the prizes yet. I happened to look up. I don't know what made me look up. I think it's just because everyone else was looking up. And then," here she paused dramatically, "you'll never guess what I saw. Pansy, can you guess what I saw?"

"Honey, the way you've been talking and this bein' Sunday, it couldn't have been anything less than an angel of the Lord."

Ruth gazed at Pansy for an instant and her face lit up.

"You're right," she screamed, "you're absolutely right! How could you have known that? I mean he actually came down out of the sky. He was beautiful. He was so incredibly beautiful."

"Then what?" Pansy asked impatiently.

"He came down out of the sky," Ruth said dreamily, "and he got in the car with me. We drove around. Then we got the prize. Then he said he only drove a Hispano-Suiza, and I said would he like to drive Poopsy and he said yes. Then he drove me on roads I'd never seen before, close up under the mountains. He drove so fast! I was afraid for my life. He said I was adventurous, Pansy. He said he'd never seen a girl so brave. Bravery is his family's code. That's why they got those old Spanish land grants. The king awarded the land to them because they were so brave."

"Sweet Jesus," Pansy said, "he's a Mexican!"

"Pansy," Ruth drew herself up imperiously, and even though she was half clad, fixed her servant with a baleful stare. "Alessandro is a member of the Spanish aristocracy. He is a member of a very important family indeed. He has eight names. Can you imagine that? And that's before he was confirmed. Alessandro Luis Antonio de Ortega de Moreno de Arellanos de Mariné y Ruiz. I think you'll find, Pansy, that it's rare to find a Mexican with eight names."

"I don't know what your father's going to say, but I have a pretty good idea."

"After a while he stopped driving. We stopped by the edge of an orange grove and a big meadow. Oh, it was so beautiful. I've never seen anything so beautiful in all my life. He showed me the wildflowers. He knows all their names in Spanish. There was a lot of mustard out there and we talked about faith. Did you know that if your faith is but the size of a mustard seed, you can still go to Heaven? His religion means everything to him. He's a very spiritual person."

"Sweet Jesus!" Pansy said.

"Yes. After that, Pansy, can you guess what he did then?"

Pansy was beyond speech.

"We went walking through the orange grove and he made me a wreath of orange blossoms. Oh, Pansy, I can't believe it. He said I would make a beautiful bride. What do you think that means? Do you think he'll come calling? Do you think it means anything? Was he—"

"I know one thing," Pansy said, as she pulled the dress over the girl's head and began buttoning up the back. "You'd better get on downstairs. And when you tell this story to your daddy, if I were you I'd change that Alessandro de Mucky-muck's name to Alex."

When Ruth appeared a few minutes later in the drawing room, her father was already standing impatiently, waiting to go in to dinner.

Clifford Creighton maintained a certain distance in his manner as he first ceremoniously seated his wife, and then pulled out Ruth's chair, with more abruptness than he had planned. But this small departure from his usual level of good manners was entirely lost on his daughter, who waited until Priest had served the first course of cream soup and sherry, and then, crossing her hands pensively under her chin, asked, "Tell me, Mother, do you think it's possible to fall in love at first sight?"

Whether it was from seeing his daughter's elbows on the table, or the effects of the champagne, or the very question itself, Clifford Creighton found himself forced to use his napkin.

The night after the *paseo,* Raoul had driven alone to San Gabriel. He had circled the adobe no less than three times. It was as impregnable as a fortress. He had used the heavy bronze knockers on the hand-carved double doors of the front entrance. The majordomo had dismissed him churlishly.

"If you have something to deliver, you go to the back entrance. If you have nothing to deliver, you have no business being here!" Clearly, what Raoul had to deliver was not meant for the servants' entrance, though he had mooned about that doorway as well, waiting for he knew not what. As the moon rose over the San Gabriel Valley, Raoul returned again to the main entrance, loitering disconsolately. They have had a fair here, he thought, or a fiesta. He tugged on a torn piece of bunting. It came down in the dirt, like his grandiose daydreams. But still he waited, as one by one the lights of the adobe went out. He had seen enough in his explorations to realize that the family he was interested in must live in this wing, if for no other reason than that the farther reaches of this vast estate were devoted to farmland and farm buildings. And the "servants' entrance" had been no more than ninety feet down from this southeast corner of the wall.

Raoul sat on his haunches and looked at the facade of the adobe. Only one light remained in a second-story room, which faced onto a small balcony. Could she be in there? Was she thinking of him now? The rest of the wall was blank, dark, swathed in shadow. There were no other windows on this side, only a trellis—a series of trellises—supporting an enormous magenta bougainvillea vine. For what seemed like an hour he stared fixedly at that one light. Enough! Had he come out here to sit like a house cat and do nothing? Was he a man of action or not?

Desperate, he trotted right across the open space where he could have been spotted by anyone, took shelter by the vine just under the balcony, and without thinking about it further began climbing hand over hand up the trellis. *Ay, Chihuahua!* This bastard plant was full of stickers. Then senselessly he remembered one of his mother's sayings. *No hay rosa sin espinas.* And in the middle of this stupid adventure he had to smile.

It seemed an eternity until he came level with the balcony. Balancing himself with a toehold on the balustrade itself, he looked avidly into the window. A wide fireplace with a triangular opening, flanked by stained glass windows on either side, a piano draped with an elaborate fringed shawl, a heavy library table covered with knickknacks and antique books, and in the near corner of the room, breathtakingly close to him, wrapped in a silk-embroidered dressing gown, a female figure doing needlework. He did not have to look twice to recognize the Señora. The scorching fear of being made to look like a fool gave him wings to shinny down this devil plant. But his heart was racing in triumph, and prowling now like an alley cat, he stepped into the shadows of the eastern wall, paced off the distance to the servants' entrance.

And there it was! Two barely discernible cracks two feet apart and another crack that ran horizontally just above his head. There *had* to be another entrance here for the private use of the family, and this was it, a secret door. He ran his fingers over the chalky surface of the wall.

Carefully digging into yielding adobe with sharp shoes, his fingers found a hold in the top of the door—No! It wasn't going to work! After he had picked himself up, he went back to the place of the booths and platforms. Deep in his project, he looked for a board that would suit his purposes and finally decided on two rickety benches, which he trundled one by one back to the secret door.

He carefully placed them one on top of the other. Trying to make himself both thin and tall, he flung himself at the wall and scrambled up. He fell back, his hands badly lacerated by the shards of broken glass that had been imbedded in the top of the wall. The next time, he threw his jacket across the jagged barrier, once again stacked up the benches, and hoisted himself to the edge of the wall.

If I lose my *cojones,* I'm not going to need the girl, he thought. He carefully lifted his left leg up and over. Now the right, and hoping for the best, he fell into the courtyard. What a noise!

Que machismo! he thought happily. *I did it.* Who would have ever thought? Catching his breath, he waited to see if anyone had heard. Then he turned his attention to the layout of the family quarters. To his left the entry hall. To his right the kitchen. In front of him a formal dining room, and adjacent to it a small chapel for family prayers. Good! That meant the bedrooms were all upstairs. But which one was Maria's?

As if in answer to his feverish question, a door opened onto the upper veranda, which ran on three sides of this courtyard.

"Who's there?"

It was she, Maria, in the moonlight, clad in her sheer sleeping gown, her hair loose about her shoulders, hanging in dark tendrils down to her waist. All that was needed was a serpent writhing under her bare toes to make her a vision of Our Most Holy Mother of God. A virgin princess. Should he answer her call? What if she screamed? *But what if she didn't?*

Even as his mind raced with these imponderables, she turned and disappeared.

It was just as well. Because the sight of her there in the moonlight had suggested a plan to him—the perfect plan. Stepping with extreme caution he moved again toward the outside wall of the adobe, found the door—which he was sure had long been unused—with a huge rusty key jammed in the lock. He tried to turn it; it creaked alarmingly. He removed it, spat upon it, swore at it, tried it again. This time the door opened uncomplainingly.

Then he was out. He locked the door from the outside and pocketed the key. After returning the benches to their places, he scuffed out the marks he had made and headed for home. *Love is stronger than the moon and the tides,* he thought. But how could this be love? He had never loved anyone in his life.

The next night, under a full moon, Raoul once again prowled through the darkness to the eastern wall of the adobe.

Silently he opened the "secret" door, silently he turned to a group of shadowy accomplices. Stealthily they slid past him into the moonlit gloom of the courtyard. The echoing night's quiet was broken by a single lonely sound; not the nightingale—the A above middle C.

Bernardo, the majordomo, hurtled from his bed and lunged for the ancient musket, which he had kept all these years as a token of his office, rather than for any real use.

The Señora awoke from a dream of a fiesta in full sway, except that it was no dream.

Alessandro flew from his bed, hardly waiting to wrap himself in his robe of purple silk, and pounded down the veranda to his sister's room, protecting her from he knew not what.

But Maria—that little white bird—had already escaped her cage. She stood leaning over the veranda, the moonlight clearly showing the contours of her firm young body as she held out her hands to the brigand in the courtyard and said, with no regard for the proprieties, "I knew you would come!"

Alessandro brusquely grabbed the lovesick girl, shoved her back into her room, and stood against the door.

"Mama!" he yelled. "Come quickly."

"I am already here." And indeed she was, concealed from all eyes in the moonlit shade of the great Mariné wisteria.

Madre de Dios! She was smiling.

"Mama!"

But she cut him off with an imperious hand. "Only once before have I heard musicians like this. When your father—now with the Holy Ones— took me on our honeymoon to Guadalajara. There in the great Plaza outside the Cathedral—the Plaza de Mariachis. He spent a fortune on me that night—more than I . . . some honest working girls might see in a lifetime. 'La Madrugada'! 'La Negra!' 'Ella'! Oh! Now they're doing 'El Gusto'! Listen, Alessandro! This is what you must do!"

Down in the courtyard the *mariachi* was on its sixth and last song. As far as Raoul could see they were playing to an empty house. Raoul was forced to consider—*what next!* He had been obsessed during the day with his quixotic quest—the *loco* idea that if he had met Maria through music he would surely win her heart through more music. He had heard of new musicians at La Tortuga. They had come from the very bowels of Mexico, from over fifteen hundred miles away, the state of Jalisco, bringing what everyone said was the music of romance.

All day long he had searched in the *cantinas,* looking for this strange new group—the men who played the violin, the *vehuela,* the *guitarrón.* Well! He had found them, he had brought them here at great expense. He had even seen Maria, hadn't he? Hadn't she called to him? But was this to be all?

With a stirring flourish the *mariachi* finished "El Gusto." As one man they all looked at Raoul. He shrugged. *"Quién sabe?"*

Then, from above, came a stern male voice. "My esteemed mother, the Señora Deogracia Ruiz de Ortega de Moreno de Arellanos de Mariné, wishes me to inform you that she is horrified. You have violated the privacy of our name and our home. You have trespassed. You have disturbed the peace. You have wakened the servants. My mama wishes to tell you that she is prepared to call the *patrulla.* But because she is a woman as kind as she is merciful, she is prepared to overlook the crudeness of your manners if—if you will play 'Arriba Jalisco'—"

The *mariachi* captain called out softly, "A woman of rare taste!" And his

194

musicians tapped their bows across the strings of their violins in appreciation.

" *'Arriba Jalisco'* with *all* the verses. And then, the Señora wishes you to know that our majordomo will have some wine for you, and then—*go home!*"

But "Arriba Jalisco" was not to be the last *son,* for Raoul had the wit to request "Amor de Madre," and it was during that song's soft strains that Maria slipped quietly out of her room and came to stand beside her mother.

All Sung could think of at this time was the power of money. He knew that outside the strict, if invisible, walls of their own enclave, Chinese were looked upon with contempt here in Los Angeles. But not now, not his family. Money is the most powerful incense. His wife and the eight children of his first family were dressed in a manner that would have done honor to the most powerful warlords or the imperial family itself. Sung realized that Lin must have been planning this trip in secret for months. Each of the children was dressed Chinese-fashion in matching pants and smock of charcoal gray silk. Six servants accompanied them. They too were dressed in silk—matte black. Their luggage numbered fifty-two pieces and two hatboxes. Although Lin's feet had never been bound she walked along the platform with the tiny steps of a woman born to the aristocracy. She was dressed for this occasion in the Western style, one of the new hobble skirts slit daringly above the ankle. Her still slim waist was cinched in, a traveling jacket of dull blue half concealed a white blouse with a Chinese collar embroidered richly with silver thread. Most outrageous, she wore a hat. A little blue hat with a silver feather, and high sandals which made it necessary to hold onto Sung's arm as she limped mincingly to the train.

Money. Sung could not fail to notice that the looks they attracted were tinged with admiration or even envy, not the careless disdain that he as a youth had come to expect from the round-eye.

Lin was almost speechless with excitement.

"Everyone is looking at us, my glorious husband, and this is only the beginning. Soon the whole world will know the honor of your name."

With an almost imperceptible flick of her lacquered nails she gestured to her embroidered collar. Sung recognized with a start the character for his family name. And quickly resting his eye on his children and entourage, he realized that each one of them wore the same symbol.

"I put it there with my own hands," she whispered, "each one of them, and all for your honor."

Sung was inexpressibly touched. "My heart aches," he told her truthfully, "to think of you and my sons—and daughters—sailing away from me on the great sea."

But she became businesslike. "I have taken care of everything. Your children will come to no harm. I have reserved four rooms on the middle deck of the SS *Golden State.* And we will have two days in San Francisco, at the home of Ming Yun Fong, who, as you well know, would be too afraid of ever crossing you to let us come to harm."

All around them passengers were boarding the train. His own servants had reserved two compartments and were handing in luggage through the window. Sung thought back to the way he had crossed the ocean. An orphan. A stowaway subsisting on stolen food. He knew that Lin was right, but still he was gripped by an inexplicable dread. A part of him felt that she tempted the gods with such a show. Another part of him, the Western part, felt keenly the shame of communicating with a woman only by siring children on her body. As he looked searchingly into Lin's proud, excited face, he saw with a pang that she was still young, terribly young. A girl in her twenties. A wiser woman would not have attempted this folly.

Then, too fast for him, he was waving goodbye to his children and a beautiful Chinese stranger in a silver-feathered hat. He was alone now on the platform with a few curious Westerners. To his amazement he gestured in the expansive, rhetorical manner of the mad peasant Bin Tang as he addressed them to their astonishment in the dialect of his home village.

"I have just said goodbye to my ugly wife," he shouted, palms up. "She is as stupid as a frog and as loud as a donkey. And those people she has with her, they are only foolish strangers of no importance."

But did the rules for warding off evil spirits have any efficacy in the crowded railway station of the City of the Angels?

"I don't want to play tennis! I don't want to go for a nice walk! And I don't want to go for a drive! I want to stay right here!"

"But Ruth—"

"No! No! No! No! No!"

Victoria looked at her daughter. Ruth hid her face in her hands and burst into tears.

"Just go away and leave me alone!"

Victoria moved to the canopied bed where her daughter lay prostrate.

"Don't touch me!" Ruth screamed.

And Victoria, after considering for a few moments, went to the window and looked out. It was a good thing Clifford wasn't here to see and hear this. This past week Ruth, never known for her calm temperament, had been almost impossible to get along with. Every time the doorbell had rung, she had raced Priest to the door. Every time the postman had come, she had wrested the letters from Priest's hand. And every time she had been disappointed, she had burst into tears.

Clifford had been anything but sympathetic and had remarked that if he'd wanted to live in a rainy climate he would have taken his fabled train trip years ago to San Francisco. This and his other heavy attempts at wit had met with the same stormy reception.

"Daddy, how could you? Daddy, you don't understand. Mother, can't you do something to make him stop?"

But since last Sunday night's ill-fated dinner when Clifford had cut off Ruth's mooning with a not-altogether-uncalled-for tirade, there had been no stopping either one of them. Clifford snorted; Ruth sighed and wept.

The most unfortunate aspect of all this, Victoria thought, was that it might be for nothing. It was all very well to argue interminably over the superiority of the old Spanish culture or, conversely, the fundamental goodness of Presbyterian values. But—here Victoria grimaced and straightened one of the gauzy curtains—none of this meant beans if the Superior Spaniard in question never made a second entrance.

The Priests and Victoria had tried to bring harmony back into the house. They had tempted Ruth with her favorite ice cream and cookies. She had stuck out her lip and howled like a child. Porter Priest had been sent to the cellar to find the rarest bottle of sparkling wine. For a moment Clifford had brightened, but when he saw it was Spanish, he had spoken so harshly to Priest that he had gone into the kitchen and hadn't come out for two days.

When this weekend had yawned before them, a stretch of time in which, by a devilish coincidence, none of them had any social engagements, Clifford had lasted two hours into Saturday morning. Then he had declared in grieved tones that he had business to attend to and grumped off to the office.

But she, Victoria, refused to play the role that this domestic dance required of her.

"For the love of God, Ruth!" she snapped. "Stop being such a bore."

No sounds came from the bed except a few muffled sobs.

"He's only one young man, and though you've known him in one sense all your life, in another you've only just met him."

Ruth began to moan. "Oh, Mother, you don't under—"

"What nonsense! Of course I understand! Don't you think I was a green girl once?"

"Green? Green! I'm not green!" The figure on the bed suddenly took shape. "Green!"

Victoria took the last approach she felt was open to her. "A woman of any experience," she said frostily, "would not allow herself to be undone so conspicuously by anyone or anybody. That is the whole point of breeding, my dear."

"Mother," Ruth said dully, "you really *don't* understand. Sometimes I think I don't even understand myself." Here she sniffed and wiped her nose on her lace cuff. "Ever since I can remember I've always adored Alessandro."

Victoria could not suppress a deep impatient breath.

"Oh, I know that you and Father never thought much of him. You may sigh all you will, but to me he's always been . . . don't you see, it was easy to control when I thought he'd never look at me. But now that he has, I just don't think I can bear it."

Victoria cut in hastily. "You don't want your eyes to be swollen when he calls."

"But I don't think he cares about me! It's been a week. And even if he does, Daddy thinks he's awful."

"There's no sense in worrying about your father until there's a real issue to worry about. And, if it does come to that, I'm sure that ways could be found to handle him. After all, Ruth, he really loves you."

Seeing the tears beginning to well up again, she hurried on. "Haven't you ever heard that a watched pot never boils? The great thing now, Ruth dear, is to go on as if nothing has happened."

Something in her mother's voice made Ruth sit up and swing her legs over the side of the bed. Her shoulders shuddered and Victoria said as strongly as she could manage, "I want you to march right in and take an invigorating cold bath. You've missed breakfast and I don't want to eat lunch alone. After that, my dear, you are taking me for a nice drive. I'll have Priest get Poopsy ready."

As Ruth began to protest, her mother said smoothly, "Your father has often spoken to me about the matter of your speeding in Poopsy."

Ruth hung her head.

"I've heard that Poopsy can go at speeds up to seventy miles an hour and your father has become so conservative I shall never travel at that speed unless it is with you."

"Why is he like that, Mother?" Ruth burst out. "Why has he become so, so *old?*"

"Ah, Ruthie, your father was quite adventurous in his day. Have I told you about the time when I ran away from the hunt and your father followed me?"

"Yes, yes, yes," Ruth interrupted impatiently. "I've heard it a hundred times. And from that day forward his name was Cliff, but I don't see what that has to do with . . ."

"My dear," her mother overrode her, "there was a night I shall always remember. We'd been married fourteen years. Frankly, I felt about him then much as you feel now. I was bored beyond belief. And then, that night, your *staid* father, your *boring* father worked late. I went to sleep and after midnight he burst in." Victoria began to giggle. "Ruthie dear, you would never have believed it. He had come directly from the oil fields. Understand me, we had many wells by that time. But this was our first gusher. He was a *black* man, Ruthie. He was *drenched* in oil. His shirt was open to his waist. He pranced across the room in the fencing position. He left great black marks across the carpet. Then he leapt up upon the bed."

Ruth's mouth hung open, her troubles momentarily forgotten.

"What did he do then, Mother?"

Victoria regarded her daughter with the most serious expression. "Why then, Ruthie dearest, he peeled off his shirt and we—discussed the price of oil."

After a long giggle Ruth said, "That just doesn't seem like Daddy."

"Your father is more complex than he appears. You mustn't forget that he's from Baltimore and he was very strictly brought up. He's spent a good part of his life trying to get away from all that, but in the last analysis I believe that those values are his touchstones."

It was the first time in many weeks that mother and daughter had been so close.

An hour and forty-five minutes later, when the doorbell rang, Ruth and Victoria were just finishing what had turned out to be a very pleasant

198

luncheon. Ruth started to get up, but Victoria put a light yet steely hand on her daughter's forearm.

"You were speaking to me, my dear, about Poopsy's transmission. Have you ever found yourself . . ."

Here Porter Priest appeared in the doorway and said in a voice which betrayed no sense of particular significance, "The Señora Mariné and her son are here."

Without looking at her daughter, Victoria said in a quiet, indifferent tone, "Do make them comfortable, Porter, and ask them to wait in the drawing room where we will join them shortly. They must be a little travel-weary if they have come from San Gabriel. Once we're a party of four I'm sure they would appreciate a little refreshment. Pansy might provide a few ladyfingers and at least one bottle of that Spanish champagne."

Victoria would remember for the rest of her life her daughter sitting as white as a sheet as she waited until Priest had left, and then saying in a strangled voice, "Four gears. Almost every car has four gears. Poopsy has five."

And then they were in the drawing room. Priest was droning. "I have the honor to announce the Señora Deogracia Mariné and her son Alessandro Mariné."

Ruth crossed the room looking splendid and carefree in her motoring skirt and shirtwaist, saying with just the right amount of regal surprise, "Why, Alessandro, how nice to see you again."

Sung had never known it was possible to live like this, and, indeed, he still wasn't sure. Sitting at their breakfast table in Katarina's chaotic kitchen, he put his hands over his ears to shield himself from the noise, then took them away, then put them back. He watched as Katarina stirred up porridge for breakfast, beating at the children with her free hand, turning every so often to give him a joyful grin. He wasn't sure how much sleep he'd had in the last two nights. His serpent should have been worn down to the size of a feeble worm, but he knew tonight it would be ready for another four hours of uninterrupted pleasure. No, that was not quite correct. Their pleasure had been interrupted several times by children who said they had to go to the bathroom, or they were going to be sick, and when at six o'clock this morning Sung had awakened from perhaps a half-hour of dreamless sleep he had felt a suffocating but not altogether unpleasant warmth. He had opened his eyes to see not only Katarina on his left shoulder, her arms and legs wrapped tightly about him, but four or five of the children, one on the pillow beside him, one across his knees, one across his feet, one on his stomach— all of them in postures of total abandon, like puppies who had played themselves to sleep, just as he had played himself to sleep.

But he was a man of dignity! How could he go on living this way for the year that Lin would be away from his side? Now more than ever he recognized that having two homes and two wives had been an act of moderation rather than excess. By giving each wife slightly less than half his energy, he had been able to keep some of his life for himself. The question was, and here he could not keep from smiling, would Lin return home to find him a sick old man, struck down in his prime from a debauched life of sexual extravagance?

In the early years he had tried to persuade Katarina to accept the help of servants, at least a cook. But none of them had lasted for more than twenty-four hours in the face of the "devil woman." Katarina insisted that they caused too much trouble and that they were spies for the other wife, which Sung had to admit was likely. While Lin required at least six servants to raise her eight children, Katarina demanded that she be allowed to do it alone. He had come to realize that although he could not understand how she did it, she must have had some secret system. The children were clean, their clothes ironed, they left for school on time with carrot-filled lunch boxes, and returned home with good grades. More than that, he could see they were devoted to their mother. They were good children. If he thought hard enough he could remember all their names, strange as they were to his tongue. Milan, Stanislav, Birgd, Jitka, Thadius, Marya, Gretel, Dynamite. Even as he named them off they launched a major attack and counterattack in the kitchen.

"Ma, he hit me! He came up from behind and he hit me and pulled my skirt!"

"I did not, you little liar!" One of the boys had raised his fist against the little girl. The little girl—it wasn't Dyna—began to sob.

Katarina turned around and grinned at her husband with an affection so strong it made him uncomfortable.

"Ask Papa," she said. "Now you ask your papa."

It was still quite early in the morning, no more than seven or seven-thirty. None of the children had gotten dressed yet. Katarina was still stirring porridge when they were interrupted by a tumultuous knocking at the kitchen door. It was Sung's relative Yun-ling.

His cousin stood shaking in silence. "Aiee-yah! I wish that the iron dragon had crushed my bones before I reached your house. But even as I lingered crossing the tracks, it spared me, to bring you bitterness to eat. But remember, Pillar of Honor, what I bring you need not be bad news."

Sung was standing by now. "What has happened?" he asked, trying to keep his voice steady.

"No one knows for sure. But the cable has sent a message from the northern city that the great tortoise that supports the earth has taken at least two—possibly three—steps. And it is said that into these cracks whole buildings have been swallowed."

The children, listening to the distraught man, couldn't understand the import of the words, but they understood the universal tone that announces disaster. And as they began to weep, Katarina dispatched them quickly from the room. She stood there silently, trying, her head cocked, to pick up enough words to learn what had happened.

Sung remembered other times the tortoise had moved, both here and in the Middle Kingdom. He knew it was true that while many people died, still there were always people that lived.

"What news of my first wife?" He knew it was a useless question.

"There is no news except what the cable says. And the cable talks of the city as a whole."

Sung spoke to Katarina. "The earth has moved in the north. I must go to see if Lin and the children. . . ."

Katarina stared at him quietly, taking it in. "Sit down," she said, "and eat. You need food for trip."

She dished him out the steaming porridge, broke in two raw eggs and stirred it roughly, together with black molasses. "You *must* eat," she said. She spoke to the cousin. "You," she said, in primitive Chinese, "*Ngi!* Go to store, buy him good Chinese food. Much food. Then come back, fast."

She stamped her foot and he scurried out.

While Sung ate, Katarina quickly made up a traveling bag with a change of clothes and a muffler against the northern cold. By the time the cousin came back, she was ready for him and efficiently packed the provisions. Sung spoke his plan out loud to no one in particular. "I have the food, I have the clothes, I go to the office, I get some money, I go to the train station—"

Katarina took his hand. "Go train station now, quick. I have money, plenty of money." She went to the cooler, scrabbled behind, and from under fifty-pound sacks of carrots, turnips, and potatoes, which she effortlessly lifted out onto the kitchen floor, she produced a yellow oilskin packet.

Reaching into it, she pulled out a wad of hundred-dollar bills. "All I have. Save for children. You take now."

There was nothing more to be said. Katarina put her arm around him. "Be careful, Wosbon. Come back fast. Be careful."

Then he was at the station, a solitary Chinese in a chaos of Caucasians. Realizing that there would be nothing like a regular schedule today, he sought out the dispatcher and pressed a hundred-dollar bill into his hand.

"First train north, I go on it."

Another hundred to the conductor, and he was sitting in a corner of a hastily improvised medical train, the first one out.

The truth was no one had any knowledge of how far this train would or could go. And after an hour or so of nervous conversation—which Sung avoided, simply by being a foreigner—the volunteers, most of whom had relatives in the northern city, settled down to an apprehensive silence.

It was after nightfall when they pulled into San José. They had been sidetracked many times, but only as the sun set had they begun to see evidence of the disaster. A window broken, a caved-in farmhouse wall, a decorative cornice of a brick building shattered on the buckled sidewalk.

San José was a shambles. Every brick building had collapsed. The station was filled with refugees, desperately trying to get a train south. The medical train was stopped; the army surgeon in charge brusquely announced that they would await official orders. Sung leaped from the train.

How strange! As he struck out, walking through the decimated downtown area, making for the main highway north, he was—even in the wreckage—overwhelmed by the dreamlike familiarity of things. He had walked this way before. Then he had been a youngster driven by hardly understood ambition and desire, ferocity and anger. He had shed no tears because he had no tears in him. His only aim had been to survive.

Now he was a man of great wealth—an oil man, a merchant, a man of substance and family with two wives and sixteen children. He had come through, he was a grown man of thirty-five.

Except, except—never, since the night he had set out from the home village had he felt so alone, so much at the whim of the gods.

He reached the strangely empty highway now and headed north. Then the headlamps of an approaching motorcar appeared behind him and he flagged it down. Knowing his visage might frighten the driver, he held up a hundred-dollar bill.

"I need a ride north."

"Climb in, bud, and put away your money."

They drove all night, exchanging, without shame, their stories. The man explained that he and his wife had moved down the Peninsula so they could raise their children outside the crowded city and away from pestering in-laws. Both their families—parents, brothers and sisters, aunts and uncles—had lived in San Francisco for fifty years. For himself and for the wife, he had to find out what had happened and see what he could do to help.

Every ten to fifteen miles left them waiting at road blocks. While it had taken Sung twelve hours to get to San José, it took at least that to go the last sixty miles. When the car could go no further, the men parted company.

Making his way through the debris, the cries, the soup kitchens, the dazed and bleeding homeless wandering aimlessly past and over tumbled buildings, Sung headed toward a Chinatown that until today had been far more prosperous than the one he had left in the south.

Fires had sprung up at several points on the horizon, and even as he walked he saw that many of them had joined, making a solid front, burning inexorably, if sluggishly, out of control.

In Chinatown the devastation was complete. Here the buildings had been older than in the rest of the city. They had simply been blown down, as if the gods had breathed once but very heavily. The cries here were much more horrifying to Sung than the others he had heard in the last hours, because the victims mourned in his native language and their laments cut him to the quick.

"My legs are gone! I have no legs!" one girl sobbed, and she was right.

One man, his face a mask of grief, begged Sung to help him move a huge bulwark of cement. "My mother is under there," he said. "With two of us I know we can get her out." But no one could have been under there and remained alive. Sung shook him off and went on.

He was searching for the home of Ming Yun Fong, but he could recognize no landmarks. The gods' awful breath had blown down what street signs there had been. Just when he had come close to giving up hope he heard the moaning of a familiar voice.

"Oh, Honorable Mother, how I have failed you and my younger brothers and sisters! Mother, can you hear me? Won't you speak to me?"

Sung looked about in the gray light of dawn. Then he saw his eldest son,

George, pulling desperately at a beam with bleeding hands. His clothes were rags now. His face was streaked with dirt, blood, and tears. He burrowed futilely in rubble that came up above his waist, rubble that had been a substantial three-story house. Sung saw with horror that George had been "successful." He had already unearthed five small broken bodies, which Sung recognized as his own children.

George looked up with no evidence of surprise when he saw Sung. "She is in there, Father, and I can't get her out. Maybe you can help me. They say many people can still be alive in the storerooms. They say there may be enough air to breathe."

Sung set down his valise, and together they freed the beam and cast it to one side. They cleared away slabs of cement, huge wooden splinters, and jagged chunks of glass. It was Sung who finally pulled away the last barrier and saw at his feet what was once the delicate bejeweled hand of his Chinese wife, now a crushed bloody pulp.

They worked another two hours to uncover Lin and the last two children, all dead. Sung cried then, the first tears he had ever shed, while his son sat down beside him and spoke in a lilting conversational voice devoid of emotion.

"Something woke me in the middle of the night and I went to the window. It's so beautiful here. The peddlers were coming into the streets. They had monkeys on a stick, and fish kites, and noisemakers. All this I could see from my room. I had the spending money that Mother had given me for the trip and I wanted to surprise them. I went downstairs into the strcct. I was going to buy something for everybody. Then, everything fell down and everybody died. I worked all day. I worked all night. I worked as hard as I could. I am totally disgraced and the gods will never forgive me." He paused and said, "Now you are crying, Father. How can I live?"

Sung looked at the face of his son, who returned his gaze with vacant eyes. Sung knew this was no time to indulge his own grief. He knew what it was to be a boy bereft.

"You did everything you could. You have been brave and truthful. I am honored that you are my eldest son and I will carry that honor until I am an old man with no memory."

When George did not respond, Sung reached out and took his son by the shoulders, shaking him, saying, "Come back to me, now. Come back to me on this earth."

But George's eyes showed no understanding. Sung, with newfound tenderness, pulled the remains of the embroidered shirt off his son's shivering shoulders. Rummaging in his valise, he pulled out one of his own shirts and the muffler that Katarina had thought to put in. These he put around the boy. Then, finding the rice wine, Sung dabbed at George's shredded hands and badly gashed forehead, hoping this would forestall infection. He bound each bruised hand in lengths of clean cotton torn from another of his shirts. He held the flask to George's lips and said sternly, "You must drink."

Sung found duck and cold noodles in a carrying dish and placed them with chopsticks in front of his son. "Now you must eat." Mechanically, George obeyed. Only then did Sung, standing up, notice the scraps of discarded gray silk that, catching the light of the sullen sun obscured by clouds of smoke, glittered with the hand-embroidered character—*Sung*. He kicked rubble over the shirt and kicked and kicked until he had created its own small grave mound.

He knew that every afternoon from three to four-thirty she went to the Mission to pray. The reason he knew this was simple. For the last week he had given over the routine of his ordinary feckless life. He had ceased gambling and drinking and staying out late. He had even stopped tormenting his mother, which he noticed caused her to cast many a worried glance in his direction. He had become a spy: a heartsick, bumbling spy.

At first the Mariné servants had looked at him askance. Then for a few pesos they had spoken to him of Maria. How she spent her mornings at lessons. How she excelled at handwriting, but was very bad at conversational French. How she was already marked for the convent. How she washed her raven tresses in rainwater and the pods of the yucca plant. How bananas made her sneeze. But after twenty minutes of this there was nothing else to be said of Maria. Her life was as pure and thin as the last few drops of skim milk at the bottom of a cup. It was just this elusive transparency that drove Raoul wild.

Now his schedule was as rigorous as hers. He spent the mornings outside the adobe, whittling or throwing twigs for the mangy neighborhood dogs to retrieve. He lived for her appearance at eleven o'clock when she went out for a short drive with Bernardo. Sometimes he allowed himself to be seen, in which event she turned away. At other times he was overcome by shyness and slouched behind the trunk of the nearest tree. With his newfound interest in the etiquette of courtship, he knew that both of these modes of behavior were acceptable. And he fancied that at least the servants of the Mariné adobe smiled upon his devotion to the daughter of the house. And thus it was he knew that after a light lunch and a siesta Maria went, between three and four-thirty in the afternoon, to the Mission to pray.

She came this time in the company of her mother in the back of the chauffeured Hispano-Suiza. Here she was dropped off while her mother spent the afternoon doing good works.

Raoul spent his afternoons in the Mission. During the last week he had said more Hail Marys than there are grains of sand on the beach. His soul was bleached as white as the boards in his mother's freshly scrubbed kitchen. He had been to Confession, not once, but five times. The first afternoon he had genuinely examined his conscience and had taken pride in the fact that Father Clement had gasped audibly during his recital. But each afternoon since he had confessed to sins he had not only never committed, but had never thought of until kneeling down in the confessional. He knew that Father Clement, from time to time, raised a polite hand to conceal a smile. But what could Raoul do? His only real sins at this time were against the Sixth and Ninth Commandments—the sins of impure thoughts, and he would have severed his arm rather than admit to that.

After receiving his penance he would kneel two pews behind that blessed form as she made one of her interminable novenas for the soul of her father. Sometimes he would be bold enough to breathe a husky "Amen" or *"Ora pro nobis,"* as she went through her convoluted invocations to the Blessed Mother above.

The question was, how long could this go on? This Friday afternoon, he knew he must make a move: Next Monday marked the beginning of Holy Week and the Mission would be crowded with processionals and *penitentes*. He would never succeed in pressing his suit against that morose background. Today Maria knelt in the lazy half light of the Mission just in front of the statue of Saint Joseph of Copertino, the patron saint of the Mariné family.

"Humblest of monks . . ."

Instead of answering "Pray for us," Raoul whispered, "Come away with me."

"Beloved of the Christ Child . . ."

"Come away right now."

"Pure in heart and tongue . . ."

"Just for a little walk."

"Lighter than air . . ."

"We'll be back in an hour."

"Exquisite in flight . . ."

"Just start to do the Stations of the Cross."

"Astonishment of the unbelievers . . ."

"And walk out the door when you get to the picture of St. Veronica."

"From all inordinate and sinful affections," she concluded, "and from all the deceits of the world, the flesh, and the Devil . . ."

"Saint Joseph, deliver us," he joined in devoutly.

She bowed her head silently and got up, made a deep genuflection at the main altar, and began to do the Stations of the Cross. His heart pounded like a trip-hammer. He in turn moved from the statue of Saint Joseph of Copertino back to another side altar, where Saint Sebastian gazed heavenward in silent complaint. Then Raoul prayed as he never had before.

"Make her go out the side entrance. *Please* make her go out the side entrance."

His prayers were answered and in a moment they both stood in the shade of an ancient pepper tree where, it seemed, hundreds of finches had made their temporary home.

In the dappled shade her dear face looked up at him.

"My mother will kill you if she finds you here."

"Then she must not find us here."

She trembled. He took her by the elbow and suddenly they were running, she ripping her comb and mantilla from her head, letting it trail behind her. Then they were in his car heading north toward the foothills.

"Oh, oh," she breathed. "My mother will surely kill you now."

His response to this was to concentrate on his driving. He drove up into a wooded canyon and parked beside a creek and a tiny waterfall. They were under a huge live oak and near a bright new spread of wildflowers. The sunshine of early mustard dotted a lupin carpet of deepest blue, and the bright orange of the earliest poppies.

"Oh," she said now in a different voice, "it is so beautiful!"

"I told these flowers to bloom for you, *dulce corazon.*"

She blushed and would not answer. His heart was stricken. Now that he had her out here what could he do with her? She could not or would not talk. What could he ask her? *What did you learn in your lesson today?* He knew nothing of French or handwriting. *I hear that bananas make you sneeze.* No, that would not be romantic enough. He could not even think of a third remark.

Her face as she stood looking at him was soft and undisturbed. She was prepared to wait forever if necessary for him to make the next move.

"I have remembered our dance," he said abruptly. "I have wanted to dance with you again."

"Oh, yes," she breathed.

And they swayed together in the first steps of a soft waltz. He had even begun to hum when suddenly the beat changed—not one-two-three, but one-two, one-two. And when he opened his eyes again, he saw her face still unworried, her mouth forming a soft "Oh" of surprise, her ruffled bodice opened to show firm and delicate breasts, her skirt flung up, her pantaloons discarded, and her body crushed into those once pristine flowers.

"*Ay, Dios!*" he cried in a terrible voice. "What have I done? I have defiled a pure virgin. Father, forgive me."

Maria looked up at him and smiled. He tried to smile back. *Your mother really is going to kill me now,* he thought.

"My beloved," she said, "now I won't have to go to the convent."

And Raoul had the sudden realization that it was not he who had been doing the pursuing.

That same afternoon another couple in another car were also pursuing thoughts of love. Alessandro Mariné, gloved hands negligently on a brand-new Stutz Bear-Cat which he had bought with his own savings, tried, with what was for him totally uncharacteristic directness, to explain himself to the girl with whom he thought he might be in love.

"It is not enough to shower you with compliments. You are too fine and good for that. Though it may seem no great favor, I would like to try to express some feelings about myself that I have never before spoken to anyone or even tried to put into words."

Ruth looked at him puzzled. This was not the same young man who indeed *had* showered her with compliments, and made sure she woke up each morning with the gift of a single yellow rose, and a Latinate poem written in his own hand.

"From the time I first began to understand my position as the only son of my parents, I have lived in the shadow of the knowledge that one day I shall be responsible for all the vast holdings of the Mariné family. But from this shadow I have yearned always for the sunlight of freedom, of carefree delight." He glanced up into the sky. "The clouds. The air. The golden warmth. These are my real world. And though I know I must accept the burden to which I was born, before I take it up I want to be one with the wind." He broke off self-consciously and said, laughing, "Probably that's why I like to drive so fast. I hope I don't frighten you."

She'd said nothing up to now, but she was able to answer him frankly and without coquettishness. "I'm not afraid with you." She too was embarrassed. "I know a good driver when I see one."

He flashed her an enchanting smile. "Ah, that is what I loved about you from the beginning. You are not a shy señorita, you are a strong American girl. When I looked down and saw you at the motor rally I knew you were different from all the rest." He hesitated for a moment, thinking that he had gone too far. "Please forgive me. It's not that I think you are forward or in any way bold. You are in all respects a perfect lady."

A fleeting frown crossed his perfect brow. "My mother has told me often that you are—"

Ruth was bold enough to interrupt him. "It doesn't matter a jot or a tittle what your mother thinks," she said hotly, "as long as you and I are friends, Alessandro."

He glanced at her with renewed admiration. "Ah, my dear Ruth, that is what makes you . . . that is what makes you a part of what I've been trying to say. It's freedom. You are freedom to me. The air. The wind."

The car began to veer and Ruth tactfully suggested that he pull over.

"Now," she said, "you may finish your sentence."

"That is what makes you. . . ." But Alessandro fell silent.

His gloved hands held tightly to the wheel. Ruth's heart melted. Her golden eagle was unable to fly.

"Oh," she said. "Oh, Alessandro, I love you." And turning up her motoring veil, she leaned over and barely brushed his cheek with her lips.

"My dear Ruth," he muttered, "perhaps my mother was right. You *are* bold." Then, flushing fiercely, he looked at her from under his long lashes. "That is no way for my wife to behave. The Mariné name—"

But her squeals of delight drowned out the last of his sentence and he felt the brim of her straw hat crumple as his hands left the wheel.

Later that day Clifford Creighton relaxed in the seclusion of the library, easing himself with a glass of amontillado, snacking on a small dish of nuts. This had turned into a private ritual, a method of unwinding, a prelude to his being joined by Victoria and Ruth. He had grown to cherish these quiet moments. Consequently, he was surprised when, after a discreet knock, Porter Priest appeared in the doorway and said, "I'm sorry to disturb you, sir, but Señor Alessandro Mariné is here, and he wishes to see you."

"I take it, then, that Miss Creighton is at home, and we may expect dinner at a reasonable hour?"

Porter Priest answered this sally with a nod.

"Since there's no escape, you might as well show him in."

In a few moments, Clifford looked up to see Alessandro Mariné, sporting lacquered hair and a suit of vulgarly expensive checked tweed, nipped in at the waist and flared at the hip. His lapels were wide and "tipped" almost to the shoulder. His roguishly pointed shoes were fashioned from the skin of an unfortunate reptile, tied with tasseled laces. A new word had recently sprung up to describe this—what Clifford hated to acknowledge as—*dress:* lounge lizard.

Clifford had to suppress all of his Baltimore instincts to say in a neutral tone, "Do come in, Alessandro, and sit down. Let me offer you some sherry."

But Alessandro, as he glided across the room into an armchair, exclaimed, "Thank you, no! I have no need of spirits! I am intoxicated with the liquor of love!"

Clifford, who had been mesmerized by the play of light on Alessandro's shoes, was not attending. "Do sit down," he murmured, although Alessandro had already done so. As the boy crossed his legs, Clifford saw with horror that someone had polished the soles of those shoes.

"Ah, sir, today I feel as if all the elements in the universe have converged and conspired to make me a happy man!"

"Are you sure you won't accept a drink?"

Alessandro sprang from his chair. "I tell you, sir, I have no need of stimulation, other than that which comes from the heart." He paused for effect. "My heart is bursting with love. Today"—here he knelt and clasped his manicured fingers over his left lapel—"today your daughter has lifted me above the dreary and trivial fate of mortal man. She has made me a demigod."

Clifford, looking with fastidious disgust at this florid performance, had time to think that with his incipient, patchy moustache, Alessandro looked more like a half-grown, begging hound than one of the immortals—but even as he formed this thought he was overwhelmed by a surge of rage.

"What did you say?" he muttered thickly. "You were speaking of Miss Creighton? You were speaking of *my daughter*?"

Alessandro leaped to his feet with unnerving speed. "You are the father of a most pure angel. And so it is that today I have the honor, sir, of asking for your daughter's hand."

Something in Clifford's complexion, an apoplectic flush as the older man emptied his glass, made Alessandro continue, with more than a touch of hauteur. "I need hardly remind you, sir, that our family has been here for twelve generations . . . as you well know, I am heir to all the plains and fertile orchards, the timber and the oil, the cattle and the vineyards, all the vast holdings of those ancient lands deeded to us by the King himself—all the land which makes up the estate of the family of Don Ortega de Moreno de Arrellanos de Mariné."

"Of course we're flattered," Clifford Creighton said with heavy sarcasm, "but there are many difficulties that would make a match like this impossible. The matter of religion is one—"

"Oh, señor! You are a man of great acuteness, to put your mind and heart so quickly on the one barrier that stands in the way of the union of your daughter to my heart. Of course my family would expect any woman who was to be my wife to be a good and dutiful Catholic, to regard marriage as the sacrament it is, and to raise our children in the true faith of Mother Church. It will mean instruction and much diligent study. But I have faith in the natural piety and good intentions of my Ruth—"

Clifford said, in the tones of his long-deceased uncle, "Of course you understand, I shall have to discuss all this with Mrs. Creighton." Here he pulled his watch from his vest pocket. "I'm sure you will agree that such delicate questions as these are best taken up within the, ah, bosom of the family—"

"Ah, *muy simpático,* señor! You are a man of true feeling! I will say farewell now, knowing that you and the mother of my beloved will be planning our future lives with parental love and consideration."

Clifford saw him to the front door himself and bolted it securely behind him. He waited until he had heard the wheels of the Stutz kick up the gravel of the driveway before he turned in the empty entry hall and shouted, "Priest! Priest! I need you here this minute!"

And barely one second later, too impatient to wait, he began calling, "Victoria! Victoria! Ruth!" He kept on shouting, punctuating his shouts with the pounding of an umbrella that he had picked up from the stand, and with which he pounded a tattoo on the polished floor until Victoria appeared on the upper landing, with Ruth close behind.

"What in the world, Cliff—"

"I will see you both in the library *immediately.*"

Porter Priest, who had appeared at almost the same moment as the ladies, saw that he would not be needed, and withdrew to the kitchen where he would spend the next hour comforting Pansy as they heard alternately raised voices and ominous silences, suffering through the sounds of the worst row in their twenty years of service in the Creighton household.

"Oh, Daddy—"

"I don't want to hear one word from you!"

"I'm the happiest woman in the world and nothing you can say will change that."

"You dimwit," her father said contemptuously.

"Clifford!"

"Don't take that tone with me! The responsibility for all this falls squarely on you and you alone."

"Cliff, calm yourself and tell me. What are you talking about?"

"That, that, that *lounge lizard* has been in my library asking—"

"Oh, Daddy," and Ruth began to sob.

"Asking—" He looked at Victoria and started again. "The supreme effrontery, the impudence, the insolence. You would not believe the assumptions that were made just fifteen minutes ago right here in this room."

Meanwhile Ruth sobbed a brokenhearted burden to his refrain. "So brave, so kind, so pure, so spiritual. To think that a man of his caliber should have been insulted in such a manner in my own home."

Clifford briefly turned his attention to his daughter. "Do you think I would give him the satisfaction of insulting him? He wouldn't know an insult if it hit him on the head. A person of his upbringing is unable to make those distinctions."

Ruth in unconscious parody of what had happened earlier rushed to her mother and knelt flamboyantly on one knee.

"Mama, Mama," she wailed, plucking at her mother's belt. "My life has been ruined. I can never hold my head up again. I am so ashamed. I will die an old maid and all because of him."

Clifford's voice came honing in, hitting a note that made Victoria wince. "The shoes, Victoria, they looked like ham ten days past its prime—orange turning to green. And the responsibility for this is absolutely clear in this case. *You* are responsible."

Ruth screamed as though she'd been shot. In the kitchen, Pansy hid her head in a dishtowel and Porter reached for the gin. Victoria meticulously unfastened her daughter's damp fingers from her belt.

"Go to your room, Ruth. Your father and I have something to settle."

Ruth took a deep breath, straightened up and flounced to the door, the very picture of girlish dignity. Something about this enraged her father.

" '*My* Ruth.' Perhaps you will be good enough to explain to me why that lizard in his peaked tweed lapels takes to himself the right to refer to you as '*my*'—"

But his tirade was cut short by the slam of the door.

Now that the two of them were alone Clifford appeared to come to his senses, at least partially. Still it was evident that he considered himself a man grossly abused.

"If I had known on that day when the Señora and that whippersnapper came to call, that you would let things get so out of hand . . . no, I insist, Victoria, listen to me. Don't turn away. I have objected all along. I have objected to her going about in this city without a chaperone. I have objected to her hoydenish ways. And you do remember, Victoria, that I seriously objected to the idea of a girl driving at all hours in her own *Poopsy* without adequate supervision, and it turns out I was right." Here a note of real hurt came into his voice. "My own daughter has turned against me and I, I cannot but hold you responsible."

Victoria walked with easy grace to the low table where Priest had placed the sherry. She poured herself a drink, conspicuously leaving her husband's glass empty, downed her sherry in one long smooth swallow, and faced Clifford with an enigmatic smile.

"This is the man who came across the country to escape stifling conventions? How could you have let this happen to you? How could the man I married turn so stuffy? Cliff, you sound like a Pasadenan."

"It breaks my heart to think of my daughter marrying a man like that."

"He's not so bad."

Then came a golden moment, one of the rewards of the intimacies of a long marriage. Each could read the other's thoughts, and each knew that the other had begun to savor the high comedy into which this match would lead them.

They began to laugh together.

"It's not just a question of his shoes. Or the way he twiddles with his moustache. Or the way he pours down *our* champagne . . . or even the question of children, and that absurd religion. . . . A marriage between Ruth and Alessandro could *mean,* Victoria, *Christmas dinner with the Señora* every year for the rest of our lives!"

"Ruth does love him, Clifford. And there's something else. It's not as though every eligible bachelor in Pasadena has been knocking on our door."

"Do you think Alessandro will be offended if I send him to my tailor?"

She thought for a moment and then said, "Would you be offended if he sent you to his?"

An air of confused foreboding had suffused the house of Katarina and her children in the eight days since Sung had been gone. In the mornings the children who were old enough left for school, but rather than racketing about the streets as they usually did, filching lichee nuts from the irate Chinese merchants and terrorizing the neighborhood with their noisy games, they walked home promptly to sit in the kitchen with their mother and the babies, counting away the hours in apprehension, anxiety, and an ever-increasing sense of impending doom. Katarina had killed a chicken, had flung its bones, blood and feathers into the dust of the backyard, and scrutinized it carefully for over an hour. When she came back into the kitchen, her face was set in a grim mask. The children dared not ask what she had found there.

Each day more news of the devastating earthquake in the city to the north had filtered down to Chinatown. Whole families had been swallowed up. Whole businesses had been destroyed in the great fire that was still burning. Each day new families, dressed in white, formed impromptu processions to memorial services. There was no need of professional mourners; everyone in town had someone to mourn.

And still they had not heard. Each morning, as they came home from school, the older children picked up a copy of the *Los Angeles Times* and brought it home. Their mother could not read a word in any language, but they did well in reading, and were able, the two oldest, to sound out the grisly reports, though this was next to getting no news at all, since neither Katarina nor her children could understand the true meaning of the words they read.

Now, in the spring twilight, Katarina energetically wielded her cleaver. Tonight they were having *piroji,* and carrots. The two older boys, Thadius and Stanislav—Thad and Stan—spread the crumpled newspaper out on the oilcloth of the kitchen table, and laboriously spelled out today's account:

> Fiends incarnate made a hellbroth of the center of the ruined district last night. Rapine and vice, assault, robbery and desecration of the dead were included in unspeakable horrors. There was short shrift for at least a score of these bestial wretches. This morning they lay stinking in the streets with bullet holes or bayonet thrusts through their vitals.

211

"Ma! Ma! What does it mean?" one of the little children asked. "When is Daddy coming back to us?"

"It does not sound good," Katarina said. "But your papa—he will come back."

"It says here they're giving out sewing machines to the women. Why is that, Ma?"

"What's a sewing machine, Ma?"

Katarina ignored their prattle. Her lips were moving, as they had been so often this week. She was praying in the language of her ancestors.

Perhaps because they were making so little noise, they heard the sound of footsteps up the driveway. Then they saw the apparition of Sung, stooped and trembling, his hands protectively holding the shoulders of the sole survivor of his Chinese family, George.

They stood in awful silence. Katarina rushed forward and with her strong arms pushed and pulled Sung over to the table. She scurried about finding a clean glass, unearthing a bottle of strong *rakia,* plum brandy, which in her village had been the sovereign, and only, remedy against tragedy.

"She tempted the gods," Sung said, half in English, half in Chinese. "I knew this would happen. She was a poor foolish girl. I have seen my children into the earth. Half of my hope is gone. But it is worse, much worse for him." Sung gestured wearily to the Chinese boy who was sitting now in one of the kitchen chairs, staring straight ahead of him. One by one Katarina's children edged up to George, some offering a toy, or a look at a favorite book, or asking a shy question: "Was it really awful?" "Did it hurt a lot?" The boy did not answer.

Some of the younger children began to cry. Although Katarina and Lin had gone eleven years and scarcely spoken a word to each other, this lack of communication had not extended to their children. All sixteen of them had had the freedom of both houses; though they tended to gather at Katarina's for their rowdier games, there was not one of them who had not received a sweetmeat from Lin's hands, or a kind word and gentle caress. Each one of them had lost a second mother; each one had lost a special playmate, a special friend.

Still George stared bright-eyed and emotionless. Sung pointed with his chin at his oldest son and said, as he downed another glass of the potent liquid, "That one has not spoken since the day I found him. He has helped me bury his mother and all his brothers and sisters. His heart has turned to stone. He . . ."

Little Dyna, whom George had always indulged with special attention, was standing in front of him now, her golden ringlets at a level with his unkempt raven locks. With her tiny hand she patted his forehead. "Do you feel bad? Don't feel bad. We love you, Georgie. Do you want to play now? Won't you give me a piggyback ride? *Please?"*

Somewhat daunted, Dyna turned to her mother. "Georgie won't play. He feels sad. Play carrot for him, Ma. Make him laugh. Please." Her lower lip trembled.

Katarina had been listening to this, seeing all of it with intelligent eyes, her own hand pressed to her brow. None of them—the wild Tex-as cowboys, the diminutive handsome man she called Wosbon, her children, the merchants with whom she joked—had ever thought to ask her about her own childhood. And she herself had done her best to cancel out her memories. To live in this world without going insane, it was absolutely necessary to forget the past, to live for the pleasures of the present. By the time she was ten she had known that the only defense was a shout and a laugh.

Her family had lived in a cave. She'd been sold at the age of ten to pay for her brother's funeral. She had worked for the town slaughterer, where she subsisted on offal and slept in the sty with the pigs. Then, when the father of that family had sneaked out to her with thoughts in his mind as swinish as his own beasts, she had broken some of his ribs with a stone and set off into the night. She had lived as an animal. She had been traded and traded again, part of vast immigrant hordes. In truth, she had no understanding of how she had gotten to this country. What she did understand was the nature of suffering.

Now all the pain she had felt was unleashed again within her. She could deal with her own pain, and even Sung's. But it made her almost frantic to see the little boy.

"Please, Ma! Make him laugh!" Dyna ran to the chopping block and brought back two carrot slices. Katarina looked at Sung. He shrugged hopelessly. She sighed and screwed the slices into her eyes. The kids gathered around George, laughing artificially. "See Ma's glasses? Look at the carrot lady! See her funny glasses?"

George glanced at the madwoman with flying white hair and great yellow eyes. He shuddered horribly, then put his head down on the table and began to cry.

In an instant, Katarina went to the boy. She picked him up as if he were an infant. She held him while he wept, hiding his face in her blouse.

"You know what we do tonight?" she said to the rest of the room. "We have Chinese dinner. Thad, you take some brothers to Lin's house. Bring back Chinese food, bring back cook. Ask him nice now! Be good boy! Bring back chopsticks. We eat with chopsticks tonight."

The older ones bolted out the door. The younger children crowded in against George and their mother.

Katarina, her eyes tormented, spoke. "Don't worry, baby. Katarina take care of you now. You be my boy now."

The boy said nothing, but he held on tight.

Magdalena spent this April afternoon in the kind of household project she loved best. A large Cecil Brunner rose trailed across the sagging picket fence that encircled her enormous backyard. Each winter she pruned it severely, and in these early days of spring she spent several hours a week carefully training the tendrils to make a solid mass of tiny pink roses, snipping some of the most luxuriant branches and bringing them in to decorate her table. Here everything was freshness, domestic order, and calm. Only one thing this afternoon made Magdalena distinctly uneasy. Today she had a helper. Her son, Raoul, was not with his friends. Instead, he stood next to her, pensively poking the tender new shoots in and out through the picket fence. Grateful as she was for this assistance, at the same time it made her apprehensive. It was a fact of her life that Raoul was never considerate unless he needed something. She kept silent, knowing the bad news was bound to come sooner or later, but it was a full hour before her son groaned audibly and said, "Mama, I think I am in trouble."

She plucked a withered rose or two before she answered.

"How much will it cost me now?"

"Money won't help me," he sighed.

"Are you sick, boy? Have you killed someone? Are you in trouble with the law?"

"It is much worse than any of those."

"How can that be?"

"I met a girl."

"Is she in trouble?"

"No, that's not it. It's worse than that."

"What could be worse than that?"

"Promise me you won't laugh. I'm in love."

His mother looked at him in disbelief. "My son, how can you know the meaning of the word love? You have never given a single thought to anyone but yourself."

"That is why it is so bad—for now I can think of no one but Maria."

"Maria. Maria who?"

"Maria Consuelo Gloria Madonna Arellanos de Mariné y Ruiz. I met her at the *paseo*. I followed her and her mother out to their adobe. I hired the best *mariachis* in town to serenade her. I went to Confession five times in one week just so I could be near her at prayers. Mama, this time I won't lie to you. I thought when I met her, here's a rich girl—maybe I can take advantage of her. I don't know what I thought. All I know is now I think of nothing else but Maria."

"But my son," his mother said softly, "the Marinés—are they not an old and famous family?"

"Yes," Raoul said. "Her family has already forbidden me to enter their house. Her brother has dismissed me like a common peon."

Magdalena searched in her heart for the right thing to say to her troubled, headstrong boy. "To love and have your love unrequited—that is not the worst thing in the world."

"*Ay, Dios,* Mama! I am in pain. What could be worse?"

Then, later that day, after he had traveled out to the Mission, after he had sat again through a rosary and the Stations of the Cross, after he had spirited away his beautiful young Maria, after he had spent his impetuous, male passion on her yielding but impassive body, she softly told him something that made his earlier pain seem as nothing—a child's dream. What she told him now made his mother's earlier phrase seem the cruel prophecy of an all-knowing female devil. Listening to Maria in that sylvan grove, his blood ran cold. Maria, wreathed in smiles, told him that he was to be a father.

"My child, we believe, just as you do, that there is only one God, in three divine persons."

214

Ruth nodded happily. With her right had she squeezed her fiancé's arm, while her left went automatically to the large gold crucifix that had been an engagement present from the Señora, and that she wore always, to the obvious irritation of her father.

"We are accustomed to make the sign of the cross, not as a pagan ritual as you may have been told by the ignorant, but as an outward sign of the mystery of the Trinity."

Ruth had trouble learning this gesture. "I've always had trouble with my left and my right," she giggled. Alessandro had his arms around his beloved's waist, holding her right hand with his own, repeating, "The Father, the Son and the Holy Ghost," while Father Clement beamed upon the happy pair, when the door to the priest's study opened.

Alessandro gaped and dropped Ruth's hands. His sister Maria stood, strangely triumphant, strangely mature. Behind her—that boy, that young man from the city, who had invaded the sanctity of their adobe.

"Father," Maria said softly, ignoring her brother and Ruth, "Raoul and I, we need to speak to you at your convenience."

The room was suddenly much too small for the five of them. Ruth spoke up clearly. "Thank you so much for the instruction, Father. Shall we see you tomorrow at the same time?" She took Alessandro's arm and firmly guided him to the door. "My dear, I believe your mother is waiting for us with tea."

It took only a few words from Maria to confirm Father Clement's suspicions. Since he was a kind man he wasted few words in recrimination. "At least you are in the church, young man. And it takes courage to admit one's wrongdoing." If he harbored any thoughts of this relative stranger as a fortune hunter he refrained from mentioning it. "God will forgive you both," he said, "in His own time. And you, my child," he said to Maria, "your penance will be the carrying of your child and the suffering of its birth."

He raised his eyebrows as he turned to Raoul. "Your penance, young man, in its own way, will be even more severe. Because you must be the one to inform the Señora and ask for her daughter's hand."

By the time Maria and Raoul arrived, the reception committee had already convened. The Señora sat straight as a rod of iron on a carved wooden chair that resembled the throne of an ancient Moorish queen. Somehow she had managed to swirl her skirts out to a diameter of five feet on either side. She presided over a tea table on which rested a small fortune in highly polished silver. These heavy pieces were used by the family only on feast days and the church's eight Holy Days of Obligation.

Ruth sat opposite the Señora, her eyes cast down in girlish horror. Alessandro lounged dangerously against the mantelpiece, one aristocratic hand nervously fingering a heavy figurine, one snakeskin boot resting on the fender.

Maria instinctively moved in front of Raoul to shield him from her family's wrath.

"Mama," she said tremulously, one hand over her heart as if to still its frantic beating, "may I have the honor to present to you Señor Raoul . . ."

215

—she hesitated as if to prepare for the recitation of all his Christian names, and then realizing, perhaps for the first time, that he had none, finished up lamely—"Ortiz. I believe you will remember him from one night last month—"

Alessandro sprang into action. "You, sir," he said, folding his arms and stepping forward, "I believe you have not been invited to this house."

In a choked voice, Raoul addressed the Señora. "Oh, beautiful mother, your daughter has this day consented to give me her hand in marriage."

"Churlish upstart," said Alessandro, "you were told never to set foot on the land of the Marinés again."

"I will make your daughter a good husband." Then, with a glance at Ruth, Raoul added in Spanish, "It is best that we get married."

The Señora watched her son as he reached up to wrench free one of the crossed ancestral cavalry sabers fixed above the fireplace. As he wrestled with it, the Señora considered the meaning of the intruder's words, putting them together with her daughter's previously unaccountable behavior of the last three weeks—her long absences at the Mission, her recent early morning lassitude.

"A million thanks for having brought this upon our family," she said bitterly to her daughter. As Alessandro pranced across the room in the galloping sidestep he had learned in his fencing lessons, grasping the sword as if it were an *épée,* the Señora clapped her hands as if bringing unruly servants to order.

"You put this very delicately, Señor Ortiz. Naturally, I give my consent." Turning to her daughter, she said, "The wedding will take place as soon as the banns are posted. I will not be able to give you my wedding gown." Here she patted her own slim waist so emphatically that the jet beads on her black costume were set ajingle. "I am afraid," she said, "that it might not *fit.*" Then she turned to Alessandro, who had maintained his *en garde* position. "And you," she said in tones of the deepest disgust, "guardian of the family honor, you can put away your sword, *lagartijo!*"

But it wasn't long before the Señora relented. There would be a double wedding, she declared to all. The ceremony would take place at the Mission and a reception would follow at the Mariné adobe. And that was that!

Clifford, who had just barely regained his calm, had never heard of anything so outrageous in all his life. "It's bad enough that they're being married in the Mission and Ruth has swallowed all that mumbo jumbo, but what will all our friends think when they find themselves invited to the wedding of our daughter by the mother of the *groom*?"

Victoria, in her own reserved way, also resented being displaced. More than once in her own mind she had planned her daughter's wedding, putting to full use the two terraces, a chamber orchestra, and the tennis court as a dance floor. She had chosen the caterers; and the cases of champagne had long been stored in the coolest corner of the cellar.

Ruth too was miffed. Her vision of being the beautiful bride, the center of attention, had been shattered by the Señora's peremptory announcement.

During all the hours of her instruction by Father Clement she had fused—and she hoped it was not blasphemous—the image of herself with that of the Virgin Mother, both of them in some way caressed by cloudlike swirls of white. And now she would have to share this with Maria, who, though Ruth hated to admit it to herself, was more beautiful than she. And despite her appearance, Maria was nothing more than a trollop. Although Ruth did not presume to understand everything that had been said that day in the Mariné drawing room, with Alessandro so bravely defending the honor of his family, she could guess at the implications. It was a tribute to her upbringing that she never voiced her complaint or told anyone what she suspected, but satisfied herself by firmly clutching her crucifix.

Raoul felt scorned, and the shame he had lived with since grade school had once again surfaced. After a few attempts at self-assertion during which he pointed out that he would be by no means a poor, poverty-stricken relative and that he could, as was the custom in Mexico, pay for the wedding, he had given up in the face of the Señora's refusal to acknowledge him. Nevertheless, he nursed a kind of secret pride that none of this would have happened if he had not been so bold.

Magdalena willingly allowed herself to be excluded from the wedding plans. On the one hand, she knew that she could bring only further embarrassment to her son. On the other, she knew she could not present herself to these two extremes of society. She was as far from Spanish land-grant aristocracy as she was from the complacent members of the Presbyterian Church. More than that, she was honor bound by a personal oath of which only two others in the wedding party were aware. For twenty-one years she had scrupulously observed Victoria Creighton's decree that she and Clifford were not to see or speak to each other. Even when Magdalena had sent Clifford that message, even when Clifford had so generously repaid her with what turned out to be a small fortune, even then both of them had kept their word. Although rumors in the city had persisted that she and Clifford were still lovers, participating in the wedding would mean seeing with her own eyes a happiness that would never be hers.

The only ones who seemed genuinely pleased were the Marinés. For Maria, everything had turned out as she wanted. For Alessandro, this was the culmination of one adventure and the outset of what he knew would be an even greater, more enchanting one. And for the Señora, the more she schemed the more elaborate and complex her plans became. The last parties she had given were the baptismal teas for her own two children. And now she decided this would be the party of the century. She had never forgotten that afternoon at the Logan-Fishers' *estancia* when Clifford and Victoria had gotten married. It crossed her mind now that their wedding even had been staged with some haste. Although she would never admit it, the Señora was determined to outdo that day, already a legend in county society, at any cost.

For this reason the Señora graciously accepted Señor Creighton's suggestion that two sets of invitations and announcements be sent: one, in the traditional Spanish manner listing everyone's titles and immediate ancestry, the other in the most conservative Protestant style. The Señora also graciously condescended to accept the twenty cases of champagne laid down years before by Clifford Creighton. She also permitted Victoria, out of her superior knowledge of the curious ways of Anglo society, to advise her on various details, such as the catering, choice of music, and floral arrangements.

The Señora herself was not totally idle. She supervised the refurbishment of the family domain. Rooms were opened and aired. New draperies were ordered. The gardens of the various courtyards were pruned and, where necessary, replanted. Two or three of the farther courtyards were put back into use. The Señora was determined that her guests would see the full glory of the Marinés. And, as the great day approached, even the huge wisteria seemed to respond by putting out a profusion of budded lavender clusters, giving softness and tender color to the very center of the adobe.

Magdalena and her son had exchanged few words since the announcement of the betrothal. All these words had ended in the same argument, with Raoul insisting that Magdalena must come to the wedding, Magdalena declaring that she would not. But today when he spoke to her he declared, "I'm not leaving this room until this is settled."

Once again, he had insisted that she attend the wedding. Once again, she had refused.

"I have reasons of my own," she said.

"And I too have my reasons," Raoul replied.

She tried a veiled truth. "I would not want to shame you."

"Shame!" he exclaimed. "Maria and Alessandro's mother will be there. Ruth Creighton's mother and father will be there. Would you have me look like an orphan? I know I haven't been the best son, but you have been my mother. We aren't penniless. You're certainly as beautiful as Señora Mariné or Ruth's mother. Who are they to look down on us?"

"You do not know of what you speak."

"That may be true. I know I have asked you for many things in the past. But if you'll do this one thing for me now, I'll never ask for anything again."

Something in his voice told Magdalena that he was as sincere as he could be.

"If I have to get married, you have to come."

She nodded her consent.

The following week she overcame her inhibitions and went to the best dressmaker in the city, who by a turn of luck had already been engaged by the Creightons. Magdalena ordered a dress that was complementary to Victoria's in elegance, taste, and color. She rejected the traditional picture hat that accompanied Victoria's costume, knowing that her own still-black hair, piled high and decorated with a tortoiseshell comb and mantilla, would not only be more appropriate to her own style of beauty, but would not compete with at least one mother of the bride.

The Señora, after many an innuendo, had brought down her own wedding dress from where it had been packed away with other family treasures. It was plainly worth a fortune in seed pearls and flounces. When María showed it to Ruth, the American girl nodded politely, went home, and burst into tears.

"Oh, Mother, what can I do? She's so beautiful! Her dress is so beautiful! And my dress is so ugly."

Victoria considered. Ruth had already been to her second fitting and the dress was paid for. But she could understand her daughter's point of view. Somehow the traditional flounces on her daughter's rangy frame contrived to make her look attractive at best, but not as radiant as any bride had a right to be on her wedding day. Without hesitating, Victoria took her daughter back to the dressmaker. Ruth was an exceptional girl and deserved a second, truly exceptional dress. The dressmaker leaped at this chance to display his ingenuity.

Since he had lately returned from a trip to all the capitals of South America, he devised a "Latin salute" for Ruth—a gown trim in its dimensions, "sporting," where María's was smothered in tiers. Over the deceptively plain shirtwaist he devised a cunning bolero, stiff with seed pearls and marcasite. Instead of the traditional band about the head to hold the veil, he suggested a charming version of the hat of the Argentinian gauchos, from which the veil would flow to a length of twenty feet. To Victoria's delighted and appreciative eyes, this costume recalled Ruth at her most vivid—on those Saturday mornings when she donned her fashionable motoring clothes to sally forth in Poopsy.

"Mr. Barnett," Victoria announced, "I believe you are a genius." And Peter Barnett, who by this time held in his mind the carefully kept secrets of half the guests who would be attending this wedding, answered, "I believe, Madame, that your daughter will now be the more beautiful bride, or at the very least, she and the other one will finish in a dead heat."

After a scant month of feverish plans, the second Sunday after Easter arrived. From early morning hundreds of families began their preparations, and by eleven o'clock the Mission was packed to the aisles, with latecomers lining the walls.

In the melee, the deacon in charge beckoned for the mothers, each accompanied by an usher. Magdalena came first, dressed in the most delicate lavender chiffon and her lace mantilla. She walked with her head held high, aware of the whispers as she proceeded down the aisle. Victoria followed, wearing traditional ecru lace and a picture hat decorated with fresh flowers. To make her own entrance even more dramatic, the Señora waited a good two minutes until after the other mothers were seated before she presented herself. Echoing her own daughter's gown, the Señora wore twenty-five yards of pearl gray arranged in six overlapping tiers.

The extensive bridal party packed into the vestibule, twenty bridesmaids giggling in two languages. All of them, especially Ruth's friends, had enthusiastically embraced the Spanish theme: They tossed their mantillas, carried small fans instead of prayer books, and finally at a frantic signal from a harassed deacon, paced together, two by two, down the long aisle.

Then it was time for the brides. Stepping in time to solemn liturgical music, Maria, radiant if pale, was led down the aisle by an elderly uncle. If sighs greeted her entrance, Ruth's appearance, striding beside Clifford Creighton, was heralded by gasps. Victoria's gamble had paid off. Ruth, for the first and only time in her life, was fairest of them all.

The nuptial mass was interminable, and Clifford was heard to groan audibly more than once as he went from his haunches to his knees to a standing position and back. When it was time to entwine the twin, enormous gardenia rosaries about the happy couples, Headsperth Bauer bleated, "What pagan ritual is *this*, Belle?" And was hissed into silence by several irate Spaniards. As the two brides moved to the statue of Our Lady, Queen of Angels, to consecrate their virginity, a muted chorus of Spanish matrons murmured their skeptical comments, and the few who had not known or guessed of Maria's condition—knew now.

No matter! They were married. The four young people came back down the aisle; the onlookers who had jammed the Mission, or sat in the blazing sun outside on folding chairs, ambled in a bemused manner to the adobe.

Alone in swirls of humanity, Magdalena strove to look more at home than she actually felt. Here in the main courtyard, the receiving line had finally broken up, and gallant men were springing to the buffets to procure refreshments for their ladies. But no one sprinted for Magdalena. She picked up a glass from one of the family servants circulating with a tray, and looked around for someone to speak to. The closest person to her, regarding her over the filigree of an ivory fan, was the Señora Mariné.

"You have made this memorable day even more lovely by your hospitality," Magdalena ventured.

The Señora looked through her, turned with a flick of her fringe, and moved away.

The circle of guests who were near them had watched this exchange. They moved back from Magdalena as though she carried an infectious disease.

Victoria and Clifford Creighton were among those who saw this, and Victoria felt Clifford's arm tense under her fingers. There was nothing he could do. Victoria moved swiftly.

"Magdalena, how wonderful to see you after all these years, and on such a joyous occasion."

"You do not need, Mrs. Creighton, to concern yourself with me."

"Tell me, Magdalena, have you thought of that other wedding day?"

"How could I not?"

"To think that brave little survivor would grow up to be such a handsome young man." Then Victoria said more seriously, "We can only wish the same good fortune for them as all of us have found."

By this time they had strolled to the buffet. To the guests who had been straining to hear this exchange, all traces of scandal were missing. Here were two handsomely gowned women, indulging in pleasantries appropriate to the day.

The Señora, miffed at no longer being the center of attention, sashayed as conspicuously as possible across the courtyard. Neither woman made the slightest effort to greet her. The Señora was forced to remark, "I think you will like the mushrooms *en croûte*."

Victoria, ignoring this, held more firmly to Magdalena's arm. "Señora Mariné, I know that you and Señora Ortiz have already met, and indeed are now related by marriage, but are you aware that we are old family friends? Magdalena and I spent hard days together in the epidemic of eighty-five. I have never seen such physical courage."

"Señora Creighton," Magdalena responded, smiling, "do you never look in a mirror?"

The Señora Mariné paled under her rouge. "I had no idea," she stammered.

"I thought as much," Victoria snapped. "But now that you *do* know, you might introduce Señora Ortiz to some of your guests, since she is the mother of your son-in-law."

Victoria sailed into the crowd, and the two women were left alone. Their awkward silence was broken by Belle and Headsperth Bauer, who were loading their plates with venison, smoked salmon, *oeufs Toulonnaise,* and various salads. "Thank God for civilized food," Headsperth grunted to his wife. "That Mexican slop always looks as if it's been eaten once before, ah ha ha ha!"

Magdalena and the Señora exchanged sidelong glances.

Magdalena broke the silence. "Shouldn't we speak directly? I know that you don't approve of your daughter's marriage to my son. Speaking as a mother, I must tell you I don't see this as the perfect match either. Raoul is a complicated boy. He is ashamed of his heritage—though it is possible his father's name might rival yours in Espagna. Raoul is not my son, Señora. He is a foundling. But I, *I* am proud of my heritage."

Magdalena held her glass high. "I am Maria Magdalena Ortiz, of the miserable town of Sonoita, and I walked twelve hundred miles to get here, *alone.*" She tossed off the champagne.

"I admire your frankness," Señora Mariné responded. "And one truth, *espero,* deserves another." She leaned forward, concealing her face with her fan, and whispered in Magdalena's ear. The guests looked with astonishment as the two great ladies staggered with laughter. Their astonishment would have been even greater had they heard the Señora's whispered words: "I was not always Spanish, *amiga,* and I was certainly not always the Señora."

A group of musicians, ordered especially by Raoul, made their way into the courtyard and began to tune their primitive instruments. They were the *mariachi,* from that first fabulous night in the courtyard. "There will be dancing," the Señora Mariné said. "*Our* kind. Will you be dancing, Magdalena?"

"There is no one to dance with. And I have not danced for years."

"All the more reason to dance now. After all, consider it. Your duty as a mother is finished." The Señora ran her practiced eye over the crowd. "Ah, I have it! The perfect partner for you. He is a *gringo,* but I think he must know the music. He lived in Mexico for many years. And he is very handsome, *también.*"

The Señora Mariné linked arms with Magdalena and moved toward the far corner of the courtyard, where a group of men and women were admiring the great, gnarled trunk of the wisteria vine, and singled out a man of some years. He was lined but handsome, dressed in a suit of immaculate white linen, a yellow silk scarf tied in a loose bow, his thick silver hair brushed back from his deeply tanned forehead.

"Señora Ortiz, allow me to present Señor John Frederick Smith. He is an American, but he speaks Spanish like one of our own. And Juan Frederico, of course you know that since this morning, Magdalena and I belong to the same family." With that the Señora Mariné withdrew.

"I'm delighted, señora."

"Señor Smith? Señor *John Frederick Smith?*"

"I beg your pardon?"

"Am I mistaken, or do you own all the land from here to Caborca?"

He laughed modestly. "I do have a little spread down there, but I haven't lived in Mexico for years. But how did you know that? Do I . . . are we acquainted, señora?"

"Yes. We are acquainted."

For an eternity, the wealthy rancher gazed at this extraordinarily handsome woman. "I am sure," he said, "I am sure I would never forget you."

"The house is big, and has a veranda on four sides. Luz works in the kitchen. The children have no one to play with. Often they aren't allowed in the house. But their father is kind, and brings them a poor girl from the worst shack in Sonoita—"

"It can't be," he interrupted hoarsely. "That girl—"

"She loved those children as her own, but she loved their father more."

"She died! Her father told me—"

"When she found she was with child she ran away. I—the child was born dead in the desert, Juan Frederico. But I lived to see you again."

The musicians had begun one of the old tunes, the harsh, cheerful strains of "El Gavilan." It spoke of miles of desert sand, and tiny shacks, no food— nothing but the will to live and the will to dance.

In a corner Alessandro and Ruth gingerly took up the beat, trying to match their steps. Raoul and Maria held the center of the courtyard, dancing the ancient story of the song in which the rapacious chicken hawk goes after the chicken, and the chicken is a more than willing partner.

Magdalena and the love of her life stood in the shade of the wisteria, not dancing, their bodies only faintly mimicking the motion of the dance. Tears streamed down both their faces. Only at the tumultuous end, when "the hawk devours the chicken," did Don Juan Frederico move and tenderly bury his lips in the crook of Magdalena's neck.

BOOK IV

1918

The lotus seeds are green like the lake-water.
She gathers the flowers and puts them into her gown—
The lotus-bud that is red all through.
She thinks of her lover, her lover that does not come:
She looks up and sees the wild geese flying—
The Western Island is full of wild geese.
To look for her lover she climbs the Blue Tower.
The tower is high: she looks but cannot see:
All day she leans on the balcony rails.

*Ballad of the Western Island
in the North Country*
Translated by Arthur Waley

$\mathcal{T}$HE world shook and Southern California quivered in response. For two years, across a vast continent and an equally vast sea, armies had clashed. The only visible manifestation in Los Angeles had been a steady comforting rise in the price of oil. But now the very civilization of which Pasadena felt itself a representative appeared threatened. President Wilson, reelected for keeping the country out of war, had suddenly made a complete about-face. The leading social figures of both Pasadena and Los Angeles felt the need to pay more than lip service to what for so long had been simply a word to them—democracy.

On a crowded station platform in January 1918, members of the Women's Auxiliary Service gathered in the crispness of a clear California dawn to hand out coffee and doughnuts to another shipment of "our boys." The naive patriotism of June 5, 1917, the "day of registration," when ten million eligible young American men had signed up in just under twelve hours, had ebbed but little. Enthusiasm was still high, perhaps because the great waves of dead and wounded had not burst back upon American shores. There was a sense of gaming, of playing war and playing soldier. If in the East they were suffering a record-breaking cold spell, and *Life* magazine was satirizing wartime austerities—

> I can not thank you for your bread,
> because there wasn't any,
> Nor any butter, either, though
> Its substitutes were many. . . .

—life in sunny, sumptuous California went on much as usual. Victoria had contented herself during this holiday season with a thirty-pound turkey instead of the usual dozen Christmas geese stuffed with cherries and truffles.

It was all a pageant, but some people took the drama seriously. Alessan-

225

ro Mariné was one of these. After a dozen years, during which he and Ruth had settled into a routine of easy, pleasant living, he found himself stimulated by the idealism of the distant conflict. Over the protests of both his wife and his mother, he had insisted on volunteering, even though at thirty-seven he was exempt from the draft.

During all this time Ruth and Alessandro had been childless. The doctors had been at a loss to explain the infertility of Ruth Mariné, except to suggest lamely that it echoed the same mysterious complaint that had kept Victoria childless ever since she had given birth to Ruth. (The only other explanation expressed in mere hints and innuendos was that it might have been Señor Mariné who was lacking, but this no one, least of all Ruth, was prepared to believe.) However it was, Ruth knew that it had been June 5, 1917, on the magic evening when Alessandro returned, euphoric from having enlisted for military service, that this new boisterous life within her was conceived.

Alessandro's prospective fatherhood had brought back all his most flamboyant mannerisms. His adventurousness in learning to fly at a time when the rest of the world considered it madness had earned him an immediate commission in the nascent United States Air Force. Almost instinctively, he was beginning to dress the part, although he would have to wait for his uniform until he arrived at his East Coast base. Today he wore a flying jacket of the finest Spanish leather, a visored hat at a rakish angle, and in tribute to what he had heard of the daredevil fliers of the Lafayette Escadrille he had slung a six-foot white silk scarf recklessly about his neck. Already he was a "fly-boy" and longed to be free of his family. Even the Señora, after shedding copious tears and praying aloud in Spanish, realized that she could not compete with her son's performance.

The entire Mariné contingent was present. Ruth wept, swollen with pregnancy. Maria, sad-eyed, held two small children by the hand. Raoul sulked. He sneered at Alessandro's scarf and looked into the middle distance, demonstrating with every shift of weight that he wished himself elsewhere.

The larger scene—thirteen hundred soldiers going bravely to what they thought would be glory and what might be death or disgrace—was observed in its depth by only one person, from the Women's Auxiliary coffee stall, which had been set up in the back of a truck at the far end of the platform.

With dispassion, with detachment, Magdalena Ortiz watched the separate dramas unfold. These boys, costumed in their ill-fitting government uniforms, recited farewell speeches to their sweethearts which doubtless they had practiced for months before their bedroom mirrors: "Amaryllis, I'll love you forever, no matter what happens. I'll be true to you. Will you be true to me?" The girls, most of them, it seemed to Magdalena, no more than sixteen, sobbed into immaculate pocket handkerchiefs: "How can you doubt me, Freddie? I'll sleep with your picture under my pillow, and I'll write you every day!"

But Magdalena wondered if under the patriotism there was not at least some despair, some terror. And what of the parents? Magdalena suspected the mothers' broken hearts, and wondered cynically if these fathers of

families weren't privately pleased to get their pimply "heroes" out of the house.

She watched the Marinés with affectionate sadness. Was it simply because Magdalena had walked twelve hundred miles to get away from such a fate that she felt marriage was not an unmitigated blessing? Ruth and Alessandro had been married for over a decade. Ruth had suffered the monthly inquiries and subsequent tantrums from the Señora—*where was the Mariné heir?* And the hard truth was that despite his flamboyant exterior, Alessandro had never done an honest day's work in his life.

And what of Maria and Raoul? Poor Maria, with her children, her tears, her incapacity to enjoy her wealth, could certainly not be described as happy. Once, in a tearful conversation with her mother-in-law, she had sobbed to Magdalena, "Your son doesn't love me!" Magdalena had done her best to comfort her, but she had thought, *you little fool! How could you have failed to notice?* And Raoul—what an accomplished actor he was. He had found his part, bitterly complaining in a filthy crib, and no matter what opportunities for happiness, riches, love, were offered him, he deliberately, like a perverse child clinging to his misery, pushed it all away. He had not really changed in thirty-four years of life. He had done his best to make Maria's life a living hell. He gambled, he stayed out late. Occasion~~ beat her, but contented himself for the most part with what h morning: sulking at the edge of things, refusing to ~~ acknowledge himself as a member of a family—a~ shrugged. Only she knew how furious her own hap Because now, after a full dozen years as the mist ~~ick Smith, she was safe from the persecution that Raou~ ~~astically inflicted upon her.

"Saint Joseph of Copertino, Saint Michael, An~ ~~el, all you saints with wings, protect my son in all his days of batt~ ~e his safeguard against the wickedness and snares of the Boches!"

Magdalena's smile widened into a broad grin. She and the Señora had never again mentioned their backgrounds, the conversation they had had the day of the wedding. But the Señora, with never a hint of judgment, had assisted in her affair with John Frederick. From the very first she had assured Magdalena that what she did was no sin, that John Frederick's wife was a whining invalid, and that he, in return for having to put up with all that for so many years, deserved everything Magdalena could give him of physical and emotional love.

How ironic that during those years when she had raised her ungrateful son by the sweat of her brow, she had been chaste—well, almost chaste—and had been sneered at by the city as a whore. Now, when she carried on an affair of passionate abandon, she had become a pillar of the community, a member of the Women's Auxiliary. *Ay, que broma!* What a joke.

She worked most mornings side by side with Victoria Creighton, a measure of just how far she had come. It could not be said by any stretch of the imagination that they were close friends, but they respected each other and that was enough.

As if in answer to this thought, Victoria Creighton appeared at the far end of the platform and began to make her way through the crowd to her place in the coffee stall. Magdalena thought that Victoria alone played no artificial role. She remained herself. Her detached composure was no act. Her cool, unadorned, aristocratic beauty had changed very little in the years, although this morning light circles were etched under her clear blue eyes. Victoria's presence was a steadying influence on all of them. By knowing what must be done she somehow saw that it *was* done.

"Jimmy's gone! Jimmy's gone! He's never coming back!"

In contrast to this hysterical outburst, Magdalena heard the cool, comforting voice of Victoria Creighton saying, "Now, my dear, you know it is our part to be strong. Think of how Jimmy would be upset if he knew that you would not be able to hold up while he was over there."

"But it hurts. It hurts so bad I don't think I can stand it. He says we're going to be married, but I know, I *know,* he's going to die."

"Now you mustn't say that," Victoria answered. "Here, take my handkerchief and dry your eyes. You must be strong at least until the train pulls out, my dear."

"But I look so awful."

"He won't even notice. He just wants you to be with him when he gets on the train."

The girl sniffed one last time and, responding to Victoria's gentle firmness, squared her shoulders and disappeared into the crowd.

With her charge dismissed, Victoria came up to the truck. She looked about expectantly and remarked to Magdalena, "I do hope Cliff gets here in time. The boys will be leaving in ten minutes and I expect Ruth will need her father."

"I'm sure he'll be here any moment."

"Well, it's true," Victoria said, "that he has been frightfully busy lately. He got the word at three this morning that a new well might blow in. He felt he simply had to go."

Then from her vantage point on the bed of the truck, Magdalena, looking over the heads of the crowd, saw the Creighton Packard. She saw Clifford get out from behind the wheel, bound around the car to open the passenger door, and gallantly hand out a beautiful woman.

"I believe, Victoria, they have just arrived."

The two watched as the couple approached, talking animatedly. Both the newcomers were splattered with oil. Clifford—still lean, still tanned, but grayer now—had loosened the knot of his tie, a sure sign of his excitement. The girl, just a girl, looked fresh, vibrant, and walked with a springing step. Her sweater and skirt fit tightly around her slim figure.

Ay, Magdalena thought, all men are alike, sniffing like dogs over a juicy new bone. But aloud she said, "Here they come."

"I can see that," answered Victoria, appearing unruffled. "I guess there's no doubt that the well blew in."

"Victoria! Victoria! We've had the most amazing night," Clifford explained. "In all my years in business and in oil, I don't think I've ever had such an experience! To stand there in the midst of the field, with the sun coming up, and feeling the ground pulse under our feet, and then—"

"Then it blew," the woman cried out. "There was oil going hundreds of feet in the air and the most profound noise. I might have gotten drenched! We both would if Mr. Creighton hadn't pulled us out of the way just in time. It was like being present at a miracle of nature."

"Well," Clifford said, "I can tell you that not many Pasadena girls would interrupt their night's sleep to go out and stand with an old man just to watch an oil well come in."

The girl stepped back and looked at him in what seemed to be unfeigned surprise.

"Old?" she said. *"You?* What nonsense."

But Clifford, remembering his manners, said, "Victoria, dear, this is the one I've told you so much about."

"Frances Hugen," she said, taking Victoria's hand.

"She's made the office a different place. She's pepped it up no end."

Magdalena smothered a discreet cough.

"Señora Ortiz," Victoria said, "allow me to present Miss Hugen."

Frances Hugen smiled warmly. "How do you do?"

Did Magdalena imagine it, or were Clifford's buoyant spirits momentarily checked?

"I hope you'll excuse us," Victoria said, "but we really must join our daughter. Her husband is shipping out this morning and we must be there to say goodbye."

"Victoria," Magdalena called down, "I really cannot desert my post here. So will you give Alessandro my final farewells?"

As soon as Victoria and Clifford had joined the Mariné clan, Frances Hugen hiked up her skirt and nimbly jumped into the back of the truck.

"You must let me give you a hand." Frances expertly poured coffee and handed out doughnuts. "There you are, soldier. Take care of yourself now. We're counting on you!

"You know, I've been trained as an artist," Frances said to Magdalena. "And I guess I can say I had some doubts about going to work in a purely business firm. But Mr. Creighton made me learn something. Here, soldier, take a chocolate one! And plenty of cream in that coffee. That'll hold you 'till lunch. . . . Mr. Creighton made me learn that business can be an art form too!"

"I can imagine," said Magdalena.

"I don't suppose there's any side of life that has to be dull, as long as you can be in the company of an interesting person!"

"So they say."

A band, which had been entertaining the crowd with a series of stirring tunes, suddenly began to play "Over There." The train gave a warning lurch and blew its whistle. There was a chorus of girlish sobs and muted masculine cheers. Silk handkerchiefs waved, except for young Dick, in the switchmaster's tower, who looked up from his breakfast and used his napkin.

Again the Señora Mariné raised her hands in heavenly supplication.

Alessandro kissed his wife, his sister, his mother and, waiting until the last possible moment, he lifted his arms to the enlisted men already on the train, who good-humoredly rose to the occasion and hauled him up through the window. Once safe, he leaned out dangerously again, arranging his scarf so that it billowed in the soot-flecked air.

"*Adios, carissima!* May God give you a safe birth and a strong son." And the train chugged away.

Magdalena felt an unaccustomed tug at her heart. Did God always protect fools?

Then Frances swung down from the truck and intercepted Clifford as he had begun rather awkwardly to pat his daughter's back. Magdalena could see that Frances addressed him respectfully and then he was following her back to the Creighton Packard. Ruth, evidently seeing herself as doubly bereft, refused any ministrations from her mother and chose to go home with the Señora.

"Clifford had to go back to work," Victoria said unnecessarily, when she returned to the stall.

"Victoria, why don't you have some coffee? I don't believe you've had a single thing to eat or drink this morning."

Victoria gratefully accepted a cup. Families drifted off the platform. Magdalena began to wonder if it would undermine the war effort if she slipped away for a few moments to say hello to Maria and the children.

Then the girl who had felt badly about Jimmy returned.

"I . . . I took away your handkerchief with me, ma'am. So I thought I'd return it now." The poor girl had been stirred by the patriotic music, and by the sacrifice she had just been required to make. "I got through it all right. Jimmy didn't see me cry. I told him I was proud of him, and I knew he'd kill lots of Germans. I just want you to know, ma'am, that I couldn't have gone through it without you."

Victoria's exhausted face brightened.

"I'll never forget what you did for me this morning," the young girl said, pressing the sodden handkerchief into Victoria's hand. "You've been just like a mother to me."

Victoria winced as though she'd been slapped.

Pobrecita, Magdalena thought.

From the moment years ago when Katarina had accompanied George to his mother's, Lin's, house to pack up his clothes and his treasured Chinese toys—his kites, his shuttlecocks, his own pictures and books which he had received on Children's Days—she had seen what a difference there was between her own haphazard establishment and this carefully planned domestic harmony.

Using the excuse that it would make George feel more at home if he had familiar objects about him, with Sung's permission Katarina removed some lacquered chests, a sixteen-sectioned screen, some silken wall hangings, and an expensive collection of snuffboxes.

She was at a loss as to how to arrange these objects. No one knew, not even Sung, that what many people viewed as chaos in her own home had been, for her, a major advancement. Again, using George's bereavement as an excuse, she asked his advice on how to use these objects, and what they meant. And when she saw what a comfort it was for George to eat his native food, Katarina made it her business to hire Lin's cook, head amah, and the number one houseboy before they slipped away into the anonymity of Chinatown.

In the beginning it seemed that this arrangement, like all the others, would not work out. But Katarina's temper had been considerably subdued by the tragedy. And there was the undeniable fact that not only did her children grow stronger with this food, but her husband had shown his approval by coming home early from work, eating a hearty supper, and spending long evenings in the bosom of his family. Then, when the children were in bed, Katarina was assured that her husband had grown stronger too.

During the three years after the tragedy, she had borne Sung another three sons—Ponko, Jiri, and Václav. For the first time she had scrupulously followed the Chinese customs for an expectant mother. She had refrained from drinking *rakia,* she had tried to cut down on her quarreling, she did not walk in the dark without company. She stayed away from lamb, and fish without scales. She had, on the other hand, practiced in the back yard with a bow and arrow, to develop the masculine spirit of the baby. She accepted a handsome piece of white jade and wore it always, so that her babies would have the look and quality of jade. And she ate *gai chao,* a soup made especially to enrich mother's milk.

She was told by several old women in Chinatown that if she looked at the drifting clouds, bubbling brooks, and graceful butterflies, the child would have a feeling for the traditions of culture and the rhythms of the universe.

When her fourth son after the great quake was born dead she was able to explain to her husband that this mishap had taken place because the child had been conceived during one of Los Angeles' rare thunderstorms.

Then, when a few months later, her second eldest, Stanislav, died from complications after all the children had been sick with the measles, Sung was moved by tenderness for Katarina and also a certain superstitious fear to suggest to her that perhaps they needed a new home in which to raise their ever-expanding family. He coupled this offer with a few shy compliments, praising her for having become, for all her wild ways, a "Chinese" wife of whom he could be proud. It was characteristic of the change in Katarina that instead of trying to cut him in two with her strong arms, she contented herself with kissing him straight on the lips, pounding his back with the strength of a longshoreman, folding her arms into the full sleeves of her mandarin jacket, and giving him a demure if somewhat demented smile.

Sung gutted one of his warehouses for this new residence, faithful to the tradition that luxury should be enclosed in a plain exterior. Katarina was allowed to decide where the partitions would be, and she took particular care over the construction of one large room between the kitchen and the servants' quarters, which would be given over to the children. Although they were better behaved now, she knew that they needed space to release

231

their high spirits, to give vent to their exuberant heritage, the Slovak blood that ran in their veins. Slowly she began to furnish this home, striving for the serenity and effortless wealth that she had seen in the dwelling of her rival, but remembering also that too much wealth was, as her husband often said, a temptation to the gods.

Her concern for the children's sense of tradition, her timid wish that they know something of their mother's inheritance as well as their father's, had been accented by a chance encounter while she was shopping in a Caucasian department store. She had heard two women exchanging remarks in her own language. On impulse she spoke to them.

"Hello, how are you? I come from close to the town of Kočisce." These kind ladies had fallen upon her with bear hugs and whoops and in their arms Katarina had felt the unexpected joy of finding her home once again. The women had joyfully taken her on the red car out Sunset Boulevard to the Micheltorena Hill. In contrast to her sedate Chinese friends Katarina saw with delight that they "walked like 'lectric," gesticulating, striding out freely.

Nestled on a neglected street called Maltman Avenue stood five or six shacks painted turkey red. Katarina was hurried into first one house and then the next, where she was greeted with shouts and glasses of *rakia*. She became friends with this little band. In the ensuing months and years she visited often, bringing the children. And perhaps most important in terms of her sense of her own burgeoning family, she found that these people were craftsmen. Each afternoon, after one of her lighthearted visits, she returned to Chinatown with a bright peasant wall hanging, a set of braided straw charms to avert the evil eye, or a pretty piece of needlepoint that held its own with some of Sung's most sumptuous embroideries.

When in the fall of 1917 Katarina gave birth to her thirteenth child, she was able to survey her home, her family, her possessions, and her beloved protector Sung with a sense of accomplishment and content. Having come from a land where life was a nightmare to be stoically endured, she had by purest chance found her way into a beautiful dream and she had proven herself equal to it.

This winter evening, just a few days after the American New Year, Katarina helped Da Se Fu, the chief cook, to prepare the evening meal. Da Se Fu thought that a decent kitchen needed at least three cooks—the third to chop, the second to allot ingredients, and the first to preside at the wok during the hour-long crisis that turned out twenty-one dishes every evening.

Tonight, for the thousandth time, Katarina hooted at Da Se Fu in elementary Cantonese. "All chief cooks are lazy, and you are the laziest! *I* will be your second and third cook in one, if you let me use two cleavers!"

"*You?*" he said in a bantering, affectionate tone. "Your cleavers would turn water chestnuts into great hunks of carrot and potato!"

"I have one use for this cleaver you might not like!"

"Just chop, Gentle Mistress, or they will never have dinner tonight."

She and Da Se Fu worked contentedly in the kitchen. The younger children played "keep away" all over the house. Her husband and the older sons spent the time before the evening meal in the living room, he going over accounts, they diligently working at their lessons.

When Katarina heard the raised voices, she put down her cleaver and went out to stop them before they started again. For the last six months, George—her adopted son, and sometimes, she even thought, her favorite—had been tormenting his father with one constantly repeated request. George wanted to fight, to be a soldier. She could see it was too late. They were already in heated argument.

"Do you see this paper?" George rhetorically asked his father. "Why do I even ask you that? You can't even read it! Do you know what it says? It says that 'Today thirteen hundred brave-hearted men left hearth and home to fight and perhaps lay down their lives for their country!' "

"Not *your* country," his father observed. "Don't you know, cabbage-head, they bring our people here to work till we die?" He lapsed into Chinese. "If we are alive it is an accident of planning. And if you would condescend to read a newspaper written in the language of your ancestors, you would know that the lice-infested American army is in the Middle Kingdom, recruiting coolie labor. Our countrymen are already in this war. They dig in the dirt like ants to make homes for the round-eye to fight in. Is that what you want? I can assure you it is not a comfortable life."

"I am not a coolie. With my education I could be . . . I could be . . ."

"At the most, and only because you could speak your own language, you might be a foreman, watching your countrymen work until they die. I have known their kind on the railroad."

"You and your railroad! Times have changed since then."

"Have they? You have much to learn, impudent frog." And against his son's bitter silence, he gave a final jeer. "Go down there, then, try to be part of their army. Tell them about your 'education.' No doubt they will make you a general."

Katarina moved swiftly to place herself between the two men. "That is enough. *My* home is not a place for noisy quarrels." She smiled desperately, hoping they might respond to her joke. "I am very . . . quiet," she said. "I do not like noise."

They stared at her sullenly, Sung entrenched in outraged dignity and George holding to his rebellious anger.

She appealed to the younger. "Your father love you, George. He no want you hurt. You are his eldest son. He—"

George spoke to her then, in choked and helpless rage. "Don't you see? He's *right!* There's nothing for me here! I'm twenty-two years old and I have no life. I should have been killed with my brothers and sisters!"

With that, before Katarina could think of anything to say, and before Sung realized what his oldest, dearest son was doing, George had jumped up and stormed out into the night, slamming the door behind him.

Raoul had chosen to live with his wife in his mother's big yellow house on Carroll Street. Maria had not been altogether pleased by this, but for Raoul it had been a kind of revenge. This was his house and his neighborhood no matter what the Anglos thought. And Raoul had taken a certain amount of perverse pleasure in taunting his mother. "When your Anglo lover tires of you, we will take you in as a boarder."

After Alessandro had made such a spectacular departure this morning, Raoul seemed to feel that *his* contribution to the war effort was to slouch at the kitchen table, read the early evening accounts of the thirteen hundred brave-hearted men who had chosen to fight and perhaps die for their country. He was on his third pitcher of beer.

Maria, watching him apprehensively, was afraid to say anything. She knew that in these moods he was at his most dangerous.

"Why are you staring at me like that?" he demanded. "You look like a pie, a cow pie. Are you trying to give me the evil eye? You already have my body, my money, and my life. Do you want my soul too?"

"I'm not doing anything," she said defensively.

But somehow her injured tone was calculated to inflame him further. She got up to stir a big pot of soup.

"Alessandro," she said in irritating little-girl tones, "looked so handsome in his uniform."

"He wasn't wearing a uniform, stupid. He was wearing a scarf that made him look like a *puto*." Raoul swished his arm in a mincing, limpwristed fashion. *"A el se le cae la mano!"* As always, he knew how to provoke her into further injured response.

"That is not a thing to say about my brother, especially when he has gone away to fight for his country."

"You know, I envy him," he said, giving her a false smile. "For as long as the war lasts he can get away from his women. It took your brother ten years to hold his nose and mount that pig of a wife. And your mother—"

"Ah! That's enough from you, lazy *borracho*! Look at you sitting there. Are you such a lover?" She swayed toward him, her hands on her hips.

That was his cue in this domestic ritual to get up and hit her with the flat of his hand. She stumbled across the room, but she did not fall. Holding onto a cupboard she gave him a bloody, contemptuous smile.

"Very brave, Raoul. Perhaps someday they will give you a medal."

His anger was murderous, but what was there to do? He could hit her again. There would be more scenes, more tears. He drained the last of his beer and stood up heavily.

"I'm going out," he said. He looked around the kitchen he had hated as long as he could remember. He saw his wife, long-suffering. Her only defense against him was scorn and an utter lack of respect. He knew that upstairs his children were listening as always. He knew there was no escape.

"I'm going out," he repeated. "Don't wait up for me and don't send Hector out for me either." He swaggered as far as the back door, then reconsidered. "One more thing," he said in a deceptively neutral tone, "I won't be wanting dinner." And with a devilish grin, he tipped the huge cauldron of vegetable soup onto the floor. Nimbly jumping back out of harm's way, he waited until Maria dissolved into tears. Then he laughed.

"Adios, chiquita," he grinned. *"Hasta luego."*

On this January night George Sung strolled aimlessly down the streets of Chinatown past the nightclub district with its gaudy electric lights and cheap, painted women who invited him from second-story windows. He kept walking to what looked like a deserted street, tightly shuttered, where no one was visible except a few apparently sleepy Chinamen taking the night air.

"Don't tell me there's nothing going on inside there," George heard a slurred voice saying belligerently.

"Nothing here, mister. Go away!"

"All my cock-fighting friends say the action's down here."

"Cock fight?" the other, Chinese, voice responded. "We no got cock fight."

George stepped into the entry. "It's all right, Fu Bai," he said. "This is a family acquaintance, Raoul Ortiz. My father would be pleased if you would show him the hospitality of your establishment."

The watchman shrugged and opened the door. "Yessee, yessee, Master Sung," he said. "You wanchee go in too?"

On an impulse George said, "Why not?" and followed the slightly unsteady Raoul into a dark anteroom.

They passed another watchman, who waved them through a small "grocery store" lined with ancient cans and boxes, and then into the back room. Harsh yellow lights blazed down on three small tables, each surrounded by a dozen Chinese. One or two Caucasians stood timidly by, trying to get the hang of the game. A Chinese bystander grinned at George, and, pointing with his chin at the round-eyes, said in Cantonese, "It doesn't matter whether they win or lose, they're going home without their money."

The sight of Raoul caused several of the gamblers to mutter disapprovingly. Other Latinos had been ejected from this place for bringing in their own *pulque*, refusing to pay the extortionate fees for rice wine, refusing to pay their losses, refusing to be cheated.

But George put his hand on Raoul's arm. "Stay by me and I'll show you how to play." George had never been in a regular "den" but he had spent many afternoons watching his father and his associates making business deals during the allegedly casual rivalry of fan-tan.

"All you do is take a handful of counters and throw them on the table. Then the house man counts them off, two by two. You put your money on odd or even."

"Then what?" Raoul said.

"Then depending on whether it's odd or even, you win!"

"Doesn't it take a long time? A cock fight is over in ten seconds!"

"The Chinese play fan-tan to spend time."

"It's gonna take me four hours to win twenty dollars."

But in four hours' time they had both lost hundreds. A surly thug informed them that the house would take no more IOUs and they had to go home.

"Tell your fat and greasy friend," the thug hissed at George, "he must pay within the week or he will find his brain in two halves, and so will you."

Out in the street in the cold night air, they tried to make sense of what had happened.

"I don't understand," Raoul said. "You bet on the odd, I bet on the even. And you're telling me we both lost?"

George's head swam from the potent rice wine. "I don't know," he answered truthfully. "It isn't the way my father plays it—"

Swaying slightly, they looked at each other.

"I can tell you one thing," Raoul said. "I don't want to go home."

"Neither do I," George answered. But after another awkward pause, with a half-wave, they parted company.

George spent the last hours before dawn in a filthy restaurant in the heart of Chinatown, elbow to elbow with the dispossessed—gamblers, pimps, delivery men—eating *jook,* a gruel made of rice cooked into white slime, seasoned with whole dried fish. It was the one Chinese dish George had never learned to stomach. He had read in dime novels about the glamorous night life. But he had not found it tonight. His thoughts shifted fleetingly to those "boys" gone off that morning in search of honor and glory. Maybe their quest would be as elusive.

Eastern sunlight poured into every corner of the Creightons' master bedroom. Pansy had already tiptoed in to open the curtains. Now she returned with twin trays on a pushcart: poached eggs for Victoria, a Denver omelette for Cliff. He took his breakfast at the table by the window, and read the financial pages of the *Star-News*. Victoria had her tray in bed.

"Steel is up, oil is up, munitions are up. You can say what you want. War is good for the economy."

"Clifford, dear, I don't quite like the idea of your investing in munitions."

"I didn't *say* I invested, I only said they were up!"

"I see here that Belle Bauer is chairwoman of this year's debutante ball. Odd, isn't it, when she doesn't have children of her own?" Despairing of engaging her husband's attention, she had opened the society section.

And when Clifford didn't answer she went on, "I wonder what Belle looks forward to? It must be rather frightening not to have children."

"She can be one of those whitehaired ladies, eating at her single table at the Green."

"Clifford, really . . ."

But he had folded his paper and moved toward his dressing room, rubbing his chin. It seemed sometimes to Victoria that just when Clifford was at an age when he should be relaxing, he occupied himself increasingly with his various enterprises.

"Roger Boulter's granddaughter is engaged to someone from the East," she said. But she spoke to an empty room.

It was a good thing he'd had the hearty breakfast, Clifford thought, because he'd worked straight through without lunch. There was something about the gamble of a thing that took hold of his blood: He hadn't felt this young in years.

Patrician Estates! The war boom had given everyone plenty of money. Suddenly the middle class had become almost uncomfortably nouveau riche.

They had money to spend, but lacked the education and taste to spend it "right." Clifford was gambling that a name like Patrician Estates—a name that would be scorned by already established families—would bring the middle class flocking in. He had bought seventy acres north of the Annandale golf course, on the west side of the Arroyo, above Devil's Gate. He would build seventy houses, each on an acre of land, and room for croquet in back. He had employed an architectural rogue, who had succeeded in making what were essentially only three basic floor plans look like seventy highly individual estates.

But it was the new girl, Frances Hugen, initially hired only to design the brochures, who had come up with the true stroke of genius. As she had been sketching interiors one morning, she'd suddenly burst without knocking into his office.

"Sorry, sir. I *am* sorry. But look!" She waved her sketch of Plan A in front of him. "Do you see what I see?"

"It's very nice, indeed, Miss . . ."

"We're selling these to the middle classes, isn't that right? All they'll see—and I know I'm right, sir—is *space,* space that they won't know how to fill up! Do they use one couch or two? Should they have a piano? What about windows? Should they use draperies? Some of these people, I'm *sure,* have had nothing more than glass curtains in their lives. And the walls? What will they put on the walls?

"What I'm saying, sir, is that you need to give them a start! You furnish the houses. Crystal, I'm sure they'd like the idea of crystal. Cut-glass chandeliers. Those new dining room sets they have and Chesterfield couches. How much would it cost, after all, to buy a hundred couches, three hundred easy chairs, two hundred beds? All in good taste, don't you see? We make them up in twenty different color schemes! And then outside—you see, sir, they're buying a dream—we can't just give them an acre of chaparral. I suggest you put in an order right now for a thousand pepper trees, just seedlings, to line the streets, and two hundred jacarandas, a hundred acacias! Optional plans for orchards in the back, or corrals, or kitchen gardens. You could *hand* them the plans, and they could take it from there. And art! You know, they *love* art, but they don't know anything about it. Did you know there's a whole new movement right here in town, the Synchronists? They're talented, sir, but they're starving. You could support the arts, and make a profit! And sir, if I'm not too bold, on my own time, I . . . paint. I could do watercolors—of California *itself,* sir. The beach, palm trees, or the desert, or just this! Pasadena! Because it's so exciting and so new!"

She paused for breath, then blushed up to her brow.

"I'm sorry! It's just . . . it's that I thought that the brochure might look nicer."

Since that day she had become, by default, his personal assistant. Their business life had turned into a constant round of exploring great musty warehouses filled with bolts of rich material, driving out for miles into the countryside to haggle under shade trees for entire orchards, pacing off each acre of Patrician Estates, deciding the dimensions of a particular grove of birches or stand of ranunculus. Ranunculuses were Frances' favorite flower. She said, "To me, they're like a painter's palette. If I were rich, I'd want at least thirty square feet of ranunculus so that I could have fresh flowers in my house every day." Then she had paused and looked at him in a way that had wrenched at his chest. "They're so beautiful," she said, "but they have such a short season."

Clifford knew that the others in Creighton and Associates laughed at the two of them in their new "harebrained" project. But if the truth were known, the oil business got along perfectly well without him. His investments increased effortlessly, almost of their own volition. Patrician Estates had reminded him of the pure fun of making money—the idea of taking raw materials, unpromising vistas, things that other people might pass up, and quite literally turning them into a dream come true.

He was astonished at how he and Frances were in almost perfect accord. Her father worked as Clifford's foreman down in the oil fields. Clifford had met Frances there one day, serene and untouched among the roughnecks, sketching the harsh machinery as a class exercise. Her father doted on this child and had saved for years to give her her heart's desire, a course of training in art school. On an impulse, Clifford had asked her if she wanted a job. He had needed an artist, he said, to help him with a new project in real estate. He had never regretted it. Frances had undeniable artistic talent, a wonderfully straight character, and a wistful sense of what was out there, if one only had the money, the wit, and the sense to get it.

He had watched with tenderness and admiration while she sketched in, as she was doing today, the furnishings for one of these homes and imagined the family to go with it.

"You see," she said, "people like these—I know some of them are going to be Irish Catholics—in the garden they'd want, oh, I'd say, elms. Maybe a dozen or eighteen of them, so they'd make a wall of green. Working people have a parlor, but they never go into it. I think we can safely assume they won't use their living rooms now. They won't feel comfortable. So I suggest, sir, that we make the living room extremely formal. Then I suggest that we invent, I don't know, we could call it a 'family room.' We furnish it—I know just the place where we can get these things—with old oak tables and comfortable couches and put the piano in there, just an upright one. . . ."

Her hair was thick and chestnut-colored. She wore it on top of her head in a bun, but whenever she became enthusiastic or excited it began to escape. When this happened she continued sketching with her right hand and made the most touching, endearing circles around her hair with her left, making certain that the locks were still safely imprisoned. The more she talked, the more they escaped. Sometimes Clifford caught himself wondering—from purely objective curiosity, of course—what it might be like to reach over, pull out those four confining pins, and watch her hair come tumbling down.

Late afternoon turned into early evening. Shyly she had shown him the painting that might go in this home. No nouveau-riche Irish in the history of the nation would be so well served as the ones who moved into this dream house, he thought, for the picture, her own, was a large soft watercolor of great beauty. Three young men in the foreground were coming home from something, or going somewhere. He and Victoria by this time had an extensive and imaginative collection of art, but never, it seemed to Clifford, had he seen anything that so clearly summed up such a sense of innocence, the lost past, the illusions of youth.

"I don't know, sir," she said. "It just seems to me that working as hard as they must have done to buy a house such as this, they'd want something to remind them—"

Clifford cleared his throat gruffly. "Miss Hugen," he barked.

"Sir?"

"There's something about this arrangement that isn't working out."

"Sir?" Her eyes were wide and frightened.

"I am afraid, Miss Hugen, that our association, useful and productive as it has become, cannot go on if you insist on calling me sir."

"Oh!" she laughed. "What shall I call you then?"

"Might I call you Frances? Might you call me Clifford?"

She blushed. "If you really want to know, sir—Clifford, at home they call me Fanny."

"Fanny! My little Fanny."

They both went off into gales of laughter, then stopped in mutual embarrassment and glanced to see who might be listening. But it was late. Everyone had left for the evening.

"Good heavens!" Clifford exclaimed. "We're quite alone here. How inconsiderate of me to have kept you working so late."

She sighed and looked at her sketches on the drafting table. "I just hate to leave without finishing."

"Frances, I see only one solution. We can get a quick meal at the Green. I won't have any trouble getting a large table so we can complete our work."

"Perhaps we should just send out for sandwiches."

"Pierre will make sure we aren't disturbed."

At the Green, just as he had predicted, Pierre showed them to a large corner table. To reach it they walked by the line of single tables known locally as Dowagers' Row. At each a discreetly dressed, whitehaired woman ate alone, assured of all the amenities by virtue of her deceased husband's insurance policy. Cliff took Frances' elbow and hurried past, leaving the ladies to follow their progress with quizzical eyes.

If Pierre felt any surprise, he certainly did not show it as he seated Frances with elaborate courtesy.

Clifford could see the delight that his companion took in these, to her, luxurious surroundings. And impulsively he decided to make this more than an ordinary working dinner.

"Pierre," he said. "We need a little extra nourishment tonight. Is there caviar?"

"Certainly, sir."

"Splendid," Clifford answered. "Bring us two servings. Don't stint. And a bottle of Veuve Clicquot."

When the menu came, she blinked. A good half of it was in French. Again, Clifford intervened. "If you don't mind, Fanny, perhaps you will allow me to order for us, with Pierre's advice."

"*Des asperges vinaigrette,*" Pierre droned theatrically, "*côtelettes d'agneau avec abricots en cognac, des petits pois, et pour le dessert, un soufflé Grand Marnier.*"

"That will be sufficient, I think. Champagne as we need it, of course." Only then did Clifford remember to telephone Victoria.

Victoria and Ruth sat in oppressive silence. Rack of lamb, oven-browned potatoes, and Pansy Priest's best braised carrots went almost untouched.

"Tell me, Ruth, what is it like at the adobe now that Alessandro isn't there? Is it lonely?"

Ruth looked at her mother. "It's not so bad," she said. "Father Clement is always very kind and you know the Señora makes a great many jokes. It's a side of her that strangers don't often see. She loves to be around and about. We spend our mornings shopping and our afternoons visiting the poor. She gets along so well with them. Often we spend evenings at the Mission—"

"Please, Ruth, do go ahead and eat," her mother interrupted. "I'm sure your father won't mind if we go on without him." She sighed wearily. "It's a shame when Pansy's worked so hard, and you've made the trip all the way from San Gabriel to see us."

"Mother . . ." Ruth said uncertainly.

"It's nothing, nothing," said Victoria. "Your father's business goes in spurts. This new development—" She brightened when Priest announced that Clifford was on the phone, and excused herself.

Within a minute she was back. She smiled at her daughter ruefully. "I'm afraid your father won't be with us tonight, Ruthie dear. He just called to say that he has to work late at the office." She smiled widely, but her eyes sparkled with tears. "Really, Ruth, it's too banal. You could hear talking and laughing behind him. It's hard to believe the whole staff is staying and having a party."

Ruth stared at her mother, who looked small and frail. There seemed to be nothing to say. In an atavistic memory of her own youthful heartbreak, it was Ruth who rang for Porter Priest, and said, "Mother and I have decided to make a party of it tonight. Won't you bring us some champagne?"

They spent the rest of the evening in pleasant chat, Ruth rather wickedly retelling stories of the Señora to make her mother laugh. When at eleven-thirty that night Victoria insisted that Ruth go home, Clifford had still not returned.

Clifford and Frances seemed to be in a circle of enchantment. They had been talking forever; they would be talking forever. Dimly he had perceived Belle and Headsperth Bauer, their heads together, gazing coldly across the room at this corner table. Automatically he had nodded and raised his hand in salute, but he had been lost for hours in his story. How her presence brought it all back to him. The young man with nothing in his pocket but a letter of credit and a heart full of aimless hopes. The land out here as it used to be. When he had told her the story of bringing the coyote to earth in the Pasadena post office it was as though it had happened again to him, but for the first time.

It was Pierre, finally, who whispered discreetly into Clifford's ear that it was past closing time, and the staff was waiting to go home.

She lay, propped up by pillows, the bedside lamp on, making a pretense of reading. If she had expected a furtive, shamefaced entrance, she had been mistaken. Clifford burst in.

"Oh, Victoria, I'm so glad you're awake! I've got so much to tell you about what Fanny and I have been doing."

"Fanny?"

"You know, Fanny Hugen, Frances. She's been doing such good work on Patrician Estates. She has such a feel for these things, Victoria. And such stamina. She's so straight! She shows such breeding. She's one of the few people I've ever been able to talk to. Do you know whom she reminds me of? In some ways she reminds me of you, when you—"

"Clifford, it's well after midnight. Ruth was here for dinner. Don't you remember? I told you this morning."

"Oh, darling, I *am* sorry. But Ruthie will recover. She's such a brick. Frances and I worked nine hours without even stopping for lunch. Don't you see?"

"And so you took her to dinner, *for seven hours.*"

"Victoria, dear, that's not like you. And that's not what happened at all. I simply took her out to dinner, and we were planning on finishing the project. But we . . . just got to talking, that's all."

Somewhere in a seedy barracks in South Carolina, Lieutenants Fitzgerald, McCoy, and "Skip" Faulkner poked distastefully at their "shit on a shingle," looked at their ersatz coffee, trying to get thirsty enough to drink it.

But Turner, ordinarily a calm and taciturn fellow, was beside himself tonight. "I knew when I drew him this morning that I was *for it!* The man's a maniac. He's worse than any drill sergeant. He can't shut up, you can't understand what he's saying, and the minute things get hot, he goes over into Spanish. Now you know me, boys! You know I'm a good flier!"

They all nodded solemnly.

"From the minute we took off I knew we were in trouble. That *scarf.* That fucking scarf! He said it was a rough takeoff. Christ! I was flying blind, his *fringe* was in my eyes!"

"Where do you think he got that scarf?" McCoy wondered aloud. "Do you think I could get my mother to buy me one?"

"He's brave, you have to say that."

"Dumb is the word for it."

"*Muy estupido,* as *he'd* say!"

"But listen! We went up there! It was supposed to be a simple lesson in slow rolls. But you know how he is. 'We do not *stroll* through the air, Turner!

241

We are not here to take *tea*!' I can see him in the cockpit in front of me, he's waving his arms like a madman. His fucking scarf is flapping out there like when Mom would chase me out of the kitchen with a dishtowel. And he pretends to be an aristocrat, but he's a consummate ninny! Do you know what he said to me?"

They shook their heads.

"He said a pilot must fly his plane like a woman. Then, can you *believe* it? Before we do the roll, he asks me"—spleen threatened to overcome Turner—"he *asks me* do I have my *seat belt* fastened. I'm a *flier,* boys!"

They sighed.

Turner could keep it in no longer.

"Well, I'm telling you, we go up there, and we go into the roll. A slow roll. And he's right in front of me. I can feel my weight against the belt holding me in as we turn over. And it does feel a little strange being upside down and you don't know quite where everything is. But it didn't take me long to figure it out, boys. Lover boy is falling out. First the ends of his scarf, then his head and shoulders. He's grabbing at the sides, but his hands slip. Then, I tell you boys, he just *fell out*!"

"Jesus!"

"So there I am. The instructor is falling to earth. I'm flying solo for the first time in my life and all I could think of was I hoped he'd been smarter about his parachute than his seat belt. I have to tell you, boys, I couldn't spend too much time worrying about that. I had to get the ship through the roll and back to the base. It wasn't the smoothest landing, but it was nothing compared to what happened when the Captain found out. They're still out looking for him."

"Or what's left of him," said Fitzgerald.

"Shouldn't be too hard to find him," said McCoy. "They ought to be able to spot that fucking scarf a mile away."

At precisely that moment Alessandro Luis Antonio de Ortega de Moreno de Arellanos de Mariné y Ruiz burst through the door.

"Comrades, I have met death and fought her off!"

He danced across the room, his boots muddy, his riding breeches torn in the seat, his jacket ripped at the shoulder. His scarf, torn into long strips, whirled about him like a flurry of snow.

"I tell you, men, I have had a great escapade today." He looked at the gawking group, sprang at Turner, and swept him up into his arms. "My pupil, my pupil, you have given me the opportunity to face the unknown, to fly like a bird, to float like a cloud. And you yourself are a hero! You are brave, honorable, truly a gentleman of the air!"

Alessandro Mariné kissed Turner on both cheeks before grounding him. Turner looked desperately at his companions.

"The Queen of Angels has rewarded me with nectar from the gods. The Virgin Queen in the person of my mother has sent me on this day a case of champagne from our very own vineyards in Cucamonga."

"Cuca-what?"

"Cucamonga, the land of my ancestors." He fluffed out his tatters with a wave of his arm and then clapped in the manner of the old Spanish gentry.

242

His batman, a beardless youth from the hills of Tennessee, grunted under the weight of a heavy box.

"Ice! Champagne glasses!"

His batman looked at him blankly, left, and returned with five heavy tumblers. "No ice, sir," he mumbled.

"It is nothing! It is the spirit we want!"

Alessandro popped one of the corks of Château Cucamonga. First he poured a finger for himself and tasted it. "Ah, the taste of my homeland!" Then he poured generous lashings of the bubbly liquid for the four other fliers and filled his own glass. He stood waiting. When Turner picked up his tumbler and brought it to his lips, Alessandro imperiously snapped his fingers. "No, no, no, no, no, no, no, *no, no, no*!"

"Huh?"

"After an adventure such as ours, *compadre,* we must stand on our feet and salute the heavens."

Like an impatient maestro he beckoned them to their feet. They found themselves standing at attention, glasses raised, looking at the ceiling to which Alessandro addressed his toast.

"To honor, to glory, to courage, to the conquest of the skies, to the life of a hero and the exquisite embrace of the most beautiful woman of all—*La Muerta!* We will meet again, my beauty!"

"Bottoms up," Turner said.

They all grimaced at the first swallow, but by the fourth it wasn't so bad, and by the eighth bottle they didn't care. It was then that the Captain discovered them, and the batman brought another glass.

In later years when Bob Turner returned to Victorville, California, as he became more and more unable to fit in at the local haberdashery, the cement plant, or the Green Spot Café, he tried to explain it was because he'd been to war and seen another world. He had kept company with heroes, he had been part of the notorious *Los Cinco Extravagantes*—the five daredevils of the sky who drank champagne like mother's milk.

At four in the morning when the Yellow Dog Fan-Tan Palace closed its doors upon the last reluctant gamblers, George and Raoul looked at each other on the sidewalk, deciding to see if they could find a drink. Both of them tacitly agreed not to try the places uptown, the Pico House, the Bella Union. They knew that those venerable institutions would not extend their hospitality to a Mexican or a Chinese at four in the morning. The saloons were closed. George thought he knew a place that served decent *mao tai,* but after walking back and forth the length and breadth of Chinatown they had been rudely rebuffed in a variety of dialects.

"*Hombre,*" Raoul said, "every place is closed to us but one. I know where can get some *pulque.* It tastes like vomit, but it gets you drunk."

The *pulqueria* was no more than a "hole in the wall" eighteen inches wide where a jar of pungent slime sat on a narrow wooden lip. A blind old man ladled them each a cup and Raoul dropped a few pennies into a bowl.

"Isn't he afraid of being robbed?" George asked.

"*Amigo,* who in this God-forsaken hole would want to rob this *anciano ciego*? You can make more money shining one pair of shoes. And God knows the *pulque* isn't fit to drink."

With these encouraging words they sat down on the curb to get drunk or wait for the dawn, whichever came first. A horse-drawn cart watered down the dusty street. Half an hour and two cups of *pulque* later, a milk wagon lumbered by. A block away a sailor hit a woman of the streets and robbed her of her night's earnings.

"You know, *amigo*," Raoul confided, "sometimes I think that life is shit."

George shrugged his shoulders. "What can you do?" he asked drunkenly. "What can you do? When my father came here, he took these bastards for all they had. A man needs a career, you know? But my father won't let me do anything. We've got these oil fields. . . ."

"You don't need to tell me about oil fields. We've got them too."

"I wanted to work there, but my father thinks I'm too incompetent to dig a hole in the ground!"

"You're lucky, *hombre*. My mother sent me out there to make a man out of me. I spent one whole summer. I smelled like a hog. No girl would speak to me."

"What are we doing *now*? We're sitting on a curb!"

"You know what I hate?" Raoul said. "I have money. When I want to go someplace, I want to *go someplace*." He gestured vaguely with his *pulque*. "No offense, *amigo*, fan tan is one dull game."

"Some of the boys I know come from Macao," George said. "They say they have roulette wheels two stories high. You know how they bet? They don't bet with counters. They bet with bricks of pure gold. They have singsong girls—every color, every size. If you win over a thousand piastres they give you a girl as a bonus."

Raoul started to say something.

"But wait," George continued. "If you *lose* over a thousand piastres, they give you *two* girls so you don't feel bad."

A cold, gray dawn began to seep through the city streets. And suddenly, in a cloud of dust, a Crane-Simplex screeched to a stop in front of them. A corpulent white man, visibly stuffed with his own sense of importance, alighted and scurried up into a warehouse where, Raoul told George, hundreds of young Mexican girls toiled their lives away, picking lint for mattresses.

"You know what we call men like that?" Raoul asked. "We call them *bolillos* because they are white and soggy inside. God, I hate those pricks."

And George, his elbows on his knees, finished off his fifth cup of *pulque*. "I'd like to take them for all they've got."

Afterwards neither could say which one of them thought of it first. When things were going well for the house, each one took the credit. When things went badly—when they took in less than five thousand on a given night— they were apt to blame each other. All either one of them could say for sure was that by eight that morning, as the city came to life around them, they had formulated the bare bones of a way to make money and take revenge; a place to gamble and win for once, and a place to stay out all night, the best possible reason for not going home.

244

They would open their own gambling den. It wouldn't be like La Tortuga or the Yellow Dog. It would be a place where the tourists they had seen so ill at ease tonight would feel comfortable—comfortable enough to lose their shirts without complaining. The well-to-do could think they were having a big night out. They would play roulette, and Mah-Jongg and poker, and craps. And blackjack. No singsong girls! They would have "hostesses." And they would serve good liquor—well, not the best liquor, but certainly a step up from *pulque*. Best of all—and this made them laugh until they rolled in the dirt of North Spring Street—they would wear evening clothes all night long.

"Can we get diamond studs?" Raoul said.

"White jade for me!"

Raoul would front the money. George would do everything else—find the tables, hire the girls, get in touch with his friends from Macao. And soon they would be free men.

It took only a few days of talking to merchants, arranging for shipments of liquor and women, of George operating lavishly with money not his own, before Sung Wing On began to pick up rumors from every quarter. Within the week Katarina had to shepherd the children from the family living room where once again father and son faced each other in anger.

"You shame me in front of the community! I have to learn from the merchants that you are spending money that cannot possibly be your own. I am told you are buying chairs, tables, screens, draperies. You are buying art objects, not from me but from Fong See On down the street. They say to me, 'Now, we *know* your merchandise is inferior, when your own son will not buy your goods!' What am I to say to them when I do not know what you are doing, when you do not tell your own father! Have you lost all sense of family? And for what can all this possibly be used?"

"It's for *my own* business."

"You can have no business. How can *you* start a business? You do not have money and you have not tried to use my credit. The merchants tell me you pay with cash. *Whose is it?*"

"My partner's."

"You have a partner who is not in the family? Your father is not good enough for you?"

"My father would not understand. I am not good enough for *you!* I wanted to be a partner in your oil business."

"But you are too young."

"I wanted to help with our import/export trade."

"But it is too difficult for a boy."

"I wanted to help in one of the stores."

"You have—"

"I wanted to go into the army," George went on before his father could answer, "but you won't let me because *I'm your oldest son!* What good is an oldest son if he can do nothing for you? Do you want me to have no purpose of my own? Do you wish me to follow in your footsteps only after your death? I've *had* to do something for myself—to show you that I can do a man's work."

Sung nodded, his expression showing a grudging acknowledgment of the truth of what his son had said.

"Father, what I'm doing can't compare to your oil business. I know it may not bring me esteem in the community to be known as a gambler!"

Sung smiled. "The middle path is not always the way to gain respect, honor, and esteem. There are times when one needs to move a little to the right or a little to the left, even to get ahead by using the ditch, but never so far as to offend the gods."

George looked at his father with astonishment.

"The road to what I have today was not always a straight one. It has had many turnings. It could even be said that at many times it has been the road of a gambler."

"Then can I hope that you will share your wisdom with my partner and me?"

"You have spoken of your partner, but you have never named him. Is it someone I know? I cannot share my knowledge with a faceless stranger."

"It is someone you know. My partner is Raoul Ortiz."

"That shiftless, no-good boy! He is slower than a turtle! The gods have laid luck at his feet and he has done nothing but step on it!"

"Father, he is as I am."

Sung remembered a legend from his home village. A wealthy magistrate, whose first and second wives gave him daughter after daughter, was finally blessed with a son. The boy child received every favor, gift, and attention. But no toy or sweet was pleasing to the pampered boy. He would break the toys and trample upon them. He spat upon the sweets. The more they gave him the worse he became. After twenty years he ran away to the Big City. His father, mother, and seven sisters mourned him until one day he returned. He stepped across the threshold briskly and his family saw that he wore clothes of the best silk, and jade of the finest quality. In his early travels the son had met an old man who taught him the true way of life. Humbled by what he had learned, the boy sought out the hardest work he could find. At the Imperial Porcelain Works he dirtied his hands mixing the clay for the potters and strengthened his muscles by turning a potter's wheel. Some days he spent ten hours stoking the hot kiln and later when it was opened taking the full blast of the heat on his face. But one night he stole in alone and made his own vase, decorated with his own designs. When the Empress saw it she proclaimed it the most beautiful in all the Middle Kingdom. And so it was that the spoiled boy child was appointed the Imperial Overseer of the Royal Porcelain Works.

"I understand that you want to gain respect," said Sung, "but you cannot have respect when you are not a full partner. If you would allow me to offer you a loan—at six percent interest, payable within five years—then you would be a full partner with Raoul Ortiz."

"It is really not necessary, Father."

"This would do two things. It would enable you to create the most elegant and expensive establishment in all the Southern Counties and it would be doing honor to your father. I would not have my son on a lower level than an orphan child. Since this is a country of equality, you should not strive to be superior, but a business does best if two strong men work together on an equal footing."

"You are always wise, Father."

"I know a good venture when I see one."

Since that evening when she and Ruth had dined alone, Victoria had mentioned nothing of her anxieties to anyone, least of all to Cliff. But during the long afternoons when she was alone, she faced the possible facts. She and Cliff had been married for thirty-three years. Their silver anniversary was already a distant memory. She knew, of course, the conventional wisdom, that after a certain number of years men "strayed," but it was hard for her to believe the evidence that it was finally happening to her.

She knew that if men did "stray," it was supposed to be either that the wives in question were physically unresponsive, or—so it said in the women's magazines of the day—the wives had "let themselves go." She had no worries on the first score, but when she looked in the mirror, she could see the possibility of the truth of the second. Her figure, she could say without false pride, was almost exactly as it had been when she was a bride. Her manner of dress had, if anything, improved over the years; she had managed at every stage in her life to make the styles her own. And yet the woman who looked back from the mirror, though meticulously made up, looked . . . tired. The carefully coiffed hair was lusterless. There were pale circles under eyes that looked . . . tired. There was a quality in her reflection of slight suffering, as if she had somehow been "under the weather."

But physical appearances were only that. They could be changed. She had, although she usually disdained those activities, spent three consecutive afternoons at Charles of Pasadena. She'd had a facial, several massages to "get the blood working," and a new hairstyle. After all this was done she had to admit she looked much the same. As her last gesture—again, she smiled at the banality of it—she had spent a morning buying new underthings, and a peach negligee that could induce a lifelike appearance in a corpse.

Today, Saturday, she had choreographed what she felt would be a day to remember. She had instructed Priest to serve them breakfast on the terrace. She had asked Pansy to cut the early ranunculuses for a centerpiece. She had asked for champagne. And now, as Clifford sat at his usual table with the financial pages, she heard her own voice, falsely cheerful: "Clifford, darling! It's so beautiful. I thought we might have breakfast on the terrace. You've been working so hard, and we both need some diversion. I thought we might begin with tennis at the Club. Then in the late afternoon, I thought we might take a drive, oh—out to the beach to see the sunset. We might have dinner at some romantic spot. . . ."

Clifford looked up to her. She saw with a pang that he too looked tired, distressed. With a sigh he pulled himself up out of his chair. She saw him look out the window and take it all in: the spotless napery, the fine china and crystal, Priest waiting unobtrusively by the tea cart, the vases filled with ranunculuses.

"I'm sorry," he said. "I'm sorry. I . . . I forgot to tell you. I have a business appointment."

"At eight-thirty in the morning?"

"I have an appointment with Shaw. I must get ready now. I can't be late. I . . . I hope you'll forgive me."

"I'm disappointed, Cliff."

"I hope you will forgive me," he repeated heavily.

Clifford drove his Packard past his office and to an address that he had committed to memory. It was a tiny California redwood bungalow that he had taken to driving past each evening on his way home from work. This morning he parked the car, and making sure no one was watching him, he strode to the door and knocked on it with more violence than was necessary.

"Just a minute! I'm coming!"

The door opened, and there she was.

"Oh! Mr. Creighton! I mean, Cliff. Clifford!"

"Good morning, Miss Hugen. There's . . . some new land that . . . out by the beach . . . I'm considering purchasing. And you have such a fine . . . eye . . . for these things. I thought perhaps . . . if you wouldn't mind. If you have the day free. You might accompany me." He cursed himself for sounding like a nervous schoolboy. "Miss Hugen, I'd much appreciate your opinion on this matter."

Frances Hugen gravely regarded her visitor. Her face paled. Then she blushed. "I'd be honored, sir. I'm glad you value my opinion." Then she laughed and clapped her hands like a little girl. "I haven't seen the beach since I was a sixth-grader."

"Well!" he said gruffly. "What are we waiting for?"

In less than five minutes she reappeared, wearing a dark pleated skirt, a starched middy blouse, and sailor tie.

She skipped ahead of him down to the car.

"Oh, I'm so excited! I thought I'd have to spend the day working!"

He followed her, his heart pounding with happiness, his gut gripped with panic. *What am I doing?* he thought, once. Then he gave himself over to the irresistible temptations of happiness, and perhaps love.

They drove for two hours through fields, the sun at their backs. He was happy to be able to say "This is my land." And as they passed oil fields to the south, "That's mine, I bought it in 1895."

She marveled. "I was just a girl then! I was learning to paddle a canoe."

"Oh, Fanny! You . . . in a canoe!"

Then, from her laughter, he was inspired to a joke of the day. "How will the French stop the Germans?"

"I don't know. How *will* the French stop the Germans?"

"They'll hold them at the Rhone. Because they'll say, *Pas de lieu Rhone que nous!*"

After a moment of sorting it out, she trilled with laughter. "You're the only person I know who would tell a joke like that."

He drove her to Venice, Abbot Kinney's new fantasy world, where against hills made of raw dirt, canals had been dug, and arched bridges hastily constructed. A host of immigrant labor, hired on to dress in native costumes, sold saltwater taffy and rented bicycles. Because it was so much like a canoe, he hired a gondola and took her for a ride.

The gondolier really was Italian, and knowing lovers left the best tips, he took them for a leisurely ride along the quietest canals, and sang sweet love songs.

It happened again to Clifford, just as it had that night at dinner. There was no one in the world but them.

He offered her lunch in a stylish restaurant, but she preferred to walk along the pier, stopping at the various concessions for corn on the cob, cotton candy, a hot dog. Instead of champagne, she expressed a desire for a Green River. If she hadn't seen the Pacific since she was twelve, he could tell her that it had been years since he had drunk a Green River. And he had not sunk his teeth into a hot dog since long before they'd stopped calling it a frankfurter.

Clifford and Frances made their dessert of saltwater taffy. And with a sense of having saved the best for the last, he led her down the dark inside stairs into the pearly gray light under the pier. Then they were out in the dazzling sunlight, facing great walls of white foam, their faces wet with salt spray.

"Oh! Oh!"

Before Clifford understood what she was doing, she had sat right down on the sand—like a little girl—rucked up her skirts, and lifting one shapely leg into the air, began to roll down her stockings.

"Don't look," she said. "I don't know what would upset my dad more—the fact that I'm taking my stockings off in front of my boss or the fact that I'm rolling my stockings with garters."

Without waiting for an answer she jumped up, and still bunching up her pleated skirt, she ran down to the water's edge.

"Oh, my goodness!" she exclaimed.

Appalled, embarrassed, stupefied almost, Clifford reached down in the sand, picked up her silken hose, folded them, and put them in his jacket pocket. He started toward her and stopped, constrained by everything—his upbringing, his conscience, perhaps most of all by his heavy shoes and socks, his expensive business suit.

"Come on," she said. "Can't you come down with me?"

"I can't," he said. "You come back up here."

And so they walked together, he precariously above the surf line, uncomfortably aware of the sand in his shoes but unable, when it came to that, to run barefoot, to roll up his trousers, to act like the boy he wished he could be. She did not so much walk with him as dance around him, chasing the long, slow suck of the sea as it ebbed, rollicking back up against him as the ocean chased her almost into his arms.

Was it the heat that made him begin to sweat, or the unusual exertion of plodding through the hot dry sand? She noticed his flushed cheeks and hesitantly said, "Excuse me for saying so, Mr. Creighton, but aren't you a little warm in your jacket?"

"Actually, I am," he said, and slipped out of it. Then, after a moment, he loosened his tie.

For the first time in years, life seemed spontaneous, unexpected, promising, unusual. It must have been this new sense of freedom that made him, the next time Frances danced up out of the waves, reach out both his arms and take her to him in a crushing grip. His lips found hers.

She went limp; it was as though every cell in her body yielded to him.

How long was it before she pushed him away? Not long enough. He clutched at her as she weakly struggled. He was starved for her love, her youth.

When he was able to look into her face, he saw that she was crimson. Her breasts heaved. "I shall . . ." Her palms, flat against his chest, burned into him. "I shall forget that you ever did that."

"You may," he breathed, "but I won't."

She replied in a strained voice, "I think you'd better take me home."

It was a long, silent ride through the bean fields. But the silence, which he knew should have been awkward, was for him electric.

When at last they returned to her bungalow, the unseasonably warm winter sun, low on the horizon, cast a lurid yellow light over the quiet residential street.

She fairly leaped from the car, but he was close behind her. "I must insist, Frances, in spite of my abominable behavior, on seeing you to your door."

Then they were on her porch. She had opened the door. He could not help himself. With one arm he roughly pushed her into the little dark parlor. With his other hand he shut the door behind him. His mouth clamped on hers, and once again, this strong little girl grew weak, unable to stand unless she leaned against him.

"This is wrong, you know." Ironically, it was he who said that, as he laid her down on the studio couch which made up part of her working-girl's suite.

"I don't care," she crooned. "Cliff, I want you."

His hands sought her breasts under her middy blouse. They were young, young!

Tentatively, he let his hands stray lower on her body. She made no resistance. And when he felt the first beginnings of response, he loosened his belt with one hand, and in a single movement freed his lower body. She took in her breath sharply as she felt his hardness against her. She was unskilled in the arts of love. But her very freshness made her infinitely alluring to him.

He helped her pull her middy blouse over her head. And after he had loosened her skirt, she even raised herself slightly as he slid it down past her knees and onto the floor. She moaned as his lips traced the outline of her undergarments. And then he freed her from those final confinements. He took her right hand and closed it around his member.

"Oh!" she said.

He was afraid that he might disgrace himself, that all this would end too

250

soon; even worse, that he might lose that passion which so far had carried him along with the insistence of the very waves themselves.

But after he was inside her, he forgot about all that. He felt her move to the slow, controlled rhythm. For a time he lived in the illusion that this could last forever. But before long he knew he could not restrain himself and surrendered to the spasms of indescribable sensation.

He could not resist resting his weight for just a few moments upon her lovely body, and as he did so, her arms tightened about him. He was exhausted with the pure physicality of their act, and the whirlpool of emotions that threatened to overwhelm him. The final surge of his passion was surmounted by an equally powerful jolt of guilt.

"Cheer up, Cliff," she said, "it's not the end of the world."

"Yes, but—"

"People have made love before when they shouldn't have and no doubt they will again," Frances said. "I won't have you spoiling what's happened between us by indulging yourself in your Protestant conscience. I was brought up a good Catholic girl, Clifford Creighton. And I know that what we just did is a mortal sin, but I also know that there's not a thing in the world that can't be forgiven if you're sorry for it." Here she gave him an impish grin, seized those wings of silver hair that usually were combed carefully behind Clifford's ears. "All I'm asking is that you please try not to be sorry for this until tomorrow."

He pushed himself up on his elbows, then rolled over on his back. Whatever speech he had expected from her, it was not this one.

She continued. "You're the most beautiful man I've ever seen, Mr. Creighton. I'm sure that tomorrow, or a month from now, I may regret this. But I don't now. And, if I may say so, sir, it's really too much," here she grinned, "to deflower a poor working girl in the first quarter of an hour and feel sorry for it in the second."

Clifford blinked. All thoughts of waves, tides, and spontaneity were far from him now.

"I didn't say a word," he said, "did I?"

"No," she answered, "but you looked as if you might."

Their silence now was stranger by far than it had been in the Packard under the sultry sun. He was afraid that whatever he said now would be wrong. And so he lay stone still on the wrinkled sheets, wondering what he should do next. She got up, put on only her middy blouse, and twitched bewitchingly into what he guessed must be the kitchen. She returned in a minute with two glasses.

"It's only sherry, I'm afraid, but we'll pretend it's champagne."

To his chagrin, he was once again inflamed. It was that damned middy blouse, he thought, riding above her rosy, glowing buttocks that had put him into this state. You're for it now, Creighton, he thought desperately.

Whether by accident or on purpose, she spilled about a third of her own glass of sherry on his chest and as he flinched from the chill of it, she bent over to lap it up, her tongue curling around the locks of silver hair she found there. Finally, he gave way to the first temptation that had made him aware

251

of her. He reached out both hands to her already disturbed hair, which kept the shape of its bun only by the help of a last two reluctant pins. Luxuriously, he slipped both hands into that springy marvel. The pins skittered to the floor and he was lost, drowning again in a shower of curls that sheltered him from every care, every worry, everything but her.

It was close on to eleven o'clock that night when Clifford Creighton let himself in the front door with his own key. Only a few lights here on the ground floor had been left on for him. The household was presumably settled for the night.

Hardly knowing what to expect, he climbed up the circular staircase, down the long upstairs hall, and saw with sinking heart that the light was on in their bedroom. He opened the door and went in.

Victoria was still awake. She lay propped against pillows reading. She wore a new peach gown, with a remarkably low décolletage revealing attractions in contrast to her somewhat dated, gold-rimmed reading glasses.

She looked up and gave him a thin smile. "Did your meeting come to a satisfactory conclusion?"

"What can I say, Victoria?"

"Perhaps it wouldn't hurt to tell the truth," she said, removing her glasses and looking directly into his eyes. "So far as I know, we have never lied to each other. Wouldn't it be ridiculous to begin now?"

He sat down heavily in the morning chair where, for so many years, he had eaten breakfast and read the financial pages, secure in the illusion that his world had been and always would be the same.

"What would you like to know?"

"I'd like to know what has happened to us. I'd like to know if I'm imagining things, or if there is another woman. And if there is another woman, I'd want to know—not your excuses, Cliff—but how you feel about her, and me."

He took a deep breath, paused, and then said, "I suppose you could say there is another woman."

"*Suppose?* Aren't you sure?"

"Oh, Victoria. Of course there's another woman, but I'd be lying if I said I knew what it meant."

"Frances Hugen?"

"How did you know?"

"Clifford, dear! Sometimes you're such a simple fool. In fact, that always has been the most appealing thing about you. You're a book that doesn't even have to be opened to be read." Her tears spilled over. "I knew it was Frances Hugen from the minute I saw you two together." She fumbled, blinded, in a drawer by the nightstand for something to wipe her eyes.

Clifford, shaken, leaped up. "Dearest! Oh, Victoria! I never meant to hurt you! I didn't think! You're right, I was a fool. I always have been a fool, except when I fell in love with you. Oh, please, Victoria, don't cry!"

He sat on the bed beside her and she crumpled against him. He encircled

252

her with his left arm, patting her awkwardly. "I've been a fool," he repeated. "Can you forgive me?"

She sobbed against his chest. He reached with his free hand into his jacket pocket for a handkerchief, and before he could stop this reflex action, Frances Hugen's two silk stockings and one perky garter came into view, just as Victoria had lifted her head in the equally automatic expectation of having her eyes dried.

They froze for one long instant.

Then Victoria said, in a tone which Cliff had never before heard, "Clifford Creighton, you *are* a fool."

Two majestic stone lions marked the entrance of what purported to be Chinatown's newest, most opulent restaurant. And there *was* a restaurant, serving an attractive variety of regional dishes, but a tourist who kept his eyes open could not fail to notice that the diners here were dressed in evening clothes. And that after they paid the bill, they exited not through the front door onto the street, but disappeared behind elaborate inlaid Chinese screens.

The Lucky Dragon had already established itself as *the* exciting new place in town, where the very rich might gamble in comparative safety—since the police had been generously paid—and spend these hours in an ambiance of exotic elegance.

Besides advancing George his share of money for this venture, Sung had lent some of his gaudiest pieces, including an eleven-foot statue of Kali, the Goddess of Lust and Destruction, plundered from an ancient Calcutta temple during the Sepoy Uprising. Gamblers had already invented the custom of touching one of the goddess's many treacherous hands before making their way to the gaming tables of their choices, whether it was roulette, blackjack, craps, poker, or the traditional fan-tan and Mah-Jongg.

George had kept to his original plan of no singsong girls, but the dealers in charge of each of these games were the most beautiful females in Chinatown, and some of the most immoral. Many of them came from Macao, and all of them wore the *cheongsam,* that most seductive of all female attire, which, slit open to the top of the thigh, showed more enticing flesh than most of these citizens of Los Angeles had ever seen in their lives.

A string trio played light songs with a vaguely Oriental air; dozens of crystal chandeliers glittered. It was a vision of high life, a vision that, once George had consulted his own fantasies, he found had been there all the time.

Raoul had fallen into this vision with rough enthusiasm. The more money they spent, he reasoned, the more they would make later. And their duties as co-owners had easily sorted themselves out. George would act as smooth host, Raoul would lurk, menacingly at the ready, in case of any encroachment by low elements. It had given him rare pleasure to give a few of his old cock-fighting *compadres* the bum's rush.

Tonight, the sixth night since the opening of the Lucky Dragon, George lounged by the larger of the two roulette wheels and unobtrusively counted the house. It was their largest attendance, but the mood was oddly uneasy.

"I just don't think we should be out in *crowds,* that's what the paper said," a woman complained to her husband, and he answered, with the inborn chivalry of the true gambler, "Will you, for God's sake, *shut up, Alison?*"

George grinned.

The evening wore on. The liquor sales swelled, the coffers of the management filled. And, George exulted, all this was actually honest money. The liquor was the second best money could buy. The house profits were not extortionate. The girls from Macao had been instructed, to their disbelief, to give the customers an even break.

Then, suddenly, there was a commotion. A redheaded girl, a heavy winner so far that night, raised her voice in hectic complaint and then seemed close to fainting. The musicians stopped playing; one woman screamed. George was there in an instant. "It's nothing," he said soothingly. "She's probably just a little overexcited. You there, sir. Would you mind helping me take her to my office?" The businessman he had spoken to pulled back, but by this time Raoul had appeared.

"Just take her on that side," said Raoul. "Come on, honey, you can lie down in the back for a few minutes." He laughed and addressed the nervous onlookers. "Usually they do this when they've been *losing.*"

At a gesture from George the musicians began again. George and Raoul expertly walked the beautiful redhead, whose lips had parted in a feverish grimace, through heavy doors into their private office. They laid her unceremoniously on the couch, where Raoul spoke to her in tones which his wife might have recognized.

"Come on, sister! Who's your date? Who brought you here? How much booze did you pour down?"

In reply, she clutched her stomach, and leaning her head to one side, vomited what looked like pure bile onto one of Sung Wing On's finest Peking rugs.

"Chingada!" Raoul groaned. "That's what women are like, man! You can thank God you never got married."

George put a hand on the girl's brow. "She's got a fever. I'd better get her out of here."

Raoul shook his head with a touch of panic. "And leave me here with all those *bolillos?* You can't do that. I don't know what to say to those people. I'll take her home. It's all in a night's work."

As the Chinese servants cleaned up the mess, Raoul disappeared through a back door with the girl.

George went out into the crowd again. They had forgotten the incident, locked as they were in a fever of their own—hypnotized by the spin of the glittering wheels, the click of the dice, the chink of poker chips, and the lilting chants of the girls in their *cheongsams,* who uttered the ancient injunctions *Faites vos jeux* and *Rien ne va plus,* in accents that somehow called up the idea of a cosmopolitan league that stretched around the entire globe—devotees of daring, chance, and glamour.

By the time George was ready to go home, the evening's profits locked away in the safe, a last nourishing meal of noodles shared with the staff, in which gossip was exchanged and the events of the night reviewed, it was close to four-thirty in the morning.

George let himself quietly into his father's house. Since he had begun this business, he had ceased longing for a place of his own, and instead had begun to relish this home for what it could be to him—a sanctuary, a place safe from the strains of the outer world.

As he made his way toward his bedroom in the dimly lighted hall, he was surprised to come upon one of his youngest half-brothers wandering, almost asleep. "Say, aren't you going in the wrong direction?" he whispered to him. "Here, let me take you to the bathroom, Pavel. That's one place your big brother George can find even in the dark."

The little boy, groggy, took George's hand. In the bathroom George undid the small pajama pants and lifted the child up.

After he had also relieved himself, with Pavel leaning against his right leg and on the point of sliding back into sleep on the floor, George said, "Say, you'd better come with me. We don't want to wake up the whole family and have Mother making carrot eyes at us, do we?"

He had to smile at his own joke, for Pavel, now being carried in his arms, was already unconscious.

George closed his bedroom door soundlessly. Holding the boy with one arm, he turned back the covers of his bed and tucked in the quietly breathing child. George slipped out of his own clothes quickly, careful to hang up his ivory jacket and satin-striped trousers—a habit he knew earned him the respect and devotion of the household servants—before he put on the raw silk pajamas laid out for him.

He slid under the covers, careful not to disturb Pavel, whose childish lips curved in a contented smile. Looking at Pavel in the subdued light from the Chinese porcelain globe lamp set on a teapoy beside the bed, George yielded to his affectionate impulse and pillowed the reddish-brown curls of the young head on his chest before he turned out the light. He kissed the boy lightly, cradling him, and as he drifted into contented sleep he thought that there must be something a little wrong with what Raoul felt about family life.

Raoul had been cruising the streets with his unwanted passenger for an hour before he had been able to determine three things. One: The redhead had arrived at the Lucky Dragon with an escort, unnamed. Two: She did not want to go home, to an address that she refused to give him. Three: She was very, very sick.

"He said he loved me! *He* didn't love me! He just wanted to use me. He wanted my body! Well, I've had enough."

"How could anyone want *your* body? All you do with it is throw up."

"You're just like all the rest of them. Where are you driving me? Are you driving me up into the hills?" She leaned her head out of the window and retched.

"That's what I'm trying to find out—where I'm driving you. You say you don't want to go home—" Suddenly his temper flared: "Tell me where you want to go, or I swear, I'll dump you right in the street."

"You wouldn't do that," she said, turning fevered eyes upon him.

"Dumb bitch!" He screeched to a halt and, reaching across, opened her door. "Get out before I push you out!"

"I don't want to go home! I don't want to go home to him."

"Don't you have a mother?" he asked contemptuously.

His question seemed to bring her into focus. "Of course I have a mother. Everyone has a mother."

"Well?"

She began to weep and hold her stomach. "Mother doesn't love me."

With his two beefy hands Raoul braced himself against her and began to push.

"Fifty-two twelve Townsend Avenue! In Eagle Rock, off Colorado Boulevard, at the end of the Five-Car line."

"*Madre de Dios! Eagle Rock!* I might have known." And through the rest of the drive he taunted her. "Some glamour girl, huh? All the way from Eagle Rock! Do they speak with a French accent out there? God!"

She was asleep again but he went on talking. "I'm in the big time now, right? I don't have to listen to any more dumb bitches! So I spent all this money. So I get stuck with a round heels from *Eagle Rock.*"

On the shabby little street he stared with loathing at the tiny frame houses with their pathetic veneer of respectability. More than anything else in the world he wanted to open the door and finish what he had started—push her right into the gutter.

Then he thought of George—and cursing, he went around the car, opened the door, and scooped her up in his strong arms. He hoped she wouldn't dirty his shirt front, but she did.

"Ah, *puta*! Slut! Dumb bitch!"

He took satisfaction in leaning on the bell for what seemed like five minutes until the door opened, and a tired woman in a chenille bathrobe said, "What—"

He jerked open the screen. "I got something for you, lady." He stood the redhead on her feet, then with both hands, pushed her as hard as he could. He heard the crash as she landed, but he was already halfway back to his car.

It was still dark. He knew he should go home. But his shirt front stank. He knew that if he went home, Maria would say something. And no matter what Maria might say, he would beat her.

In spite of his new venture, his fancy clothes, he was trapped, still trapped, by his mother-in-law, his wife, his children, his life. He couldn't go back to it right now, it stank.

He drove toward downtown. And suddenly, without having thought much about it, he realized he was in his mother's neighborhood.

The last ten years had been kind to Magdalena. She, of all of them, had come up smelling like a rose. After all the years that he'd been after her to give up the boardinghouse, it had taken a *gringo* to persuade her. Now she lived, without a care in the world, on the top floor of a big apartment house with her Señor Smith. Of course, she said she lived alone, because he was married. But she was happy!

"Is that just?" he asked himself. "Is that right?" And suddenly it seemed imperative that he wake his mother, ask her how she had played this cruel trick, how she had managed to escape from everything in the world he had most hated, and managed in her "sweet" way to slough it all off on him.

He tried the same trick, leaning on the bell. But she was there in an instant, her hair combed back and fastened with tortoiseshell combs, decently clad in a morning gown of dull gray taffeta which rustled even as she stood still. She looked at him with no particular surprise.

"Raoul. *Que tal?* Come in. Can I get you some coffee?" She surveyed him appraisingly. "Aren't you a little overdressed for this hour?"

"What are you doing up?" he blustered.

"I have always risen early, *mijo*. First to work, and now to enjoy the dawn."

Raoul peered past her into the spacious penthouse. "You mean *he's* here," he said rudely. "I don't want to interrupt your enjoyment, Mama."

"You always had a bad mouth," she said impassively. "Do you want some coffee or not?"

They sat together at a small breakfast table that overlooked the entire city, watching in silence as night turned into chilly dawn.

Finally she said, "I am up early, Raoul, because I am waiting for news. They called John Frederick away in the night." She permitted herself a small smile. "His wife is sick."

He was drawn into it in spite of himself. "But she's always sick, isn't she?"

"She has had headaches. But this time it may be the influenza."

"So?" Another sick woman. Was there no end to this female conspiracy?

"There was something in the paper last night. They said it couldn't come out here, but then they said it might already be here. . . ."

When the *Times* was delivered, it confirmed her fears. Overnight, emergency wards had begun to fill up.

Magdalena looked up and said, "I don't care if that woman dies or not. But I am afraid for John Frederick. They say it is very contagious." She paused, and sighed. "Do not accuse me of telling old stories. But I know what something like this can do to a city."

Raoul did not answer. He had been reading. His earlier rage congealed into nausea and fear. "My luck is holding, Mama," he said. "You see this stain on my shirt?"

She nodded.

"I've been exposed." He got up to leave, but she put herself between him and the door.

"Where do you think you're going?"

"Home, where else?"

"Where else?" she echoed. "Almost anywhere else. You are always the same, Raoul. You think only of yourself. I can understand you wanting to give this sickness to your wife, but do you want to take your children with you?"

He couldn't answer. Was it his imagination, or could he feel the sickness starting? He put his hand to his forehead. It was hot.

"You will stay here," she said dispassionately. "I will send word to Maria. I will do my duty, and you will do yours, whether you want to or not."

Los Extravagantes had shipped out together, landed at Cherbourg, flown to the air bases behind the French lines in the same squadron. For the five days they had been here, they had insisted on flying as a group, and had accounted for seventeen downed planes. *Los Extravagantes* flew together or not at all, and when keeping score, a Fokker didn't go to the credit of Turner, or Faulkner, or McCoy, or Fitzgerald, or Mariné, but to *Los Extravagantes*. They all wore the white scarves now. One by one the laconic Anglos had succumbed to the insane Latin exuberance of this madman who gave them lessons in good humor and courage.

On the ship coming over they had stolen a fresh sheet from sick bay, torn it into five impossibly long white scarves, and drunkenly made the extra tears for fringe. Then they had staggered aft, this time with bottles of contraband whiskey, and held their glasses aloft as Alessandro Mariné doffed his tattered silken banner and wound the torn bedsheet around his neck. They cheered as his old scarf floated off in the wake.

"Goodbye to the past," he shouted. "Hello to new adventures! We are part of the same fabric now, my comrades-in-arms!"

On their sixth day in action, the squadron, having taken evasive action against a superior formation of Fokkers, had been drawn dangerously far into enemy territory. With fuel running low, *Los Extravagantes* had turned back toward their base. It had not been a bad morning. They had downed three German planes. They had buzzed a marching column of Boches as they left the front, but disdained to fire—because Alessandro had told them that that was not the act of a gentleman.

Then, between them and the bright morning sun, there were fully a dozen Fokkers, guns blazing. What happened next remained in their minds forever. Alessandro Mariné went into a slow roll, gained altitude, and gliding gracefully, as if there were all the time in the world, did the impossible; he veered straight into the leading planes of the German formation. He must have taken out the first two. The middle plane dove beneath him. The rear planes, displaying rigorous Teutonic training, began to fire, and before they realized what they were doing, had destroyed three of their own.

There was nothing for the others to do but watch as the last of the Fokkers peeled away in panic, and Alessandro's plane went down in a white trail of smoke.

After they had landed, as Turner made his report, he broke down and cried like a baby.

Two weeks after the opening of the Lucky Dragon, attendance had tapered off considerably. The spreading influenza had discouraged people from circulating in public places. Raoul was down with the infection himself; and George, though the sickness had apparently skipped him, had his own reasons for staying at home.

Within twenty-four hours little Pavel burned with fever. George sat endless hours by the child's bedside, blaming himself for carrying the disease home. Once again, fate had decided that George would suffer only vicariously.

"I'll pay anything," George declared, "to get the best medical treatment." But here he found himself up against the stony opposition of both Katarina and Sung.

"Doctors kill you," Katarina insisted. "They no good for my baby boy! I know from the old country the only way to expel the evil spirit."

Katarina scurried about the house exclaiming angrily over the servants' efficiency. "They clean this house too good! They don't know how to run a house. Every house needs some spider's webs." It was only when she thought of the storeroom upstairs reserved for traveling trunks and an overflow of merchandise from Sung's store that she let up on her tirade. In the storeroom she found a great wealth of cobwebs and wound them in threads around her hands. In the kitchen, she mixed the webs and ashes from the stove, and mustard. For a moment she hesitated. Would the Chinese mustard be too hot? But she decided this would probably work for the good, because the little boy, after all, was himself half Chinese. She applied the plaster to the toddler's chest. He whimpered and vomited.

It wasn't until the Chinese herbalist arrived that Sung's plan became clear. The herbalist invaded the kitchen to brew an infusion. When the water came to a boil he opened several small containers, and taking a pinch of material from each, he cast them into the bubbling water. When George asked what was in the mixture, the herbalist hastily condescended to respond in Chinese, "Tiger's dung, buffalo testicles, dried phython's blood, and bats' eyes!" George tried to reassure himself that there were no tigers, buffalo, or pythons in California. Even if these truly did come from China, he hoped the trip had weakened their power and the boiling water destroyed it. But George could not deny that the fumes smelled like nothing less than the claims made for them.

Although Pavel's condition didn't improve, neither did it worsen. But by the following day when Jitka and Gretel began showing the earliest symptoms of the infection, George took matters into his own hands and left the house in search of a western doctor.

Since Clifford's indiscretion, the Creighton household had taken on the atmosphere of an armed camp. Victoria had retreated to the guest room. Clifford, still uncertain as to the ultimate outcome, held himself in reserve. Without forming any clear plans Clifford went to work early and stayed late, a tactic that did little to resolve the situation.

The Priests, meanwhile, played the role of discreet observers. Pansy had more than once lashed out at her husband, "Everyone knows the way men are!" But Pansy had to grudgingly admit that Miss Victoria was looking downright awful. Her eyes were ringed with red. Her skin was drawn tight over her cheekbones. She ate little and her hair had lost its luster. Even her fine clothes seemed to lose their shape and hung loosely on her.

As on every Sunday, Ruth, after attending early Mass with the Mariné entourage, joined her parents for brunch. Ruth did little to take the strain off the conversation. She was well into her ninth month of pregnancy and had religiously followed the latest obstetric fad. She had gained no less than fifty pounds and complained bitterly of swollen ankles, excessive perspiration, and the increasing activity of the Mariné heir.

"And you know, Daddy, sometimes I think he knows right where my kidneys are!"

"Oh, Ruth!" her mother was moved to exclaim.

"But it's perfectly natural, Mother. Dr. Barstow says. . . ."

To Clifford the lunch seemed interminable. He couldn't look at Victoria; he couldn't look at Ruth. Clifford made it a point not to listen to his daughter's medical reports and only half heard her continued ritual complaint over Alessandro's failure to write. Finally, Clifford just couldn't take any more.

"Ah," he began, "I have some important matters left over at the office that I really should attend to."

"Why, Daddy," Ruth said, jarred out of her self-concern, "nobody works on Sunday."

"Times change," he said, offering the first lame excuse that came to mind. Clifford pushed himself away from the table and stood up.

But before he had a chance to go farther, Porter Priest came in and announced, "Miss Ruth, Colonel Victor and Major Trent of the Air Force are here to see you. They are waiting in the drawing room."

For a moment Ruth was frozen. Then, in a quavering voice she asked, "Mother, Daddy, won't you come with me?"

Clifford held Ruth's elbow as she heaved herself up and Victoria led the way to the drawing room.

The two officers stepped forward ceremoniously and introduced themselves. Then Colonel Victor said, "Mrs. Mariné, we went to your home in San Gabriel and were told we could find you here. We come on the least pleasant duty, but we are obliged to carry it out. It is with deep regret that we must announce to you the gallant death in combat of Captain Alessandro," here he glanced at the telegram, "Captain Alessandro Luis Antonio de Ortega de Moreno de Aıellanos de Mariné y Ruiz. You have our deepest sympathy. The only comfort we can offer is that, as his comrades report, he died bravely in the service of his country and his death was instant. Your husband will no doubt be decorated for conspicuous gallantry in giving his life to save his comrades from certain destruction."

Ruth, after a moment of silence in which all five of them stood motionless, said, "Colonel, I appreciate your taking the trouble to give me this news personally. I want to thank you—" But she could not go on.

Her father took over. "Gentlemen, I too wish to thank you for your consideration. Perhaps it would be best if we left my daughter with her mother. Won't you come with me?" He moved toward the door to the entrance hall, the officers, visibly relieved, following him.

As he reentered the drawing room he saw Victoria doing her best to cradle Ruth, whose whimpers had grown to a steady wail.

"My Alessandro, my Alessandro!"

Victoria stroked her daughter's hair in unconscious rhythm with Ruth's cries and joined in with her own quiet chant. "Now dear, now, now, my dear."

Clifford hesitated before crossing over. His movement drew Victoria's attention from Ruth and when he stood beside them he was met with nothing but her steely stare. Clifford stood there awkwardly.

"You can be of no help here." Victoria's voice was hard and merciless. "If you really have work waiting for you on Sunday, perhaps the best thing for you to do would be to go and attend to it."

Whatever words had been forming in his mind died stillborn. He looked helplessly at his wife and his child, aware that by unspoken agreement they had already closed him out.

With Victoria's eyes still upon him, he spoke. "All right, if that's the way you want it. The least I can do is obey."

When she said nothing further he turned on his heel, crossed to the door, and closed it behind him. But even as he did this his parental heart was torn with the sounds of his daughter's mourning.

Clifford wandered aimlessly through the lush offices on the executive floor of his building. Thinking back to his beginnings, he remembered how his first sponsor, Logan-Fisher, had spoken to him of the nature of life. Just when you believed that your life was safe and secure, disaster might strike. This was still a wild, unpredictable place with its own primitive lures. A man had to be careful here or he could lose everything.

The evening wore on. Clifford couldn't, wouldn't go home. There was nothing he could do for Ruth. And Victoria? How had he let his life get so out of control? By midnight Clifford had fallen into a fitful sleep on one of the office couches. Surely things would seem clearer in the morning.

Inside her room, Victoria lay in bed in a cold sweat, too sick to move. It was unconscionable, she thought, when her daughter needed her most that she herself had been taken ill. There was no place for the young, pregnant widow to go but home alone to the Mariné adobe.

For Victoria, it was as if her body had taken perverse control, replacing her customary will and determination. This feeling was confirmed when waves of nausea forced her to the bathroom. As she retched, she realized that she'd eaten nothing since the ill-fated lunch. Her only relief came, and even that was minimum, when she was able to bring up a mouthful of bitter bile. Too weak to stand just yet, she lay down on the cool tile floor and wept.

As on every Monday morning Creighton Enterprises bustled with activity. The new oil well had come in with a flow even higher than the original prediction, which meant that it was necessary to reestimate all of their plans. Sales for Patrician Estates were going splendidly and it would be less than a month before the entire project sold out. But Clifford had no time to consider these developments.

He spent the first part of the morning trying to get through to the Señora. After speaking to several weeping men and women he had finally been permitted to offer his condolences and, once again, give some comfort to Ruth.

When Clifford called for Frances Hugen to be sent to his private office, it was left to one of the underlings to explain that the girl wouldn't be coming in today. In fact, she'd called in just that morning to say she was quitting.

Clifford was at Frances Hugen's door within minutes. She answered his ring wearing a silk kimono. She paled when she saw him.

"Oh, Clifford, you shouldn't have come here."

"I have to speak to you."

"Please don't say anything. Just go away. Go home."

Clifford shook his head.

"Mr. Creighton, when I called the office they told me about your son-in-law. You shouldn't be here. Your family needs you."

Clifford touched her cheek. "You're a wonderful girl. I don't feel any great personal grief about Alessandro. In all honesty I never really took to the boy. But his death made me think. If I were younger, or a different person . . . but I'm not."

"You really don't have to go on." She tried to smile and then said, "I'm in quite a hurry. You see, I'm leaving Los Angeles."

"Fanny, let me in. We must talk."

She shrugged, tightened her kimono around her, and stood back. Her tiny bungalow was in complete disarray. Drawers had been emptied into trunks, paintings covered with butcher paper, and books piled into cardboard boxes.

Even before Clifford had a chance to speak, Frances cut him off in her hasty way. "I've been thinking, too. I was brought up to do the right thing. The Hugens don't break up families. Believe me, I have no regrets. You and I never had a future."

"Do you have any definite plans?"

"I'm going to New York, get a job, and save my money until the war is over. Then I'm going to go to Paris and learn how to paint. My parents will think I'm crazy, but I know I have some talent. I've got to give it a chance."

Clifford stifled a wrenching sense of loss and a somewhat shaming sense of relief. "If you're sure you think that's best," he said cautiously.

"I do."

Clifford reached into his vest pocket and pulled out a packet of bills.

"I'm not that kind of girl!"

"Of course not," he said, "but I want you to think of this as a bonus for making the Patrician Estates development the great success it has turned out to be. After all, it's really your work, and yours alone, that was responsible."

Frances considered for a long moment.

"I feel that I shouldn't," she said. "But I accept on the grounds that I know you'd want me to be the best artist I can. I won't spend this on anything frivolous. I'll put it away—for the future. Now, you'd better go before . . ."

While Porter took the car to the garage, Clifford looked for Victoria. Finding the drawing room empty, he sought out Pansy in the kitchen. Even to his untrained eyes her face showed the signs of strain and he suspected that she'd been crying.

"Pansy, is Mrs. Creighton down in the rose garden?"

"No, sir," her voice quavered and Clifford wondered what he had done to inspire such fear. "Mrs. Creighton hasn't been out of her room all day."

"Oh, well," Clifford cleared his throat. "Thank you, Pansy."

Clifford climbed the stairs and spoke through her door.

"Victoria, we simply cannot go on in this way. I have something to say to you and unless you have locked the door against me, which I cannot imagine you doing, I'm coming in."

"No, please, go away," he heard her voice from the other side of the door.

He opened the door and walked in. "Truly, I'm sorry that I have to do this, Victoria." But he stopped when he saw his wife. She lay limply across a velvet chaise longue, an afghan over her legs. Her hair hung in matted strings and her brow glistened with sweat. "Victoria!" he exclaimed. "You aren't well."

"Go away and leave me alone. No, wait a minute!" Victoria pulled herself up with visible effort. "*I* have something I want to tell *you!* I've had a lot to mull over in the last few days."

Clifford tried to interrupt, but she raised her hand and went on with difficulty.

"I'm aware of what's called for in a situation like this. I'm also aware of my age and station in life. I presume from what's happened that you find I've become boring, but why don't you take a good look at yourself? I'm supposed to be interested in your business. But after all these years, your business is tedious to me. How many times can I show enthusiasm when you make a killing? How can you expect me to show fresh, girlish excitement when you make another million after all the millions you've acquired? Why, you've already made enough to insure our great-great-grandchildren the best possible futures."

He tried once again to interrupt, but she was not to be stopped.

"I'm supposed to spend two or three hours a day trying to look young and pretty. But I'm not as young and pretty as I once was. I'm supposed to smile when you come home late, with sunburn marks on your back. I'm supposed to sit at home quietly while half of Pasadena talks about your infatuated behavior. But we're both too intelligent for that kind of charade. And you've got a long wait coming if you think I'm going to try any feminine wiles to win you back. Now, if you'll excuse me. . . ."

Victoria fell back in an exhausted heap. Clifford rushed over to her.

"Stay away from me," she said. "I must have the influenza."

"I'm going to call Dr. Bradley and see that you're properly taken care of."

Clifford reluctantly left his wife's side, and going to the library, called the doctor; then he sent Pansy up to look after her mistress. He longed to be by Victoria's side, but he didn't want to upset her any further. He paced restlessly until Porter Priest appeared with a glass of Scotch.

"I hope you don't think I'm presuming, sir," Porter said to him. "But I've found that there are times when all men need a little help."

"Thank you, Porter."

Encouraged by this response, Porter went on. "Mrs. Priest and I want you to know that we have every confidence that these difficulties will pass."

Before Clifford had a chance to answer they saw the lights of Dr. Bradley's car coming around the driveway and Porter hurried to open the door.

Twenty minutes later—during which Clifford paced through every room on the ground floor trying to find a comfortable chair, rejecting them all—Dr. Bradley had returned with Porter to the library.

"Will she be all right?" Clifford asked, trying to read the answer in Bradley's face. Bradley's expression puzzled him. And when Bradley failed to answer immediately Clifford felt that his worst fears might be coming true.

"Actually, Clifford," Bradley began seriously, but then his face cracked into a wide grin, "we'll know in about seven months."

"Why in the world should it take that long?" Clifford demanded indignantly.

"Well," Bradley said, "to date, nine months has been normal term for the human species."

"What are you talking about? What does the human species have to do with this? I just want to know if Victoria's going to be all right."

"It has everything to do with it, Clifford. You are a sly dog pretending you don't know what I'm talking about. Come on, Papa, drink a toast to the new baby Creighton."

Clifford looked bewildered. *"What?* Do I really understand you're telling me I'm going to be a father again after all these years?"

"That's right," Bradley said, lifting his glass. "Even for Creighton Enterprises some investments take a long time to mature."

As the realization finally hit him, Clifford turned to Porter and said, "You've got to get yourself a glass and the three of us will drink to the future."

As soon as they had toasted and drunk to the new life, Clifford excused himself sheepishly, ran up the stairs, and burst into the guest room.

"Victoria, my darling, before you say anything, I want you to know that I see it all clearly. Whatever has happened has already ended. That's what I've been trying to tell you.

"Oh, Cliff!" Victoria gasped from her bed.

"You're the only woman in my life. You've always been smarter about things than I have. You're right, I have become stuffy in many ways."

"Oh, Cliff," Victoria repeated, her eyes filling with tears.

264

"No, there's no point in denying it," Cliff said. "But from what Bradley says it looks as if we haven't become *completely* stuffy."

Her eyes lit up. For the first time in weeks Clifford saw in her a reminder of the liveliness of the old days and he felt a spark of renewed fire in himself. Taking her hands he put them to his lips and said, "Look, we have a young life to look after now, and if you're willing, I'm willing too, to try to be as young as we were when we first rode out on Apple and Black Barb."

It had been a week since Pavel had come down with the influenza. Since then nine other children had succumbed to the disease and of those, four had already died from complications. Now Katarina could no longer prepare her peasant plasters for she had taken to her bed with a high fever, chills, and frequent attacks of nausea. Sung still summoned the herbalist, not for his healing abilities but for the sake of both their standings in the community.

George had won out in the end and an American doctor—who charged triple his normal fee to come into Chinatown—now came to the house twice a day. But Dr. Blitz had little to offer other than standard advice on the intake of liquids, cleanliness, and ventilation. And he insisted on cloth masks for the children who were well and wore one himself at all times.

After little Pavel had died in George's arms, Dr. Blitz had said, "Why don't you hold off on funeral arrangements? Chances are you will lose more before it's over." George was too grief-stricken to do more than look at him with contempt.

When Katarina had sickened, George, together with two of the older girls still uninfected, had taken over the immediate running of the household, the supervision of the servants, and the nursing care for the sick ones. Sung had tried to go about his normal business. But even though it was not proper for a Chinese husband to show concern he had spent hours at Katarina's bedside. In addition he had made arrangements with the Chinese mortuary for the temporary care of the bodies and preparations for the family funeral, whenever it would take place.

George had compulsively watched over each of his half-brothers and sisters. He had read them stories, wiped their foreheads, spoon-fed them, and stayed with them through their sleepless nights. George had grown weaker, but he did not come down with the disease. One morning, after pronouncing two more children dead, Dr. Blitz took a good look at George and said, "You've got to get some rest or you'll pass out on your feet and be more of a burden than a help."

George regarded him through narrowed eyelids and said, "I can't. I'm responsible for too many deaths."

As on every day, the two señoras Marinć attended noon Mass and were now spending the afternoon on their knees in the family side-chapel dedicated to Saint Joseph of Copertino, where they had placed Alessandro's Congressional Medal of Honor beneath the statue.

"Truly, it is God's will," the Señora sighed. "Has not Saint Joseph

265

become the patron of all aviators? Though my darling has been taken from us he has flown directly through the upper reaches to his eternal home."

Ruth sobbed, but the Señora continued, "And in the wisdom of our own saint and the Holy Trinity you have within you the fluttering wings of his successor."

Ruth's sobs lessened but she was still unable to speak.

"My dear," the Señora went on, "I have brought today a memento of our own Alessandro, commissioned before his birth by his father, the Señor Alfredo Jesús Luis Ortega de Moreno de Arrelanos de Mariné, and crafted by the best goldsmiths of Oaxaca." From the engulfing folds of her black gown she brought forth a six-inch gold crucifix on a heavy chain. "This symbol of His suffering stood guard over our Alessandro's cradle. And now I give it to you to protect the precious life within."

Ruth took the crucifix, kissed it, and clutched it to her swelling breasts. "I will keep it, Mama, for the child, forever."

As the servants picked up the newspapers Magdalena had insisted on spreading over the entire apartment to prevent the germs from infesting the furniture, she and Raoul ate one last breakfast together. He had regained his strength slowly once he had passed the most crucial phase. The illness had hit him hard, and he had gone through periods of delirium. Magdalena would never tell him that during these sessions he had called to her like a baby, the baby she had loved unconditionally.

For two weeks they had been almost isolated from the outer world. Magdalena had given daily telephone bulletins to Maria on Raoul's condition. Maria, alone to make her own decisions, had kept her children at home and perhaps it was because of this that they escaped untouched. When news of her brother's heroic death reached her, Maria was free to give herself over to grief and frequent visits to San Gabriel.

Magdalena had received daily telephone calls from John Frederick. He had offered to send a doctor, to help in any way, to take her from the sickbed for an afternoon. But all of these she had refused for fear that he would fall ill himself. Wanting to wait until Raoul's condition was resolved, as well as thinking that he should add in no way to the pressures under which Magdalena was already working, he said nothing of an important development in his own personal life. Thus it fell that Magdalena read in the *Times* that the long-ailing Mrs. John Frederick Smith had herself succumbed in this epidemic. Magdalena reacted to the news with mixed feelings. On the one hand, his wife had been suffering from a series of vaguely mysterious illnesses for as long as she could remember. Even in Sonoita, the household servants had argued about the Señora's chances of surviving one season over the next. Only Dolores, the Señora's personal attendant and the only one, in fact, to see the Señora, refused to take part in these speculations. She would say scornfully, "Have no fear, my friends. The Señora, for all her sicknesses, will live longer than the rest of us."

On the other hand, Magdalena was not sure how this would change her relationship with John Frederick. She was not even certain that she wished for any change. And so, even though they spoke frequently over the telephone, she made no mention of his wife's death.

Now as she and her son sat across from each other, she looked at Raoul's face; it had grown far thinner than she could ever remember. The clothes that Maria had sent hung baggily on his no-longer-stout frame. Magdalena realized that he'd changed in other ways as well. Maybe it was his brush with death that had washed away the contempt he felt toward his family.

"I owe it all to you, Mama," he said. "I have everything to live for. George and I will make a real success of the Lucky Dragon. And it is good of Maria to have shown so much concern during these days. She has been a good wife to me. I have neglected her and the children terribly."

"I'm happy to hear you speak this way," said Magdalena. But to herself she wondered how lasting this change would be.

"You were so brave, Mama, to keep me here, especially when you could have sent me to the hospital. You have more courage than Pancho Villa, and you're prettier too."

Magdalena laughed as they rose from the table. At the door, Raoul embraced her for the first time in ten years and then he was gone. In her heart Magdalena wished him well, but she suspected it was not to be.

The funeral procession marched from the Sung residence to the local temple where the death ceremonies would be carried out. As the chief mourner, Sung, dressed in the traditional coarse white robe, walked behind the blaring brass band hired for this occasion. Katarina followed a few steps behind him. She too wore mourning white. Sung, remembering a tradition of the home village, had had their new white cloth shoes trimmed with red piping. Red was the color of happiness and this seeming forgetfulness was an indication of the deepness of their grief. Next in the procession came the several professional mourners, carrying large framed portraits crudely touched up with pink tint by the photographer's assistant. The photographs showed the seven faces of the dead children as they had been in life. For at the end of three weeks, Pavel, Gretel, Ponko, Binki, Marya, Vaclav, and Birgd, ranging in age from three to twenty-one, had been taken by the disease. Out of Katarina and Sung's twelve living children only five remained. The coffins, each supported by four to eight bearers, swayed as they were borne forth.

Immediately behind them, George and the rest of the children—Milan, Jitka, Thadius, Dynamite, and Jiri—led the other mourners, hundreds in number. Thirty more professional mourners among them wailed in abandon, tore their hair, carefully ripped their worn robes as they cried out against the bitter fate that fortune had dealt this noble, wealthy family. The others behaved in a less extravagant manner, but many among them openly wept. As the sea of white-clad mourners made their way down Alameda they were accompanied by men who carried poles wound about with strings of firecrackers, adding to the general din as they crackled, punctuated by the louder explosions of every twelfth cracker that was five times the size of the others.

Here and there appeared dark-clad figures. Raoul and Magdalena were there, as well as certain Caucasian merchants and some men from City Hall, including old Jordan Espey. The Creightons had sent a telegram of regrets, excusing themselves because of Victoria's condition and fear for her well-being in crowds while this infection still raged through the city.

Bringing up the rear of the procession, incense-bearers and the family servants carried trays of candy and red paper envelopes enclosing coins. These would be given to each of the mourners at the conclusion of the rites. The money symbolized good fortune, and the candy was meant to wash away the bitter taste of death.

"You know, Victoria," Clifford said as they drove through the bean fields to the west, "this is a little like traveling the Great Plains. Sometimes I think when we're in Pasadena that we haven't quite left the East behind us. We still live in echoes of Baltimore, Philadelphia, Boston, though nobody would dare admit it. But now driving west is like crossing the continent. We'll know we've truly arrived when we can see the ocean itself."

"Goodness, Cliff," Victoria laughed, "I never thought to hear you make a speech like that."

It really wasn't like him, she reflected, to take her out simply to look at property. When he had asked her to "look at some houses in Venice," she had been more than willing to make good the pretense; for it was a beautiful day, she was feeling well again, and by now she was going a little crazy from Cliff's insistence that she stay in the house. And she knew the sea air would do her good.

"It's just that I've been thinking, Victoria, about our new life," he said as they drove down the narrow Venice streets. "I've spoken with Ruth and told her that she would always have a home with us, but I really think that she now prefers to be in San Gabriel, with the Señora, close to the Mission."

"Yes, Ruth seems to find a center there."

"Well, be that as it may. . . ." Then he continued in his previous light manner. "You see, Victoria, it's that old house, that old Pasadena house. It's not that we'd ever want to give it up, but we've become almost as much of an institution for our time as the Logan-Fishers were for theirs."

"I suppose I've never looked at it that way."

"The house almost takes over, and we have to act in a manner appropriate to it. Not that I regret any moment of our lives together, but I do think that after thirty-three years we shouldn't be afraid of adventure. I'm not suggesting an African safari," he said as he drove the car under the porte cochere of a large handsome seaside villa, "but I do think for our new life we need a cozy little beach cottage."

Clifford turned off the motor, got out of the car, and came around it to open the door for Victoria. She could see that he was tremendously pleased with himself and said, "You're certainly full of surprises today."

He held her hand as they walked up to the front door. He took the large master key from his pocket, unlocked the door, and let it swing open. Then he swept Victoria up into his arms and carried her over the threshold. He set her down in an empty, airy, light-filled, glass-paneled entrance hall. The spacious rooms that she could see beyond had dark hardwood floors, beamed ceilings, and open bay windows that let in the tangy sea air.

"This *is* a nice little place, isn't it?" Victoria said, as they strolled through the rooms, her heels clicking on the pegged floors. "It really has a style of its own."

Clifford grinned smugly. "You always have noticed the important things, but would you have any idea who has designed this?"

"Well, my dear," she said, smiling up at him, "I haven't been so far out of things as not to recognize what the future will certainly consider one of the Greene Brothers' masterpieces of domestic architecture."

They commented on the individual details: the hand-carved mantelpiece over the ample fireplace in the large living room, the bay windows in each bedroom of the second floor which looked out on the Pacific Ocean, the arched passageways between the downstairs public rooms, which themselves offered a variety of vistas. Here and there an alcove offered a suggestion of intimacy and seclusion.

"You see, Victoria," Cliff said, "we ought to have a place that's smaller—just for the three of us."

"Yes," she smiled, radiant with the flush of maternity, "and a nurse, and cook, and the Priests, of course."

BOOK V

1929

And from the floating bodies, the incense
 blue-pale, purple above them.
Shelf of the lotophagoi,
Aerial, cut in the aether.
                            Reclining,
With the silver spilla,
The ball as of melted amber, coiled, caught up, and turned.
Lotophagoi of the suave nails, quiet, scornful,
Voce-profondo:
        "Feared neither death nor pain for this beauty;
If harm, harm to ourselves."

                            Pound, *Canto XX*

ITH the end of the war the entire country had prospered. A few private banks had failed because of overextended credit, but none of this had touched Southern California. More and more people were drawn to it—first coming as visitors and then staying on as enthusiastic, permanent residents. Real estate had burgeoned; community after community sprang up in areas that had originally been thought good only for bean fields, walnut or citrus groves.

The one deterrent to happiness—and this in some measure affected the Creightons—was the passage of the Volstead Act, "Prohibition." Most Angelenos were forced to use the products of doubtful bootleggers and to frequent night spots and speakeasies that opened up throughout the city. A strip of Sunset Boulevard was the safest place to go for liquor since it crossed an unincorporated area between the cities of Los Angeles and Beverly Hills.

But the Creightons, like a few other families of equal wealth and shrewdness, had had the foresight to lay down vast supplies of vintage French and California wines and spirits. The already ample cellar in their Pasadena home was enlarged to twice its original size and one room at the beach cottage had been converted, fitted with racks, shelves, and electric temperature control. Porter Priest had been right when he said, "We should be able to ride out the whole rough voyage on these liquids."

The first signs of possible disaster came late in the summer of 1929 when a few abrupt movements in the stock exchange took most of the country by surprise. The Creightons felt no great personal concern, though Clifford could see the cramping effect a serious disturbance in the money market would have on his holdings.

On that fateful October night, the Creightons kept an engagement with Headsperth and Belle Bauer and their niece at the Ambassador Hotel's

Coconut Grove. After paying the sizable tips to the maître d' and waiter, they sat drinking illicit champagne at a corner table underneath papier-mâché palm trees. An orchestra played the popular tunes of the day, and couples crowded on the small dance floor in the center of the sophisticated nightclub lit by indirect rose-colored lights. Black ties and either cocktail dresses or evening gowns were the accepted dress, and the scent of gardenias perfumed the air.

As the three women chatted, Headsperth leaned forward eagerly toward Cliff and said, "I don't suppose I have to tell you what a fantastic opportunity today's action on the market has opened up."

"You always were a great joker," Clifford said.

"No, I mean it. After this shakedown the market's certain to rocket up," said Headsperth. "Old boy, this is a time to be aggressive. The market's bound to go up farther than ever."

Clifford shook his head. "I've never been one for buying on margin. What I own I really own, no strings attached. And it looks to me as if things could get more than a little worse."

"You're going to miss the boat this time," said Headsperth. "I know what I'm going to do. I'm going to borrow every dollar I can and buy right in. . . ."

The rising tone of his voice attracted Belle's attention and she listened for a few moments. Hearing this last statement of her husband's, she sighed, looked at Clifford with a resigned expression, and returned to the conversation she was having with her niece and Victoria.

Iris Bauer, at eighteen, was an attractive blonde. Some might have called her slight; others, like her uncle, called her "bean pole" and kept encouraging her to eat. But Iris was the kind of girl who didn't like to take orders or even follow suggestions, and the more her Uncle Headsperth urged her to eat, or do anything else for that matter, the more she'd stubbornly refuse. Since Iris had come for her extended visit, Belle had had to play the role of mediator between her husband and her niece, and, childless herself, found she was delighted to have a daughter at last.

Victoria was quite taken with the girl's simple, charming ways and could see that Iris was torn between curiosity and delight: the opulent life she was seeing for the first time, and her loyalty to certain standards that had been instilled in her during what had clearly been a more severe and less privileged youth.

"Mrs. Creighton, Auntie Belle, this is the prettiest room I've ever seen. We didn't have anything like this in South Dakota or Colorado," the girl said, taking in all the details of the room. "I only wish Mama could have seen this," she added without a hint of sentimentality. "It looks just like a movie. It's not real at all."

"Some things don't have to be real," said Victoria.

"Yes, but everything in Los Angeles looks like a painting, a fairy tale. People spend so much money for just the front of a building. I suppose if they get tired of it they throw it out and get a new one."

"Humph!" Headsperth grunted. "Little girl, you don't know a darn thing!"

"All I'm saying, Uncle," Iris said innocently, "is that where I come from people work hard for very little. Here people don't seem to work at all and they have everything."

"My brother was a fool. If he'd come to California he could have had every success I've had. But no, he worked that rocky acreage until it broke him and he died."

"Headsperth, please," begged Belle, "don't get started on that again."

"It's my own father you're talking about, Uncle Headsperth. He left us enough to go on for ourselves. And, let me say, Uncle, that a lot of things about you have reminded me of him."

"What? You think I'm like brother Burt?"

Victoria, noticing that her husband was on the point of breaking into laughter, said, "Why, Headsperth, this city wouldn't have been big enough for both you and your brother Burt."

Everyone laughed except Headsperth, who after a moment of puzzlement, said, "Victoria, you have always been an astute woman."

Iris made no response to this comment. She'd been distracted by the sight of an elegantly dressed, handsome Oriental man in the company of a bleached blonde clad in what Iris considered a very loose manner. After seating his companion, the Oriental looked about the room, and to Iris' surprise apparently recognized their party. With a brief word to the blonde, he started across the room. As he approached, Iris felt more and more strongly the attraction of his fine features, his flashing dark eyes.

"Good evening, Mr. and Mrs. Creighton," said George Sung with a slight bow. "It's pleasant to run into you here. It's been a long time since we've met."

Clifford rose and shook George's hand. Headsperth made an abortive movement, but instead of standing he sank back uncomfortably in his chair. His face colored in confused irritation.

"It's so good to see you," Victoria said. "We think of you and your family often, but now that we have a second home down on the waterfront we rarely get into town."

George permitted himself a slight smile. "Ah, we are practically neighbors then."

Clifford, still standing, said, "You must let me introduce you to our old friends Mr. and Mrs. Headsperth Bauer. And this is their niece, Iris, who has recently come to our city."

"I know your reputation, Mr. Bauer, from my father," George said smoothly and seemed to be on the point of extending his hand when he realized that Headsperth was not even looking at him. With scarcely a pause, George bowed to Belle and Iris, saying, "And it is always a pleasure to be introduced to beautiful women."

"Oh, Mr. Sung," Belle said, "you know how to charm."

Iris murmured an almost inaudible thank you.

"If it wouldn't shock the patrons, Miss Bauer, I'd ask you to dance," he said, in what was to her the most beautiful voice she'd ever heard.

"I, I . . ." Headsperth blustered.

"But," George went on, "I really must return to my companion. Do be seated, Mr. Creighton. And please give our family's greeting to your young son."

"And you, George, must give our best to your mother, father, and all the rest of them," said Victoria.

The Oriental bowed one last time and went back to his date.

"How many do they have now?" Victoria asked. "Seven?"

Clifford said to Iris, "It's really only the remnant. The Sung family has an interesting history."

"Interesting!" Headsperth sputtered. "It's disgusting the way those Chinks breed."

"Why, Uncle, I thought Mr. Sung showed wonderful breeding and good manners," Iris teased.

"Don't you know anything?" Headsperth asked scathingly. "He's Chinese! They carry disease! They live in sin! His father lives openly with a Caucasian woman! It's against the law to marry a Chinaman here in California and I think it's a good thing too! And this one, this George Sung, is the worst of all! He's more crooked than his father and that's saying a lot, young lady! He lives off respectable people by running a gambling barge! The Lucky Dragon! We don't allow gambling in the city anymore, but he's beyond the law out there on the water right off the Santa Monica pier. And his partner is almost as bad! A Mexican! It's unforgivable!"

"Now, Headsperth," Belle said. "You know perfectly well that both the Sung and Ortiz families are among the wealthiest in the city. And Clifford will tell you that they've helped to make Los Angeles what it is today."

"Oh, I don't know about that," Headsperth grumbled. "Really, Iris, I think I should say I felt uncomfortable at the way you acknowledged his admiration."

"Uncle, I've hardly understood what you've been saying. To me he seemed very nice."

"I'm just trying to warn you that this city is full of scum. A young woman of our social class should be very careful whom she's seen with."

"Headsperth," Belle began, and even her husband recognized the change in tone, "when it comes to the Sungs, no one could call them scum. And as to his partner, you seem to have forgotten that Raoul Ortiz is the son-in-law of Señora Mariné, and thus related by marriage not only to one of the oldest land-grant families but also to our host and hostess for the evening."

An embarrassed silence fell over the party, and once again it was left to Victoria to restore at least an appearance of harmony.

"There's a great deal to see, Iris," Victoria said. "Clifford and I would be delighted if you could spend some time with us at the shore."

"Oh, I'd love to do that," Iris answered. "But I owe so much to Auntie Belle, and I know she's planned a number of things for us to do."

"You mustn't let that stand in your way," Belle said. "A trip to the shore will do you good. Victoria, I'm sure you won't forget to show her the big bathhouse and the fading splendors of Abbot Kinney's folly."

Clifford ordered another bottle of champagne and on the surface the evening went on as though nothing had happened. Victoria and Belle did their best to keep up the conversation. Clifford wondered why they were still under any social obligation to entertain the Bauers, though he felt sorry for Belle, who must have had to listen daily to Headsperth's obtuse comments. Victoria, looking at Iris, sympathized with this attractive, fresh young girl and looked forward to giving her a few days of freedom and entertainment. Iris spent the rest of the evening stealing glances at George Sung.

George slipped a few more bills to the headwaiter, who was quick to return with two dry martinis served in plain tumblers. Claire, as always, drank hers a little too swiftly. She was a regular customer on the Lucky Dragon and George had allowed her to amuse him.

"Who are your friends?" she asked.

"Those are the Creightons of Creighton Enterprises. We've had a long association with them, especially in the early days."

Claire was satisfied with the answer. She never pressed and she never made demands. She seemed perfectly content to go back to her filet mignon.

George smiled at her and asked, "Shouldn't we take advantage of the orchestra?"

They drew several curious and some hostile stares as they glided over the dance floor. Many could not help admiring the accomplished performance of the handsome Chinese man and his blond partner.

The dark figures of two young men cautiously approached the rear entrance of the luxurious Oriental art store. In the murky light it was impossible to distinguish their features. The only sound that could be heard was the soft click of a key turning in the lock. Glancing nervously about them to be sure that they were unobserved, they quickly slipped through the open door and closed it behind them.

"That wasn't so hard, Hector."

"No, you were right about that part all along. I just hope the rest of it is as easy."

"Come on, turn on the flashlight. I want to get out of here as fast as we can."

Hector Ortiz focused the beam on the carved outlines of a statuette.

"Look at that," Hector said. "That ought to be worth thousands."

The other man snorted. "You'd better leave this to me. That's just the thinnest gold leaf over clay. We need something we can turn over fast. What we need is *real* gold."

He opened a glass case with another key, reached in, and pulled out solid gold bracelets, a gold butterfly pin weighing an ounce or more, its wings decorated with rubies and diamonds, and a necklace of lavender, green, white, and amber-colored jade. Then his fingers closed on a cabbage-green jade ornamental buckle. He slipped the jewels into his pocket and locked the case.

He looked around, picked up a statue worth a fair two hundred dollars, raised it above his head, and brought it down fiercely, shattering the glass case.

"Let's get out of here!"

Before leaving, they went to the heavy window closest to the rear

277

entrance and Hector swung the flashlight against the glass. It took him two strokes to break the large pane and then a few more moments to get rid of the jagged edges to give it the appearance of a break-in.

Then they unlocked the door, crept out, closed it carefully behind them, and with a sigh of relief turned to face the street.

It was then under the light of the streetlamp that they first saw the stocky frame of a blue-uniformed officer of the law.

The cop waited until the boys were abreast of him before he stepped forward, grinned, and said, "Just hold it there, you punks!" He pushed his red face up close to theirs. As they looked at his piglike eyes sunken in the folds of his flesh, they could see the hatred as he spat out, "Well, it looks as if I've caught a greaser and a slant-eyed Chink."

At first the boys were not afraid. But as the policeman began to taunt them they looked far younger than their twenty-one years.

The officer lumbered around them in clumsy circles, laughing as he took an occasional jab at one or the other of them, pushing his fat fingers against their backs or tweaking their carefully knotted silk ties.

"And just what are you dark-skinned, slant-eyed, greasy bucks doing out here at this time of night?"

"I'm afraid you don't know who we are, officer. I'm Mike Sung, son of Sung Wing On. Anyone down on this beat must know who *he* is. And this is Hector Ortiz, whose grandmother knows a lot of persons in City Hall."

"And allow me to introduce myself. I am the owner of the Castle of Killarney and the Keeper of the Blarney Stone," the policeman answered.

Mike cleared his throat. "My father has sent us here on an errand, and I'm sure even now he waits for his merchandise—"

"You lying yellow belly. And I suppose he also told you to improve the ventilation of the premises by breaking out a window?"

"We had trouble with the keys," Hector Ortiz ventured nervously.

"My father is an impatient man, as well as a powerful one. And I think, sir, that we should be on our way. I wouldn't like to answer for his temper if he is kept waiting too long."

"How much do you think an Irishman can swallow?" the officer asked. "If you're really so eager to return to your father, I'll be happy to take you there."

The young man hesitated before he said, "That really isn't necessary."

The cop roughly shoved Mike ahead of him. He pushed himself between them and put a viselike grip on their upper arms, propelling them down the street.

"I look forward to being introduced to the great Sung Wing On of Chinatown."

Within five minutes the young men and their custodian arrived at the warehouse that was Sung and Katarina's home. The elderly servant who answered the peremptory ring of the doorbell did his best to show no surprise as he saw the son of his master and his best friend in the hands of the law.

"I wanchee speakee you boss," the officer said.

278

"Certainly, if that is your pleasure," the servant replied and slowly turned.

The preternatural calm of the sumptuous living room was broken. Sung rose to his feet.

"Don't bother getting up," the cop began. "I just wanted to bring by these two hoods before I take them down to the slammer."

"Sir," Sung began, "to whom have I the honor of speaking?"

"Sergeant James Daly, if it's anything to you."

"Perhaps you would be good enough to release my son and his best friend. I see no reason for them to be charged with anything."

"He may be your son, but he's nothing more than a common thief," snorted Daly. He patted Mike's full pocket and said, "You might be interested in what's hidden in here."

"Father," Mike said, reaching into his pocket and pulling out a handful of jewels, "I believe these are yours."

Sung's eyes glittered. "They are indeed," he said. "They are the property of our family."

"I know this is a strange time to bring them to you," Mike said.

"Strange time is right! *Bring* them!" Sergeant Daly exploded. "Real people call it breaking and entering. They're robbing you blind. You're going to have to press charges."

Sung allowed himself a slight smile. "Sir, I have found in my life there is nothing I *have* to do. Certainly I have no need to bring charges against my own son for being in possession of the family gems."

"What about the spic?"

Hector shifted his weight nervously from one foot to the other, afraid to look at Sung, Katarina, or the mad Irishman.

"If I understand your manner of speaking, you are referring to my son's friend."

Sergeant Daly's rage had grown out of control. His face swelled. "Listen," he said, "don't think we don't know all about what goes on in Chinatown. And don't think you can slip through my fingers. I know all about you."

Sung's lips tightened in a controlled smile.

"Let me tell you," Daly went on, "you're going to get caught one of these days and in the worst way. And don't expect any mercy when I catch up with you."

He ran out of words and stood shaking in frustration.

"We appreciate your concern over our affairs," Sung said, "and I want to thank you for providing my son and his friend with an escort during these dangerous night hours." He paused and then went on. "Would you allow me to offer you some refreshment?"

"Just remember, someday I'll be coming back." And then he was gone.

For a moment calm was restored. Sung—giving the appearance of a kindly, unworried, dignified king—stood looking at the young men. Katarina, in her modified Oriental silk pajamas, her hair in a neat bun, sat quietly waiting behind her husband. The two culprits tried to act as if nothing had happened.

Then Sung shouted, "Can it be I am the father of a turtle's incestuous abortion, a filthy sow's afterbirth? Have I crossed the ocean and slaved under the whip of these barbarians only to be shamed by a creature beneath even them?"

"Really, Father, we were walking by and we saw the broken window. We saw the thief, but Hector and I chased him off. The jewel case had been smashed. I was looking after our family welfare. I was only trying to save the most valuable pieces."

"I have taught you well, my son. Those *are* the most valuable pieces. And truly no common thief would know that." Sung turned to Hector and asked, "Is that not right, Hector?"

Hector blushed and stammered, "I, I—"

"What is worse? To have a son who is a corrupter of others, a son who is a liar, or a son who is a thief? There is no need for you to answer for I know now that I have a son who is all three of these." Sung's voice choked as he spoke these damning words and abruptly left the room.

Released from her assumed Chinese dignity, Katarina leaped up from her chair like an avenging fury. Grabbing her son by an ear, she tugged at it, shrieking, "Milan, what have you done, you wicked boy?"

"Mother, what I said was the truth. Just ask Hector."

"I do not need to ask," she screamed, giving his earlobe a sharp tug that made him cry out in pain. "Like your father says, you are a liar. Do not make your friend a liar too. What do we not give you that you would be a robber?" By now her hands were busy working both of his ears and he yelped, pulling away in protest. "You have good food! You have good clothes to wear! You do not know what hard work is! *I know!* Your father knows! But you know only to be *bad, bad, bad, bad boy!*"

"You're always hitting me, Ma," he cried out as her slaps turned into blows of real force. "It's Hector's fault too!"

And without missing a beat, Katarina turned her wrath equally on Hector.

"Spoiled brats! Bad boys! I beat the devil out of you! How can you do these things to your family, Hector? How can you do these things to your father, Milan?"

"I'm Mike, *Mike.*" The young man shook himself out of her reach, and retreating behind a chair, assumed a defiant stance. "Why don't you call me by my real name? I'm Mike! What do you expect from me? You can't even speak English. My father's a millionaire, but I live in a warehouse. I'm a freak. Nobody even knows my name."

Katarina looked at her son with steely peasant eyes. "I don't care what they think. And to me, you are Milan. That is the name we give you. It is a good name. A true name from the old country." She started around the chair toward him and he circled away. "You, Milan, look at you! Look at the robber afraid of his own mother! Look at the coward!"

From the beginning Victoria had loved her beach cottage. The air was always fresh and crisp and salty. The open rooms led naturally to a more relaxed, informal style of life than the great mansion overlooking the Arroyo. Instead of the formal sitdown dinners in Pasadena, Pansy often packed them a picnic basket and the Creightons would have a light supper right at the ocean's edge.

This morning in particular Victoria enjoyed this freedom as she sat in the sun porch watching Iris and Gary playing catch. Gary, just approaching adolescence, gave promise of growing up into an exceptionally handsome young man like his father. For the last ten years he had delighted his parents with a natural inquisitiveness, a quick wit echoing his mother's, and a gift far beyond the ordinary for music. Although Victoria could see that Iris and Gary were having fun—her tomboy responses kept him from looking at her as a mere girl—it was the thought of his special talent that finally moved her to interrupt their carefree pastime.

"Gary," Victoria called out just after he had caught a particularly hard-thrown ball from Iris, "I think you'd better practice before your lesson this afternoon."

"Ah, Mother, please," said Gary as he crossed the lawn to her.

"You know how Mr. Krisel counts on your progress from week to week. You wouldn't want to disappoint him. And you certainly wouldn't want him to become angry."

Gary winced. "You can say that again."

Iris joined them. "Don't worry, Gary, we'll have plenty of time to throw the ball if we feel like it before dinner. Anyway I've heard you practicing and you can't tell me you don't really enjoy it."

"Sure," he said, as he went into the house, "but I don't want everyone to know that."

"You're really wonderful with him, Iris."

"I'm so grateful for all you and Mr. Creighton have done for me," Iris said as she sat down on the porch. "It's not that Uncle Headsperth and Auntie Belle haven't been kind."

"Belle's heart's in the right place, but she's never had any children of her own," said Victoria. "As for Headsperth, well, I've known him a long time."

"He makes fun of me," Iris blurted out.

"But, my dear, that's just the way he is. Especially when he's dealing with something he doesn't understand."

"Maybe it's because he's lived out here so long that he's forgotten what it was like back home. Uncle Headsperth says things like, 'What's so important about a pair of shoes or a new post-hole digger?' But I can tell you when we were in Colorado, warm shoes *were* important if you wanted to keep your toes from freezing off. And I remember back in South Dakota when we got our post-hole digger. After Father died, we had to let go the hands. That post-hole digger kept us from being eaten out by the range cattle." The girl sighed. "Oh, I don't know what's wrong with me. I have no reason to complain."

"I too came here when I was eighteen. You mustn't think that life here is completely aimless. It's just that we have a different style."

By this time Gary was crashing through a series of arpeggios, sometimes holding the tones with the pedal, sometimes cutting them off abruptly.

"If I could do something like that," Iris said, "I would understand where I was going."

Victoria's eyes lit up with surprised appreciation. "Except for Mr. Krisel and me," she said with delight, "you're the first person to hear what Gary's real direction in the future may be." She smiled ruefully. "Certainly Cliff's ears are deaf, but then he has his own qualities."

"I envy Gary. I envy all of you."

"You know what you need," Victoria said suddenly. "You need to get out for a while. You could begin by taking my car. Explore. Have a good time. A girl your age needs to get out. Don't come back until . . . after midnight." Victoria laughed again. "We won't tell Headsperth and Belle."

Iris looked disbelievingly at Victoria.

Later that day Iris was driving up the Speedway in Victoria's coupe. At first Iris had been reluctant to drive at all. She had two strong legs and could walk to anywhere she wanted to go. Victoria had found that amusing. "My dear, you'll need to go a lot farther than that," she said, "before you find what you want." So Victoria, after a few demonstrations, had insisted she take the wheel.

Iris appreciated what Victoria had said only when she felt the ocean breeze whipping her hair into her face and back behind her at the same time. As the rays of the lowering sun glanced off the water and tinted the sandy beach orange, she realized that she was entering into a private world to which her sturdy feet and legs could never have brought her.

She had driven north no more than two miles when she saw the first signs reading "This way to Lucky Dragon." She parked near what she knew was the Santa Monica Bay Pier and walked to the merry-go-round, which was housed in the first building.

A calliope playing lively circus music wheezed to the end of a piece as the carousel slowed. A crowd of children with their laughing parents climbed down from the gaily painted horses. Iris bought a ticket for the next ride. The attendant came by and said, "Be sure to fasten yourself securely, miss."

She laughed, one foot in the stirrup. "Don't worry about me. I've ridden some mighty rough broncs."

"Just the same," he said, "be careful. We have our own breed of horses in California."

When the ride came to an end, she slipped down and walked to the exit feeling exhilarated and eager for whatever might come next. She flashed a smile at the attendant as she passed him and said, "You were right after all. That horse has its own stride."

Starting down the length of the pier, she saw food concessions where children pleaded with their parents to buy great swirls of pink cotton candy, shooting galleries where young men tried to win teddy bears for their sweethearts, and, finally, again, a sign that read, "This way to Lucky Dragon."

She walked toward the water taxi booth inside which an attendant lounged. She hesitated. Perhaps she should have just gone on and looked at the waves and the fishermen casually tending their lines. But as she was on the point of moving away she remembered Mrs. Creighton's instruction.

"Can you take me out to the Lucky Dragon?" she asked the attendant.

"It's a little early for that, miss. The real action doesn't begin until after dark."

"Oh, well." To herself she thought, so much for my adventure. "Well, I know that, but I happen to be an acquaintance of Mr. George Sung."

The name acted upon him like an electric current and he jumped to attention. "I beg your pardon, miss," he said. "I should have known that you weren't just an ordinary tourist. I'll be happy to telephone Mr. Sung on the barge, if you give me your name."

Iris, frightened by her own audacity, went ahead with a sense of adventure. "Just say that I'm the one he didn't dance with."

"Whatever you say, miss," the attendant said, looking at her with both surprise and ill-concealed curiosity. He went into a back room of the booth and within a few minutes he had returned. "The boss awaits your arrival. He'd send his own personal boat except that would make for an extra trip. I'll have one of the boys ready in just a couple of seconds to whiz you out there."

As the pier receded, Iris marveled at the expanse of blue water. Since she had been staying at the Creightons' beach house she had gone to the ocean shore every day and had played with Gary in the surf. But she had ventured into this vast new element only ankle- or knee-deep at best. Now she rode over the true depths. The young man steering the taxi was so intent upon his job that she felt herself quite alone during this magical transition. Then he startled her out of her reverie.

"There she is!"

For a moment she could see nothing through the iridescent spray.

"There, right there ahead," he said.

And then her eyes caught a dark shape that looked like a domino. And a few moments later she saw above it a square cloth sail decorated with a large red Chinese character.

"Oh!" she exclaimed.

"It really is something to see, isn't it, especially for the first time."

He steered the taxi skillfully in a large arc that brought them to the base of a gangway. As they pulled up alongside, he quickly reversed his motor and then cut it off. He tossed a hawser to the waiting sailor, who said, "You're out on an early trip, Joe."

Any reply that Joe might have made was silenced as they all caught sight of a nautically dressed figure watching them from above. Joe and the sailor handed Iris up to the platform, and the handsome stranger from the Cocoanut Grove with his yachting cap tipped at a rakish angle started down to meet her.

"Miss Bauer," he said, fingering the bill of his cap, "I hoped that it was you."

Joe and the sailor exchanged looks that did not escape Iris' notice.

"I was just passing by. . . ."

George rocked with laughter. "How lucky for me!" Then he was at her side helping her up the gangway and taking her elbow as she stepped over the high edge of the deck.

"I know it sounded foolish to say I was just passing by," she said, "and I shouldn't have come unannounced, although in South Dakota no one ever announced anything except the coming of snow."

"But this is perfect," he said. "It gives me a chance to show you around before the crowd arrives."

"I can only stay a short time."

"We'll see about that. Before we start our tour, can't I offer you a glass of champagne?"

They left the deck and stepped into the main lounge of the barge, a nightclub with a huge dance floor and a revolving mirrored reflecting ball hanging from the ceiling. Carved Oriental tables and chairs encircled the dance floor on two levels. The walls were hung with scrolls and Oriental tapestries. An arch decorated with a carved, five-clawed gilded dragon stretched across the bandstand. The bar was a temple altar filched from a monastery in the western hills above Peking.

George went behind the bar and, opening an ice chest, drew out a bottle of Mumm's Cordon Rouge. He poured two glasses.

"To our first dance."

She blushed as they clinked glasses.

"My goodness," she said, "I don't know much about champagne, but this tastes better than anything Uncle Headsperth and Auntie Belle have given me."

"We bring our wine and champagne from small villages in France, across the Atlantic, up through the deserts of Mexico and across the border. With things the way they are now it's easier to get the best than take a chance on something second rate."

"Is it really true that people can gamble here?" Iris asked.

"Why else would I be out here three miles off shore? Come on, I'll show you around."

He refilled their glasses and took her elbow. It was eerily quiet as they entered a room containing four roulette tables. She exclaimed at the luxury of the equipment, the wall hangings, and when they came to the bar at the end of the room she said, "Gee! It looks almost like a marble boat."

"You have a keen eye," George said. "That's exactly what it is. It's a miniature reproduction of the Empress Dowager's marble boat in the grounds of the Summer Palace outside of Peking."

She ran her hand over the smooth surface of the cold stone. "I'm not sure I'd want to risk a ride on this."

"Only the Chinese would think of making a boat out of marble," he said.

"But could it really float?" she asked.

"Of course not," he chuckled. "The Empress—they called her 'The Old Dragon' behind her back—was angry because her ministers told her that China needed a navy and they voted enough money to start one. The Old

Dragon was so furious that in her high-handed way she gave them their navy in the form of a marble pleasure house at the edge of one of the lakes in the Summer Palace gardens. She and her attendants would go out there for tea and refreshments and to enjoy the breeze off the water and the sight of the western hills rising behind the imperial yellow and purple tiled roofs of the pavilion."

Iris looked at him in disbelief. "I think you're teasing me and just making it up."

"No, on my honor," George said.

He led her on through four more rooms, each furnished with tables for poker, blackjack, and craps. The last room was for the players wealthy enough to put no limit on their bets. George explained to her how he and Raoul had gotten started downtown with the Lucky Dragon, how after a few years the pressures of the law, the racketeering that had grown out of Prohibition, had forced them to move to this floating barge masquerading as a junk. And it had all been for the best. It had given his family a chance to diversify their business interests and George a chance to strike out on his own. They'd had two rivals, but neither equaled the Lucky Dragon in quality and patronage. At first they'd been a little disturbed by the threat of this competition, but now they were grateful for it. The other two enterprises operated on a shoestring and attracted the kind of clientele that could afford nothing better. The result was that the Lucky Dragon had a reputation for wealth and square dealing.

Because of George's tour they missed the sunset. Iris knew she should go. As the colored lights that illuminated the deck were turned on, she said, "It's really been wonderful and I'd love to see it sometime when you're open for business."

"Of course you'll be staying for dinner with me."

Iris looked down at her motoring skirt and sweater. "I'd feel so out of place in this."

"You don't have to worry about that. Sometimes we've had pretty rough water out here. It wouldn't be in the spirit of the Lucky Dragon to let our customers go home bedraggled."

He took Iris below deck to an elegant suite and opened the closet to reveal perhaps fifty evening gowns that made a sparkling rainbow of shiny silk and satin.

"I'll wait for you in my quarters across the passageway," he said, making a half bow, and left, closing the door behind him.

She'd never seen so many beautiful gowns before. She rejected the persimmon-colored chiffon, the cream-colored body-clinging silk with the low neckline, and the elegant black satin with sequin trim. They seemed to her too provocative for this occasion. She finally settled on a dress that she felt would blend in with the decor, an emerald-green silk gown cut on Oriental lines with a high Chinese collar and a long skirt slit to the knee. She slipped off her street clothes and put on the dress. It fit as if made for her.

She began to giggle at the sight of her sturdy walking shoes, looking like small boats themselves in contrast to the delicate quality of the green silk.

Stepping out of them, she tried a second closet and to her relief found a rack of evening sandals. And there she selected green silk slippers embroidered with a red dragon's head.

At the dressing table she picked up the silver-backed brush and fluffed out her blond curls. She dusted her cheeks lightly with powder but rejected the pots of lip rouge and mascara.

Taking a deep breath and glancing at herself one final time, she crossed the passageway to his half-open door. She knocked lightly.

"Just a moment," George called.

Then he was at the door, knotting his black tie. But he stopped as soon as he saw her.

"I had hoped that you would choose a gown of that style. You are absolutely beautiful."

She didn't know what to say, but secretly she was delighted at his pleasure.

"You're perfect," he went on, "except for one thing. Please come in." He held the door for her and she stepped through, her green embroidered slippers sinking into the rich deep mat of a Peking rug.

She saw that the room was furnished in the same elegance, taste, and luxury as the rest of the barge. But although this was his personal sitting room, there were no mementoes, family pictures, or any clues to his private life.

"You're perfect," he repeated, "but you would do me a great honor if you would wear something that is very private in its meaning to me."

"If it would please you," she murmured.

He turned and walked toward a cabinet. She followed silently. He carefully lifted out a very old Oriental headdress and placed it over Iris' blond curls, saying, "It was my mother's."

His mother's wedding headdress, the yards of red silk long since removed. Now all that remained were the gold circlet and strings of tiny beads, seed pearls, and gold leaves that still tinkled delicately. For George, the transformation was complete. Before him was his bride for the evening.

"Your mother's," she whispered. Before she could say anything more, two waiters in white jackets entered, pushing a cart, and began to set a square teak table for a dinner for two.

One of them opened a fresh bottle of champagne. The other removed the covers of silver chafing dishes and served pheasant and wild rice. George dismissed the waiters and then they were alone.

"I have told you about my life and the work I do," he said, "but I know nothing of you."

"My life is not nearly as glamorous as yours."

"But I want to know all about you. That is, if you don't mind."

"Papa died when I was thirteen. Mama and I had to work the farm by ourselves. Some of the hired men wouldn't stay and then others had to leave when Mama ran low on money. I guess it was too hard on her. All I noticed at first was that she'd get terribly tired and we decided that the work was too much. Land values weren't all that high even in those days, but I guess we got a fair price. We decided to go southwest to Colorado where we'd heard women could find jobs at the mining camps."

"What about the rest of your family? Why didn't they help you?"

"Mama didn't want us to be a burden and we didn't want to ask for charity."

To Iris he said, "You were very courageous," but to himself he thought, family obligations were the most privileged burdens a man could carry.

"Well," she said matter-of-factly, "we really had no choice."

"What kind of jobs were there?"

"Almost everything you can imagine. We shaved the miners when they came into town ready for a big weekend. We washed clothes. We wrote letters for them. We did their mending. Sometimes a miner would want us to read to him from the Bible. And we could provide a home-cooked meal that they always said was just like the ones their mothers used to make."

"I always thought miners were tough guys full of booze and hard to handle."

Iris, looking demure in her finery, said quietly, "There was that kind too, but they preferred the hospitality of Madame La Grande." She flicked a quick glance at him. "Of course, they didn't get any buttons sewed on there."

"I can understand that," George said as he refilled her glass.

"In some ways it wasn't such a bad life," Iris went on, "but Mama never really regained her strength. She began to cough a little each morning. I didn't think much of it at first, but when I saw how thin she was getting I started to worry. I suspect she knew what it meant a long time before I did. After an especially bad spell, I said she had to go see old Dr. Walker. After he examined her Dr. Walker just shook his head and said, 'Mrs. Bauer, I think you already know what I have to say.' 'I think I do,' Mama said. And then there was nothing else for me to do but keep going on. I tried to make Mama rest but she didn't want that. Before she passed away Mama wrote to Uncle Headsperth. I could have taken care of myself! But Dr. Walker and the other people we knew in town insisted that I should at least come for a visit after Mama's death. So here I am."

"I, too, have lost my mother and many brothers and sisters," he said quietly, "and I know there is no greater pain to be endured."

"But you can't just stop living and suffer. Last year I was getting ready for another harsh winter, chopping wood and trying to keep the house warm for Mama. This year my Auntie Belle tells me my only worry is whether I should have white gardenias or camellias for my coming-out corsage at the Valley Hunt Club."

"That's a change," George said, "but I'm not sure everyone would call it progress."

"You're right, things do change, don't they? I still can't get used to having people do for me what I did for others. I'll never forget how upset Uncle Headsperth was when I offered to help Sylvie do the dishes. Sometimes I feel that they're trying to make me over, make me into something that I really am not and don't want to be."

"As for me, I wish you would stay just the way you are now," George said daringly.

She laughed. "Well, I certainly couldn't scrub floors in this outfit."

"I think you will find when we go back to the club that you are the most beautiful and exotic woman on board."

"I can hardly imagine that."

But upstairs she did notice that people turned their heads. Surely, she tried to convince herself, it was her costume or her escort that had aroused admiring stares, rather than the farm girl from South Dakota. But as she felt herself being swept up into the magic of the evening, she considered the possibility that maybe, just maybe, George had been right.

"How are we doing tonight, Bill?"

"Just fine, Mr. Sung, just fine."

"Have you ever played roulette?" George asked Iris.

"No, but I have to admit I have seen it played."

"Play the seventeen," George whispered, handing her three blue chips. "I know you'll be lucky."

"Messieurs, mesdames, faites vos jeux," the croupier chanted as he started the wheel and the ball rolling.

Iris placed all three chips on number seventeen. The croupier glanced at George, caught his quick nod, and continued with his chant until a substantial number of bets had been placed. And then as the wheel began to slow he announced, *"Rien ne va plus."* All eyes followed the circuit of the ball and a collective gasp went up as it settled into the slot for seventeen. The croupier pushed to Iris what looked to her like a mountain of chips.

"My goodness!" she exclaimed. "This really must be beginner's luck."

"Do you want to keep on playing," George asked, "or quit while you're ahead?"

"Oh, I'd like to play a little longer," she said. "What should I choose now?"

"Seventeen seems to be your lucky number," he said, "but you shouldn't risk it all."

Once again seventeen came up, and again and again. Her run of luck had begun to attract attention. Among those who gathered around the table Iris recognized George's companion from the evening at the Cocoanut Grove.

"George," the woman said. "They told me you were busy tonight." She fondled the back of his neck.

"I *am* busy tonight, Claire," he said uncomfortably.

Following his look, Claire took in the green gown, natural blond curls, and the headdress which she had seen but never worn. Claire let her hands fall to her sides.

"I quite understand, Mr. Sung," she said politely. "Perhaps another time."

"Perhaps," George said absentmindedly, hardly noticing that she had already stepped away from him.

By the time Iris had finished playing she had turned her thirty dollars into five thousand. She wanted to give it all back to George, but he accepted only his original investment.

Later, slightly tipsy from champagne, they promenaded alone on deck, under the moonlight, floating on the Pacific. The lights of Los Angeles twinkled like a faraway fairyland.

"This has been an unforgettable day," she said as she looked at the stars and then back at his face. "I never realized life could be so . . . I owe it all to you."

George gently tilted back her head—the beads tinkled softly—and then kissed her with firm but brief pressure on her lips. "I hope I haven't offended you," he said as he released her.

"This sure beats South Dakota!"

And George Sung, suave man-about-town, found himself for the first time in his life totally dumbstruck.

At the breakfast table next morning as soon as everyone had been served, Victoria turned to Iris and asked, "Did you have a pleasant day? You seem to be in better spirits."

"I had the time of my life."

There was something in the tone of her voice that made Cliff look up from his scrambled eggs and bacon. Somehow he was reminded of another occasion and it finally came to him that it was the evening long ago when his Little Ruthie had come in late from that fateful car rally.

"What's this?" he demanded.

"Mrs. Creighton let me take her car yesterday—"

"I knew it!" He looked accusingly at his wife. "You know, Victoria, that it's been my belief for years that unescorted girls and automobiles can take some very strange turns."

"Now, Clifford," Victoria said, "I just wanted Iris to get out a little on her own and enjoy the shore."

Before anyone could speak all four of them were distracted by the sight of a black limousine gliding up under the portecochere.

"Boy, is that some wagon," Gary exclaimed.

"You didn't tell me you'd be conducting business at home today," Victoria said. "I'll have Pansy set another place or at least we can offer them coffee."

"That kind of car has nothing to do with me. I'd think it was a bootlegger making a delivery if I didn't know better."

As they all craned to look at the driver of the car, they saw a black-uniformed Oriental, carrying something under his arm, disappear as he made his way to the door. In a few moments Pansy came in, holding a package wrapped in gold and red paper.

"I don't know what to make of this, Mrs. Creighton," she said, "but the Chinese man who brought this said it was for Miss Iris. I asked him to wait if he needed my answer, but you know how those foreigners are. He just shook his head."

And indeed, even as Pansy spoke they could see the delivery man sliding under the wheel of the long, gleaming automobile and driving away as quickly and smoothly as he had arrived.

"What's in the package?" Gary asked. "It looks like a Christmas present."

"I can't imagine," Iris said.

"Perhaps you should open it," said Cliff sardonically. "That would be one way to find out."

"But how exciting!" Victoria exclaimed, as Pansy in one motion removed Iris' breakfast plate and replaced it with the present.

Iris carefully, slowly removed the paper, opened the box, and lifted away the top sheets of tissue paper.

"Oh," she murmured, and the Creightons leaned forward to get a better look.

She held up a necklace of gold with a pendant of carved jade surrounded by a sea of tiny diamonds.

"Holy Toledo!" exclaimed Gary.

"Victoria, what *is* the meaning of this?" Clifford demanded.

Even Victoria was somewhat taken aback. "My dear," she said to Iris, "all I wanted you to do was get out and see the world. I didn't expect you to bring back its treasures."

They all waited as Iris laid the necklace down on the table. Then she looked up.

"I did just what you said," she began. "I took the car and went up the coast. It was all so new and different to me. I stopped at the pier and I just couldn't resist riding on the merry-go-round. I'd seen the signs for the Lucky Dragon and the next thing I knew I was there. It was so exciting! It was really a different world! And he was so kind."

Clifford stared at her. "He," he said. "Who is this *he?*"

"Why, that friend of yours that I met at the Cocoanut Grove. Don't you remember? He said he'd like to dance."

"Please don't tell me you're talking about the Sung boy!"

"He showed me around the barge. You know it's designed to look like a junk. Do you know what that is?" When they didn't answer, she went on. "He let me change my clothes and we had dinner together. And then he taught me how to play roulette. He gave me three chips. You'll never guess what happened."

The Creightons waited.

"I won five thousand dollars. Can you imagine?"

Clifford choked.

"I never thought I'd see that much money in my whole life and I couldn't help wishing that I'd had it when Mama was ill. But you know, now I have a stake. If I'm careful I'll never have to shave another miner." She giggled. "I tried to give it back, but Mr. Sung would take only his thirty dollars. He said the money was mine, that I'd won it fair and square, that it was a real case of beginner's luck."

"Beginner's luck," Clifford moaned.

"Oh, I know it's a lot of money, Mr. Creighton. And I hope you'll help me invest it properly. I can't think of a better person to ask advice from. That's what George said I should do, I mean Mr. Sung. I did just what Mrs. Creighton said. I didn't come home until after midnight—" Iris looked at them defiantly. "I know what you're thinking and it's absolutely off the mark."

"Wow!" Gary sang out.

"Victoria, it's worse that I thought," Cliff said.

"My dear, you should think things over carefully, and then do what you think best," said Victoria.

Iris picked up the necklace. "Of course, I know I should send it back."

Clifford breathed a sigh of relief.

"But I'm not going to. It would hurt him. He's so sensitive."

"Damn!" Cliff exclaimed.

"Oh!" Victoria chimed in.

"Leaping lizards!" Gary concluded.

As always on the last Sunday of every month Magdalena Ortiz had gathered her family about her. It had gone as well as could be expected. She'd long since given up the formal dinners. Instead they served themselves from a generous buffet that made it possible for them to chat casually, to circulate freely, or even to sit down all together on the soft sofas and easy chairs of her solarium.

After she had seen to the clearing of the dinner dishes, Magdalena sat out on the roof garden and waited. How was it, she thought, that she, who had never wanted a family or a domestic life, found herself at the center of these relationships and responsibilities?

Her son, to her surprise, had really turned over a new leaf since his bout with the influenza. At forty-four, Raoul took great pride in his family and his work. The partnership with George Sung had been a success. Raoul handled the shoreside aspects of the business with real energy and responsibility and rarely, if ever, risked the ocean voyage to the Lucky Dragon, for he had discovered almost immediately after they had chartered the barge that the slightest motion of water made him seasick. Though George teased him about this, he had accepted the situation with sympathy and understanding and a bond had grown between the two men that went far beyond the terms of their partnership. They'd long since forgotten differences of race and background.

Maria, at thirty-nine, had turned into a stout matron solicitous of her children, but still afraid of her husband. Her daughter, Chata, was, at fifteen, soon to be a mother. The family had objected to Max Rodriguez but had permitted the marriage to avoid any further shame and public humiliation. For his part, Max, a sullen and unappealing sixteen-year-old, said he regretted ever meeting Chata or her family, but once he recognized their wealth, had decided to make the best of a bad bargain.

Hector, son of Raoul and Maria, Magdalena's only grandson, usually the most animated member of the group—the one who could be counted upon to tell jokes and smooth over awkward silences—had seemed strangely sub-dued tonight. Each of the family members took turns questioning him, but to no avail. What, she wondered, could have dampened him so much? She knew it must be something more serious than just a casual setback—another in a series of speeding tickets, some disappointment in an affair, or a family dispute over money. If he couldn't talk to his own grandmother, who could he talk to?

As for herself she knew there was only one person she could discuss it with, and she waited for him with more than ordinary eagerness. For he was the only one not physically present at the family dinner, though, in one way or another, everyone there had been conscious of John Frederick Smith. Over the years she'd tried to include him, but her family resisted, especially her son. By now this was the only thing she and Raoul disagreed about. And her son always made it a point to embarrass her, perhaps in hopes that she would give up her lover of—off and on—forty-four years. "Say hello to your boyfriend for me." And it wasn't what Raoul said but how her son looked at her. For no matter how rich and happy she was, or how much Raoul had changed, he still thought of her as a *puta*.

To her surprise she, who had crossed the Sonoran desert and made her way into the upper reaches of Los Angeles society, dissolved into tears. The more she tried to get control the more they poured down her cheeks.

Then John Frederick was there behind her, his arms about her, holding her tight against him.

"Tears," he said, *"carita,* tears as we look over the lights of the City of the Angels. Is this a way to welcome your lover?"

But she could not control herself, and though she tried to suppress her sobs she continued to weep. He turned her in his arms and said tenderly, "You must know better than I the old saying that I learned in your country, the only cure for tears are the kisses of true love."

She felt his lips against the lids of her eyes and then his lips following the wet salty course ending at her mouth, where he caressed her without insistence.

"You must tell me, my little dove, what has caused you this sorrow?" He held her face softly in his hands so she could not, even if she had wished to, escape the gentle captivity. When she looked into his eyes this way she knew she could not lie.

"Oh, it is nothing really and truly. I am a *vieja* to let it bother me so," she said. "But my son was so cruel. He does not respect me."

"I had no idea he still felt that way about us."

"He means nothing against you," she said, dashing away a tear with a bejeweled hand. "He has always thought of me as a loose woman. We are lovers and we will always be lovers no matter how much it offends him."

"Who is he to be offended? Who gave him his life? He should go down on his knees before you."

The notion of Raoul with his stocky figure making an obeisance before her brought Magdalena to her senses.

"What a vision!" she exclaimed, laughing, wiping the last tears from her cheeks. "I'd have to help him back up onto his feet."

He walked over to the roof garden railing. As he looked out over the city he thought of how his own children had done little more than tolerate his relationship with Magdalena. Their first ten years together after he had found her again had taken place in secrecy behind closed doors. During their last ten years she had been by his side constantly and had, in fact, been an asset to him in public. To see her suffer now was almost more than he could bear.

He turned and saw her waiting quietly for him. She was more beautiful to him than when he had first seen her all those years ago. Her hair was still jet black and full of luster. As a girl she had been like a ripe papaya; now she was even more of a woman. She was more than any man could hope to possess. She was charming, handsome, rich in her own right.

"I can't allow us to go on this way, my dear," he said as he walked to her and once again took her in his arms. Then surprising even himself, he said, "Will you do me the honor of becoming my wife?"

At first she laughed. But when she realized his sincerity she was scandalized.

"Even if I had ever wanted to marry I could never marry you."

"Can you give me one good reason?"

"*One?*" She laughed bitterly. "Look at us, my beloved. We are old and that alone should be enough. But there are other considerations. Think of your business associates. I may be an acceptable companion, but I am not a wife. Think of your children, let alone mine. How would they be able to show their faces in society when their father takes a servant for a wife?"

"Are we not free spirits from the harshness of the desert that knows no age? And, Magdalena, don't forget. I'm only five years older than you are. It was your childish misconception that made me seem older than I was. When I'm with you I'm a boy again and you, my dear, are nothing but a giddy girl. It's our children that are old. They can't be any more stuffy and intolerant if we are married or not. As for my business associates, they're all secretly jealous of me anyway. For who among them has anyone to equal you?"

"Ah, my Juan Frederico," she purred, "though I shall not marry you I will never leave your side." She put her arms around him and ran her fingers into his silver locks. Her lips met his and then he was lost to her, her warm breath engulfing him like the hot demanding desert winds, her hands enveloping like the shifting sands.

She pulled a silk quilt from a rattan chest and laid it on the rough canvas of the chaise longue. To John Frederick she seemed more lovely, more willing, and as greatly concerned for his satisfaction as for her own.

"I still won't marry you," she said as she lay back on the chaise and brought him to her.

"We shall see," he said. And he removed each of her rings from the fingers of both hands, lingering at each for teasing kisses.

That same night, Hector Ortiz walked quickly to his new car, a flashy Duesenberg, which he had parked a block away from his grandmother's and the watchful eyes of his parents. Within yards of his prized possession he felt rough hands closing on his shoulders. He knew better than to resist.

"You're coming with us," a voice rasped.

"I have connections," Hector said in a slightly quivery voice.

"Yeah? So what?" the gangster said as he slammed Hector into the back seat of his car. To his driver he said, "Come on, let's get out of here."

The black Cadillac Straight Eight screeched away from the curb and sped down the street.

In a matter of minutes they had pulled up in front of a house that looked like every other house on a standard middle-class residential street in East Los Angeles. Hector's escorts hurried him up the short flight of front steps and in through the door. Instead of being ushered into a standardly furnished living room, Hector was thrown to a bare floor.

"Ortiz, you have wasted my time long enough." Hector recognized Giuseppe Marinetti, the king bootlegger and drug runner of Los Angeles. "I have a big business and I don't have time to spend on a punk like you."

Hector tried to sit up. Immediately the thugs were by his side. Hector cringed, expecting a boot to his ribs but was instead dragged to his feet and shoved across the room.

"Easy there," Marinetti said. "We don't want to bruise the merchandise. Bring in the other one."

Hector, already sickened by what he knew he would see, looked at the corner door where Mike, despite the efforts of a flunkie holding onto his arm, stepped forward independently, his bruised and bloody face held high. His defiant eyes took in the scene and when they came upon Hector the lids narrowed.

"Look," Marinetti said, "it's no good your trying to fight us this way. Of course, you could give us a lot of trouble. You might ruin us, but sure as hell you'd ruin yourselves and your families."

"I'd like to know how you think you can possibly hurt my family?" Mike sneered.

"How about a headline in the paper like this: 'Sung and Ortiz Heirs Linked to Drug Ring'?"

Hector whimpered.

The man leaned forward confidentially. "C'mon, boys. I gave you seventy thousand dollars' worth of cocaine. I want to know where it is. Where's my money?"

"It's all Mike's fault," Hector said, his eyes welling up with tears.

"Shut up, Hector. Just keep your mouth shut. Let me handle this," Mike snapped.

"You said that before and look what it's gotten us."

"That's right, Ortiz. Tell the truth," Marinetti said in a friendly manner. "You might even get out of this alive."

"Don't listen to him, Hector!"

Mike's words were stopped by a kidney punch.

Hector blurted it out. "Look. We took the cocaine. We went to parties just like you said and sold it to our friends. So then for once in our lives we had money."

"You *had* the money," Marinetti prompted.

"And then we saw those cars. Duesenbergs. We," he hesitated, "we used the coke money to buy them." Hector tried an ingratiating smile. "We got a good deal buying two at once."

"Is that a doozie?" Marinetti said with heavy irony. "A double doozie if I ever heard one."

"We couldn't drive them home," Hector continued. "We couldn't drive them anywhere we'd be seen. And we couldn't just leave them on the street. So we had to rent our own garage space. It took us a little more than we'd expected so we played the numbers. Mike said he knew the places to go, but we lost. We were really behind now. We needed a sure thing. We put the last ten thousand into the stock market."

"Jesus," Marinetti said.

It was Mike's turn now. "Don't think that we were going to welch on you. I was going to steal from my own father, but our bad luck held out. Can you believe it? We were caught by a cop. But don't worry, we'll get the money."

"Yeah, we'll get the money," Hector echoed. "Somehow."

"You have twelve hours to go home and ask your fathers to pony up for you," Marinetti said.

"I'd rather die than ask my father," Mike said proudly.

Hector paled.

"Well, then," Marinetti said, "I only know one way for you to get out of this without getting your four legs broken. It'll mean a little travel time for the two of you."

"I'd go a long way to keep this from my family. How about you, Hector?"

"Sure," Hector said. "Whatever you say."

At his broker's, Headsperth Bauer dropped in confidently to confirm his recovery plan.

"How many points have we gone up today?" he asked, taking no notice of the general air of gloom that fought against the autumn California sunlight streaming through the slanted venetian blinds.

"Mr. Bauer," his broker said, "I don't think you've grasped the situation. As I tried to warn you last week, you've done nothing but send good money after bad. Everything bought on margin is being called in. If you were a Vanderbilt, a Morgan, even a member of a solid New England family you could put your cash down and hold on. But to be perfectly frank, you haven't that kind of hard money left. For that matter, I've got very little myself. Of course, there are people like the Creightons, the Rosecranses, and the Bedloes, but you and I know we're not in that class—financially."

"I could raise more money, I'm sure," Headsperth said.

"It might be best, Mr. Bauer, if you held on to what you have left."

"I hardly know what you mean," Headsperth said. "You make me sound like the next thing to a pauper, as if the only thing left for us is the poorhouse."

"Frankly, Mr. Bauer, all you do have is your own house. It's certainly not a poorhouse, but if I were you I'd hang on to it for the present."

After his broker had shown Headsperth his file on investments and explained all of his losses, it finally became clear. Headsperth Bauer had, indeed, lost everything but his house, his father's house at that. Dazed, feeling sick to his stomach, Headsperth got into his car and pulled away from the curb. He couldn't go home yet. He couldn't face Belle or his new ward. Drawn by memory, he drove west along Colorado Boulevard and automatically turned south on Orange Grove as if he were driving to the club. He slowed to a stop at the corner of Del Rosa Drive and turned off the motor. There, across the Arroyo, the terraced stone of the Creighton mansion glowed in the evening's rose-colored light.

He remembered when they were all young. He had been a gentleman of means, the son of a respected banker. Everyone said he was a promising poet and all the blossoming young ladies had clustered about him. Then that handsome young adventurer from Baltimore had come bursting into the hunt and everything had changed.

It wasn't Headsperth's fault that the Eastern editors had failed to recognize the merits of his work. And with his father's insistence on the need for every young man to make his own social contribution, he had been forced into a variety of community services: Executive Secretary of the Rose Bowl Committee, Honorary Member of the Mount Wilson Observatory Association, and a Trustee of the Pasadena Community Playhouse. Meanwhile, he realized, Clifford Creighton—the glowing facade of the mansion seemed to look at him with a mocking grin—had ridden off with the golden girl of his dreams, effortlessly picked up land that doubled in value by the year, even married his daughter into one of the most aristocratic of the Spanish landgrant families.

No, it wasn't my fault, he thought as he started up the motor, I worked hard and Creighton had the luck.

Later that night after their formal dinner, as they were taking their coffee and liqueurs in the library, Headsperth felt that he must speak.

"I don't know if you've looked at the stock quotations for the day," he began and paused as he became aware of Belle's skeptical gaze. He went on, "I felt I ought to stop by the broker's. I'm sorry to have to tell you that things don't look good."

"Yes," she said noncommittally.

"I guess my idea of reinvesting wasn't as smart as I thought it was." He still felt he could not tell her the whole truth.

"Maybe you could ask Clifford for advice."

"Clifford," he said, thinking of his late afternoon vision of that blatant prosperity shining from the other side of the Arroyo.

"Why not?" Belle replied. "After all, we've known each other for years."

"You're right about that." But the thought of going to Clifford and revealing the full desperation of his condition kept him from saying anything further. "Well," he said, "I just wanted you to know that things are bad. They're bad for a lot of people." But he could not bring himself to tell her how bad things truly were for the Headsperth Bauers.

It was on rare occasions that Ruth Ann Creighton de Ortega de Moreno de Arellanos de Mariné swooped down on her parents' beach house, which she considered a folly of their middle age. As she had confessed to Father Clement, she called it their self-indulgent, late-dated love nest.

Ruth no longer drove through the country in anything as girlish and undignified as Poopsy. Instead, fingering her cross in the rear seat with eleven-year-old Lex fidgeting beside her, she was chauffeured in the Señora's latest Hispano-Suiza limousine.

Widowhood became her. She had almost eclipsed the Señora, if such a thing were possible, with her air of perpetual loss and lamentation. As in this visit to her parents, she had turned all her energies into acts of piety and devotion. Now that the Señora was ailing, Ruth felt it her duty to visit the poor at the Mission, giving them lectures on hygiene and the value of protein for their children's health, bringing with her baskets of citrus fruits from the Mariné groves, leaving these surplus crops as if she were conferring a papal favor.

"Mother, I have brought you some fruit," she said, as she marched in. "Now that you and Father are getting on you mustn't underestimate the value of fruit for digestion and the general encouragement of the body's functions. And Gary and Iris no doubt need an extra supply of vitamins, the importance of which we are only beginning to understand."

Victoria was aware of the frivolous contrast she presented in her colored print blouse and lavender walking skirt to her daughter's severe widow's weeds. "Thank you" was all she could find to say.

"Now, Lex, Gary, you two boys can head out for a brisk, and I mean brisk—no lallygagging and skipping stones on the water—hike right down to the end of the canals."

The boys in question looked as if they had just received a sentence of service on a chain gang.

"That's really a wonderful idea, Ruth dear. But the fact is Gary woke up this morning with a slight sniffle and a sneezing fit. It's probably nothing important, but I really think he should stay in and I know you wouldn't want Lex going out alone. Why don't we just let them entertain themselves in the music room?"

"Well," she said, "if you choose to live down in this damp air, you have to expect this kind of thing, Mother."

The two boys retreated before Ruth could formulate her policy in the face of something she obviously disapproved of.

"Now, Ruth," Victoria said, "do take off that dreary veil, and let's have a cup of tea together or something stronger if you wish while we visit in the sitting room. Your father is out having a talk with Mr. Kinney about why the canals keep silting up and Iris has taken my car for an afternoon excursion."

"Mother," Ruth looked extremely shocked, "you really shouldn't let a girl go about unchaperoned, especially in a place like this . . . this *Venice* dedicated to hedonism."

"Dear, aren't you forgetting something?"

"What?"

"The way you and Alessandro met?"

"Oh, Alessandro," Ruth said. "You're so good to remember him. I've made provision that two candles are always lighted for him in the shrine of Saint Joseph of Copertino."

In the music room, Gary rapidly ran through his exercises for both the major and minor scales. Lex, sprawled on the floor, stomach down, had a drawing pad in front of him on which he drew quick sketches of his young uncle.

As he finished his last scale, Gary swung around on the piano bench and said, "All right. Let's see what you made me look like this time."

The scions of two of California's richest families grinned at each other in shy comradeship. Both of them only sons, both of them groomed to be "different" by doting mothers. The boys had been educated by private tutors. Each of them had been for as long as he could remember uneasy in the company of "ordinary" children. Close as they were in age there were yet important differences between them. Gary's parents, Clifford and Victoria, showered him with attention. He was the sunlight of their golden years. Lex, Ruth's son, had been almost a prisoner in the somber adobe that had become a monument to his father's memory. His only outings were to the Creighton beach house. At home, he pored over his drawings of Venice as reminders of a life forever closed to him.

Lex put a protective hand over his work. "How is it you always know when I'm drawing you?"

"Well," Gary said, hesitating, "when you draw it's the same as when I play the piano. I like playing catch with Dad or taking tennis lessons or fooling around in the ocean—"

"Me too," Lex said.

"But there's just something different about the music," Gary said. "Of course I'm sick of going through these dumb scales, but old Krisel says I have to keep at them. What I really like is tackling the hard stuff he's letting me try now or even trying to make up something of my own."

The boys stretched out on the floor together. Lex slowly turned the pages of his sketching pad. There were pictures of the servants of the adobe, of the view from his grandmother's veranda showing the front of the old mission, and a few from his visits to Venice. He laughed at one of his morning's efforts. "I sure messed up on that one. Your hands are bigger than your head."

Gary laughed with him. "I guess so," he said. "But that is the way I hold my head when I have to do those scales, isn't it? And I'd better get back or your mother will be in here telling us what to do."

This time he struck a few tentative chords and then worked into a melody that Lex had never heard before. Lex worked hastily, concentrating on Gary's head and neck.

Even so, their brief silence must have been noticed, for Porter Priest, after a knock on the door, came in carrying a tray of chicken and egg-salad sandwiches, milk and pound cake. He put it on the center table and said, "Miss Ruth won't be happy if this tray isn't empty when it comes back."

The boys groaned. Porter smiled at them and closed the door behind him.

"Why," Lex asked, "*why* can't they just leave us alone?"

Meanwhile in the sitting room, Ruth continued her long monologue. "You know, Mother, he came to me like an angel with wings and he left the same way. Mother, truly he must now be with his own kind in heaven."

"Ruth," Victoria said, "it has been eleven years. You should try to give up your grief. You have a son, a wonderful boy—"

"That Lex!" Ruth said petulantly. "You couldn't possibly understand."

Victoria knew better than to interrupt.

"His father was a gentleman and a hero. Lex just wants to stay in his room with a pencil and a piece of paper."

"You're talking about an eleven-year-old boy who may have a real gift."

"Oh, Mother, if only you knew the depths of my sorrows. Every day I suffer, every day I endure the pain of earthly life. My son is a problem child. I fail in my responsibilities to the adobe. The older family retainers are one thing, but the younger people we are forced to hire are flippant girls and irresponsible youths more interested in themselves than in the honor of the household. I hate to think of what may go on when I am not there to supervise their activities. The Señora's arthritis has made it almost impossible for her to tend to things in the way she used to. And the burden falls upon me."

All this was old news to Victoria, but she was quite unprepared for Ruth's next complaint.

"Up to now," her daughter said, "I have at least had the comfort of coming to see you and Father, either at our real home in Pasadena or your whimsical cottage here. But," Ruth drew herself up, "I've come today especially to tell you that the conduct of your house guest is close to becoming a matter of common gossip. Really, Mother, what can any of us say when word reaches the Bauers? And how will any of us be able to live down the embarrassment and humiliation of *that girl, that necklace, and that Chinaman?* Even *I* know it's been three days and she hasn't sent it back. How could you have allowed this forward behavior to happen in front of Gary? And what, Mother, what are you going to do to restore our family name?"

Iris had begun to think of Victoria's car almost as if it were her own. Parking it at the entrance of the pier, she began to walk out to the water taxi station, but before she'd gone far she saw George Sung, dressed in sporty tweeds, making his way toward her. He waved to her and she waited for him.

"What luck," he said. "I was thinking about you as I came in from the Lucky Dragon."

"I felt I should thank you in person for your hospitality and your extravagant gift."

"Did you like it?"

"Like it! It's the most beautiful thing I've ever seen."

"I can't tell you how glad I am."

When he failed to say anything further she realized that this early morning meeting was making him feel awkward.

"You mustn't let me keep you from your business," she said tactfully.

"I'm busy enough on the barge," he said. "But Raoul really handles everything on this side of the water. No, my day is free."

"Wonderful!" Iris said. "I have a whole day too! What can we do? Where can we go? Maybe we could have an early lunch. Or maybe a stroll along the boardwalk. There's so much I haven't seen. Or we could go for a swim at the bathhouse—"

"Well," he said, distracted. "Well . . ."

"Maybe this isn't such a good idea. I can just tootle along on my own."

He brightened up. "Do you like horses?"

"Do I! The ranch hands in Colorado used to say that if only I were a boy I could ride the range and help break in the yearlings every spring."

Almost before she knew it George ceremoniously ushered her to the passenger seat of a sand-colored Cord roadster. As he turned left to go up the coast, he said, "What we're going to need to get where we're going is the front-wheel drive traction of this little number."

The Speedway bordering the ocean front turned into a narrow roadway. George drove skillfully as they moved along between the Pacific Ocean on the left and the palisades on the right. After about four miles he turned right up a dirt road which very quickly led into a steep canyon. As they climbed, George with great expertise used his front-wheel drive on the sharp inclines and avoided the deeper ruts and potholes.

The hills were covered with sage, chaparral, and a few sycamore trees just beginning to turn yellow and orange.

"I can't believe it," Iris said. "There's a lot more to California than desert and ocean, oranges and lemon trees."

They had reached a fork in the road.

"I guess you could call this the center of town," George said, "if there is one. This is Topanga Canyon. They say that outlaws have used this place as a hideout for the last hundred years."

The "center" was nothing more than an old wooden shack that functioned as the United States Post Office, and another equally small structure, a general store, which served the frugal needs of the community and rented tents to weekend campers. Iris saw no other signs of civilization.

George took the left fork, rattling across a rickety bridge spanning a deep gully. Iris saw here and there what looked to her almost like the summer shacks on the lower slopes outside Colorado Springs. But she was more concerned with George's confident maneuvering of the luxury car through the narrow gap where the primitive dirt road was pinched between a rocky cliff on the right and a shaded dirt slope on the left. As he steered through this she said, "Wow, I'm glad there was nothing coming the other way."

"You get used to this kind of driving up here."

Before her Iris saw a cupped valley with a great rock outcrop thrusting up.

"Everyone around here calls this Big Rock," George said, "but my stepmother calls it Big Potato. Her ranch, Dragon's Den, is her own place. She doesn't get much chance to come up here, but she'd never let my father sell it."

They drove up to a gate. Before George could move, Iris had jumped out, run to open it, pulled back the bars and swung it open. George drove through and Iris closed the gate behind the Cord.

300

George had a slight twinge of irritation that she had anticipated what he had thought of as a demonstration of gallantry. But he was more pleased that this wasn't just another Caucasian girl who had to be waited on.

Frank, the crusty old caretaker of Dragon's Den Ranch, spat out his tobacco and banged the side of the Cord as soon as George stopped the motor.

"Well, goddam, if it isn't little Georgie and a pretty little gal. Howdy, miss," he said, circling the car to open the passenger door.

"Howdy to you, too," Iris said. "You look like a real wrangler."

Frank, who had wrangled very little but his salary since finding this posh job in the Santa Monica Mountains, smiled sheepishly, and said, "I can see you're no stranger to this kind of rough life."

"Rough?" Iris said, looking at the sprawling ranch house and seeing two corrals above on the slope behind it. "I hope it's not too rough for you to have some coffee and a pot of beans simmering on the back of the stove."

Frank slapped his thigh. "Well, goldarn, you're a sharp-eyed young lady. You can see through me just like a bottle of purple-colored glass. I guess I'd better get inside and warm up those cold beans."

Their primitive meal seemed to be ready in no time at all. And although George was skeptical, it wasn't half bad. As he wiped his lips on his paper napkin, George decided to take control again.

"Frank, saddle up a horse. Miss Bauer can find what she needs in the tack room. Show her the way."

George waited for Iris on the front porch. When he saw her emerge in blue jeans and rough cotton blouse he was reminded of Katarina. Frank, who stood nearby holding the reins to a chestnut gelding, let out a low whistle.

"Surely," Iris said as she came up to George, "you're not going to ride in those tweeds."

"I won't ride. I'm going to watch you."

"Nonsense," she said. "We came out here together and we're going to ride together."

Frank grunted.

"I *don't* ride," George had to confess.

"Well, it's high time you learned. Anyone who could bring that Cord up here the way you did should be able to manage a horse in a little under fifteen minutes."

"I've got some half clean things in the bunkhouse," Frank interrupted, grinning slyly. "I'll go saddle up Old Pokey. He doesn't even mind which side you mount from."

In the cool of the bunkhouse, George fastidiously stepped out of his tailored tweeds and pulled up over his narrow hips a pair of faded loose-fitting jeans. Once he'd added the Pendleton and boots he felt that with luck he might just pull this off. He did his best to strut out to where Frank was holding the chestnut and Old Pokey, a faded roan.

Iris gracefully swung up into her saddle. George, after two or three clumsy attempts to imitate her, was happy to accept Frank's forceful boost that almost sent him sprawling to the other side. Balancing himself with diffi-

301

culty, he got both feet firmly settled in the stirrups. Iris had already headed her horse up a trail that circled the big rock and George, holding on to the saddlehorn, knew enough to kick the horse's flanks. He was soon trotting uncomfortably beside her.

"You know," he said, the words coming jerkily, "some people say—that—this is really—the worn-out crater—of an old volcano. Of course—there are fossils around—marine fossils—so we know that—millions of years ago—it was under water."

"Mr. Sung," Iris said, her eyes taking in the embarrassing sight of the slack reins and his hands clutching the saddlehorn, "you might be more comfortable riding at a faster gait. There's something about a trot that takes getting used to."

"As I was saying—the big rock—itself—was probably—the plug of the crater."

"Speaking of plugs," said Iris, on the edge of bursting into open laughter, "that's certainly one you're riding."

"Oh—I don't know," George said.

"Well, Mr. Sung, I do," Iris answered. "Listen, you'll do a lot better at an easy gallop."

"A—gallop," George said, doing his best to control his voice.

"I know it sounds crazy," Iris went on. "But truly, it's an easier gait."

"I'm—perfectly—comfortable," George maintained.

Iris pulled up a little, letting Old Pokey get ahead of the chestnut and then, slipping her right foot out of the stirrup and bunching the ends of her reins to use as a whip, in one deft movement both lashed and kicked Old Pokey's solid rump. The horse shifted into a gallop.

The trail led to a clump of live oaks near the summit, and as they reached it Old Pokey began to slow down.

"I did it!" George exclaimed in triumph and turned his head to smile at Iris who had followed effortlessly. "I really did it!"

"Look out!" she called warningly, but too late.

Old Pokey had headed straight for a low branch and the next thing George felt was a sharp blow that sent him flying off his mount and rolling down a dried brown grassy slope. When Iris saw him lying motionless at the bottom of the hill, she reined in and hiked down to where he lay. Her amusement had turned into worried concern. She knelt down beside him.

"Oh, George, I never meant anything like this to happen. Please say something." Looking at his smooth, clear skin, she found herself kissing him lightly on the temple. "Please say you're all right." When he made no response she slid her hand between the buttons of the Pendleton shirt to feel his heart and was reassured by its rapid beat.

He slowly opened his eyes and blinked.

"Oh, George, thank God!" she said, and without thinking kissed him tenderly full on the lips.

To her surprise, he pulled away. "I shouldn't have let you go that far. I'm sorry," he said.

"No," she said, "I'm the one who's sorry. That was forward of me."

"You don't understand," he said.

Iris sat down beside him and waited for him to continue.

"I decided to bring you up here," he said, staring out at the brush-covered hills, "because I couldn't submit you to the humiliation of what could happen to us if we went out in public."

"What do you mean?"

"I'm Chinese, Iris."

"But you were flirting with me at the Cocoanut Grove."

"That's not the same thing," he said. "That's a night spot where money counts. But you come from a good family—"

"Oh, poppycock!"

"No, listen to me," he went on, "we have no future. You must know that I'm in love with you. The oil wells, the houses, the Lucky Dragon, the money—they don't mean a thing. I'm not a real Chinese, I'm not a real American. I'm an untouchable. *We can't be together.* You have to know that."

Her shoulder touched his and she made no effort either to lean against him or to pull away.

"We're together now, aren't we?" Then she added, "I'll tell you a secret—you mount a horse from the left side."

Not since the turn of the century had anti-Oriental feeling run so high. It was as though after thirty years of blissful ignorance the good citizens of Southern California had looked around them and suddenly seen that the docile race they had imported as servants had, through their unremitting industry, gained property, standing in the community, and relative riches. Ironically, it was not the wealthy who most resented these exotic foreigners, but those at the bottom of society's ladder. Poor whites hated the Chinese with irrational ferocity, blamed them when there were no jobs, feared their "pagan" ways, imagined untold sexual vices. Now that hard times had come, this long-suppressed hostility simmered on the brink of overt violence.

For this reason, Sergeant James Daly relished his frequent invasions of the Chinese community. At the slightest provocation he forced his way through shopfronts where he deliberately knocked over tables of merchandise and containers of precious ginseng root. He broke through to back rooms, claiming that he had smelled opium fumes or heard the click of dice or fan-tan counters. When he found nothing, he would spit contemptuously on the scrolls of the household gods, leave the shops, yanking down ropes of *lop chung,* overturning a rice barrel, and pulling the hair of wives and daughters.

It was this final insult that prompted a delegation of concerned Chinese merchants to seek the help of Sung Wing On.

The Sung family had prospered during the last decade. Katarina had had two last little ones and between them and the many grandchildren she was kept busy, happily ruling her household in her own imperial way. Snug, fifty-four, bored now by merely making money, entertained himself and kept the household in a constant state of agitation by making daily visits to the local matchmaker, muttering to everyone who would listen about the possibility of taking another bride.

In truth, the last thing Sung needed or wanted was another wife. What he yearned for, in these days, what he brooded over during sleepless nights, was the possibility of eligible and decent women for his sons. More than that, he worried increasingly about where and how his grandchildren might be raised. His father had told him that "a good family flourishes in a good village," but Sung knew that Chinatown now with its crime and the threat of outside persecution was far from being a good village. Therefore, he was more than glad to welcome the group of beleaguered merchants.

"Oh, Honorable Benefactor," their spokesman said, bowing deeply, "we come to you because you alone of us all can hope to influence the powers who should control this round-eyed madman. We have tried every method we can think of. We have offered money. We have prayed to the gods. But this man, this barbarian, is not even a human. He is truly a devil possessed by a spirit from some other planet."

"Echoes of this have indeed reached me," Sung Wing On responded with grave dignity. "You flatter me when you say that I may be able to be of help to you, my countrymen." As he spoke the household servants appeared with cups of tea for the members of the delegation. Sung Wing On continued, "It is indeed a matter of concern to us all and I must tell you openly that I have no explanation for it. I ask you to be patient and I assure you that by the end of the week this round-eyed devil will no longer be a problem in our community."

On the Lucky Dragon, Claire shook up martinis as George lounged moodily on the couch of his private suite. He knew he should be more talkative, but he was preoccupied by thoughts of Iris Bauer. He had not seen her since their outing to the ranch three days ago. When they got back into town, she had told him that she wanted to see him, that conventions really didn't matter. But he had not called her.

Claire crossed over to him with his drink. She tried to rub his neck but he shook her away.

"What's wrong, baby?" she whispered in his ear. "It's been over a week. That's not like you."

"Something's changed," he said.

"You don't have to tell me," she said and gave him a comrade-in-arms punch. "You really got it bad. Anyone can see that."

"It's a hopeless case."

"Nothing's hopeless," she said, standing up. "It's been a lot of fun, but love hits the best of us. Call me if it doesn't work out." She gave his shoulder a comforting pat, refilled her glass, drained it in one swallow, and left him alone as she closed the door behind her.

George poured out the dregs of the pitcher. He ambled across the room and looked at himself in the mirror. A wave of pure self-hatred swept over him. He threw his glass at the mirror, shattering it to bits and gazed at himself through the oily tears that the gin left there. He knew he was a coward and a liar. When he had held himself aloof from Iris he had said it was because he was Chinese. When he had told her even earlier that he worked alone on the barge because Raoul was prone to seasickness, he had been lying then as well. Raoul *said that*, sure, but George knew what he was—what he had become—to everyone around him.

He was a pariah. He had not deserved to survive the death of his mother and all his brothers and sisters. When Katarina had taken him in and treated him with love, he had betrayed her by depriving her of half of her children. She had never reproached him, but he could scarcely bear to look upon her careworn face and rarely made visits now to Chinatown. And he had repaid Raoul's gruff friendship by infecting him with that almost fatal disease. Although a part of George's mind insisted it could not be true, all his life's experiences told him otherwise. When he reached out to anyone in love or even affection his embrace carried the kiss of death.

Hector Ortiz and Milan "Mike" Sung had been best friends for ten years, half their lives. When George and Raoul had become partners the boys had been of an age to be sent on errands. The gambling den changed both of them from a feisty half-breed and a skinny little *cholo* into a pair to be reckoned with. If the new street gangs just springing up in downtown L.A. even thought of picking on Hector Ortiz, they had Mike Sung to deal with, and behind him rumors of a crime world as big as the Mafia.

The boys loved it. At the ages of twelve, thirteen, fourteen, they had carried themselves like bantam roosters, Mike always leading, Hector his strutting sidekick. Now hovering at the edge of "real manhood" they needed only money and power to make those rumors true.

In the last year they had begun to deal in drugs. It was dangerous, stylish, and easy money. Marinetti had been more than happy to put these two punks to his own uses.

Even their own parents preferred to leave Hector and Mike alone, ignoring their insolence in the hope that it was a phase, that it might go away.

Hector Ortiz and Mike Sung had each asked their parents to let them go for a weekend "vacation" across the border into Tecate, Mexico. Sung Wing On, already preoccupied with the troubles Sergeant James Daly and his like had brought upon Chinatown, granted his son's request with little thought to the consequences. Katarina had gone into one of her tantrums only to be cut short by her husband when he said, "Are you not aware, old woman, that all of my own community here is looking to me for help?"

But Maria and Raoul had not been as easy to convince. "Why do you need a holiday from work that you never do?" Raoul had demanded. "You do no work to take a holiday *from*."

Maria had wept, saying, "You are but a baby, my son. You cannot leave me."

"I'm not leaving, Mama. I am only going for a weekend."

"But to a strange country," Maria protested. "They say you get typhoid there. They say you can't eat or drink for fear that the meat is tainted and both the water and the wine are unhealthy."

Hector glanced at his father. Even Hector was familiar enough with Raoul's activities in supplying the Lucky Dragon to realize that he crossed the border many times, often staying up to a week in the Sung family's hacienda in Tecate.

Taking advantage of this he said, "I know, Mama, but your own husband was born in that 'strange country.' People go down there all the time." He could see from the slight smile on his father's face that he had hit upon the right line of persuasion. Before his mother had a chance to answer, he said, "Didn't Grandma *walk* here from that country? She was only a girl. And I am a man of twenty-two."

"But you are still a baby to me," Maria said.

"Even a boy, a boy of twenty-two," Raoul said with sarcasm, "needs an adventure. After all, *vieja,* what could possibly happen to them?"

"Vieja!" Maria exclaimed, and Hector knew that he'd won his battle and he and Mike would soon be on their way south.

The grandmother who had walked fifteen hundred miles across the desert to leave behind the disgrace of her affair with the Anglo ranchero was now involved in a more elaborate courtship than if she had been born into one of the original land-grant families. As it continued she wondered if any woman even in the days of knights and dragons had been so inventively wooed.

The morning after their romantic evening on the roof when she had protested against the possibility of marriage, she was not surprised when a florist appeared at her door. Señor John Frederick Smith had always indulged her delight in hothouse flowers, especially the more delicate, exotic, and fragrant varieties.

But when she'd opened the box she had found a small cactus planted in a rough clay pot. For a moment she was sure that the florist had blundered and confused his deliveries. Then her eye was caught by a jeweler's case tied with a piece of ordinary string to the base of the plant. With a delicate caution that went back to her childhood in the hostile desert she untied the knot, avoiding the painful thorns. She opened the satin-lined lid and saw a tiny lapis lazuli scarab set in a gold circlet.

She saw that it had been resting on a bed of the most ordinary notepaper. Her beloved instructed her that this ring was for her right little finger. There were no words of love. In fact, he had not even signed the note. It wasn't until his other gifts began to arrive that she realized what this first ring symbolized and remembered the occasion it represented.

The first time she had lain between the cool linen sheets of his bed, he had casually brushed away a scorpion that had crawled out from under the pillow next to him. In the village they had only known fear of the deadly *alacrán* and here was a blond godlike man whose readiness for love was not to be diminished by any intrusion. Later, during their few weeks together he had teased her that her kisses were like the sting of the scorpion with sharp honey replacing the venom.

306

She had not expected a gift two days in a row. But the following morning the florist's delivery boy presented himself again. This time he carried a newspaper-wrapped bouquet of cuttings of rosemary, oregano, and sage—herbs that flourished in the hostile Sonoran desert. There were no blooms, but another ring, this time for her right ring finger, had been tied to one of the branches as a solitary flower. Señor John Frederick's first present to her had been a small, insignificant opal he had brought back from a business trip to Querétaro. But she gasped as the light flashed from this iridescent large central opal, mounted richly but austerely in plain gold.

She had been puzzled by the third token. A single long-stemmed red rose and a matching solitary ruby in a simple setting. But then she had broken down and cried when she realized that this stone was for the blood of their lost child.

For her index finger the delivery boy presented her with an emerald ring resting in a spray of green orchids, a refreshing and promising renewal—a new life after the harshness of the cactus, the dryness of the desert plants, and the blood-red suffering of the rose.

She wondered where he found such perfect stones, where he had found the accompanying flowers and plants, not all of them in season. She could not ask John Frederick, for his only communication to her during these days were his gifts. And she knew better than to get in touch with him before this extraordinary courtship had reached its end. And even then she suspected that he would wish it to remain an unsolved mystery.

As it happened, she had plenty of time to ponder all this. Having become accustomed to the daily rhythm of these extravagant presentations, she could not understand, this morning, the failure of their continuance. As the early afternoon wore on into evening she began to doubt her lover's intention and her own interpretations of his wishes for their future. At ten in the evening, after a solitary meal, she consoled herself with a strong drink. Just as she was ready to retire, her doorbell rang. By the time she had thrown on a negligee and answered the door no one was there. Instead, at her feet she saw a small white-flowered plant in an elegantly glazed ceramic container. As she stooped to lift it up the intoxicating odor of the night-blooming jasmine instantly flooded her mind with memories of his late-night visits. She carried it into the room and eagerly opened the tissue-wrapped box. It was a simple ring, no decoration, just plain gold as far as she could tell. As she slipped it on the first finger of her left hand, she saw that it was an old-fashioned locket ring held shut by a delicate clasp. Flicking it open, she was dazzled by the brilliance of a deep-blue star sapphire. Ah, she thought to herself, our passion which has only been able to flower in the night, in secrecy, behind closed doors. What next, she wondered. What a subtle *hombre* her Juan was revealing himself to be.

But even her wildest speculations were eclipsed by the next delivery. She could take no meaning from the three pungent stalks of the commonest flower in California. Geraniums after jasmine, what could it mean? And the ring. The rough, unpolished triangle of semiprecious stones, one set apart from the other two, were only vaguely attractive. Not until after she had put it on her middle finger did the pieces of the puzzle fall together. Their three

307

disapproving "children" came between the secret passion and the love of the blue sapphire and the possibility of being united forever through marriage.

The following morning she waited mesmerized for the messenger who she felt sure would deliver a diamond engagement ring. But instead, from the florist's boy she accepted a bouquet of forget-me-nots and a tiny gold ring whose only ornament was a delicate loveknot. Even before she tried to slip it on the ring finger of her left hand she knew it was too small. No, this ring was for her little finger, and whatever the future might bring.

That afternoon, as she looked at the seven rings on her fingers that represented their forty-four years together, she had no doubts of his love or commitment or intentions. But it was she who still hesitated, and for two reasons. She had been independent, she had been alone. At the age of sixty-two, could she be flexible enough to change the pattern of her days? And even if she was, how would she be accepted into his world?

She was still turning over these questions in her mind—feeling foolish that at her age and after all the decisions she had made throughout her life, she was as nervously uncertain as a girl—when, to her surprise, her maid entered with a huge box preceded by its own fragrance. With trepidation and excitement she opened the box to reveal five dozen long-stemmed white roses with an accompanying note cushioned on the blossoms.

"My beloved *corazon*," it read, "can I hope to expect you here tonight at eight o'clock? Unless I hear from you to the contrary my chauffeur will be in attendance upon you well before the appointed hour."

In the years since they had been reunited, and even after Mrs. John Frederick Smith had died, Magdalena Ortiz had entertained her lover at her penthouse, had accompanied him to the theater and performances of the Philharmonic Orchestra, and had been his companion on more than one public occasion, but never in the last twenty-three years had she been invited to his town house in Hancock Park.

George had known since the day at the ranch that he was totally lost to Iris Bauer. Finally, he convinced himself that if he saw her one last time that would be that. He called the Creightons and was abruptly told by Porter Priest that Miss Bauer had returned to her uncle and aunt in Pasadena. Iris herself answered the phone when he called the Bauer residence. No, she wouldn't let him pick her up. She would take the red car to Santa Monica.

He hadn't wanted things to get out of hand, but once she was aboard the Lucky Dragon and in his arms, he had forgotten the promises he'd made to himself.

Now George lay in bed with the girl that he loved by his side. Their lovemaking had been swift, ecstatic, and inevitable.

"I didn't plan it," he said.

"Well, I guess I've been planning it even if I didn't know it, since the minute I saw you."

"I just don't know what you see in me."

She kissed him below his ear. "You may look a little different," she said, "but you have everything that my mother told me to watch for in a man."

308

"Just what was that?" he asked tentatively, touching her.

"Well," she said, "to begin with, you work hard. You're close to your family. You have good manners. You know how to have fun and you're even brave."

"I never knew it before I met you."

"And," she said, caressing his cheek, "you're wildly handsome and everything that goes with that."

"Gee whiz!"

After a long afternoon of love, he drove her back to Pasadena. She had said she would go home in the red car, the way she came, but George had insisted. Her aunt and uncle would have to know sometime and he couldn't let her go through it alone.

Headsperth Bauer sat by the radio listening to the day's final report from the New York Stock Exchange. For a long time he sat there motionless doing his best to deal with what he had heard. He was hardly aware of Belle as she came into the room.

"Is something wrong, dear?" she asked.

As the words finally entered his consciousness, he answered, "Nothing."

Belle poured him a drink, but he didn't touch it.

"Nothing can mean more than one thing," she said.

He lifted his head, responding to the commanding tone of her voice. But before either of them had time to react, they were interrupted by the sound of the front door opening. As Belle went to the library door and pulled it back she saw George and Iris holding hands in the entrance.

"Oh," Belle said in a startled voice.

"We lost track of time," Iris said, "and Mr. Sung was kind enough to drive me home."

"Sung!" Headsperth leaped from his chair. Brushing past Belle he yanked Iris away from the handsome Chinese.

"Forgive me, Mr. Bauer," George began, "perhaps it would be best if you and I sat down and talked this out."

"I have nothing to say to you," Headsperth said, pulling Iris with him into the library and slamming the door.

"It is true then what I've been hearing, that you and Iris have been seeing each other," Belle said.

"Mrs. Bauer, please," George pleaded.

"No, not now," said Belle. "My husband has been under a strain and it would be better if I tried to reason with him myself."

He bowed courteously. "My father has always told me that a woman's reason with a man is stronger than any other persuasion."

Belle smiled wanly. "I only hope you're right. Now, if you'll excuse me. . . ." And Belle disappeared into the library.

George settled himself on the lower steps of the sweeping staircase. He was prepared to wait all night if necessary.

In the library, Headsperth declaimed, "Listen, this is no way for a young girl like you to act. We had no idea that you would behave in this manner."

"What manner is that?" Iris asked innocently.

"To embarrass us in front of our neighbors, to bring in broad daylight someone of that race!"

"Headsperth, try to calm yourself," Belle said.

"Calm myself?" Headsperth sputtered. "Iris has a responsibility to us and the way we expect to bring her up."

"Oh, really?" Iris asked. "For your information, Uncle Headsperth, I've grown quite fond of George. Frankly, I'm not used to being told whom I can bring home and whom I can't."

"While you're living under my roof you'll live by my rules and you'd better be a little more respectful to me," Headsperth went on. "When Belle and I took you in you were penniless."

"What your uncle is trying to say is we're delighted that you came to live with us."

"That's not it at all!" Headsperth contradicted. "You've come from a side of the family I'd just as soon forget."

"Isn't it *our* family, Uncle?"

"We may have been related by blood, but not in spirit. When the Bauer family came out West we made something of ourselves. But your father, my brother, stayed behind on that rundown farm, just plowing himself under the dirt."

"What makes you so much better?"

"Don't you realize that Belle and I, in return for very little, are willing to give you all this?" He gestured about the comfortable library.

"What's the very little?"

"Respect. Living the way we do."

"And just what way is that?"

"Well," Headsperth said and then rushed on, "not bringing home a—"

Iris stiffened. "It's too late for that."

"I'll disown you," Headsperth shouted, the blood rushing into his puffy cheeks.

"Wait a minute," Iris yelled back, "you can't disown me, Uncle, because you never owned me in the first place."

Iris turned on her heel and walked out of the room before Belle, who held out a restraining arm, could stop her.

George jumped up as Iris approached. "Are you all right?" he asked.

"If it wouldn't be too much trouble, could you drop me off at the YWCA?"

"I'll take you there if you wish," he said, "but there's something I think you should see first before we make any decisions."

"I'll be down in a few minutes," Iris said. "I need to get a few things together."

In the library, Belle and Headsperth looked at each other in strained silence. This was finally broken by Belle, who said, "I had lunch with the girls at the Green today."

"So?" Headsperth responded belligerently.

"They said the market is even worse than it was before. Much worse, as a matter of fact, than anything you've indicated, Headsperth."

"What do a bunch of bridge-playing women know?"

"Actually, if you're a good hand at bridge, you're no fool," she said, keeping an even tone. "They can keep track of stock as easily as they can count the cards in the four suits."

Headsperth glared at her without replying.

"Speaking of suits," she continued, "they all said that copper, railroads, steel, and even gold have fallen. Aren't those our four main investments, Headsperth?"

"I don't want to hear any more."

"You said you would disown that girl." Her voice rose slightly. "What were you going to give her? We don't have anything left, isn't that right?" She paused and then went on. "All these years I believed everything you said. The Cycle Way. The chariot race. The eucalyptus grove. 'Don't buy real estate.' 'Oil is a flash in the pan.' 'Buy on margin.' What I went through. And through all those years, I knew I was your second choice. You wanted Victoria! I felt so privileged when you finally chose me."

"Belle—"

"I love that girl. And you've lost her just as you've lost everything else."

Instead of answering, Headsperth turned on the radio. The news only confirmed the increasing disaster on Wall Street. One stock alone, though moderately depressed, seemed to hold steady—Coca-Cola.

Her first thought, as the Rolls-Royce drove her into the curve of the half-circle drive of the porticoed town house in Hancock Park, was one of relief. The driveway was lined with the latest models of Cadillacs, Duesenbergs, and Daimlers. The house itself was brightly lit and through the windows she could see groups of people in evening dress. Thank God, she murmured to herself, for she had hesitated as she was dressing, between her ultra-fashionable low-cut cream silk and a more formal velvet dinner dress. She had settled on the velvet, not knowing what the evening would bring. She had on all her rings and wondered once again how she would answer his question if indeed there was a question.

As the car stopped and the chauffeur rounded the front of the Rolls, opened the door and handed her out, the butler came quickly to escort her into the foyer.

"Ah, you have beaten me to it, Jenkins," she heard the familiar voice of John Frederick Smith as they entered. "This was to have been my own duty."

"I'm very sorry, sir," Jenkins replied. "I do my best to please. Perhaps you should have warned me."

John Frederick laughed. "I suppose I should have," he said. Then he led her into the gaily lit drawing room which she had already glimpsed during her arrival.

Jenkins had somehow preceded them and as they reached the short flight of steps leading down to the room itself, his almost too cultured voice announced in ringing tones, "The Señora Maria Magdalena Ortiz."

Then she was surrounded by guests coming to greet her. First among them came Don Benito Wilson and his wife, the Dona Wilson, who said, "I'm so

311

happy that John Frederick has finally yielded to our wishes."

"You are very kind," she said as Don Benito lifted her hand to his lips.

As couple after couple of the cream of Los Angeles society presented themselves, she acknowledged their formal recognition. And to her surprise she heard herself responding easily and naturally to their cordial remarks. John Frederick Smith took pleasure in seeing the fruits of his efforts, for he had schemed as ardently over this gathering as he had over his courtship.

He had decided almost from the first that their children were no longer of any concern. Children, indeed! They were already middle-aged, married, complacent. Sometimes he found it hard to believe that he had sired two such conventional and unadventurous offspring. Even if his children never accepted this match they could—in a phrase he had recently heard at the Athletic Club—stuff it.

He had opened his campaign two weeks before with a lunch at the California Club honoring Don Benito Wilson. John Frederick had known from the beginning that the men in this rarefied world presented no real problem. It was their wives who made the ultimate social decisions. He knew too that the Dona Wilson, to whom Don Benito owed all his prosperity, was a Dominguez, and if he could only win her approval, that of the others should not prove too difficult. But he had not left it at that. He had dropped by the Valley Hunt Club for a Saturday brunch, and, after ordering his eggs benedict, had drifted from table to table, paying particular attention to the wives, dropping gallant hints that if they were not already married he would be happy to pay them suit, and then suggesting that he was romantically involved and sought their approval.

"If I understand what you're saying, John Frederick," Mrs. Ronald Laselle Knox had remarked, "I can't tell you what a relief it would be not only to me but to many of our friends when it comes to sending out invitations to know precisely how to address them."

"Ah, Edith," John Frederick had said, while Ronald, looking vaguely puzzled, took another drag from his Bloody Mary, "I always knew you were clever. And being clever, you must know I have only one woman in mind: the lovely Señora Ortiz."

Edith Knox had smiled up at him. Before she could say anything his waiter had tapped him on the shoulder. "Your eggs benedict are served, sir," he said.

Edith's laughter was almost too strident. "How Shakespearean of you!" she had said. "A wedding after five acts. Benedict—Benedick. Beatrice and Benedick. I think it's a wonderful idea."

As he went back to his table, saluting his friends who waved to him, he knew that with the Dona Wilson and Edith Knox on his side he had only one woman left to persuade—Magdalena herself.

Looking at her now as she received his guests he knew how right he had been. As the last group paid their respects, he signaled to Jenkins, who in turn signaled to the musicians. The quintet began the soft strains of a waltz. John Frederick led Magdalena onto the center of the floor as the others withdrew, and said, "I think that this dance is mine—or dare I say?—ours."

312

He took her in his arms and she surrendered herself to his lead. They circled the floor to the sounds of muted applause, bubbles of laughter, and music. After they had completed one turn the floor filled, as couples joined in the dance and then almost before she knew what was happening John Frederick had swept her through one of the open French windows and out onto a terrace bordering the side of the house.

"Here we are at last," he said.

"Oh, Juan Frederico, what have you done? What is happening to me?" Holding out her hands, the jeweled rings catching the light from the ballroom, she said, "At first I did not understand them, but now I think I see them all." She gestured with her hands in a winglike movement. "From the thorns of the cactus to the forget-me-nots of the golden bow."

"You deserve them all and more," he said, "and that is why we are here now."

"Juan Frederico, I don't know. I—I am afraid."

"But *I* know, my beloved Magdalena, and you must know too."

"I have seen many changes since I have come to this city, but will they allow us to be happy together?"

"Allow us!" he exclaimed. "They are eager to embrace us, as you must have seen. And even if they didn't approve, would you not be happy with me?"

"I have always been happy when I have been with you."

"Then it is only right," he said, reaching into his pocket, producing a diamond ring, and slipping it on her finger, "that we should be together always."

As her eyes began to well up with tears, he said, "You have always told me in the old proverb of Sonoita that there is no rose without a thorn. But is it not true, *mija*, that there is no rose without its fragrant and soft petals? You have told me—sometimes in jest, it is true—that a woman's life is a bed of stone. But from now on, Magdalena Ortiz Smith, your life truly will be a *cama de flores.*"

Just what he had meant by "there's something you've got to see" had puzzled Iris. She might have guessed he meant to show her his real world—Chinatown. And she felt, even with his reassuring grip firmly on her arm, that they had entered into an altogether foreign land. They had passed by red lights, dancing girls in dimly lit clubs, hanging duck carcasses in windows, and clumps of gossiping old women. From the streets came a rich aroma of roasted pork, garlic, ginger, hot peanut oil, and garbage.

George parked the car just beyond the entrance of a building that looked to her like a warehouse, except that it had two stone lions flanking the entrance.

"Where are we?" she asked.

"This is where I grew up," George said. "For me this is home."

Before he had a chance to help her she had opened the door of the car and jumped out onto the sidewalk.

"This isn't a field trip," he said harshly, trying to crush her enthusiasm.

313

'Adventure is one thing, but this is how we live."

"Trying—before it's too late—to bring me to my senses? Uncle Headsperth would approve of that."

George shrugged. "Well, Iris," he said, slipping a key into the double doors, "here we go."

He led her through Sung's downstairs offices and up the back stairs. Iris, without saying a word, took in the quiet, elegant living room with its lacquer, silks, and embroideries. But even as George led her, Iris was drawn by the most ungodly noise. Iris followed George into the kitchen and total pandemonium.

Several small children chased one another around a large kitchen table in a game of tag. First they ran in one direction. Then, without any kind of signal that she could grasp, they reversed themselves and, screaming with laughter, ran not only in the other direction but took detours into the corners and rejoined the circle with shouts of triumph in a language she knew she would never understand.

Several Chinese men, stripped down to sleeveless undershirts, not only egged on the children but teased and provoked each other, not hesitating to handle one another without embarrassment.

The women, mothers and daughters and servants, gossiped in shrill voices as they kept an eye on their offspring and half pretended to ignore the raucous behavior of the younger men. Nevertheless, as Iris could see, they giggled among themselves and made what she felt sure were comments on their men's private capacities. At the same time, the women chopped water chestnuts, red cabbage, and thin slices of pork with a rapid rhythm, using cleavers that looked dangerous enough to sever a grown man's arm with one stroke. An older woman with frizzy blond hair orchestrated this symphony with the *slam slam* of her pots.

"George! George!" the kids shouted as they ran to him, throwing their bodies against his legs, and climbing over each other to get into his arms, almost throttling him with their embrace. But when they caught sight of the blond stranger they fell silent. The young men and women at their work, becoming aware of the children's sudden quieting, broke off their banter. The pandemonium instantly turned to paralyzed silence.

She had not lived on the Western frontier for nothing, and seeing George still encumbered by the children clinging to him, said to the group, with her eyes focused on the other Caucasian woman, "Hello. I'm Iris. Iris Bauer."

The other woman stepped forward, a pot in either hand. "I am Katarina, and I make you welcome."

Iris, advancing to Katarina, took one of the two pots from her hand and said, "What can I do to help?"

"Yippee!" Katarina shrilled. "George bring home a girl who can work. Here! You take cabbage. I take pork. The other girls cook fish." And even as she spoke the inhabitants of the kitchen sprang back into their devilish play.

"Who is she?" the children screamed at George.

And the young men in a mixture of Cantonese and their own accented English began to welcome the girl with a series of suggestive comments.

"Broad hips!"

"Good for kids!"

"She looks like a real cook. She can feed your belly and we can see the babies won't starve!"

Iris turned to this last brash speaker. "Do *you* have a wife?"

He recoiled and said to George, "She'll give it to you, boy!"

And the family joined in with high-pitched laughter as they introduced themselves and did their best to explain their complicated relationships.

"Help!" Iris said, after she had heard the names of George's half-brothers and sisters, their wives and husbands, his nephews and nieces, a few stray cousins. "You know I'll never keep this straight. You'll have to tell me again and again who you are and you mustn't be offended if I get your names mixed up."

And then the little children were grouped around Iris, repeating their names, reaching up and touching her hair, asking her questions.

"Where are you from?"

"South Dakota," she answered.

"My teacher says South Dakota is a *bad land!*"

The kids giggled and blushed and asked more questions until finally Katarina said, "Enough of this. Bring Papa. It is time we eat."

And out of this apparent chaos Iris could see that a substantial, almost elaborate family meal had been prepared. The servants, remaining in the kitchen, waited for the others to enter a large dining room where three large round tables—already set with plates, bowls, and condiments—barely accommodated the entire family group. Iris wondered at first why everyone held back until she, with Katarina on one side and George on the other, was escorted to the entrance. Then she saw that the three or four older men in the family were awaiting them. George and his stepmother led her to a distinguished man of late middle age who, letting his eyes inspect her with a rapid glance, calmly stroked his mandarin beard.

"Father," George said stepping forward, "I respectfully introduce you to Miss Iris Bauer. I had the good fortune to meet her when she was a guest of the Clifford Creightons."

"Ah," said Sung Wing On, "Bauer. I know that name. Headsperth Bauer in Pasadena."

"We are related by blood," she said, "but my father and his brother followed different roads."

"Ah," Sung Wing On said, smiling cordially in a way that she could not understand. "You will do me great honor if you sit by me."

"I'm delighted." And as she spoke the rest of the family came crashing in and took their places at the three tables.

During dinner Sung Wing On asked her cryptic questions. She struggled not only with her dinner conversation but with her chopsticks as well, sometimes using her fingers when all else failed. She realized that she was being put to the test when Sung himself placed the head of the fish on her bowl of rice.

"For us," he said, "this is the true delicacy. You will enjoy especially the crunchy taste of the eyeballs."

"How good of you," Iris said, rising to the challenge. After she had

315

emptied her small glass of hot rice wine she nodded to him slightly and said, "Gee, back in South Dakota they never let me eat the eyes of the walleyed pike." Summoning all her courage, and counting on the comfort of the wine, she bravely attacked the fish head.

And Sung Wing On, turning to his eldest son, winked an acknowledgment of his approval. George, for the rest of the meal, beamed like a temple lantern.

After the meal, George sought out his father and the two of them went to Sung's office. Over tea George reported the news from the Lucky Dragon and asked why Mike had not shown up for dinner. Sung said only that the boys had gone off for a little vacation in Mexico. Though George said nothing directly in reply, he thought of how his father's attitude had changed. Certainly George at that age would never have been allowed such freedom.

"But enough of business and family," Sung said. "This is the first time you have brought a woman to our home."

"She is not Chinese and yet she is the one person I wish to bring here."

He was hardly prepared for his father's burst of ironic laughter. *"Not Chinese?* What meaning does that have here?" And then going on with intense seriousness, Sung said, "I know you have not forgotten your mother and neither have I. But have you not had a second mother? Although her ways are still strange, Katarina has been a faithful wife in all her duties. And *she* is not Chinese."

The two men exchanged affectionate glances.

But the women in question were not so reticent. As the servants and the others cleared the tables in the dining room, Katarina moved to a chair beside Iris.

"You like my son?" Katarina asked.

"I like him a lot. I haven't known him very long."

"It is not important. You meet someone, you *know*. He is your wosbon."

"How did you meet *your* husband?"

"He buy me off ranch. I am second wife. He give me good life." Seeing Iris' questioning look, Katarina went on, "I have much unhappiness. I have sixteen children and nine die. But in the old country it was worse. Happiness? We do not know this word. Sung is a good man. We never hungry. He is good father. He never beat me."

"George says you can't get married in California. That a—" here she flushed—"a white person can't marry a Chinese."

"We are not married with the right papers. But, yes, you can get married. You go to Mexico. My wosbon has house in Tecate for work. You get married there." Katarina whooped. "I have too many children. *I* have no time for wedding bells."

Iris joined in her laughter.

"Your family," Katarina asked. "What they think?"

"I have no real family," Iris answered. "My mother and father are dead."

"Poor girl, don't worry. We have plenty family here," Katarina said, patting Iris on the back. "George not my own son, but he is good boy and I love him just like the others." Suddenly she said, "Why not *now?* Why not go now, down to Tecate?"

As if on cue, George entered the dining room and asked, "Have you decided where I should take you?"

That same night, Clifford and Victoria were awakened by the imperious ring of their bedroom telephone.

"The Creighton household here," Clifford said.

He immediately recognized Belle Bauer's voice as she said, "Thank God I've found you at last. I kept trying the Venice number but you weren't there."

"We had to come back to town for a few days to keep in touch with the financial situation. Belle, what is it? What's wrong?"

"It's Headsperth. We've had a few words. He's finally admitted where we stand. He says . . . he says's he's going to kill himself."

"We'll be right over."

They quickly pulled on clothes and drove to the old Bauer place. When they approached they saw the house brightly lit on all three floors and a lone figure sitting on the edge of the slate roof.

Belle greeted them at the door in tears. "What am I going to do? What would I do without him?"

"Belle, I'll take care of this," Clifford said.

"No," Victoria interrupted, "I think this is really for me."

And without waiting for their protests she climbed the curved staircase, and in the third-story hallway found the ladder that Headsperth had left leading up to thc attic. She kicked off her shoes, hiked up her skirts, and made the ascent to the roof. The slate felt cold and damp on her feet, but without hesitating she slid out on the roof next to Headsperth.

"Well, Headsperth, what sort of performance is this?"

"I might have known they'd send you," he said miserably, his teeth chattering with cold. "You always saw through me."

He pulled his flannel pajama top closer about him, shivered again, and slipped a yard down the slick, wet roof. Victoria reached out for him.

"Don't come any closer," he threatened.

"Well, then, come in and we'll talk."

"No. No, you don't take me seriously. No one's ever taken me seriously. Everything Belle told me was right. I've never made a right move in my life. I gave up my poetry. I let you marry Creighton. I saw a city full of bicycles. I thought the motorcar wouldn't last. I spent a fortune on eucalyptus trees. They have yet to saw down one tree for anything but cheap firewood. And my idea for the chariot race. I made an idiot of myself that day."

"Perhaps that wasn't wise. But you were also quite brave under the circumstances."

"I've had a wonderful wife," he continued. "I've never appreciated her the way I should. I finally had a chance to have a daughter and I drove her off tonight."

"You shouldn't have done that."

317

"Oh, Victoria, I'm an idiot."

After the silence that followed, Victoria said, "In many ways you're right." She paused while Headsperth thought *that* over and then said, "But that's no reason for sitting out here and catching cold. And that's no reason for jumping off this roof. Besides, it's only three stories high."

"I'd be better off dead."

"You might be, but what about Belle? Do you think she's loved you all these years for your financial wizardry?"

"Well . . ."

"You're going to come in before you catch your death of cold. And while you're at it, you're going to help me off this slippery roof before I catch mine. Then we're going downstairs, have a drink, and talk this whole thing out."

In 1929, Tecate's one main street was lined with makeshift frame buildings—newly set up legal offices, markets fronting for dubious activities, brothels, and gambling houses. For hapless Chinese swindled into crossing the ocean and unable to enter the United States by legal means, Tecate offered both a temporary haven and a chance to arrange for getting over the border. For others Tecate was a safe place to conduct underworld business, for this town was virtually ignored by the Border Patrol, the State Police of Mexico, or any other law enforcement officials. For a few, Tecate had the answer to their romantic woes. Here anyone could get married without question for a few pesos.

And for Iris and George as they drove down the tawdry street, this fact alone gilded the shabby town with an aura of love and promise. George chose to stop at the self-proclaimed service of Señor Pablo Ignacio Ramirez, "marriage judge." Within ten minutes they were man and wife, with documents stamped and signed safely in George's breast pocket.

They would spend the next few days at George's father's hacienda just out of town. George hoped Iris believed him when he explained it was merely a family investment with an eye to the future. For himself and Raoul the deep-dug cellars held cases of champagne, cognac, and the premier wines of Europe which had entered Mexico at Veracruz and made the long, tortuous trip clear across the country to this hideaway.

He could tell her later that they used the *ranchero* as a holding place for Chinese immigrants who paid healthy sums for Sung Wing On's assistance in entering the United States. Though immigration seemed easy now with the establishment of legal entry through Angel Island in San Francisco Bay, for the Chinese themselves, the truth of the matter was that this had become an added terror. Without consideration of the Chinese traditions of personal privacy, members of both sexes were humiliated by being forced to submit publicly to what purported to be medical examinations. For the women in particular this was a degradation beyond endurance. And more than one girl of good family had taken her own life after this barbaric treatment. What Sung Wing On did here in Tecate might have seemed like lawlessness to the white community, but to himself and the other Chinese it was the most honorable service he could offer his countrymen.

318

All Iris was aware of after the long dusty journey, the perfunctory ceremony, was her appreciation of the solidity of the thick adobe walls, the traditionally furnished *sala* with its beamed ceiling, the conventional yet comfortable colonial furniture, and the immediate attendance of the household staff that brought them refreshments.

On the other side of the property, Mike Sung and Hector Ortiz, hidden in a dark outbuilding, worked desperately at stuffing pounds of heroin into the door panels of Mike's Duesenberg.

"We'll never get away with this," said Hector, as he wiped away the nervous sweat that ran down his face and soaked his collar.

"That's the trouble with you, Hector." Mike spoke in a feverish burlesque. "You brown boys really haven't moved into anything on your own. You're lazy like they say and you're more yellow than we are."

Hector tried to laugh. He was used to Mike's acid humor, but still he felt doomed. "All right," he said, "we'll keep at it. We don't have any choice. But I'm telling you, after this I'm going clean. This could make me an old man."

"What's the big deal?" Mike asked. "We drive across the border, we deliver the stuff, it's over."

The shack lit up with bright pink light. A flare blazed at their feet.

"Stop where you are and give yourselves up, you slimy scum!"

Hector's face pantomimed imbecilic astonishment.

"You little pricks!" Daly's voice went on. "I've been following you for weeks. Your Chink father ruined my life by going straight to the mayor." Daly laughed maniacally. "I'm going to pay him back the best way I know."

Mike hit the dirt floor, grinding his face into the dust with desperate intensity. A blast of machine-gun fire tore through his shoulder, whipping him over on his back. He lay rigid and helpless as the neat row of bullet holes stitched a seam in the wounded Duesenberg and moving on, cut Hector Ortiz precisely in two.

George knocked over the lamp and flung Iris to the floor. In the dark he listened intently, trying to make sense of the voices, the bullets. Crouched by the window he saw a lone figure capering in the loose dust of the courtyard, shooting random patterns where his victim had taken precarious shelter. Then George caught his breath. The entire north wall of the building shuddered, buckled. A car burst through with tremendous speed and mowed down the lone gunman. Then there was silence.

George, shaking, got up. "Wait for me here," he choked out. He opened the door, walked down the stairs, and stood in plain view.

"Mike," he called out, "is it you?"

His brother's voice whimpered and George ran to the Duesenberg.

"I've killed him. I never meant to kill anybody. It was that cop, that crazy cop."

"Come on, let me get you inside." George carried his younger brother into the main room of the hacienda and called for the servants.

"Hector," Mike sobbed. "Is Hector all right?"

A servant quietly disappeared and returned with the news.

"Bury them," George said. "Bury them both. Give them decent graves."

By this time Iris had brought hot water and was quickly and efficiently binding Mike's wound.

It was strange, George thought, how easy, how routine this should have seemed. This was a simple smuggling job, like so many others that were remembered in his family. He spoke quickly to the little circle of scared faces that surrounded him in the lamplight.

"Tsiang-li, drive this car to the chief of police. Tell him crooks used this place for a dope drop. Be sure he sees what's in the car doors. Tell him it's his. Then walk away."

Even as he spoke, George riffled through the contents of a wall safe. "Mike, can you travel? There are papers and money here. We've got to get you out right now."

Not until they were on the road did George remember he hadn't even said goodbye to Iris.

The morning wedding in John Frederick's garden had been an intimate affair, just the children and grandchildren. John Frederick's family had put a brave face on it. Raoul and Maria, to Magdalena's surprise, actually seemed pleased. Magdalena's only regret was that Hector was away. Raoul had tried to cheer her up. "That's what you get when you have a shotgun wedding."

After the guests had gone home Magdalena had rested in the library until the man who was now, to her growing astonishment, her husband, appeared in the doorway and said, "My darling, what are you doing here? Shouldn't you be putting a few things in a bag?"

She had not understood his meaning.

"My beloved," he had said, taking her by the hands and helping her to her feet, "can we have a wedding without a honeymoon?"

"We're not spending the night here?"

"I am a man of my word. Have I not promised you a bed of flowers?"

"Where are we going?"

"Ah, *mi corazon,* that is for me to know. We shall leave in fifteen minutes. The car is already at the door."

Then they were on their way in a shining new Lincoln coupe, not only driving to the coast but heading south.

She thought they were going to Laguna, but when they passed that resort she decided that the Hotel del Coronado in San Diego would be their destination. In one sense, this was true. They spent their first night as husband and wife there. But in the morning they were off again.

Within an hour they crossed the border into Magdalena's homeland. Before long she began to feel the tremor of something close to panic. She had not been here since she had walked away from her home all those years ago. The miles of desert, the wretched little towns, the starving animals reminded her all too clearly of her past. But seeing how happy John Frederick was, driving next to her, she said nothing and tried to keep the

320

conversation light. Hours later, when she could stand it no longer, she asked if they were going back to Sonoita.

"Heart of my heart, rose of all roses, unless it is your wish to return to the first flooding of our passion, I have made other plans."

She said briefly, "It would be no wish of mine."

"Our path is a new road for both of us." And even as he spoke he turned off the main highway, if it could be called that, onto a lesser road that took them directly to Puerto Penasco, a tiny fishing village. In the middle of the protected bay a gleaming white yacht awaited their arrival.

One of the crew members was there to greet them in the captain's gig and within minutes they were on board the elegant vessel.

"I'll show Mrs. Smith to our stateroom," John Frederick said to the crew. "You can take care of the luggage later."

Magdalena noticed that the men smirked at each other. How presumptuous of her countrymen she thought to herself as John Frederick led her along the deck to their door. He paused, grinned at her as he took her hand and lifted it to his lips. Then he opened the door.

She gasped. The entire stateroom was layered with roses and rose petals. Huge bouquets hung from hooks on the ceiling, baskets with at least five dozen roses in each lined the walls, every available surface had its mantle of roses. As she stepped inside she could not keep herself from looking, even though she knew it was ridiculous, to see if those roses had thorns. But of course there were none. Just as she realized that her feet were standing in a thick carpet of petals John Frederick swept her into his arms and in two strides crossed to the bed where he tenderly laid his Magdalena on a bed of blushing pink roses.

As George drove toward the coast, Mike fell in and out of consciousness. But for a few moments he was lucid enough to get angry with his brother.

"Hey, we could be millionaires," Mike said. "We can keep the stuff. We can sell it."

"I've gotten rid of it already."

"How could you be so stupid? Marinetti will never know and I know how to turn it over fast."

"You just don't see it, do you, Mike? It's not our family way."

"What do you mean? Father—"

"Don't you see the difference?"

But Mike blacked out again.

By dawn they reached the small sleepy port of Ensenada. For a generous fee George found a fishing boat, sailing down the coast of Baja, then past Manzanillo to Acapulco, that would be willing to take on Mike as a passenger.

"Where will I go?" asked Mike.

"From Acapulco you can board a ship for anywhere. Just don't come back. Not until you hear from me."

The two brothers shared a last anguished embrace. The fishermen were eager to cast off, and as soon as Mike had boarded they reeled in their hawsers. George saw Mike, still on deck, drifting away from him on the ebb tide until the motors caught hold and the boat veered away from the dock, heading out to sea.

The drive back across the barren desert took a full ten hours. At first he cried and then he hit his hands against the steering wheel until the pain in them congealed into numbness. It had happened again. If he had been his father he would have cried out to the gods. But a man such as he had not even the gods to comfort him. Another death, another brother lost. George would have to tell Raoul, he would have to tell his father. But beneath this pain there lurked another, far more excruciating. He had not been straight with Iris. He had drawn her into a marriage which had already become a death trap. What could he say to her if she was there when he returned? He had not even said goodbye and how could he face his life if the only woman he ever loved was lost to him now?

At the end of his return journey, under a blazing sun, George drove up to the hacienda. He glanced at himself in the rear-view mirror—dirty, blood-stained, dog-tired.

"There you are, darling," Iris called out as he came up the steps. "There's coffee waiting and some fresh rolls. The police have been here asking questions, but Tsiang-li seemed to have the right answers."

He smiled at her and took her hand.

"You don't have to tell me anything," she said. "All I want you to know is that I'll be there for you forever, always."

Iris and George Sung began their second day of marriage.

BOOK VI

1945

Dry the pool, dry concrete, brown edged,
And the pool was filled with water out of sunlight,
And the lotos rose, quietly, quietly,
The surface glittered out of heart of light,
And they were behind us, reflected in the pool.

Eliot, Burnt Norton

The first Sunday in July found the Creightons having breakfast on their Pasadena terrace. What had begun as a wartime contingency—their eastward migration across the city—had settled into an uneasy "permanence." Victoria sometimes considered wryly that their lives might end before the war would; that this elegant, if austere, Pasadena life might be, after all, the way she and Cliff would end their days.

They had given up their beach house for myriad reasons. It had not been part of their romantic vision of themselves to look out of the bay windows of their home only to see the crazy glitter of barrage balloons. Clifford had worried so visibly about his wife's safety after the first bomb scare that all her protestations could not restore him. Ruth had peppered them both daily with phone calls, reminding them that by staying where they were, they were interfering with military maneuvers, that if a Jap bomb were to take their lives, she would feel personally responsible to her Creator, and finally that "Daddy wasn't up to it," that "the damp would hurt Daddy's chest," and that Daddy, brave as he was, "would be physically unable to withstand the invasion when it came."

Secretly Victoria had to agree with some of this nonsense. Cliff was wiry and full of quiet fun. But the other truth was that when the Japs had bombed Pearl Harbor, Cliff had been seventy-seven. He had been brave and calm about this terrible new turn of world events, but the sunny afternoon when Gary had appeared for tea in a crisp army uniform, had broken the news that he been accepted for Officers Training School, Victoria had watched Clifford's eyes fill with tears, even as he smiled his approval.

And so they had moved back to the old house—just the two of them now—and given their Venice home to the Red Cross for the Duration. The Duration. How long would it endure? They had moved for the fear of invasion, for Clifford's health—although no one except Ruth would call it that—and for pure survival. Although they were determined to live within the strictures of rationing, Priest was able to work relative wonders with the tradesmen in Pasadena.

The Pasadena to which they returned had also been scarred by war. Posters warning of loose lips and sinking ships adorned every public building. Suicide Bridge was swathed in, to Victoria's eye at least, pathetically amateurish camouflage. Even the view from their terrace had changed dramatically. Across the Arroyo, now littered with all the careless debris of modern civilization—bungalows, roadsters, incinerators, ratty palm trees, buckling sidewalks, and the like—the elegant grounds of the Vista del Arroyo Hotel which through the decades had provided an emerald green oasis for their pleasure was itself now wrapped in festooned camouflage, and the wall that topped the Arroyo cliff had been painted with a glaring red cross. The hotel had been turned into an army hospital, for the Duration.

Victoria sighed, then realized that Clifford had been speaking.

"I said," he repeated gently, "wouldn't it be wonderful if we could spend the day galloping down the Arroyo?"

He sat wrapped against the morning chill even though it was a summer day. He was always cold now. But his face was still strong and fine.

Again, Victoria sighed. "My dear, it would be wonderful, wouldn't it, simply to take a drive? But you know I can't. I'm signed up for work today."

An expression of peevishness fleetingly passed over Clifford's face. "I don't know what you make such a fuss about, Victoria. You're just a volunteer. You're not a real nurse." A flash of feeling came into his voice. "Don't you think I need you too?"

Victoria's heart melted, and beyond her initial concern she felt every bone in her own body cry out for a measure of repose, quiet days spent in the companionship of her beloved.

"Darling," she said, "I *want* to stay here. Surely you can see that. But don't you see, I just feel that as long as Gary is still gone . . . well, until he comes home, I feel I have to do my part."

"The war's almost over," he rapped out. "There's just an island mop-up left to do."

"You only want company," Victoria said and got to her feet.

Alone in the hall she donned a smock and pinned on a jaunty Red Cross hat which Pansy ironed crisp and fresh every night. She rejected Priest's offer to drive her to work, telling him to keep an eye on Pansy, meaning that he should keep an eye on Clifford.

Even the Priests seemed old to Victoria now. She had lightened their work by bringing in day help over their not very vigorous protests. It amused Victoria that by evening there were four elderly people rattling about the mansion.

After Mrs. Creighton had left, Priest went out to the terrace and stood unobtrusively by the old man as he watched his wife's rakish prewar roadster zip across the bridge and turn right into the Vista del Arroyo Hotel.

326

The hotel courtyard into which Victoria drove seemed almost to have approached a prewar state. Behind the brisk nurses intent on some errand, the occasional bandaged soldier in a wheelchair, there was an almost palpable air of festivity, excitement, even glamour.

After all, Clifford had been right. The war was nearing its end. Off-duty nurses taught willing "boys" the intricacies of Ping-Pong and shuffleboard. The music of Tex Beneke blared from a portable radio. Along the westward wall a group of volunteers worked on their tans while writing letters and playing checkers with soldiers not yet ambulatory.

Victoria headed, as she always did, to New Admissions. She had learned in these past five years that while boys loved to flirt with the pretty ones when they were getting better, they needed motherly attention when they were truly ill and frightened. It was quiet in the anteroom of Ward 23. Liz Devers, who had nursed here for the last four years, greeted her with relief.

"Honey, am I glad to see you! I thought for a while you wouldn't be in today. God knows why, you always show up. We've been swamped since four this morning and there are at least fifty more kids coming in from the Pacific. I think if you held them up to the light you could see through them. They're nothing but human colanders."

Then she stopped, seeing the stricken expression on the older woman's face.

"Oh, hon, I'm sorry. I forget sometimes." She gave the tiny gray-haired woman a gruff hug. "Don't you worry, Mrs. Creighton. The war's almost over. You," she raised her voice, consciously changing the subject, "you'll be having a new helper today. She's a pretty thing. We tried to put her outside, but she says she doesn't know how to play games. At least she's quiet. Just take her along with you and give her the idea she's helping."

Victoria looked around and in the half gloom saw that a young woman, her dark eyes heavily shadowed, had been waiting to be taken into the conversation. Had she heard the way Nurse Devers had so curtly dismissed her efforts? If she had, she seemed not to care.

"I'm glad for the help," Victoria said with quick courtesy. "I'm Victoria Creighton."

"And I," the young girl responded, "am Tovah Toffias. I am very pleased to make your acquaintance." She spoke with a marked accent and with the stilted English of a well-schooled European.

The two made a strange pair, but they had in common an aristocratic mien. Nurse Devers took a moment to watch as the old woman and the young girl walked off together down the corridor. Both of them were the kind of woman she would never have met if it hadn't been for the war. She was brought back to reality by the rude snap of gum directly behind her. An orderly, 4–F, lounged on a gurney.

"That old lady is hot shit, isn't she? Where do you think she gets it?"

"She's working off her worry, Phil. She's still got a boy in the service. Say, don't you think you could do a little of that?"

He gazed at her, uncomprehending.

327

"You know, *work.*"

At the door of the first room of her accustomed rounds, Victoria paused. There were four beds inside. One held a double amputee, one boy had lost half his face, another had suppurating stomach wounds that required constant cleansing and draining, and one held a man who was a man no longer.

"My dear," Victoria said gently, "it's not too late for you to learn the game of Ping-Pong or the simple moves of checkers. Some of what you will be seeing is most unpleasant."

The young girl smiled politely, sadly. "I am afraid," she said, "that your lovely California sunshine does not yet seem quite real to me. I believe there is still some work to be done here." And, with respect, but still with the quality of speaking to an equal, she said, "I would imagine this unpleasantness would hold no surprises. I have just come from Austria, where I have seen the worst of atrocities."

Even though it had been sixteen years since the event itself, Raoul woke from a nightmare that had haunted him at irregular intervals. He was sitting at his desk in the downtown office that served as headquarters for his and George's operation of the Lucky Dragon. George, without knocking, had thrown open the door and stood looking at him, his face reflecting mixed emotions.

"What is it?" Raoul asked, already apprehensive.

"I have the worst news I could bring you," George said. "The boys won't be coming home. Hector—"

And with the terrible futility that attends the worst nightmare, Raoul leaped forward and tried to grasp George even as he faded, screaming, "What have you done to my son?"

Raoul woke drenched in sweat and choked by a terrible thirst. He had drunk too much the night before, as usual. He was alone in the bed. He pushed himself up on one elbow and drained the last of the stale beer which he'd taken to bed with him. He rubbed the back of his fist over his bleary eyes and with distaste surveyed the room.

Ten years ago Maria had invested in a seven-piece blond-wood bedroom set. He had recognized it as a pathetic attempt to get him interested in her and the marriage again. The wood had cracked. His distaste for her was as firm as ever. Since his son had died he had found no reason for living.

Not only the law and the repeal of Prohibition had led to the dissolution of the Sung–Ortiz partnership and the disappearance of the Lucky Dragon. But Raoul had punished himself every day for sixteen years. Without his connection with the Sungs, Hector might not have been led into the life and death of a criminal. And yet, Raoul thought feverishly, what else could the boy have done? What could any Mexican do? How had he, Raoul, managed to spend his own *pendejo* life? In trouble.

His mind, tormented by a crashing hangover, skittered over his life's possibilities like a desperate rat. If he hadn't gotten mixed up with those scheming Chinks. If he hadn't married that cow. If he had invested his money wisely. If he hadn't been cursed with a selfish mother. But a quiet voice reminded him that Maria had been beautiful before he had touched her, that Magdalena had done everything in a woman's power to help him and if she chose to avoid him now it was simply because he made himself intolerable. He had more than enough money in the bank even if he chose not to spend it, perversely denying pleasure to himself and those around him. And as for Hector's death, who could know? If Raoul blamed the Chinese, if he blamed the *chingada* police for their insane persecution and deliberate torment of a lost and lonely Mexican kid, at least that way he would not have to blame himself.

He sat up on the side of the bed. His stomach protruded from his pajama top and spread halfway to his knees.

"Maria!" he shouted.

When there was no answer, he muttered to himself, "Stupid bitch."

Only after he had heaved himself up and shuffled into the bathroom to relieve himself noisily did he realize that this was Sunday. Maria would be in church. She'd left coffee for him in the kitchen and fresh tortillas kept warm for him under a towel. He had already eaten two of them doused with beans and laced with fresh chiles, and opened his second beer when she returned.

She was stout now. Her green rayon Sunday suit pinched her like a sausage. A white lace veil was draped unbecomingly across a modified pompadour.

"Aren't you ready yet?" Her voice held exasperation, resignation, and scorn. He didn't know what she was talking about and tried to remember *ready for what*? "Your mother," she reminded him. "The first Sunday of every month we go over for lunch at your mother's."

"Why don't you ever take care of yourself?" he lashed out. "Why don't you lose some weight, buy some decent clothes? You look like a real beaner today. I'm ashamed to take you over there."

For a long moment her eyes speared him. She answered his outbursts with silence and seemed at these times less like the Spanish aristocrat than Indian and ancient.

"What do you expect from a pig but a grunt?" she said casually. "Come on, get ready."

The house was gleaming white stucco built in the ultra-modern fashion of the late thirties. A double garage faced directly onto the boulevard. Above it a spacious living room was placed so as to take advantage of the view of Silver Lake, a small body of water to the northwest of the central city. It was a sophisticated address. The district combined the very best in suburban living. Fresh air, ample room for children to play up the rough slopes of the hills, and facing Silver Lake Boulevard, a line of trim, anonymous urban exteriors, each one closed off against its neighbors. If the children of the Silver Lake District played together, its adults preserved a polite privacy. The houses were occupied by a great variety of artists and businessmen, Hollywood writers and academicians. Silver Lake was perfect for George and Iris Sung.

The last five years had not been easy for the Chinese in Los Angeles.

329

More than once George had been hissed off the street and called "a Jap." They had left their last home, a cozy redwood bungalow at the top of the Micheltorena Hill after Lloyd's seventh birthday party. George had hung a red paper carp to celebrate the occasion from the chimney of the house. Some neighbors had thought that Mr. and Mrs. Sung were taking advantage of their ocean view to signal twenty-six miles across the city to the Japanese submarines that everyone was convinced lurked in the bay. Iris had tried to reason with George. Everyone was fearful of invasion. In fact, a Japanese submarine *had* surfaced off the coast above Santa Barbara and lobbed three shells into what the Japanese Navy thought was an oil-loading pier. Still George would not be placated. The humiliation of being interviewed by the police and the subsequent examination by the military authorities were too much for him. It was bad enough, he told Iris, to be discriminated against all these years for being Chinese; to be persecuted now as a Jap was preposterous.

Accordingly, they had moved off the hill and into this relatively new and certainly more tolerant district, purchasing the very best treatment that money could buy.

Beyond these events of the world, Iris thought, as she stood now in her elegant living room, putting the finishing touches on her daughter's hair, life had been good to them. She'd always felt that personal happiness was not a particularly reasonable expectation.

When she had met and married George Sung she had done so out of passion and a wish for love and glamour. It had been a quixotic gesture bathed in blood and disaster almost from the beginning, and yet, and yet . . . The years had followed each upon another, bringing them the children, possessions, and a family life that Iris delighted in.

If she conjured up her Aunt Belle in her mind and tried to explain to her why she, Iris, felt that she had made the right decision, these thoughts became less frequent. She had a husband, children, money, and a home, and she was happy.

George appeared in the doorway dressed for their family Sunday dinner. He lounged elegantly, his handsome mouth turned in a sardonic grin as he watched her fuss with the last recalcitrant curls of Elizabeth's hair and fasten a huge white puffy bow just above the perfect part.

Iris looked up a little defensively. "I don't want Katarina to think I'm neglecting them."

"I wish you didn't have to go down to the station on a Sunday."

"George, dear, we've discussed this before. All the women decided to take turns on the weekends because none of us want to be away from our families. We don't think it's right, you see, when a troop train comes in, for none of us to be there."

George countered with the argument that thousands of American men were using to their wives these days. "It doesn't really matter, does it? You're just a volunteer."

Iris looked at him. "Yes," she said. "I think it does matter. It matters very much."

Twenty minutes later saw her at Union Station, where she had worked three days a week, since the beginning of the war, for Travelers Aid.

George had always felt resentful about the grandiose halls of Union Station, though he admitted the architecture fit in well with the Spanish colonial inheritance of the city. He could never forget that its construction had meant the tearing down of the heart of old Chinatown, his home. For herself, Iris could feel only gratitude that the city fathers had completed this ambitious project before the war broke out. Having spent many hours of pandemonium within the station's vast reaches, she shuddered to think what would have happened to bewildered boys, heartsick wives, wretched children, without its protection.

Today the cathedral-like waiting room was filled with anxious relatives who had received word of the incoming train. Iris recognized worried faces; some mothers who had sons missing in action had not missed a train in months.

Iris leaned into the small open cubicle right in the center of the great hall, where for five years good women had measured out strong coffee and sweet doughnuts, meal chits and information.

"We don't need you here, dear. We've got our coffee brigade set up. Why don't you go on down the line and wait for the train?"

Iris was passed through the barriers, and hurried down the long tunnel. Emerging onto the platform, she found herself in the company of at least a dozen newspaper men, relatives with platform passes, and a radio crew. A balding commentator was killing time with repetitious patter.

"Now that the Rising Sun has almost set, we won't be seeing quite so many of our heroic boys as we used to, but we'll remember them like this— our boys!—coming home from land, from sea, from air, and those of us who stayed can only be—"

He was drowned out by the roar of the incoming train.

Iris' heart began to pound. No matter how many times she saw it, she was always unprepared for the stark emotion with which a mother greeted a son, a young father in uniform touched a child he was seeing for the first time, the gruff tact with which an aging dad made light of his soldier-son's injuries. . .

And they began to flood off the train. There were so many wounded in this contingent! In this first hush, Iris heard women begin to cry.

The balding commentator gripped his microphone and raised his voice.

"Here they come, as they have from Truk, from Guam, fron Saipan and Guadalcanal! The brave, the weary and the maimed. Oh, folks, if you could see the terrible sacrifices these boys have made to keep America free—Son! Son! Wait a minute, boys, put that stretcher down right here. Let that hero say a few words to America's home front."

The "hero," Iris could see, was a boy no more than nineteen. His left arm and leg were bandaged stumps.

"Well, fella, how does it feel to be home?"

The boy blinked. He was obviously in pain.

"Tell them all how it feels to give everything for your country!"

The boy, the stretcher-bearers, froze as the man droned on.

"If you could see what I see, a boy who used to be in the prime of life and the pink of condition, a boy who used to play baseball, football—"

In a frenzy, Iris snatched the microphone from the commentator's pudgy fist, and with an authority that made him step back, she hiked up her skirt and knelt down beside the boy.

"Where are you from, soldier?"

His voice was a whisper. "Alhambra."

"Alhambra," Iris repeated clearly. "That's close enough for you to talk to your mom. What's your name, dear?"

"Billy Roney. William Hamilton Roney the third."

"Mrs. Roney," Iris said into the microphone, "I do hope you're listening to this broadcast. And if there're any neighbors of the Roneys listening, I hope they'll get her on the phone. Bill's back, Mrs. Roney, and he has something to say to you."

Something in Iris' voice had given the boy courage. And he took the microphone with his good arm and held it close to his lips.

"Mom? Mom, I'm home." His low voice gathered strength. "They did their best to kill me, Ma! I don't think they've told you, but I've left an arm and a leg over there. They say I'll be in the hospital for a while. But I'm all right, Ma." His voice broke. "I'm all right."

Iris dashed what might have been a tear from her eye and said, "Well! I think that's about enough, Billy. The sooner you get out of here, the sooner you'll get home."

She stood and handed the microphone to the broadcaster, but he refused it. "Listen, lady, you go ahead and talk to them. Talk to them the way their wives would, their sweethearts would. . . ."

She turned to the next wounded kid.

And when, a full hour later, she again returned the microphone to the broadcaster and he'd signed off, he took her arm before she could get away.

"Where'd you learn to interview like that?"

Now it was her turn to be wordless.

"Of course, I can't be sure what they'll say back at the station, but this is the best show of this kind we've had. I feel pretty sure you could have a job for the rest of the war, if you want it."

"I'm not a professional. This was just an accident. I don't think my husband—"

"Look, this is an awful job. I mean, it requires what you might call a woman's touch." His face flushed. "Do you have any idea how *I* feel, an able-bodied man, facing these kids? Anyway," he said, after a pause, "here's my card. Give me a call at the station tomorrow."

It was two hours before Victoria and her new assistant were able to take a break. The girl had shown remarkable stamina. She was stoic in the face of the worst physical suffering, but had managed to respond warmly to each patient's needs. Now, at the coffee stand, Victoria, admiring the girl's bravery, felt at ease enough with her to compliment her on her hard work.

"I wish more of our volunteers were as devoted as you. And I know you will forgive the inquisitiveness of an older woman. This is obviously not your first experience in a hospital, and I can't help wondering. . . ."

"Mrs. Creighton," the girl said, "you have been so kind. Feel free to ask me anything you wish to know. It is true that I spent some years before the war studying medicine in Vienna. Then, when the war came, my mother and I pleaded with my father to recognize what was happening, but he, like so many others, felt himself privileged as an artist. By the time he came to his senses, Hitler's army was, as you know well, completely entrenched in the capital. By then, it was too late. They were rounding up the Jews. Papa paid for us to be taken off in an ice truck."

"Good Heavens!"

"Papa stayed behind as a decoy. And it was just like him to give the moment a final touch of realism and defiance. He flung open the windows of the music room and gave what I shall always consider to be his finest performance. Our trip was too much for Mama. She felt she had no life without my father. She died in North Africa. And Father? I only know if he is alive, he still has his music."

Victoria hesitated. "My dear, now I understand your endurance and dedication. Because, from what you have told me, I realize that I must be speaking to the daughter of Stanislaus Toffias."

"You knew my father?"

"Not personally. But my husband and I heard him play the last time we were in Europe."

There was a moment of quiet recognition between the two women who esteemed control above almost every other virtue. Then Victoria went on, "My son is a composer as well. He greatly admires your father's work. Especially the Third Etude—"

Their conversation was brought to an abrupt end by the approach of a familiar creature who Victoria, shuddering inwardly, thought was almost the equivalent of a human Sherman tank. She wore a kind of improvised uniform that appeared both religious and military. The floors trembled under her relentless tread.

"Come along, ladies, this isn't a tea party. You can gossip later."

The two women put down their coffee cups and followed the rustling martinet into the next ward. The soldier in the first bed groaned at her approach.

"Hello, Edward, how's the leg? How are *you* doing, Stanley? We don't want any malingering! There's a war going on. Now, Frank, who do you want to send a letter to today?"

"Nobody," the bandaged figure croaked.

"Everyone has to send home at least one letter a week. For the war effort!"

Victoria closed her hand over Tovah's upper arm and surreptitiously pulled her back into the hallway.

"Who *was* that?" Tovah breathed.

Victoria smiled and sighed. "I am sorry to have to say—that was my daughter."

Ruth's voice boomed after them. "Now, Johnny! Father O'Day tells me you haven't been to confession since Friday before last. What would your mother think about *that*?"

Tovah and her companion began to giggle. "Quick!" Victoria said. "We've got to escape and I know where. If Ruth is here, that means my grandson is too."

She hurried her charge down the hallway to the Solarium. A few men in wheelchairs drowsed in the sun. An extraordinarily handsome young man had set up an easel and seemed to be amusing the convalescent patients by painting simple watercolor likenesses of them.

"Tovah, my grandson, Lex."

Priest hated the days when Mrs. Creighton went to the hospital. It was not that Mr. Creighton complained or in any way made a fuss, but that as the day went on his energy began to wane. He sat alone in the drawing room. No books could comfort him. He refused the solace of radio or records with an impatient shake of his head. Occasionally Priest would look in on him and ask if there was anything he could "do." The answer was usually no; sometimes there was no answer at all.

"I hate the way he just sits in there by himself," Priest would tell Pansy when he went back into the kitchen.

She would look up and say, "Honey, what else is there for him to do? He's eighty-one years old."

Not until Clifford heard—or fancied he heard—the crunch of Victoria's roadster on the graveled drive did he pull himself out of his chair, automatically run an ivory pocket comb through his silver hair, pour two sizable slugs of sherry, and greet his wife standing up casually with one elbow on the mantelpiece.

"Did you have a pleasant day, dearest?"

He would answer with enthusiasm and vigor, making up some pleasant tale about the garden or the servants or the book he had been reading.

In these last hours before Victoria returned Priest's heart melted for the man he had served so long.

This afternoon when the telephone rang, Priest hesitated, wondering if Mr. Creighton might prefer to answer. But the old man sat motionless in the quiet drawing room. Thus it was Priest who heard the news first and, knees almost buckling, tears streaming down his cheeks, Priest who had to say, "Mr. Creighton, it's the War Department."

Cliff was too shaken to drive and had to ask Porter Priest to take him to the Vista del Arroyo. When they arrived, the sun was setting and the volunteers had gathered in the lobby to sign out for the day and ask for their new assignments.

As he entered Victoria felt a momentary pleasure, thinking that he might have come to escort her to dinner. But when she saw his face clearly and noticed with what effort he was walking toward her she hurried to meet him and said, "Oh my God, is it Gary?"

He took her hands and said, "It's bad. That's all they were able to tell us."

When several blocks of old Chinatown had been razed to make room for the construction of Union Station and its surrounding outbuildings and parking lots, the warehouse in which Sung and his army of descendants had made their home for so long was one of the inevitable casualties. Several of the children had expressed their concern about the effect it might have on the "old folks." That gutted warehouse, filled with priceless antiques, rare objets d'art, and hordes of happy, noisy children had been a bastion against the outer world. It had been a wrench for most of them to leave that sanctuary, but they had underestimated the resilience of Sung and Katarina.

Sung, in particular, took special enjoyment in planning New Chinatown, where he personally supervised the construction of his own store and insisted on the use of the true curved and Oriental-roofed Spirit Gates which designated the boundaries of what was to be both dwelling-place and lucrative tourist-trap.

With almost transparent glee, Sung had set about selling perhaps ninety percent of his inventory, wailing that the city fathers had conspired by this construction to deprive him of everything, and using this "disaster" to turn over many objects of decidedly dubious origin. When the brash architect of Barnsdall Park, young Frank Lloyd Wright, heard about this extraordinary clearance sale in the depths of Chinatown he swaggered in wearing his cape and carrying a malacca walking stick. When he tapped it against a three-foot porcelain jardiniere, testing perhaps for authenticity, Sung drove him from the store with a cascade of insulting Cantonese.

"Heathen frog! Red-faced masturbating giant! Will you barbarians never learn respect for the true art of Han?"

It was the only time that the noted architect was reported to have retreated in complete confusion. A few days later the purchasers of the jardiniere for three times its value were rumored to be his emissaries.

When Sung had finished, he was left with one-tenth of his inventory, but that tenth represented his best stock. His store in New Chinatown was tiny and exclusive, his hours impossible to ascertain. And if a customer was lucky enough to make his way inside the tinkling curtains of pure white jade, chances were ninety-five out of a hundred that he would find himself on the street again in minutes, a rain of curses ringing in his ears. Sung kept the store for the sheer amusement of driving the round-eye to distraction. Every older man, he told his wife, should have a hobby.

Sung and Katarina, as part of their return to the "simple life," lived above the store in a small luxurious apartment of extreme elegance. Now that their last children had left the nest they could enjoy each other's company without respite. Their children were astonished at their seeming contentment, but they would have been even more astonished at the lengthy hours of sweaty pleasure in which their parents now indulged themselves without interruption. "At long last," Sung would say from time to time as he bantered with other elders on the streets of New Chinatown, "I have my yellow-haired she-devil to myself."

Only once a week on Sundays did they, in traditional fashion, gather the

335

entire family for a lavish early evening dinner in the upper floors of Chinatown's best restaurant. Scores of their descendants marched up the stairs, the mothers herding their children before them. There were in-laws of every description, both Chinese and Caucasian, aged mothers, aunts and uncles here on a visit, college friends who surveyed this spectacle wide-eyed, and close to the floor squadrons of tiny mechanical toys and un-counted buzzing grandchildren and great-grandchildren who shouted and ran between the tables, secure in the knowledge that Grandpa Sung and Grandma Kate would protect them from their parents' discipline and indulge them in all their favorite foods.

"Hey there, you, hurry up," Katarina shouted in the direction of the kitchen. "Or do I come back and help you?"

The waiters cringed at the thought and brought out great cauldrons of steaming winter melon soup. Close to a hundred gathered here, an almost unimaginable triumph of family, and the restaurant owner knew that if things didn't go as the crazed blond woman wanted, he would lose both face and money.

When George came in with little Elizabeth and Lloyd, most of the relatives had already begun to eat.

"Iris is going to be late," he said to Katarina. "She's working down at the Travelers Aid."

"Iris fine girl. Too good for you. Ha! Ha!"

George busied himself with his children's rice bowls, selecting delicacies for them with his own chopsticks, while Sung and Katarina greeted a steady stream of relatives who came by the table to pay their respects. Sung knew every configuration of his vast family and welcomed the most lowly second cousin not only by name but with a tactful reference to his place in the family. Katarina could not be bothered. She had her reputation as a barbarian to keep up and did so with gusto, pounding unsuspecting men upon the back, catching timorous girlfriends in an iron embrace, and sometimes honoring important visitors with the blank stare of a demented peasant. "Who are you?" she would shout. And turning to her husband would say, "Who is he anyway?"

And if Sung looked stern at this she would hug him too and query in tones audible throughout the room, "When will they all go home, my handsome wosbon, so that I can be alone with you?"

After the distant relatives and most of the guests had left, twenty or so stayed behind, exchanging family news and gossip. Only then did Iris arrive, out of breath, her cheeks flushed.

"Hey, Iris!" Katarina boomed. "When we go riding again? I beat you any day!"

Sung and George exchanged a glance. This was the price they had to pay for taking as wives Caucasian beauties, women who were not content to stay quietly indoors. Once a month at least they dragged their husbands to Dragon's Den Ranch at the foot of Big Rock in Old Topanga Canyon and bullied them into riding the trails for hours at a time, the women galloping recklessly ahead, the men following with what dignity they could preserve.

It was a mark of the women's strength that they had finally persuaded Sung himself to straddle the meekest mount in the stable. But once in the saddle he had laughed and said, "When I was a small boy I rode on the back of the worst-tempered water buffalo in my village."

George had to fight against the rising tide of irritation that had begun that morning. Iris had sat down without properly greeting his father or responding to Katarina's challenge, and had begun telling him a story that he could scarcely hear over the din of his brothers' and sisters' conversation. He waited for her to pause, but she went on and on. Finally, in an unexpected moment of silence, she ended her harangue: "And he says I should come down to the station tomorrow. He says it will be a good salary. He says I can name my price."

The silence deepened around them. George flushed with shame and rage, aware of his father's eyes.

"My wife," he muttered, the words choking him, "my wife work for money?"

Iris stared at him, then sought the glance of the one who had always been her ally in the family. But Katarina's eyes were hooded, and for once she too kept silent. The whole family quivered under the disgrace of it.

Paco Ramirez had never seen anything like it. His father had told him when he'd enlisted in the army that he'd become a man and see the world, but *Dios mio!* Papa himself could never have imagined a thing like this. The bad part was, Paco thought, that back in El Centro they'd never believe him. He'd been killing time in the USO down by Union Station, where he'd found a few *compadres,* from Yuma, from San Antone. They'd been talking about going out into the downtown streets to see if they could find a meal of tacos and enchiladas, each of them trying to cover up the fact that they were a little bit afraid of the *pachucos,* who, they had been told, held a bad place in their hearts for Latinos in uniform.

They'd been standing there talking, trying to get their nerve up, when the white lady, old as their mothers, had approached them. "Excuse me, boys, but are you—I mean, would you call yourselves Mexican?" As they turned to look at her she blushed. "We, we have a card in our files, Sunday dinner for up to four boys, but they especially request"—her old cheeks streaked red—"that the boys be of Mexican descent."

Sunday dinner for a soldier. Just like John Hodiak and Anne Baxter. But this made the movie look punk. It seemed like as soon as they'd said yes, joking that at least they'd get a free meal this way, a huge car like in the movies—a limousine!—came gliding right up to the door and fifteen minutes later here they all were. In a palace. In a castle.

The boys had gone into the entry hall as if they were in a dream. A servant had come up to them with four frosty mugs of *cerveza,* and as they sipped, an old Anglo, *abuelo,* came into the room. *"Buenas tardes, muchachos. Cómo estas?"* His accent sounded as if he'd been born not a mile away from Yuma. "My name is John Frederick Smith, and I'm more than honored to have you all for dinner."

337

They stared at him, but before they could think of anything to say, a door opened, and there was a grandmother like they'd never seen. She was Mexican all right but—well, they'd never believe it in El Centro. She wore a long lace dress and rings on every finger, her hair was bright silver, and her fingernails painted red.

"*Bienvenido!* I'm so glad you could come. I've been cooking all day. Do you like *chiles rellenos?*"

"Oh, señora!"

Without waiting for a further answer she led them into a big room, with rugs all over and a big piano and doors that opened up onto a lawn. Everything was strange, man, except for the smell, and that was just like home. "*Gorditas,* I have made some *gorditas,* in case you got here early. But save some room now, we're having a big dinner later."

They hung back, but then the old man started to ask them about their families, and called for more beer. It was so wonderful to be talking their own language again, about families, and home towns—not just acting tough. And the people were great, funny, you know? They laughed at each other's jokes.

They just sat there for about an hour and talked. It turned out that the boys had all grown up in about the same place, give or take a few hundred miles. They talked about the desert, and fiestas, each trying to outdo the others. They told how back home they'd danced the girls off their feet. It was then that the old lady got up, grabbed the poker from the fireplace and went through the motions of the Adelita dance, the dance of the women soldiers of the *Revolución.* Her husband was laughing, they all were laughing, and then the servant came in, followed by a family. They all stopped laughing.

There were five of them. Paco's mama had relatives like that, the kind that always showed up but nobody was glad to see them.

A young couple, looking scared, walked in stiffly. Señora Smith introduced them as her granddaughter Chata and her husband Max, who owned a car dealership in East L.A. They had a kid, a real zoot-suiter. He was wearing a modified drape and a sneer on his face. His name was Emiliano. He sat down on a couch and looked out of the window.

It was the other couple that gave Paco the creeps. Señora Smith said, "This is my son, Raoul Ortiz, and his wife, Maria." Paco had seen such people before—too many of them. Raoul was like old guys in El Centro who hung around gas stations drinking beer, who beat up on their kids, who tooled over the border on Saturday nights and paid twice the going price to get laid, then came home and kept the whole house up until they passed out. All the young guys made fun of them. But when they looked at those men with their torn T-shirts and big bellies, it made them afraid to grow up.

This one didn't have a T-shirt. He wore a two-tone sports jacket and yellow slacks. Both were a size too small. His hair was slicked back with a pound of grease. His hands were puffy. His fat pushed out against his shirt. But it was his face—*que feo!* What a hog. And mean! He didn't speak and he didn't shake hands. And his wife looked like she'd been crying. She looked like a human wet mop. Well, didn't they all?

The thing was, the old people didn't seem to mind. It was like they'd planned this party and they were going to have one, no matter what. They all went into a huge dining room where a servant gave them homemade *tamales* and *carnitas* and *menudo*—they knew *menudo* was good for hangovers, and the guys took a lot of kidding about that.

All Señor Smith wanted to do was talk about the old days in Mexico—he got a real kick out of it. And the Señora egged him on. It seemed she had worked for him about a hundred years ago. And so the dinner went on, even though half the people at it looked like they were going to die or kill somebody.

Señor Smith kept talking to the Army guys about what it was they were going to do after the war. And it was interesting, you know? It turned out they all had their plans. One of them was going into contracting. When it came to his turn, Paco said that his dad had some acres and he'd be either farming or—

That's when the pig in the yellow slacks said, "Just marry a broad with money. That's the only chance a *beaner* will ever get in this rotten world!"

The *pachuco* kept looking out the window. You could tell he'd heard it all before. The young married couple exchanged glances. But the guy's wife began to wail and moan, and the tears started coming down.

The fat guy pushed himself away from the table and left the room. Paco figured the Sunday dinner was almost over and automatically reached for his beer. But Señor Smith stood up as if nothing had happened.

"The gentlemen will be taking brandy and cigars in the drawing room."

The guys jumped up. Paco tried not to look back, but he couldn't help it. The young wife was patting her mother. "Don't you worry, Mama, don't be afraid of that big gorilla." But "Mama" was crying like a fire hydrant. Señora Smith just sat there with a sad look on her face.

Raoul was standing by the liquor cabinet when they came in. He'd already poured himself about a cup of booze.

"I tell you, that woman is running me ragged. *Raoul, do this! Raoul, do that! Raoul, why aren't we happy any more! I'll pray for you, Raoul!*"

He drained off the liquor in a single gulp, and coughed.

Señor Smith ignored him. "What you were saying about the GI Bill, that's good, I think. The price is right. And an education helps—"

"The trouble is, señor," one of them broke in, "my English isn't so good. If they had their classes in Spanish—"

"They're never gonna do that," the *pachuco* burst out. "They laugh when you can't speak their *pendejo* language. The only way for a *Chicano* to get what he wants is fight!"

"There're different ways of fighting, *mijo*," Señor Smith said. "The way *you* fight you lose either way. The *gringo* fixes it so we end up killing each other."

Paco felt himself nodding, *yes*.

339

But Raoul burst out, "It's never been different! It's always been the same! Life is *shit*."

Señor Smith tossed off his brandy. "Do you always have to sing the same tune? How many years have we all had to hear it? You've had everything a man could want—and one tragedy. Your mother took you in when—"

"Ah, shut up," the pig growled. "You think you know about life? You think you know about Mexicans just because you sleep with one?"

The old man finally got mad. "That's enough! Don't you have any pride in that worthless piece of cartilage you call a spine? Do you have to pick on women and old men? If you don't like your life change it!"

The fat guy turned purple. He opened his mouth to say something but the old man waved him off as if he was a bad smell.

"Save it for the women and children, Raoul. Don't bother the *men* with your problems!"

There was nothing more the fat guy could say. He turned around and left. Then Señor Smith looked at the rest of them with a big smile. "Tequila goes better after a dinner like we had, don't you think? And, Max, don't you think Emiliano can have one beer?"

Max grinned. "He's had more than *one* beer, I bet." They all laughed with relief. Then Señor Smith rang a bell. A servant brought in salt, lemons, beer, tequila. Then Señor Smith put on a stack of scratchy Lucha Reyes records. They had a wonderful time after that, and it must have been close to three in the morning before the limousine took them back down to the USO.

First he drove, racing through red lights, gunning the motor, hoping a cop would stop him, hoping he'd run over somebody, hoping his brakes would go out, and he'd crash into a building and die. Then he ran out of gas. He barely managed to get the car over to the curb. He pounded on the steering wheel until somebody passing by on the street gave him a funny look.

There was nothing to do but get out of the car and walk. But walk where? He started off, looking for a bar. But it was Sunday night. Everything was closed. He was downtown, close to the Plaza. Maybe he could get a drink. A dim memory of better days flashed through his mind. Maybe they still sold *pulque*. He passed some sailors on the street, and some hookers. Everyone steered away from him. When he got to the Plaza the first thing he noticed was that even though it was Sunday night and still early, there was no *paseo*—no circles of young men going one way, and the girls with their *dueñas* going another. The whole place was empty except for a few winos, some old newspapers that caught the raw wind and sailed a few feet. A couple of rats! And every once in a while, two or three sailors, or two or three *pachucos* carousing past, one of them holding a bottle, their mindless jokes carried away on the wind. What could have happened here? Where was the *mariachi*? Where were the dancing girls, with their ruffled skirts and trailing ribbons? Where were the guys with their *machismo* and their crazy tricks? Raoul dogtrotted across the parched grass to the gazebo, which didn't have a band now, only a couple of bums who raised their heads groggily and peered at him. Then he ran, across the Plaza and over to the church, which was locked up. There wasn't even a sign out, saying when Mass was.

What is it? What's happened here? he wanted to ask someone, to cry out, to scream, but there was no one to ask.

"Hey old man, got a match?"

Three *pachucos* stood behind him in the shadows, their faces almost hidden by their wide flat hats, their watch-chains glinting in the light from the single streetlamp.

"What happened here?" Raoul said.

The guys looked at him blankly.

"The *paseo*. You know, on Sunday night, when people come down here."

One of them burst into laughter. "You got to be out of your mind, Daddyo. There's no *paseo* here. Go back to Mexico where you came from."

"Yeah, but give us your money first." The youngest one said it. His switchblade flashed.

Raoul went crazy. "Go ahead and *do it,* crazy punk! Do me a favor. Give me an excuse. Go ahead and kill me, if you can! See how many of you die first. Come on, come on! I want you to. I'm waiting for you. Get tough with me. Show me what men you are!"

He glared at his attackers, but what he saw was his wife's tears, his daughter's look of contempt, his grandson's scorn, his mother's calm indifference.

"Come on, I can't wait all night. If you're going to kill me, hurry *up!"* Awful words came back to him. "Or are you waiting for some women and children to pick on?"

"Take it easy, grandpa—"

He went after them like an enraged bear. He snatched the switchblade from the punk, loving the feel of the knife as it cut into his palm, and threw it, clattering, into the street. He butted the largest one with his stomach, and sent him tumbling. "Come on, fight, *fight!"* he yelled, but the last one turned tail and ran.

After he was alone Raoul went over to the knife where it lay in the street. He picked it up, wiped it on his pants, and put it in his pocket. Then he smiled.

Late that night, he swaggered into his bedroom. Maria was still up, praying in front of their statue of the Infant of Prague.

"Where were you?" she whispered apprehensively. "I was worried."

"I was down at the Plaza."

"You could get in a fight down there."

"I did," he said casually. He took the switchblade out of his pocket and tossed it on the bureau. "And I won."

Maria got up off her knees.

"I decided something. That Plaza looks like shit, you know? It looks like a real pigsty. Somebody ought to do something about it. I got a feeling the *gringos* want to do with it what they did to Chinatown. Tear the whole thing down. But you know what? I'm not gonna let them do that to me."

"What can *you* do?"

341

"I don't know yet, but I'm going to stop them."

"Oh, Raoul. Be careful. I don't want you to get into trouble."

He patted her awkwardly on the shoulder. "Don't worry, Mama." Seeing her anxious face, he gave her a rough grin. "Do you think I'd let them tear down the place where I met you?"

Over her husband's shoulder, Maria's eyes met the Infant of Prague's. Was this the answer to her prayers? Or had drink finally softened her husband's brain? Anyway, she knew by tomorrow he would have forgotten all about it.

The next three days of waiting were the most painful that the Creightons had endured in their half-century of marriage. Victoria tried to keep up a brave front for Clifford, but the truth was that this blow had all but broken her spirit.

She thought of death often, not Gary's but her own, with a kind of bitter longing. What was the point of any of it, if your son, your only son, died, or worse? At times in the night she would wake up, turn on her tiny bedside lamp so as to exorcise those demons, and see with a pang that Clifford, wide awake, had been lying immobile staring into the darkness. There was nothing either one of them could say.

When on that Wednesday morning they received word that Gary would be arriving at the hospital at Vista del Arroyo, Victoria experienced a sense of utter relief. At least now they would know how bad it was. At least now they would know what it was they had to fight against.

Most of the family were there that morning. They waited uneasily by the side entrance at the portecochere. Victoria and Clifford sat together on a bench, looking frail and old, holding hands. Lex tried to keep up bright chatter, and Tovah, who had been sent by the head nurse to be of whatever use she could to Victoria, brought coffee. Ruth paced up and down, her uniform swishing, gazing ostentatiously from time to time at a sturdy man's watch which she had bought at the beginning of the war. Perhaps it was sheer impatience and frustration that made her cut into Tovah's civil murmurings.

"You see, Lex, I was right. You did the right thing by staying home. You had your responsibility to the family to think of. This way even if the name is lost the blood will—"

"Shut up, Mother."

Ruth took a breath as she stopped dead in her tracks.

"Yes, that's right. Speak to your mother with disrespect." Tears formed and she jutted out her chin. "There wasn't this kind of fuss when poor Alessandro died. People were brave enough about that!"

Her speech came to an abrupt halt as an ambulance skidded up the drive. Victoria and Clifford came to their feet as two medics alighted, went round to the back, opened the doors, and wheeled out a stretcher with a body on it wrapped like a mummy. Only the face, curiously unscathed, was in full view, his expression preoccupied, his eyes unfocused.

"Gary," Victoria breathed. "Oh, Gary." This time it was Clifford who was strong and put his wife's head onto his shoulder.

Lex assumed a role for which he had been bred since birth. "Mother, why don't you see to Grandma and Grandpa? Tovah and I will see Gary settled into his room." Then, motioning to the medics to follow, he and Tovah led the way to the bed that was waiting.

His mother's voice followed them as she ministered to her parents by saying in commanding tones, "Now don't break down! We can't have any of that! Get hold of yourselves!" But even as she spoke her voice broke, and it was Ruth who in the end lost control and wept.

As they wheeled Gary down the hall, Lex tried to make contact. "God, Gar, it's good to have you home." And when he got no reaction he went on with elaborate irony. "Old buddy, we've got a pretty one for you this time. Miss Toffias, wow, she's a looker."

Tovah leaned down in front of Gary's passive, expressionless face. She smiled and said, "Hello."

Lex bravely continued his one-sided conversation. "We picked out the best room for you. In fact, you can see the old house right across the Arroyo. Now I know that's not too exciting, but you've also got a view of the pool. Just one look will tell you we've got the niftiest nurses in California. . . ." Lex's voice trailed off as his eyes, too, filled with tears.

Tovah, seeing Lex's despair, took up the patter. "Your mother tells me you're a pianist and a fine composer."

As they wheeled Gary into his room the Austrian girl continued with what was to become a very long monologue.

That same evening about five o'clock, while George helped the kids with their homework and Iris supervised the making of the family dinner, the telephone rang.

"Where have you *been?*" a brash, familiar voice boomed out. "I've waited around three days for you. What do you want to do, make me look like a jerk?"

"Who is this, please?" Iris asked primly, but even as she spoke she knew the answer.

"Come on, sweetheart, don't play hard to get with me." Then the voice took on a fake pomposity to match her own. "This is, ah, your sometime friend and occasional sportscaster, A. J. Cassidy, from down at the radio station."

"Oh, that," Iris said weakly. "Well, I talked it over with my husband and we agreed I can't do it."

"What do you mean you can't do it? You already did it and you were great. Look, they thought you were pretty good down here. Not terrific, but pretty good. I told them that I had you in the bag and they said that's fine."

"But—"

"I already told you. Don't make a monkey out of me. We've got women out there," his voice faltered, "dying for a chance like I'm offering you today."

"Mr. Cassidy, I have family obligations."

"They want you to come down tonight. Back to Union Station. The Super Chief's coming in and Frances Perkins is on it, the only broad in the cabinet.

If you think any of us is going to go," again his voice changed and to her chagrin she heard him mimicking her own prim tones, "Well, miss, if you think any of our he-men are going to waste time with a chunky New Dealer in a print dress, well, then, you've got another think coming. So there!"

"How long would this take?"

The voice was crisp and businesslike again. "Fifteen minutes, max. You'll meet the crew at the station. The equipment's already set up. How did a nice girl like that get into a job like that, and is she screwing the President?"

Iris laughed in spite of herself.

"Be there at seven and you'll get a check in the mail. More than enough to pay the sitter. Ha! Ha!"

Iris stood a moment staring at the dead phone. Then she went into the living room. George looked up with an expression of faint inquiry. His long slim fingers held a child's protractor. How handsome he was. How kind he had been. She knew that however casual she made this sound, he would not be fooled.

"I know you're not going to like this. I'm not even sure I'm going to like it myself."

"Yes?" he said.

"That man from the radio station called."

"No."

"I told him that's what we'd decided, but he—they want me to talk to Frances Perkins tonight." Her sentence trickled off. "You know, the first woman Cabinet member."

"She's the next thing to a socialist."

"So I won't be here for dinner," she said bravely. "But I'll be home in time to put the children to bed."

"You're not going," George said flatly. "Chinese wives don't work."

"I'm not Chinese."

She would never forget the terrified look on the children's faces. Her careless words, she knew, had cut him to the quick. With a horrid sense of burning her bridges she said airily, "I can't talk about it now. We'll discuss it later." And with that she was out the door, barely remembering to pick up her purse.

When she got there she was amazed that in spite of her anxiety over leaving George in that way, she was assailed by an intense wave of well-being as she once again became a part of the casual swirl of newspaper reporters, and recognized the men from the radio crew. Certainly this wasn't work, what these people did, but some kind of luminous fraud. These men had somehow jimmied their way into the position of having fun and getting paid for it. Although she hadn't thought he'd be here, she recognized A. J. Cassidy, accompanied by a portly man in a cream-colored garbardine suit.

"Fred, I told you she'd show up," A. J. Cassidy said. "There you are, my little moppet."

Iris went over to them nervously.

"Look, honey," A. J. said, "we don't have much time. You know something about this Perkins woman?"

Iris grinned. "My husband says she's the next thing to a socialist. Sure, I know about her. She's terrific. She closed down all those sweatshops in New York."

"Just be sure you ask her how she's helping the women of America. Before you set up I want you to meet our manager, Fred Kirkpatrick. Fred, this is Iris . . ."

"Iris Sung," she said

"Sung," Kirkpatrick said. "She can't be Sung."

"Sure she can! Anna May Wong. Chiang Kai-shek. You know, those brave little yellow men over in Chungking!"

"No," Kirkpatrick said. "What's your maiden name, sister?"

But the roar of the train drowned out her answer.

The children knew that it was a mark of their father's distress that not only had he decreed they eat dinner in the kitchen with the maid while he ate in the dining room alone, but that after dinner he put on his purple smoking jacket with the Chinese dragon. As he pulled out his carved ivory cigarette holder they knew they were in for it. When he was mad their father never yelled, but he turned into somebody out of a bad fairy tale.

He slanted his eyes and pulled his lips over his teeth, flicked the ashes off his cigarette and said, "Oh, really." When he sent them to bed they knew better than to make one peep of protest.

George paced the living room in his smoking jacket. A part of his mind knew that on other occasions like this he would begin to laugh at himself sooner or later. But now he was aware only of his cold fury. *That woman was nothing before I met her.* And he knew with bitterness that his own father would have locked up a wife, even Katarina, if she ever dared talk to him the way Iris had. Each time he paced the room he passed the radio. Each time he passed the radio he looked at his watch.

Seven o'clock came, then five after and ten after. Then he could bear it no longer and flipped the switch.

"And so what you're saying then is that you don't have to be a rich person to help the economy."

"That's exactly what I'm saying. Each and every housewife can do her bit. Right now our country is working at peak production. But the war will be over soon and we'll go through a period of transition. Experts have said that domestic products will carry us through this potentially difficult time. I would ask every housewife to start saving now—"

"For what you've wanted all through the war," Iris broke in triumphantly. "That way, you tell your husbands you're not being extravagant, just patriotic!"

"Exactly!"

"That's all the time we have, Madame Perkins. . . ."

George was conscious that he'd been listening with an involuntary smile. But it froze when he heard the words "This is Iris Bauer, signing off."

George waited for her in the living room. The sound of her approaching clicking heels on the floor only added to his inner turmoil. In spite of his

345

anger and frustration he was momentarily surprised to see that she was even more upset than he, if that was possible.

"Don't even say it," she said, tears filling her eyes as she burst into the room. "*I know!*"

"How could you do that to our family? How could you?" He spoke through bared teeth.

"I had no choice. It wasn't my fault," she said. But then she gave in. "It *was* my fault. They told me I couldn't use Sung, but I wanted to do this so badly. I wanted to do something on my own. Something I could be proud of, and you and the children too."

"How can we be proud if you deny our family name? It's not as though we're Japanese."

"But everyone is suspicious. And you want to know the really terrible thing? They're afraid people won't know the difference between a Japanese and a Chinese name. The men at the station say they want a nice woman! Someone who can talk to people. They told me I can do a good job. It's only for the duration."

George saw that she had calmed down now, but even so was struggling for words. She had always had a mind of her own, but she'd always been fiercely loyal to him. She'd given up her Pasadena connections because they'd disapproved of him. She'd given up *her* family, and now, he thought to himself, who was he to deny the woman he loved so much the one thing that she had ever asked of him in sixteen years? He didn't know how he was going to tell his father, but he'd work out something.

"I listened," he said in a stiff, grudging voice. "You were very good. I'm sorry too that you can't use our name. But if it's truly just for the duration—"

He was rewarded as she rushed over to him and kissed him. It was more than gratitude. It was an expression of deep love and an acknowledgment of what he had had to go through. He smiled wryly. He wasn't losing her. In fact, he was surprised at the passion he felt for this new, complex woman.

Maria Consuelo Gloria Madonna Arellanos de Mariné Ortiz finally had to admit to herself that she didn't understand her husband. For thirty-nine years she had ridden on an emotional roller coaster controlled by her husband's changing tempers. At first he had been a romantic youth, only to descend into self-pity, self-hate, and contempt for her. Then she had felt blessed during those "lucky years" of the Lucky Dragon. Nothing could go wrong, she thought. But oh Heavenly *Dios,* why did you take away my son and leave me alone with his father? For too many years her Raoul had neglected his daughter, his grandson, his wife. Oh, *Madre*!

But nothing in her sixty-four years had prepared her for this new change. He had stopped drinking. He was alert, full of energy and purpose. He had begun to lose weight. And almost without realizing it *she* had begun to take an interest in her own appearance. One day they had gone out together shopping. He had bought a pinstripe three-piece suit that took years off his age and she had, giggling, bought a silk negligee. That night! Oh, all the saints in the heavens! That first awkward pat had revived in him the memories and then the practice of his youthful skills from the days of his most ardent lovemaking.

But she was merely a human on God's precious earth. She could not understand His ways. She could scarcely believe Raoul's transformation and his repeated proclamations that he would save the Plaza and fight City Hall. Though Maria was afraid, her only comfort was a phrase remembered from her childhood. Truly, it is the will of God!

Raoul had made good on his word. And now she sat with Magdalena in the visitor's area of the City Council watching her husband address the assembly. He had told her he knew how city politics worked. He couldn't run for office. Mexicans had no chance. But even this didn't upset him. He didn't *want* to run for office. The most powerful men in the city, he told her, were not the elected officials. He drew on his boyhood memories from his mother's boardinghouse—all the overheard conversations of how affairs were handled in City Hall, Jordan Espey's speeches over plates of chicken and dumplings, the way in which city policies were formed in the parlor over snifters of brandy.

"I will change this city," her husband had told her. "We Mexicans were here first. I'm going to make the *gringos* remember that and pay attention to us."

Oh, Mother of Mercy, that's what he was telling them now.

"And so you see a lot of the crime we're having now and the way people are afraid to go down to the Plaza even in broad daylight, some of that comes from war fever, but some of it comes because the Plaza has just let itself go. Ever since they started fixing up Olvera Street, people aren't as afraid to go down there. And so what I'm saying is, the city doesn't have to spend a lot of money on the Plaza. All we have to do is remember what it used to be like with the trees and the dancing and the music and families coming there to spend a Sunday afternoon. Because," his voice rose, "the Plaza is the heart of the city. And if you take away the heart, the city will die. Not all at once, but little by little it will get ugly, because no one loves it. The city is like a woman. It deserves respect."

Maria blushed with pleasure as the onlookers and the Council applauded. The old men on the platform whispered a little bit among themselves. Then one of them spoke into the microphone.

"Thank you very much, Mr. Ortiz, for taking the time to come down here to alert us to this problem. To be perfectly frank, the downtown Plaza doesn't rank first on our list of postwar priorities. But we'll put it on the agenda. And what we suggest that you do, sir, in the interim, is head up an ad hoc committee in ways and means whereby you can put this project into action. Thank you again, sir, very much. Next."

Even Maria knew, although she was unskilled in these matters, that they hadn't really been listening carefully to her husband. And so she was bewildered to see that his face as he came back down the aisle to rejoin his family was wreathed in a big happy smile.

"They think I'm going to forget about it, but I'm not. Now I'm in a

347

position to go ahead and do something. Those *bolillos* were stupid enough to go ahead and put it on record that I can save the Plaza. So now I'm going to."

Her husband was crazy, but she loved him.

There is an afternoon time in California when the whole world seems balanced in a golden sunlit glow. If it is true that Paradise once existed on this tear-drenched earth, it might have been precisely on the soil of the wide soft valley that pushes westward fifty miles from the Cajon Pass and stops only when it meets the Pacific. Balmy breezes sift through the aromatic leaves of the eucalyptus. The only sound is the occasional cooing of the mourning dove, the barely perceptible scrabble of a lizard's claws, the tick-tick of tiny red peppers as they fall one by one from those commodious, feathery trees.

In the cheerful rooms of the Vista del Arroyo time had come to a halt. The hospital was filled to capacity. The chaos and excitement of new arrivals had ceased. Doctors and nurses did as much as they could, and, having done that, stood back and waited for Nature to commence her healing work.

It had been four weeks since the ambulance doors had opened and the Creighton family had received its wounded son. The war was ended now. The suffering was almost over. The reports that came from Japan were only the cries of a sleeping unfortunate not yet wakened from a nightmare. Here in California even grief assumed a calm and seemly pattern.

Each morning Victoria arose, and as she had all through the war, drove the short distance to the hospital where she spent the mornings by Gary's bedside. But she was careful to spend no more than three hours. Her husband now demanded her major attention. If she cried no one saw it. And she left the room each morning around eleven with a look of confidence and disciplined serenity, reminding the staff that she, Clifford, and Ruth would return for tea.

"I think he heard me today. I sang him all the old songs from when he was little. I reminded him how he used to climb out of his bedroom window and go for a swim when we were still living at the beach. . . ."

Then she would be gone, and it was Lex and Tovah's turn. The brilliantly sunny, endless afternoons stretched ahead of them as far as they could see. The only thing for them to do, the doctors had told them, was simply to spend time with Gary, to never let him be alone. The wounds he had suffered were grave. His body was lacerated with shrapnel, but his mind had suffered even more. Acute traumatic shock was what the doctors called it, a poor phrase for a phenomenon they had no real words to describe. All they knew was that Gary Creighton had not spoken or given evidence of hearing since he had been admitted to the hospital. Whether this condition might change was purely a matter of conjecture.

This afternoon Tovah and Lex had wheeled Gary into the hospital solarium.

"I wish you could have met my father, Gary," Tovah said. "Lex says you know his work. It's strange living with a genius. There were times when I

348

heard those trills at the end of the first bars of the Third Etude when I really thought that I wanted to take my father and shake him. Put his hands in mittens. Do anything so that he wouldn't practice anymore. Was your family like that, Gary?

"Did you fill their poor ears with music until they begged for mercy? My best girlfriend in Vienna, when we were still at the *gymnasium,* decided that the only way she could be happy was if she took up the oboe. Of course, her father denied her nothing, but I believe she did it simply to spite her mother. She practiced two hours a day from three to five in the room next to her mother's parlor. And, Gary, never in a hundred years could I convey to you how very, very badly my friend played the oboe."

Her inconsequential words fell like tiny pebbles into the wide pool of sunny silence. Gary's face, eyes wide open, his mouth set in weary repose, gazed into the dappled green of eucalyptus just outside the solarium. Lex, his easel set up just a few feet away from them, smiled faintly at the thought of afternoons spent with reed squeaks and sour notes, but his real attention was turned to the disabled young man and the grave and beautiful girl who sat next to him chatting in such a civil and decorous manner. There was no end to her charming stories. In these past weeks he had learned a great deal not just of Tovah Toffias but of a life perhaps gone forever now—a life of courtesy and culture and kindness, of endless discipline ignited by the incandescent light of creative genius, of concerts, of new compositions made all the sweeter by a loving family and close domesticities. If Tovah grieved because of her losses, she never showed it, and seemed to take quiet pleasure in re-creating all the love that she had known as a child.

Lex's hands moved swiftly over a wide sheet of drawing paper. He was making a series of watercolors of all the wounded men in these sylvan surroundings, but especially of Tovah and Gary. He intended to present these paintings to his uncle when he recovered if, indeed. . . .

Tovah's voice faltered and came to a halt. It was Lex's turn.

"Well," he said to Gary, "I never had an oboe. All I had was Mother. It used to drive me wild that *your* mother's idea of fun was to drive us over to the club to play tennis and that *my* mother's idea of fun was to make a novena for the protection of all the virgins in the San Fernando Valley. Do you remember the Debutante Ball when you and I were both escorts and your mother and my mother were chaperones? And your mother came dressed as Katharine Hepburn and my mother came dressed as Our Lady of Guadalupe? We had a pretty good time, though, didn't we? Remember when we took out those girls from Eagle Rock High and we got them to play truth or dare? What was that girl's name? Theresa Kataptha? When you kissed her she'd sneeze. And you kissed her so many times that she said she'd blown out an eardrum. And then if we had to go home to the adobe my mother would ask you if you had had impure thoughts. Remember that time you had Theresa in the rumble seat?"

Lex may have agonized during the long nights of the past five years—nights when he felt that not only his youth was slipping away from him but also the one great adventure of his generation—about whether or not he was a devoted son or merely a coward. But he was not stupid. When he talked now he was not merely trying to awaken his handsome uncle, that golden boy who so many times during his youth had effortlessly lived a life that Lex could only yearn for. A dark and unacknowledged part of his soul wished that his uncle might never wake up, that he, Lex, might stay here in this glowing room forever reflecting upon his own life, making himself understood to a woman who satisfied his strictest standards, a girl who had lived life as he never would, whose intelligence illuminated his own and whose soft beauty had made his nights another kind of agony.

"Remember that time your father invited Mother and me to go skiing with your family and my mother wanted you to wrap your fingers in bandages because she said your fingers were a gift from God? You tried it that first morning and—"

Victoria, Clifford, and Ruth came into the solarium. Lex knew that it was time for afternoon tea. It would be Tovah who brought it. Lex cherished these moments in the waning day when Tovah sat on the low wicker settee and poured tea for them all with the unconscious delicacy of a princess.

After greeting the visiting relatives, Tovah excused herself to bring these refreshments but before she did she brushed a lock of hair from Gary's eyes. Lex heard his own mother's swift intake of breath. Gary's parents sat down on either side of him. Each took one of his hands, each gazed intently into his eyes and began a low and loving conversation. Lex's chest tightened.

He may not have known the exact words that would fall from his mother's lips, but he could guess their content as surely as he knew his own limitations. Ruth strode across the room, placed herself between him and the other three, and in a hoarse whisper, wheezed, "Who is that woman and why won't she leave our family alone?"

The next day there was a constraint among the three of them. If he hadn't known better, Lex would have thought that Gary felt it too. His eyes were troubled and he sat like a stone. Lex thought that Tovah must have heard his mother's remark and he sensed besides the hurt a kind of flittering contempt. Desperation drove his comments today. His jokes held no lightness and finally he broke off.

"Tovah," he said, "you are very beautiful."

She laughed and said casually, "What is Gary to say to that when he wakes up?"

"Tovah, tomorrow perhaps, just from twelve to one, we might go out to lunch. You shouldn't be cooped up here all day."

Her answer was an ironic glance.

"I know what you must think of me," Lex blurted out.

She moved her wrist. It was a polite, wordless disclaimer.

"I may as well clear it up now," Lex said. "The question is, why didn't I go into the service, like Gary, like everyone else my age? The story is I have a bad heart, but that's a lie. The truth is that my father died in the last war and I'm an only son. My mother and grandmother pulled every Mariné string to make sure I wouldn't be drafted." He grinned crookedly. "Have you ever heard my full name, Tovah? There are seven or eight names in it. The names of all the great land-grant families from three hundred years ago. It was my mother's feeling that if this body you're looking at got shot full of holes, it would shoot down those names too. She sets great store by that, Tovah."

"But you didn't have to do what she—" She stopped herself and blushed.

"I thought I might take you to the Stuft Shirt," he said hurriedly, "or maybe get you out of Pasadena entirely. You've been here almost two months and I'll bet a nickel you haven't even seen Hollywood."

Tovah smiled at him sadly. "You're right," she said, "I haven't."

"Tomorrow, then," he said, "I'll take you to the Pig 'n' Whistle and Brown's for a hot fudge sundae. What do you say?"

They played hookey the whole day. She was enchanted not only by the oddity of the names but by the variety of choice offered at that strange restaurant. She asked if she might take a pig mask, even though they were for children. He laughed at the way her nose poked out and dared her to wear it on the street. Since it was only two o'clock, they decided to roam the boulevard. She loved Grauman's Chinese, as he'd expected, but her real favorite was the Egyptian theater.

"Why," she kept asking, "why would anybody want to construct a building so strangely styled?"

"Well," Lex said, "ever since they began the excavations of King Tut's tomb in the twenties, Hollywood seems to have gone through a series of Egyptian and Babylonian crazes. There's a tire factory between Pasadena and Long Beach built like an Assyrian fortress."

"A *tire* factory!"

"Yes," he said, "we'll go and look at it one of these days."

They turned down a side street. He had repeatedly and considerately asked if she was tired, but she said no, it was wonderful to be out and moving. And everything here was so fresh, so new. The bungalows on either side of them were small and well kept, with tidy lawns. Here and there the owners had let their imaginations run riot, in reproducing what looked like Arthur Rackham illustrations of children's stories. Lex stopped before one of these and said, "I don't suppose the Land of Oz means anything to you— *would* it mean anything to you?"

"The land of what?"

He spelled the name for her and went on. "It's from a series of American fairy stories, and for some time the writer lived in this house. It's called 'Ozcott.' Oz is a kind of Paradise, you see. An American fantasy. A place that you can get to by—"

"By wishing," she said.

"So that's why these theaters, these houses, always seem touching to me, even though some outsiders don't like them."

He offered her the choice of a drink at the Hollywood Roosevelt or a hot fudge sundae at C. C. Brown's. She chose the sundae. It had been four or five hours since either of them had spoken of Gary, or the war, or the future. Tovah watched Lex as he ate his sundae—the boyish way he saved the

351

whipped cream for the last, the intensity on his face as he savored each bite, as if he knew that treats were few and far between.

"You ought to get out more often," she told him. "You look happier, Lex."

"I am," he said after a moment. "I am happy."

During the next two weeks Lex took it upon himself to show this beautiful young woman the city. Although their afternoons belonged to Gary, they claimed their mornings for themselves. Lex showed this European visitor that his home, too, had a culture. One morning he took her downtown to Bradbury Building, where she exclaimed over the ironwork in the central enclosure. Other days he took her to the Public Library, designed by Bertram Grosvenor Goodhue, and in contrast to that, drove out on West Adams and conducted her through the intimate, private library of William Andrews Clark's self-indulgent, stylized monument to copper, the seventeenth and eighteenth centuries, and Oscar Wilde. Each day held a new surprise and gave them conversation for their long afternoons. In Pasadena itself, there were the Art Institute, built in the style of an aristocratic Chinese courtyard, the Huntington Library and Art Gallery.

One morning he said, "If we hurry I can show you something between this kind of building and what everyone makes fun of us for—the hot dog stand like a hot dog, the hat of the Brown Derby, the cement tepees of the Indian Motel."

They drove down Wilshire Boulevard to the ocean front and turned north. He stopped in front of a restaurant that they entered through an elaborately tiled arched doorway.

"This was originally built by an actress you've probably never heard of. Her name was Thelma Todd."

They ate a light lunch at a table by a window overlooking the ocean. Afterward, they took the footbridge crossing the highway and walked down on the sand.

"This is so open, so free," Tovah said. "Your air here is like sparkling wine. Back in Austria a city is a city, and the country is the country. Here you have combined the two so beautifully."

The next morning, inspired by this comment, he picked her up armed with a blanket, a picnic basket, and a chilled bottle of champagne. He turned aside her every question about their destination and drove north into the mountains on a carefully graded road. He didn't stop until they'd reached the peak of Angeles Crest. If possible, the air was even more like wine, and below them they could see the entire basin all the way to the lip of the sea. And it was there, once they had spread their blanket and opened the champagne for a first bubbly drink that what Lex had been dreaming about for weeks finally happened.

It was a bittersweet experience. From now on his city would seem intrinsically feminine and enchanting and bound up with the sight of the alabaster body of the woman he loved. Even when they were the most close, he felt within them both a sense of regret or loss. And afterward as he looked at her—she staring into the clear sky with an expression he could not fathom—he remembered with a pang their first afternoon at C. C. Brown's, how he had stretched out that sundae to make it last, but that even as he tasted it, it was gone.

Tovah said nothing. She reached into her purse for a comb, smoothed her skirts over her knees, and put her hand on his shoulder.

Curiously, he found it impossible to talk to her about what had just happened and retreated as he so often did into the perception of life as a form of art.

"You can see from up here," he said, "exactly how the city grew. It was born just down there beneath us. How strange it must have been then. Now that the war is over, the city will be moving out to the east. They'll be tearing out the orange groves. But that's not its natural movement. Its great thrust is to the sea. The boulevards stretch due west. Do you see that section out there? They call it the Miracle Mile. Can you imagine that? The Miracle Mile." He turned and looked directly into her eyes. "I know I've got to get out, Tovah. I know I've got to get free, but I just don't know how."

Tovah looked at him with troubled amusement. "I don't believe," she said, "that you could ever understand my feelings at this moment. I have spent years, my dear Lex, five years hiding in closed dark houses in fear for my life and now you make love to me on a bed of pine needles in the bright light of morning. I am a woman, my dear, who has lost everything. My parents, my family, my fortune, my home. Sometimes at night in the little room the Red Cross has rented for me I hold on to my bed with both hands. It seems to me the world is spinning so fast that it will spin me away too. Now I see you, an intelligent man, unhappy because of your bondage, and your bondage is simply all those things I have lost. It is a joke, don't you see?"

"Tovah," Lex said desperately, "you have to understand. This has never happened to me before. I've never met anyone like you. I—"

"Wait," she said, cutting him off, "don't say anything more." She patted his cheek. "Dear friend. I can make no promises now, no protestations of love. You must understand, dear Lex. I cannot allow myself to be too happy all at once."

That day was the happiest of his life. They stayed on their mountaintop until it was time to go to the hospital. Their conversation that afternoon was dotted with silences filled with affection. His mother's arrival in time for tea could not blot his sense of euphoria, even though Ruth drilled him with a series of baleful glances. He drove back to the adobe early that evening, and was surprised that his usual feelings of dread were not with him.

He spent this part of his circumscribed day, bound as it was by family duty, with his grandmother, the Señora Deogracia Ruiz de Ortega de Moreno de Arellanos de Mariné. She was waiting for him in a handsomely carved wheelchair, and blinked rapidly at him like a little bird.

"Who is this? Who has come to see an old woman?" she chirped and, fluttering the fringes of her silken shawl, motioned for him to come over to her.

"*Abuela*, it is Lex, your grandson. Have you had a pleasant day?"

"I'm old now," she said, "I'm very old now. No one comes to visit me. They only give me puddings to eat. There's a woman here, she shouts at me, she makes me take exercise."

"I know, *abuela*."

"Then she goes away and leaves me alone every day."

"I know."

"Have you seen my husband? He is a handsome man, and very rich. He said I was like a ripe peach. And he didn't care if I was poor. He said he would raise me up—and he did. But now he's gone. Have you seen him?"

"No, *abuela*, I haven't."

"Have you seen my son, then? He too is handsome. And he is as bright and kind as an archangel. He was raised to be an aristocrat, a carrier of the name. But he doesn't come to visit me. Have you seen him?"

"No, *abuela*."

"Who did you say you are? You could almost be a member of the family."

"Ah, *abuela*, you are so clever. I am your grandson, Alexander Luis Antonio de Ortega de Moreno de Arrellanos de Mariné y Creighton."

"Lex," she said. "You are Lex. Of course." She reached over to touch his hand with a shaking motion. "Will you tell the rest of them I'm here—and waiting?" Recognition lit her eyes for a moment, then her attention wandered, and he knew the audience had come to an end.

Ordinarily this nightly interview filled him with hopelessness and despair, but this evening he carried his happiness with him, fragile but still intact.

He went into the study, poured himself a Scotch, and sat down with a copy of Ezra Pound's *Personae*. It was there, two hours later, that his mother found him.

She stood before him and tapped her foot impatiently.

"The cook has told me all about it."

"All about what?"

"I'd just like to know, young man, where and with whom you are sharing a picnic basket, champagne, and," her voice grated over the last word, "a *blanket?*"

"Don't worry, it wasn't one of the maids, Mother."

"Perhaps it would be better if it had been." She fingered her cross. "Are you aware that what you are joking about is a mortal sin?"

"For God's sake, Mother, I took a girl on a picnic. That is *not* a mortal sin in anybody's book."

"Don't make light of this, Lex. Do you think I'm blind? Do you think I can't see what's going on under my nose every day? That girl is a penniless fortune hunter. She's common. We don't know her family or what she's come from—"

"Why don't you stop beating about the bush and say what you're really thinking?"

"All right," she said coldly, "I will. The girl is a refugee. She's a Jewess. Any alliance between the two of you would be absolutely out of the question. I am not an unreasonable person, Lex. I know that family obligations require you to spend time with my brother Gary. But I want you

354

to think! Remember your position! Resist the temptation to get involved with the first pretty girl who flings herself at you."

All through that night, as he sat and smoked and paced and looked out his window onto the dusty fields below, Lex reviewed in his mind all the answers he could have given. But all the wishing in the world could not change the fact that what he had said was "Yes, Mother."

Weeks had passed since Raoul had addressed the City Council, the dizziest, most exciting weeks in his life. Every day Raoul had been up at dawn. An informal group of Mexican businessmen had already come together to discuss what steps could be taken for not only the preservation but the restoration of the Plaza. Though this appeared to be the immediate object, everywhere Raoul looked he saw conditions that needed improvement for the *cholo* community. He spoke to sympathetic Anglo lawyers, many of them native Angelenos, about forming a legal aid society. And he looked up the successors of the city hall officials who had for years been his mother's boarders. Just by dropping a few names he had really gotten the ball rolling.

But by far the most important event was today's meeting at the California Club at a luncheon both sponsored and partly organized by John Frederick Smith. He had been delighted to discover that he could give pleasure to Magdalena while at the same time contributing his services to the people and traditions that in his heart had become his own.

At first Raoul had felt ill at ease during what John Frederick had laughingly warned him would be a "regular three-martini business lunch." But as the second martini took hold, and John Frederick had introduced him to the members of the group as his stepson, Raoul relaxed and found he could talk comfortably to men he had always thought of as contemptuous and condescending fat cats. He decided he enjoyed the elegant, conservative decor, the good but standard chicken à la king luncheon. And after two hours he realized that he had received financial commitments from men representing local, state, and national interests.

What surprised him most of all was the approach made by a Creighton Enterprise representative, Howard Keene. He took a temporarily empty seat beside Raoul and said, "Ortiz, there's a group of us that's concerned about what's happening in your community. No matter what they say back East, Los Angeles is one city and we have to work together to support each other's interests."

"I appreciate the interest that has been expressed here today," Raoul said noncommittally.

"What's really called for, and I'm speaking not just for myself, is the need for an elected city official," Keene said. "There's a seat coming up on the City Council and you should know that Old Man Creighton is willing to back you a hundred percent."

"I have had the opportunity in the last few weeks to look at the history of our people in Los Angeles." Raoul allowed himself a smile. "The last time a Mexican was elected to any seat in the city government was back in 1881."

"But that's just the kind of thing that would tickle Old Man Creighton."

"You may be right," Raoul said, suppressing a momentary twinge of resentment and childhood humiliation. "But I'm not your man. The city isn't ready yet and neither am I. What I'll be best at is working behind the scenes. We could work together, Keene. We could get someone elected who would be acceptable to both communities. He should be younger than I am. He should have his degrees from a good local school. He probably ought to be a lawyer and, the way things are now, he should have a good war record. And he should be someone," Raoul put a conspiratorial hand on Keene's shoulder, "someone we can control."

"Ortiz, you've said it all."

Raoul was amused by the genuine respect with which the other man spoke.

Sometimes, Iris thought, working just wasn't any fun. It was all very well to talk about independence, but when you were assigned to cover something as dull and routine as a meeting of the regional stockholders of Coca-Cola, where was the independence in that? And where was the fun? Her boss wanted a feature story on Coca-Cola's local business interests. Iris couldn't see spending an hour talking about it, even if the company had weathered the Depression and had become an almost international political concern. Where was the human interest in that?

With mild distaste Iris Bauer Sung and her crew trooped down to the Biltmore Hotel for what she felt sure would be an excruciatingly dull meeting. The officers of the company, on the other hand, were enthusiastic and greeted her with what she thought was exaggerated courtesy.

"We're flattered that KQIX has sent its most distinctive interviewer to cover this meeting," the media liaison said. "We have other members of the press here today. And it's a tribute to Coca-Cola that you feel that we're of national importance."

"Um," said Iris.

The man led her down the arcade decorated with fine murals and the coffered ceiling, each section lovingly detailed in gold, red and green paint. She was shown into a meeting room with its *trompe l'oeil* painting of cherubs and vestal virgins. On the walls swans floated endlessly on a silver pond, and all was illuminated by great water lily lamps.

"You see, Iris—may I call you Iris?—we've come to realize that our western stockholders really control the balance of power in our company and that's why we've set up this special meeting. Now, if any of it seems too complicated for you, you just come to me."

"I think I can manage."

By this time the room was filling and he had conducted her to an alcove close to but partially concealed from the podium.

"From here if you keep your voice down you can comment on what's going on and—as I'm sure you know—by using the amplifier you can pick up comments from the floor. I'll send over the people who really count. You'll get your scoop." And with that he was off and courting the newspaper men.

It didn't take long for Iris to recognize the real reason that KQIX had sent her down to cover the story. As soon as the meeting began a woman's voice boomed out new objectives, cost analyses, and plans for a postwar division in Mexico. Though Iris couldn't see the woman's face, her back, her voice were hauntingly familiar.

"It's like this, boys, my husband always said those, ah, south of the border sure have a sweet tooth." From her alcove, Iris could see the serious businessmen who hung on the words of the woman in the hat. "We're going to have to get the locals involved. . . ."

"Yes, madame, you're always right about these things."

And so it went on until matters were settled in the woman's favor. Iris did her first interview with the secretary, her second with a vice-president sent out from New York.

"What do you think of shifting part of your control to Los Angeles in a matter like this?" Iris asked the New Yorker.

"We really don't have a choice. Our stockholders make our decisions." The man laughed ironically. "Mrs. Bauer is the real boss around here. She's our policy maker. You talk to her, she'll set you straight."

Then there was only time to interview one last person and the media liaison ushered in Mrs. Headsperth Bauer. It wasn't the smoothest or most inspired interview Iris had ever done, but both women got through it without any serious breaks or even a hint of their relationship.

But as soon as Iris signed off, Belle Bauer—dumpier, stumpier, richer— reached out and shook Iris' hand. "I listen to your show all the time," she said. "And you really brought this one off like the pro you are. I'm so proud of you." Then, not waiting for Iris to respond, Belle took her niece by the arm and led her out of the room, calling back to Iris' bewildered crew, "Boys, you look after the rest of this. We're going down to the bar for a couple of quick ones."

As soon as they were settled in a booth and after Belle had taken a long drag on her Scotch and soda, she said, "It's so wonderful to see you, sweetie. It's been a long time. I've wondered about you."

"I thought you didn't want to hear from me," said Iris.

"I thought you didn't want to see me either, but," Belle beamed, "here we both are. I've kept track of you. I was overjoyed when Elizabeth and Lloyd were born. If Headsperth had lived to be a great-uncle, maybe he'd have seen things differently."

"My only excuse is that you must remember how Uncle Headsperth reacted to George. He never would have come around."

"Well, perhaps you're right," Belle said. "Toward the end, he was really," she hesitated, "he was really . . . eccentric."

"Oh, Auntie."

"You don't know," Belle explained. "Your Uncle Headsperth lost everything in twenty-nine. But I'd made a few investments of my own. I never wanted to hurt his feelings. It's just that I looked around during those hard days and it seemed to me that the more people lost the more they depended on the little things they liked. After all, anybody could dig up a quarter for the neighborhood movie, or a nickel for a Coke. On the income from my investments we were able to live very comfortably. I was able to save the house, but I suppose it was too much of a shock for Headsperth. Your uncle was a wonderful man, but he didn't have much of a head for business. His luck held to the very end. They even spelled his name wrong in his *Star-News* obituary. That was a long time ago and in most ways I've gotten over it. He may not have seemed like much to others, but he was my Prince Charming. My only consolation after his death was that I could do something for myself, just like you're doing now."

Iris laughed bitterly. "It isn't easy. Every step I take, I lose another friend and I get farther from my family. The other day George came down to meet me at the station and after we left somebody stopped me for my autograph. George and the kids didn't speak to me for the rest of the day."

"Ah, don't give up. A woman needs her own life. By now investment is just a hobby with me and I've become a very rich woman in my own right. But without my taking those risks, where would either one of us have been? You gave up everything to get what you wanted once before. You still have gumption, don't you? Aren't you willing to gamble?"

"The stakes are higher now. I don't want to lose my family."

"Don't you see?" Belle asked. "Anything you want badly enough you can get."

A couple of rounds of drinks later, after they had reviewed the past and promised to keep in touch, Belle said, "I hate to break this up, but I've agreed to meet someone over at the Green tonight." Belle blushed. "He's just a friend, of course." And as they stood to leave, Belle said, "No matter how they act, just remember that your husband and children are secretly as proud of you as I've been. The day will come when they'll let you know." And the two women embraced.

The lovely clear nights of Pasadena took on an almost imperceptible chill, and in the same way the sap of deciduous trees retreats in healing, numbing autumn, the Creightons closed in upon themselves. Gary, beloved only son, the sweet bloom that had turned their middle age into an exciting youthful adventure, was, in fact, dead to them. One by one the veterans at the Vista del Arroyo recovered and left. There were whole rooms now that were swept clean, waiting not for more soldiers but for the hotel's regular life to begin. The worst cases were to be moved soon to a new hospital out in west Los Angeles, and already articles in the *Pasadena Star-News* had made several calls for a speedy return to a "peaceful" economy.

And still every day Victoria made the short drive across the bridge to spend the morning with her son. And still every day Lex Mariné and Tovah Toffias performed the obligations of duty and of friendship even as their own feelings for each other expanded. Their hope, however, ebbed as the days passed.

This afternoon was like fifty or a hundred others. They had come in sated with love, sat down, each one with a guarded sigh, and looked at the handsome man in the wheelchair, still hung with tubes as a handsome mountain climber might rig himself with pitons to the sheer cliff of daily life.

"Good morning, Gary," Tovah said.

"Hello, Gar," Lex echoed. Then he smiled. "You're not much of a conversationalist, are you?"

"You really ought to get out more," Tovah said, trying to imitate an American accent. "Meet some new and interesting people . . . I think he's bored with us, Lex."

This time Lex's sigh was gusty. "God knows I'd be," he said.

"What did he used to do?" Tovah asked. "How did you and he spend your time? What was he like then?"

Lex met the question with silence and then said, "We were the best of friends, but we never talked much at all. We don't have much in common. We spent time with the family, of course. And countless afternoons playing tennis, but when I think of how we spent time together, really, what I remember is being in my grandparents' house. I'd be painting or reading a book and Gary would be at the far end of the room practicing. He looked at that piano, oh, I don't know, as if it were a partner or another physical being. He thought of practicing as staying in shape. He—"

"Lex," Tovah said, "is there a piano anywhere here?"

"Sure, there's one down in the rec room. Sometimes the boys sing around it. It's in pretty bad shape."

"It might not be a bad idea to try that."

"Tovah, are you sure that you—"

She put him off with an impatient gesture. "If you're thinking of my father, darling, or that the sight of a piano might hurt my feelings, you are suffering from an excess of consideration." She smiled sadly. "I have seen your Hollywood movies and I know that when Joel McCrea is wakened it is by the voice of love and not conversation. This young man," she said, gesturing to the immobile figure in the wheelchair, "has no Shirley Temple to wake him up. And he has no wife. But you and I have both learned in school that music is the voice of love."

Lex shrugged and left the room, returning in a few minutes wheeling a remarkably rickety upright piano.

What she proposed now was a test not for this young man that she barely knew but a gauge of her own recovery. When she had first come to this sunny, pleasant little city, she had been as dead inside as the man in the wheelchair. She had looked at these tanned and healthy California people with amazement and contempt. Their ignorance of life as she had led it was a mockery, blasphemy, a grievous sin. She had sought out this hospital not from any impulse to "do good," but to find a place that at least approximated her view of reality. But in this land even blood and suffering were swathed in laundered linen and there was always enough to eat.

That afternoon a few weeks ago when Lex had penetrated her she had felt nothing, thought nothing, had submitted to the act dutifully as a sick man downs his medicine, knowing that in the long run it will be good for him. And Lex *had* been good for her. These past weeks, laced as they were with fantasy, performed a subtle and benign magic. There were whole hours now when her mother's face tightened in the rictus of death did not blot out every other sight.

In touching a piano, she would, literally, be laying hands upon the past. She would emerge victorious or defeated, but at least she would no longer retreat from it. She said nothing of all this and simply asked Lex if he could find her a straight-backed chair. Her hands stretched across the keys and one long chord hung in the air. It was as if she had sustained a mortal wound. Her chest was open and was bleeding.

"I remember," she said, "that when I first met your grandmother, she said Gary was fond of the Third Etude."

And with no more talk she began. The first bars came to her as from a great distance. She thought, yes, it was a great distance, halfway around the world. A neighborhood park in Vienna, her father swinging her higher, higher on a Sunday afternoon. It had been her father's pleasing task in writing this piece to double and triple its complexity while still keeping the rural simplicity of the initial melody. As she attempted this part, her left hand faltered. She could hear the false notes. Behind her she could hear Lex's voice low and intense, "That's the part that always used to give you trouble, Gar. Do you remember the recital when. . . ."

She remembered her own father, elegant and meticulous, on a Paris engagement in the Salle Pleyel, bringing even the blasé Frenchmen to their feet as they shouted their approval and he acknowledged their cheers with the merest flicker of a smile while he went on with a lilting arpeggio, which— he had told her often—he had written for her when she was still an infant. She noticed with detachment that the tears streaming down her face were staining her new bright blue blouse with dark blots.

"Go on," Lex said. "Don't stop."

But she had no intention of stopping. It was as if by this act she was challenging all the world's suffering. She thought of explorers setting forth in small boats on the wine-dark sea. She thought of her father's music pouring out of open windows even as the Nazi troops drove up the deserted streets. She could see the end now in her mind and stepped up the tempo, knowing her father wouldn't approve. She heard uneven husky breaths behind her and felt Lex's hands dig deep into her shoulders as she played lightly, delicately, the last sixteen notes, and fell against him, her face buried in the flesh just below his rib cage, and felt there as strongly and physically as she had felt her own, the almost palpable pain.

"Oh, my dear," he said, "how brave you are, how good you are. And I must tell you, Tovah"—here his voice broke and he was crying too— "Gary's fingers moved. He was with you almost all the time. He heard it. I know he heard it."

He stooped down to her and drew her up. She locked her arms around his neck. Her whole being was racked with sobs. She wept for all of them. Her father's headstrong defiance, her mother's stoicism in the face of death, Victoria's indomitable strength, Lex's healing kindness, his sweetness which had been so wasted in his short life. Her knees buckled and it was in a kind of swoon that she heard what they would later describe as literally a voice from the dead.

"I beg your pardon," it rasped, eerie, and scarcely human, yet still with a miraculous tinge of irony. "Excuse me," Gary's voice said. "Am I intruding?"

The events of this afternoon would be told and retold in the joyful blur of days that followed. Despite their precautions Gary talked so much in the first few days that he developed severe laryngitis and was sentenced to silence again. Lex and Tovah were almost always with him now, trying in this first stage of consciousness to keep his mind from the nightmare events that had first injured him. They took him for shaky walks down the halls. He was as rubbery on his pins as a new baby. They strengthened first his hands and then his fingers by bringing in a dart board and then a set of jacks. They whiled away long hours playing five hundred rummy.

Lex bundled his uncle into his car and took him to almost all the places that he had earlier shown Tovah. It was simply the exigencies of nursing, he told himself, which decreed that Tovah should sit on the outside next to the window with Gary carefully sandwiched between them. They took Gary to the movies and fed him malted milks. They carted him out to the adobe to pay a courtesy call on the Señora, who was so animated by his return that she imperiously asked for her fan and rewarded them all with a few flirtatiously demented remarks. They took him everywhere except to that enchanted spot on Angeles Crest.

Soon the time came when Gary was rolled ceremoniously in the wheelchair he no longer needed to the car where his mother and father waited to make the final drive across the bridge and back to the Creighton mansion. The beloved young man, mourned for so long, was finally home from the war. There, in a flurry of domestic preoccupation, Gary sat curiously unmoved, as if in the eye of a storm.

"How does it feel?" Lex asked him.

"I . . . I don't know how it feels. It feels good, I guess." His hand automatically reached out, and Tovah's just as automatically reached out to touch his.

Lex saw this with a pang. Gary looked around with a slow smile of awakening contentment.

"You know what I'd like to do, just for an hour or so—I'd like to get out on the court again. How about it, Lex?"

"We'll play doubles," Lex heard himself saying. "You and Tovah against me and I'll still beat you silly."

Gary's hand tightened over Tovah's small fist. "We'll see about that."

And so the rhythm of life at the Creighton household fell, once again, into its accustomed pattern. But inside the house, from different rooms, Victoria and her daughter Ruth watched the young people, each with her own closely held thoughts.

It was with a feeling of some dismay that the mayor surveyed his day's agenda. A prayer breakfast. Then luncheon with the Brentwood Garden Club. Then he had to beat his way back downtown, where the air had recently been filled with a mixture of smoke and fog that some journalist who

had it in for him had shortened to the totally unappetizing acronym "smog."
The afternoon held nothing better than a perfunctory twenty-mintue "inau-
guration ceremony" for the downtown Plaza.

He knew that the air would be bad for his allergies and he could look
forward to speeches that he had already heard a hundred times over. He
would be giving one of them himself. For not the first time he considered his
wife's suggestion that he might be better off in private practice.

This whole project as far as he was concerned was crackbrained, idealis-
tic, and a bow to a constituency that simply didn't exist. The area across
from Union Station was potentially valuable property and would have lent
itself perfectly to one of the modern new skyscrapers. But somebody
somewhere on the east side of town had blocked those plans. So what he
faced today was óne large irritation at the end of several small ones.

His chauffeur had trouble parking, so the mayor came late to the Plaza,
puffing and grumpy. Then surprise blotted out his ill-temper.

The run-down gazebo had been decorated with bunting and ribbons. A
few stalls had been moved from the confines of Olvera Street out onto the
Plaza. His practiced politician's eye spotted several tables that had been set
up inviting Latinos to vote, reminding them that this was their city too.
Instead of the lackluster handful of committee members he had expected,
the Plaza was filled with at least five hundred people. And these weren't just
Mexicans. He saw members of the City Council and the County Board of
Supervisors. He recognized two of the richest women in town. One had over
the years secured herself a place on the Coca-Cola board of directors. The
other one, was she one of those aristocrats, or was she the one with the
shady past? All he knew was she lived in Hancock Park and made the
society columns at least once a week. It looked like half of Chinatown was
here too. Whât could their interest be in all this?

There was a smell of tamales and tacos in the air. What seemed like a
million little kids scurried about carrying ice cream cones. And one of those
God-awful Mexican bands stood waiting. Then somebody stuck a microphone in front of him. He straightened his shoulders and smiled.

"Mr. Mayor, you must be very proud of your city today."

"Yes, I am. Certainly, yes. It's a great day for all of us."

"Do you think that this reclamation is part of a new urban awareness, sir?
Frankly, some people have expressed surprise that you haven't given in to
big business interests. . . ." She was grinning at him impishly and his own
smile became genuine and a bit flirtatious.

"You must remember that I originally ran on a reform platform. I would
never allow big business, as you call it, to blot out the picturesque heritage
of our great city."

Then she was drifting away from him, but he heard her chattering into her
mike, "There's such an air of festivity and excitement here today. I wish all
of you could come down. So many families have brought their children.
Even the politicians seem happy. Everyone is in their best clothes. They've
cleared a place for dancing. And, wait a minute, I think they're going to
begin the speeches."

Someone had mercifully told the little clutch of officials to keep their words down to three minutes and they uttered their platitudes to a crowd that did not get bored simply because it wasn't listening. The mayor sized up the crowd, knowing that he would be last, eyeing the short but consistent lines in front of the voting-registration tables, trying to remember what he knew about East Los Angeles.

A portly, prosperous businessman in a pinstripe suit mounted the platform and held the microphone up to his lips. A ripple of recognition went up. A few scattered yips and shrieks came from some of the young men. Housewives held up their arms and waved. Applause gathered and held. The mayor stood blinking as the man on the platform began.

"Most of you know me by now. I've been knocking on your doors and calling you at night. We've been working on this project for months now and we're not finished yet. But at least we've started. Today marks the real beginning of that start. So, I guess you could call this a victory speech, and it's been a long time in coming." He hesitated. "This victory isn't over the City Council; they were more than willing to listen to my ideas. It isn't over the juvenile delinquents in the area. Those delinquents—we know them—they're just our boys." Here the crowd began to cheer and some zoot-suiters who had come to heckle grinned a little sheepishly. Raoul's voice boomed out. "It isn't over big business and it isn't over the white man. Working on this Plaza has really been a victory over ourselves. What I want to do now—if you'll let me—is be a spokesman for the Latino, because for many years in my life I was deaf to those voices. I couldn't hear my mother, who was in search of a better life. I couldn't hear my wife, who helped me in the best way she knew. Instead, I heard white voices that blotted out everything. They say that L.A. is a city without a heart, but I say L.A. is a city with many hearts." He paused, waiting for the applause to subside. "I know I've talked enough. You didn't come here to listen to speeches, but before I get down there are three people I want you to meet. The first is a young man, a hero, just home from the war, young Ed Roybal. They say the Latino can never have a voice in city government, but this guy will prove them wrong."

A nervous GI got up and took a bow.

"And then, a woman who has done more than anyone I know to show that the finest parts of Mexico and America can be united. My mother, Maria Magdalena Ortiz Smith."

The mayor's eyes narrowed. So that's where that guy got his money.

"And finally, a lady who is very private and shy, who has done nothing in her life except be a good wife, a wonderful mother and put up for over thirty years with a husband who for most of the time was nothing but a very big pain. My wife, my beautiful wife, Maria Ortiz."

He reached down and pulled up to the platform a pretty Mexican woman who hid her face at first and then waved and smiled as the crowd went wild.

Across the Plaza the band must have been given a signal by Ortiz, because it began a strong introduction to a piece that even the mayor found familiar. He knew he'd have to move fast and he did. He scrambled up onto the platform, pounded Ortiz on the back, and stood in the maelstrom of applause as if it belonged to him.

"No one could follow a speech like that," he shouted. "Let me just thank all you good people who made this possible and," as the trumpets began to drown him out, "have a wonderful—"

By this time the crowd had surged away from him and were crowded around Ortiz and his wife as they went into the first steps of "La Negra." He looked around for the radio broadcaster and was surprised to see that Ortiz's speech had gotten to her. She wiped her eyes and he heard her say, "This is Iris Bauer Sung, signing off."

Sung. Could she be related to *that* family?

He didn't have time to think of it, because Ortiz's mother came up to him and demurely said, "Will you honor me with this dance, señor?" And how could he say no to a campaign contribution like that?

He spent the rest of the day there and got his picture in all three papers. Not a bad afternoon. Certainly better than the garden club.

Late that night, after a long and sensual evening of love, George reached for two cigarettes, lit them, and passed one to Iris.

"Paul Henreid couldn't have done it more suavely," she said. "I'm very impressed."

"It's you," he said in a faint Viennese accent. "It's you, my darling. You turn me into a beast."

"Well, something's happened," she said. "I don't feel like one half of an old married couple, I can tell you that."

"You're the most beautiful woman in the world," he said, and his voice told her that he wasn't pretending. Then, after a pause, he asked, "Did you have a nice day at work?"

"It was fun. I should have brought the kids. Everybody was there—the mayor and all. And it was nice to see Raoul and Maria after all these years. You know, George, if you wanted to, if you thought it was the right thing. . . ." She let it drop. It was for the men to decide.

And then she felt him smile all over his body through the darkness. "Iris Bauer Sung. I like that. It's so refined. Like Mary Roberts Rinehart or Harriet Beecher Stowe."

She waited.

"My father and I . . . well, he has an interest in this Plaza scheme. And just because we don't want you to work doesn't mean we don't listen to your show. Do you know what my father said today, Iris? He said you brought honor to our family name."

"They've asked me to stay."

"Well, I've been thinking about it. We have the maid, and the kids are in school. Because of your job we get free tickets to the theater and never have to wait in line. And since we get extra gas coupons . . ."

"Yes?"

"I've been thinking that it really wouldn't do any harm if you wanted to continue now that the war's over."

"I told them I wouldn't make a decision without asking you."

"I say go ahead, but I have to ask. What would you have done if I'd said no?"

"I would have chosen my family, but I'm glad I didn't have to make that choice."

"You're a barbarian and you have no respect, but what you do, you do well." And with that George took Iris back into his arms.

Cliff Creighton fumbled with the wing collar of his evening shirt, and stepped to the door of his dressing room as he began to knot his tie.

"Why do I always have to dress for dinner?" he grumbled across the room to Victoria, who was putting the final touches on her hair. Her peach-colored evening gown accented her still-fresh complexion. To Clifford she had never aged. She turned her head toward him.

"For one thing, my dear," she said, "you know very well that you secretly enjoy changing for dinner, because you look your very best in evening clothes."

He grunted.

"But even if that weren't true," she went on, "you would want to dress tonight. Gary's officially discharged and home now and I know you want to make that a real celebration."

"You're always right, my dear."

He did want it to be a celebration. His son was home and safe and well. He knew Pansy had worked for two days on this meal and he and Porter had gone down to the cellar together to pick out the choicest wines. Of course Lex would be here and his new friend, the girl whom Victoria had praised so frequently. And Ruth. And the Señora. God, the Señora! Why, he asked himself, did every red-letter day have the Señora marked in? Well, he supposed, after fifty years it wouldn't be a celebration without her.

He joined Victoria, who had finished dealing with the clasp of her double strand of pearls, and they went downstairs to the drawing room.

"I think, Victoria, that we could begin, just the two of us," Clifford said as he opened the first bottle of the vintage champagne, poured two glasses, and handed one to her. "You're as lovely as ever, my dear," he said, lifting his glass to her and sipping the wine.

"And you," she replied, "are as handsome as you've always been."

He kissed her on the forehead and sat down on the arm of her chair. He felt better than he'd felt in weeks and it pleased him that Victoria had regained her strength as well.

"Gary has recovered so swiftly," he said. "We can never thank Lex enough for all the hours of his care and attention."

"And Tovah."

"Yes. It seems she came into our family at just the right time. Out of this tragedy it seems Lex has found himself quite a girl."

Victoria looked pensive. "I wouldn't count on anything, dear."

Before he had a chance to question her, Gary was there, crossing the room to greet them with only a slight limp, resplendent in his evening clothes.

What could Victoria mean, Clifford asked himself. He wasn't so blinded by parental affection that he couldn't see that Ruth had a terrible hold over her son, but surely she could never do anything to mar his happiness.

Victoria was just imagining things. But he wouldn't think about it now. This was Gary's evening.

"Aha," Gary said, crossing over to the champagne bucket, "you two thought you'd steal a march on me, but it won't take me long to catch up." He poured himself a glass and raised it to his mother. "I can't tell you how marvelous it is to be home again."

The three of them enjoyed a few moments of intimacy and silence. There was no need for speech. Clifford knew that this was one of the golden moments of his life, one that he would never forget. He also knew that it could not last forever, and even as he savored this fleeting vision, he heard the stir of their guests' arrival. Reluctantly he stood, and with Gary beside him, walked toward the thick, highly polished drawing-room doors. He knew that one or the other of them would have to help Porter Priest support the Señora in whatever mode of entrance she had decided upon.

Once in the entrance, with Porter taking care of the older ladies' outer garments, he saw that the privilege was to be his; for Gary, after a perfunctory bow to the Señora and Ruth, went directly to Tovah. Was it his imagination, or did Gary's arms linger about her slim shoulders as he helped her remove her wrap. . . ?

The Señora looked blankly about her. "What is this place? What an interesting piece of architecture. How wisely the early *padres* built. . . ."

So that was the line she was going to take tonight. Clifford bowed, and took her arm.

Ruth's voice rose irritably. "Don't be silly. This is *my* house! I grew up here. My father built it. You've been here a million times."

Cliff shuddered. He could not but notice that the four of them—Ruth and the Señora, Lex and Tovah—appeared to be under some tension.

"Your comparison is very flattering," he said, as they all moved toward the drawing room. "The *padres* did indeed build well."

The Señora's eyes lit up in a demented way. "That is what I was saying." And with a high, piercing giggle and a look of contempt at Ruth, she added, "Of course you are the *padre* here."

"Well, I've been called a lot of things in my day," Cliff said, laughing. Luckily he didn't have to go on, for Victoria was there to greet their elderly guest and help her husband lead her to a chair by the fireplace.

Gary, plainly enjoying his role as both host and guest, assisted Porter Priest with the champagne. As he handed the heavy leaded crystal glasses to Lex and Tovah, Clifford—with a wave of the same intense joy that he had felt earlier in the evening—looked at the young trio. Gary, tanned and strong now, Lex, more slightly built, but his keen intelligence lending him an almost tensile strength, and the young nurse, who, Clifford now realized with a shock, resembled a nurse no longer. Tovah had dressed for this evening with a strange exoticism. She wore black, with a severe yet daring neckline. She had flung over this austere, revealing gown a narrow vest of red satin bordered with rich gold embroidery. Long pendants hung from her pierced ears, dull silver with hundreds of marcasite chips in an exquisite design. She had lost weight and strength in the past weeks even as Gary had gained it, and under her tan she seemed pale and drawn but very lovely.

Feverish, that was the word for it! She had used rouge tonight, and something on her eyes. Her hair was drawn up in an elaborate bun. Cliff recognized an aristocrat, someone dressed perfectly for a Viennese salon, but definitely a foreigner in this Pasadena drawing room.

His thoughts were broken into by the Señora, who was not yet willing to surrender her theme of the evening. Holding her crystal goblet with both hands she sipped the bubbling champagne, and pronounced grandly, "Ah! You have given us holy wine! Wine from the vineyards of the new world!"

"Not exactly," Clifford said diplomatically, but he was spared the effort of further invention by Priest's announcement of dinner.

Perhaps there was no perfect way to seat such a disparate group, but Victoria had done her best to solve the problem by going against convention and placing Tovah between Lex and Gary on one side of the long table and Ruth and the Señora on the other. And Victoria had shown her customary thoughtfulness in seating Ruth on Clifford's right, so that he might be spared the considerable pain both of watching the Señora eat and of listening to her conversation. This meant, on the other hand, that Cliff came under the immediate attention of his daughter, and she did not fail to take advantage of this.

Priest, with evident pride, served them each six oysters on the half-shell embedded in shaved ice, oysters that had been flown down by chartered plane from British Columbia just this morning. Clifford could hardly wait for everyone to be served, anticipating the cold, smooth succulence of the delicacy in his mouth, but he had no sooner taken up his oyster fork when Ruth looked at him and said, "Really, Daddy, do you think it's wise at your age to indulge yourself in such risky food? I understand that the elderly are prone to develop allergies, especially against seafood, and most particularly against shellfish. Don't you want me to ask Porter to see if he can't serve you a soft-boiled egg?"

Clifford lifted his wine glass and deliberately drained it. As he ate his first oyster, he turned to her and said, "Ruth, have you forgotten that your father is a Baltimore boy? Don't you know that all Baltimorians enjoy a particular affinity for oysters, a lifelong affinity? Not only that, there seems to be some truth in the tradition that oysters are an aphrodisiac."

"Daddy!"

"A soft-boiled *egg*," Clifford said, putting the second oyster into his mouth. "If *you* want one, I'm sure Priest will be glad to oblige you, and I'll be happy to finish your plate."

But, as he noticed, Ruth was herself already on her third oyster. More gently, he went on. "Ruth, don't think I'm unappreciative of your concern. I know you're . . ."

Their exchange had been listened to by the young people. Tovah had trained her full attention on her plate, but Gary and Lex had been unable to suppress their mirth. Lex had foolishly said something in a half-whisper that, whatever it was, clearly infuriated his mother.

"Yes, of course, laugh! That's your answer to everything. Laugh when your father dies! Laugh when it's time to find a profession! Laugh when war breaks out! Laugh every day when you go out to play, and your mother stays

367

home alone!"

Even as she spoke, she somehow managed to finish off the last of her oysters, but as she did so, the table was stunned into silence.

"Really, Ruth," Victoria said in a deliberately light tone, "that's laying it on a bit thick, isn't it?"

But Gary, with quick loyalty, responded hotly. "Look, Ruth, don't for the love of God put it on Lex. You know he'd have been off like a shot if you hadn't pulled every string to keep him home, in that prison of an adobe—"

Lex made an involuntary movement, but Ruth cut him off. As Porter Priest brought on the mock turtle soup, she sneered, "You don't know what you're saying. Your mind isn't what it was. You ought to keep your mouth shut until you recover from your shell shock."

"*Shell* shock!" Clifford exclaimed indignantly, but Victoria's voice cut through it all. "That will be enough, Ruth, for the time being."

"Amen!" the Señora brought out, from the private world in which she was continuing to live, though she too had eaten her oysters without difficulty. Before taking up her soup spoon, she smiled vaguely, looking about the table.

Priest passed among them with more champagne; all of them reached for their glasses.

"Tovah, my dear," Victoria began again, drawing upon all her reserves of good manners and serenity, "I hope that the boys have been showing you something of the city and the countryside."

"It must be terrible for you, Miss Toffias," Ruth interjected, "living here all alone with no one you can really talk to, no family, no—"

"We've had a marvelous time," Tovah responded quicky. "We've been to the Huntington. I found the gardens especially charming. I had no idea that the cactus grows in so many different forms. We've been to the Philharmonic, of course. Last night the three of us went to your Pasadena Playhouse. The production was quite fine."

There was a momentary hush as Priest entered again, bearing, with ceremonial aplomb, an enormous rib roast. Pansy followed him with a platter of Yorkshire pudding cut into large slices. This had been Gary's favorite meal since boyhood, and he said, "Now I know I'm really at home, at last."

Even Ruth smiled as Clifford stood to carve with swift efficiency. The family lull that comes at such times—the passing of Pansy's fresh rolls, the clink of their glasses, the exchange of relishes—filled the next moments. Perhaps only Victoria guessed at the depth of Tovah's feelings when she murmured across Lex, "I never thought the time would come again when I would be part of a family."

And Gary said, huskily, "Thank you, Dad, and Mother, for all of this, for still being here when I came home."

Again, it fell to Victoria to take the lead. "Well, Tovah, I hope it hasn't been all architecture and libraries."

"Oh, *no.*" (What was it that made her blush, Clifford wondered, fleetingly?) "We've been to the . . . mountains, and all of us have been to the beach. I think I must have seen everything that I've heard talked about here, except for—what is it you call it?—the Valley Club? The Hunt Club? The Valley Hunt Club!"

"Ah," Clifford said.

"How thoughtless of you, boys," Victoria said, after a barely perceptible pause. "You must take her over and introduce her around. It's not fair of you to keep her all to yourselves, playing tennis on our court—"

"But that wouldn't be possible, Mother, even today." It was Ruth again, and this time no one had a ready answer for her.

"Ruth, for God's sake!" Gary burst out.

"No, it's true, and there's no point in pretending such things don't exist." Tovah put down her knife and fork. Clifford watched as the blood drained from her face, leaving the rouge on her high cheekbones in two hectic spots.

"While everyone deplores what went on in Europe, there are probably very good historical reasons for keeping certain traditions alive." Ruth's hand, in the old gesture, went to her cross.

"Mother!" Lex exploded. "That's unconscionable."

"Oh, you! You don't know anything about it. I know what you're thinking and I know what you're doing. And that's just exactly why rules like that have been made."

Now Ruth addressed Tovah directly. "I have nothing against you personally. But if my husband were alive, it would fall to him to tell you both that your 'friendship' . . . that society is kept alive by each kind keeping to its own."

"*Ruth!* Hold your tongue. We're all the same kind here," Victoria said. But suddenly the room had become a horrible place.

Out of endless stillness, Tovah, sitting very straight, looked at Ruth. "Is that what you think, Mrs. Mariné?"

But Ruth, conscious that perhaps at last she'd gone too far, was speechless. She looked, Clifford thought, like a big baby, and sulked, toying with her food.

"May I ask then," Tovah repeated clearly, "is that what you all think?"

"You *idiot!*" Clifford said to his daughter, and Victoria said, "No Tovah, no! Never that!"

The girl pushed back her chair, strangled a cry, blindly flung open a French door, and disappeared into the darkness of the terrace.

"Lex!" Gary said. "Go after her!"

Lex sat paralyzed, looking at his mother.

"Lex! Go now or you'll lose her forever!"

And so it was Gary who went after her.

In the silence Victoria waited as Priest gathered up the "public dishes." As the door shut behind him she said coldly to her daughter, "To use the language of a younger generation, you certainly bitched that up."

"You're all hypocrites! None of you would want that kind of foreigner in the family. But of course it falls to *me* to say it. I'm the one who—"

Through most of this unfortunate dinner, Clifford's only solace had been the champagne.

"Almighty God!" he exclaimed. "That you, of *all* people, should bring up such an objection."

369

Ruth looked at him with an air of injured innocence. "You have to admit, Daddy, that she'd never fit into the Club."

"The Club! I'm not thinking about the Club! I'm thinking of all that Latin mumbo jumbo we had to go through for you. Those men in skirts! That choking incense! Why, to this day you wear that tasteless cross."

Suddenly the Señora sat up. "What is it you are saying?"

"And those names!" Clifford raved. "You couldn't marry somebody named Tom or Dick, you had to bring in *Alessandro!*"

"It was a terrible day when our land grant fell into your hands," the Señora said. "I know who you are now! You are Clifford Creighton! The money-grubbing Anglo who came out and spoiled everything he touched. It's because of you that my last days are cursed with this woman, this ungrateful daughter-in-law."

She slumped in her chair, gibbering in Spanish.

"You see," Ruth said, quietly, bitterly, "it doesn't really matter whom a person marries, does it? Because it comes to this in the end. Have either of you ever thought, really thought, about what it's been like for me these last years?"

The Señora suddenly found the strength to stand up. "No! Don't touch me! No one shall touch me." She gathered her silken rebozo about her. "I can no longer breathe the air of this house!" Ruth and Lex automatically moved to support her.

"The Monsignor shall hear of this," the Señora hissed. "Perhaps even *el Papa* himself!"

When, moments later, Priest emerged from the butler's pantry, proudly displaying before him the flaming baked Alaska, he found his master and mistress alone, facing each other from either end of the now-deserted table.

"Oh, Priest," Victoria quavered. "You must tell Pansy it's beautiful, but I'm afraid we won't be taking dessert."

"But you may," Clifford sighed, "bring in another bottle of champagne."

There was no moon this night. Even the starlight was obscured by the fragrant leafy trees that blanketed the grounds of the Creighton estate. Gary heard his own uneven footsteps on the terrace, his own ragged breathing. He knew she was out here, he knew she was watching him.

"Tovah, please! Come back so I can talk to you. Come back so I can explain."

No answer.

"It isn't fair of you to leave like this. You have to give us a chance. You have to give *me* a chance."

There was a sound then so slight that had he not been listening hard he would have dismissed the faint crunch of leaves as nothing but a vagrant squirrel. But his senses, sharpened by combat, picked it up immediately and he lunged blindly in that direction. Then she was in his arms, struggling to get away.

"Let me go. Let me leave," she said. "Show me the way out of here."

He held her to him, telling himself in a corner of his mind that it was only to calm her down, to keep her in one place so they could talk. Her cheek was against his neck. He felt the warm wetness of her tears. Then they thrust themselves from each other, their only communication the sounds of their trembling breath.

He tried desperately for a conversational tone. "I guess now you can see, like the rest of us, what's been happening to Lex all these years. His mother is a truly terrible woman. I have to say that even though she's my own sister. But come on, Tovah. Nobody pays any attention to Ruth. She's nothing but a family joke."

"Is it true? Is what they said true?"

"Is what true?" he asked cautiously. His eyes had gotten used to the dark and he could see her outlined, pale against the bark of the huge eucalyptus.

"Is it true I couldn't get into your club?"

He thought for a minute, then said with a certain air of surprise, "No, no, you couldn't, but you could be my guest." He was aware of the ludicrousness of the situation. How supremely silly for a group of people to keep a woman like her off their tennis courts, and how supremely silly for her, after her untold heroism, to care a damn about it. But perhaps that was why wars were so popular. Heroism was easy then. It was daily life that was the killer. He plunged his hands into his pockets and made a speech.

"Look, Tovah, no one out here except Aimee Semple McPherson thinks this is Paradise. It looks like Heaven on Earth, but we're not perfect. Intolerance and stupidity and greed are everywhere. A war might change some of that temporarily, but everyone on earth wants to stick to the old patterns. The best thing about life out here is that it's just possible that you can change the pattern. At least in California everyone has a fighting chance. But when you look at Ruth or even my parents, well, there's something about people—they like to keep their old ways."

"Are *you* like that?" she asked.

"I used to be," he answered. "But the war has changed the way I think, and the last three weeks."

She gazed stubbornly into the distance and, thinking about it, he knew there was nothing more he could say.

"Come on," he murmured, "I'll drive you home."

The next morning Gary ordered breakfast in his room. He practiced for an hour and waited until he knew his father was settled for the day in the drawing room and Victoria had left the house. Then he drove out through the San Gabriel Valley to the Mariné adobe. He went into the old courtyard where the gates swung open now, and up the back steps to Lex's austere room. Gary knew he'd find him there and he did, sitting in a chair looking out a window, a cup of coffee and an ashtray full of cigarette stubs by his side.

"Lex, let's go for a drive."

"Why not?"

They drove along Foothill Boulevard, the mountains on one side of them, the vast green jungle of orange trees on the other. Every few miles they saw bulldozers and other heavy equipment uprooting the trees, shaving the ground, making ready for the postwar building boom. They talked cautiously of the night before, Lex making mordant family jokes about his mother and grandmother. When the Señora died, Lex said, if, indeed, such a thing was possible, he planned to have her stuffed and would donate her to the Historical Society—either that or put her in Bullock's window, her arms and legs moving, as an example of what children might expect to get for Christmas if they hadn't been good. There was a wretched hangdog feeling in everything he said. Finally Gary pulled up at one of the last fruit stands that dotted the dusty highway. They each ordered huge paper cups of orange juice and began to walk along the shoulder of the road.

"Lex, we have something to talk about," Gary said.

"I know."

"You're my oldest friend. We're more like brothers than nephew and uncle," Gary said. "All those weeks when I was unconscious I knew you were there. I heard your voice and I heard Tovah's voice too. I guess it's not too much to say that you gave me the reason to wake up. And when I woke up, there you both were and you were happy. And that was the way it was. Until last night I was never going to say anything, but now I have to know. Lex, what are your plans about Tovah? What are you going to do?"

Gary would always marvel in the years to come about how life—people's lives—were decided in a seemingly careless minute, in a few seconds. Lex shrugged.

"What *can* I do? I'm stuck, Gar, I've had it. You were right last night when you said I should go after her." He threw his cup on the ground and smashed it with his foot. "You don't know what it's like to grow up in a house with nothing but women, and, Jesus Christ, what women! There's nothing I can give Tovah. As long as my mother and the Señora are alive they're my responsibilities, whether I like it or not."

"Well," Gary said, "let me ask you this. No matter what happens, will we still be friends?"

"Always."

It was a few minutes after noon when Gary got to the hospital. He entered it as a returning hero, smiling at all the nurses and USO hostesses who made much over him. He stopped to give a good word to his buddies who still had days or weeks to spend in this lovely sunlit prison. He found Tovah at the far end of the garden, her head bent in intent concentration over a game of Chinese checkers with a rawboned young vet.

"Hey," Gary said roughly.

She looked up hastily.

"Are you free for lunch?"

"No."

"I knew you'd say that so I already got you permission. I'm sorry," he said to the kid, "but this is urgent family business. She'll have to finish the game later."

He kept a strong grip on her wrist and half dragged her through the grounds. Once in the car neither of them spoke until they got to the Stuft Shirt. He had called ahead to reserve the best table.

"I'm not dressed for this, Gary," she said to him, and it looked as if that was all she planned to say.

Gary waited until two martinis had been placed in front of them. Then he took a deep breath for his third speech in less than twenty-four hours. He put both hands flat on the table and began.

"I'm not going to mince words. I just came out of a terrible war and I've seen terrible things."

She lifted her drink and drained at least half of it.

"Vraiment?" she said with heavy sarcasm.

"Oh," he said, "I know you've seen terrible things too. Been through hell and all that. We could both sit around and worry about it for the rest of our lives. But that would be a waste of time, wouldn't it?"

"So?" Her eyes had begun to water. She took out a handkerchief and unceremoniously blew her nose.

"We both know our lives can end tomorrow. This new bomb they've got proves it if nothing else does."

"So?"

"I talked to Lex this morning."

"Gary, please—"

"Tovah, I love you. I love everything about you. Your eyes, your hair, your kindness, your loyalty, your dignity."

She was crying in earnest now. "You don't have to—" she said, and then she was on her feet.

His voice rang out through the restaurant. "Tovah, the thing for us to do is get married. That way you can get into the Club and we won't have anything more to fight about."

She turned on him in a rage. "How dare you make fun of me? Ha, ha, ha," she spat out at him. "Very funny, you Americans."

Gary saw the faces of a score of Pasadena matrons turning toward them in their wide-brimmed hats, like flowers to the sun. He knew it was now or never.

"See if you get a laugh out of this," he growled and, not even getting up, he pulled her roughly down onto his lap and stifled her words with his lips.

Though she implored him not to, he drove her straight from lunch to his parents' home.

"Gary," she kept saying, "you're not well yet. You don't know what you're saying. You're mistaking a physical attraction for love. Two people can't go against the way of the world. Oh, you *do* think it's funny, don't you? Well, millions were killed because of it . . . I can't do anything until I find out what's happened to my family."

All Gary knew was that his hands gripped the steering wheel until his knuckles were white, and all he could say whenever she paused to take a breath was "We're getting married and I don't want to hear anything more about it."

Finally she subsided into grim and unbelieving silence. He pulled the car up to the front of the house in a whoosh of gravel, kept hold of her wrist even as they went in through the wide stately doors. Gary knew he would find his parents in the drawing room. They sat there together deep in conversation. Gary stood before them like a man possessed.

"We don't care if you approve. We just want you to know we're getting

373

married."

Instantly Victoria folded Tovah into a maternal embrace. "My dear, I'm *so* pleased! This was what I'd hoped might happen all along."

His father's response was more in accord with what he had expected. "Gary, this is impulsive and precipitous." And then to his wife, "Why am *I* always the last to know?"

Victoria addressed her husband with a loving smile. "Precipitous, Cliff? Haven't you always told me, dear, that you declared your intentions to my uncle on the first day you met me?"

"That was different," Clifford said. Then, with a touch of the old charm, he said, "I guess it's always different." With quiet ceremony he kissed the girl. "Welcome to our family."

Something about this reception had put Gary off balance. "I know the world is in terrible shape—"

"Turmoil," Tovah chimed in.

"We don't want much. A civil ceremony."

"I can't do anything until I find out about my family."

"I know there will be some elements, Mother, Father, that will be bound to disapprove, but I—"

Victoria cut them off. "Nonsense. Nonsense. Nonsense. You don't give in to those people. You defeat them by staring them down." She rang for Priest and then said, in the clear, almost haughty, voice with which she used to ask for the horses to be saddled up, "We'll be having a wedding soon, Priest. Rather a grand one, I should think."

As Priest began to beam, she went serenely on, "I know that we're still in the grip of shortages, but I'm sure you can put something adequate together. A sitdown dinner for five hundred. Dancing, of course. Iced swans. Champagne fountains. That sort of thing."

"Just like the old days, Mrs. Creighton!"

"Five hundred?" Cliff echoed. "Victoria, really!"

"We'll combine the marriage with your eightieth birthday, dearest."

"I'm eighty-one."

"Round numbers are always nicer. I want everyone to come. Tovah, I wish I could offer you my own wedding dress, but let me tell you the story of what happened to it. . . ."

The next three weeks were filled with the kind of arrangements that plague any family that decides upon a big wedding. Victoria's elegant desk in the drawing room overflowed with list upon list. Pansy and Priest called in their children and their children's children to run errands all over the city. The house was full from morning till night with caterers, dressmakers, pastry cooks, bandleaders, engravers, florists. Tempers flared. Priest had his first tantrum in over a decade. "I will not," he proclaimed, "I will not allow Spam, in any form, to be served under my roof. I don't care how much brandy it's laced with."

"It's not your roof," Pansy snapped. And he wouldn't speak to her for a week.

Clifford found it convenient to enjoy a revived interest in his financial and

374

real-estate holdings, and though the office on Green Street had been functioning smoothly for years without his personal supervision, almost every day now he felt called upon to check on one detail or another.

Victoria, accustomed to triumph in all things, went through her own dark night of the soul on a fateful Tuesday morning when armed with a yardstick and in the company of two cantankerous caterers, she realized it couldn't be done. The terraces of the Creighton estate were simply not large enough for a sitdown dinner for five hundred. She went into her bedroom and locked the door, emerging an hour and a half later dry-eyed and determined. She called the engravers, canceled the invitations, and sent out telegrams for a reception and dance, not for five but six hundred people.

It would take shape then as an autumn wedding with a groaning buffet, the most lavish they could procure, and banks of golden chrysanthemums—not just a beginning of a new life but the harvest of the old.

And another crisis was averted almost before it had begun. Victoria and Tovah had been deep in discussion about wedding apparel—Tovah insisting that because of the war she didn't want, didn't need, and couldn't use a wedding dress—when three messengers from Sung Wing On struggled in with a huge chest of silks. It was the first wedding gift, and another twenty-five telegrams went out to every last relative of the Sung clan that Victoria could remember.

Then the day came—a sunny, golden Sunday in late October. The wedding, a private one in an upstairs study, was gone in a euphoric tearful instant. The festivities began.

Belle Bauer strode in a half hour early, huffing under the weight of a twenty-pound sack of sugar. "No, no, get out of my way. I don't need any help." She went straight through to the kitchen and dropped it with a thump at Pansy's feet. "I don't know if your connections are as good as mine," she whispered to the startled woman, "but Coca-Cola keeps pretty good control of some things."

The gates of the estate were swung open and on either side of the gravel drive photographers gathered to snap distinguished guests as they arrived. The Huntingtons, the Chandlers, the Pattons, the Dominguezes, the Wilsons, and here was Paulette Goddard on the arm of a smiling Indian. "Paramahansa Yogananda," she told a reporter. "And be sure you get the spelling right." Four Englishmen arrived together—three of middle age, one a startlingly young boy. They relished the ohs and ahs that went up about them. "That's Christopher Isherwood and his boyfriend. Can you imagine him bringing a child like that along? And there's Huxley and—what's his name?—Gerald Heard. I hear he's the second most intelligent man in the world." "Yeah, who's the first then?" an impudent reporter queried. It was A. J. Cassidy, replaced as a broadcaster by Iris Bauer Sung, working now "city-side" for the *Daily News*.

"I don't know. He must be the only one who isn't here."

Huxley fixed them with an elegant, nearsighted stare. "Laughter is a sign of sexual attraction," he informed them primly, and went on in to discover what he could about California society.

Victoria had been serious when she had said this was to be a tribute to

Clifford as well as the young couple. Her guest list reached far back into the past. As the grounds filled, the party seemed to be made up of three parts: the White Protestant cream of Pasadena society, the remnants of the Spanish land-grant families taking strength now from new Mexican blood, and glamorous representatives of the East. Sung Wing On, his family and friends, including Anna May Wong, held glittering court at the far end of the terrace.

And it was from opposite ends of that fabled promontory that Raoul Ortiz and George Sung caught sight of each other at the same instant. Each walked forward to greet the other. As they met their hands joined involuntarily, and it was Raoul who turned it into an *abrazo*. Then, their wives were at their sides.

"I hear your show all the time," Raoul said to Iris. "You're good."

"I read about *you* in the newspapers. You've got a big foundation now," George said to Raoul.

Raoul reached for Maria and squeezed her to him. "I couldn't have done it without this one. She's the one who does the work."

Maria smiled and delivered a little joke. "The hens are beginning to crow," she said softly to Iris.

"That's a good line," Iris said. "Don't be surprised if you hear me use it soon."

George said quietly to Raoul, "You want to have lunch next week?" And Raoul nodded yes.

A small army of waiters assaulted the guests with every manner of refreshment. Down on the tennis courts the first of two bands struck up. The young people started to jitterbug. Raoul's grandson, Emiliano, and his date for the day quickly became the center of a circle of admirers as they demonstrated the Latino variations on the Lindy. The older generation shrewdly took this opportunity to find the best seats along the edge of the terrace where they could look down on the dancing.

Victoria, as she circulated, making sure everyone was content and taken care of, came suddenly upon Maria Magdalena Ortiz Smith. The two women gazed at each other with frank enjoyment.

"My husband is with your husband, I believe," Magdalena said. "But I thought I would stay out here and watch the dancing. What a celebration. Thank you for inviting us."

"How could we not?"

Magdalena silently acknowledged the truth of that and drained her glass. Their eyes went together to Raoul, who with the force of his personality had created a little eddy in the glittering crowd.

"He looks fine, doesn't he?" Magdalena said.

"Very impressive," Victoria agreed.

Shyness perhaps, or circumspection, kept them from saying anything further, but each woman remembered the squalling brat flung up to these latitudes on a Mexican freighter. Their heads turned then and they looked down at the tennis court to where the young people were dancing.

At the further end of the court, away from Emiliano's zoot-suit display, a tiny whirling dervish was the center of a frenzy of motion.

376

"Who *is* that person?" Magdalena said.

It was a diminutive blonde dancing with one of Gary's veteran friends, who, they could see from this distance, was already red-faced and out of breath.

"Doesn't that have to be Katarina Sung?"

"It can't be," Magdalena said, but it was.

The two women watched until the music ended. In the relative calm that followed they heard Sung's voice, clear and unmistakable. "You want to sit down now?"

Katarina stamped her heel and shook her head with an emphatic no.

"I teach those boys how to dance," she shouted. "They don't know old country steps. Ai-ya."

Was it their imagination or did the old man answer, "Ride 'em, cowgirl"?

Stealing a few moments alone in the gazebo, Gary and Tovah looked out upon the throng.

"I think what my mother meant to do was show you all of it at once. The diversity, the change. I don't know how to say it. It needs somebody to say it."

"There's an irony in this," his bride said. "If my family were here, I'm not sure that they'd approve."

"Do you miss them, dearest? Are you unhappy?"

"No, today I'm not. I want to live for a hundred years."

But in life as in parties it is fated for some people not to have a good time. Ruth Creighton Mariné hated this afternoon and all that it meant. She was disgusted with her family and disappointed with her son, who had hung back and sulked and not done his share with her mother-in-law. She beckoned Lex imperiously and greeted him with "Why must it always be *I* who must take the responsibility? Why must it be I who always cares for your *abuela*? You must look after the Señora for a while. I still follow my duty to our boys."

The boys of whom she spoke were Gary's friends from the hospital who were taking every advantage of the drinks and refreshments.

"Ah *shit!*" one of them exclaimed as Ruth approached them. "Look who's bearing down on us." They had no place to hide their champagne.

"Come on, this is a party. She can't say anything. We'll present a united front."

They had reckoned without Ruth's determination and their front collapsed under her strong artillery.

"Boys, what are you thinking of?" she volleyed at them. "You must not endanger your recovery by this kind of indulgence. Wait here without moving and I'll see that you're brought some warm milk and soda crackers."

But as soon as her back was turned they beat a fast retreat to a secluded vine-covered arbor beyond the tennis court where they spent the rest of the day sending out scouts for additional supplies.

All great celebrations have a life of their own—nervous beginnings, ends sometimes tinged with melancholy. With luck and the right guests there may come a moment when time is enchanted. And this enchanted time came over the party now. The first band, exhausted, packed up and went home. The second one came on, fresh, with new tunes. The cake was cut, more champagne opened. The bridal couple were waved away in a blizzard of rice. Priest moved urbanely through the crowd, lighting up banks of Chinese lanterns which lent a pink and golden glow to the violet twilight. Some guests, the duller ones, began to go home. Those who were determined to enjoy themselves settled in for what they hoped would be a very long evening indeed. The noise level increased. Suddenly a pack of little children, who had been invisibly on their best behavior, started up a game of tag—or was it keep-away—which took them to the farthest reaches both of the mansion and of the grounds. Mrs. Otis Chandler was scared out of her wits when, as she wrestled with her corset in a luxurious powder room, one of the youngest of Sung's great grandchildren sprang from under the ruffled dressing table with a Chinese war cry.

Out in the arbor Gary's buddies were blotto. One of them had disgraced himself in an adjacent rock garden. This led them to realize that they were cut off behind the lines from any normal exit. Remembering their more active days in the service, they began to plan a tactical foray down one of the old Indian trails that would take them across the slope to the foot of the Vista del Arroyo. Precisely how they were going to do this with their canes, crutches, and one wheelchair was not yet clear to them, but they were confident that a few more reinforcements in the shape of a further supply of champagne and wedding cake would provide the necessary inspiration. And they sent out another runner.

Down on the tennis court the two stars of the floor, Emiliano Ortiz and Katarina Sung, had been forced for an hour or so to take a back seat to the radiant bride and courtly groom who had requested many a romantic ballad and Viennese waltz. There had been the obligatory family dancing: Ruth Mariné propelling her reluctant father from one end of the court to the other. The bride in the awkward arms of Lex. And Gary gallantly holding the Señora in a modified version of the bunny hug—both her bony hands on his strong shoulders, both his strong hands spanning her still slim waist, lifting her so that her feet dangled a full four inches off the ground, sweeping her in a gentle waltz. But now all that was over.

Katarina eyed the elusive Emiliano with a bold challenge. "I want to fly," she rasped at him. "Fly me in the air like you do the others." And soon they were out there, the perfect couple. Emiliano's drape-shape moved like flamed lightning as he hurled Katarina's compact little body through his knees and over his head. The crowd on the court went wild.

Victoria's feet hurt. Her face kept its calm beauty as she moved among the older contingent, stopped to give charming interviews to Matt Weinstock, Erskine Johnson, Virginia Wright, and other journalists. The "movie stars" had already, of course, dealt with Hedda and Lolly. Although Clifford was bearing up bravely, it was Victoria who saw the Huntingtons and Chandlers to the door. Now, returning to the terrace, she sought out Clifford and found him already seated with Magdalena and Sung.

"I don't know how you do it," Magdalena said. "I'm ready for the old folks' home by now, but you look as fresh as the bride herself."

"You'd better watch out for your husband." Victoria gave her a hoydenish grin. "He's giving quite a rush to the Señora."

They looked tó where the urbane and lanky Mr. Smith was doing his best to respond appropriately as the Señora tapped him on the cheek with her fan. Even from this distance their gestures showed they were exchanging compliments in Spanish.

Sung, who had dressed for this occasion in long blue silk skirts, let out a raucous laugh and deliberately thickening his accent, said, gesturing to the courts, "My wife act that way I send her to Srlave Marlket."

As they looked at him a trifle askance he laughed a full-bodied laugh of total contentmcnt, "And I get good plrice too. You bet."

"I'll get some sandwiches to go with that champagne," Victoria said a little drily and moved away from them, her steps firm, her figure graceful and still young.

Clifford's eyes misted over. "That woman was the girl of my dreams." Then he said with quick kindness, putting his hand on Magdalena's arm, "You, too, my dear, you were a very good dream."

· "We both got what we wanted," she said. "I'm so happy now."

Sung looked at them with shrewd understanding and, dropping his accent, said quietly, "The gods have smiled on us, but we have made this place our own Mountain of Gold."

Lex Mariné, leaning against the balustrade in the half-shadow, had watched the trio and had caught a few of their words.

They had done it. They had "gotten out." But these thoughts were rudely interrupted, as most of his thoughts were, by his mother.

"I can't count on you to do anything," Ruth said.

"She's having a wonderful time, Mother," he said wearily. "I would only be *de trop*."

She cut him off. "It's time to go. We've made our appearance. I can't lend my presence to this travesty any longer."

He tensed himself. "Mother, I'm not going home."

In a gesture that was to haunt him and infuriate him for the rest of his life, she clamped her fingers around her heavy gold cross.

"What is it this time? A chorus girl? Mountaineering? Retirement to Death Valley? I can't spend the rest of my life—"

"You won't have to, Mother, because I'm not going home at all."

Ruth looked at him aghast.

"I loved that girl, Mother, and you knew it," Lex said. "You won that, but I can't let it happen again. Suppose there's no one else for me to love."

"What are you saying?" Ruth demanded. "You're insane. Have you been drinking again?"

"Three glasses of champagne in four hours. I'm leaving, Mother."

"You don't have a penny," she railed. "Not of your own. Your father left all his money to me. And the Señora is incompetent, as you well know. Don't look for any money from your grandfather!"

"I don't care," he said.

"You can't go anywhere. *You* can't do anything! You're twenty-nine and

379

you've never done a day's work in your life. What makes you think you can earn a living?"

"Maybe it's time for me to start . . . a lot of things." Lex gestured about him. His left arm extended down the Arroyo and his right pointed due west. "It's all out there, Mother, the rest of the world is out there. This whole place is a story, and it's something I own. That's something you can't take away from me. It's our story and I can tell it. And I can tell it to all of them."

She stamped her foot in exasperation. "What are you going to do," his mother said scathingly, and he could hear the ten-year-old spoiled little girl in her voice, *"paint it?"*

"I'm not sure yet, but I know where it is and I know how it starts."

A look of cunning crossed her face. Lex realized with a flash of inward amusement that it was she who had been drinking, not he. As plainly as if she had said it he read her primitive thoughts. *I'll let him tough it out for a few days. He'll have to come crawling back.* She turned on her heel and walked away. He heard her voice as she rudely interrupted the Señora and Mr. Smith.

"It's time to go," she rapped out. "We've made our appearance. I can't—"

Lex began to make his way through the diminishing crowds to say goodbye to his grandmother. Victoria was at the center of an admiring group, a picture of charm and dignity, the perfect hostess. But for a blinding moment Lex saw her—he saw her with the radiant vision of all the family stories—Victoria Landon, a "new woman," shocking the Valley Hunt Club with her riding breeches, starting new lives over and over again, stepping onto the porch of her romantic beach cottage at the age of fifty-one, glowing triumphantly with the flush of new life.

Lex turned to leave. His mind tentatively touched the problems of tomorrow. He had two thousand dollars in a personal bank account and no more than fifty in his wallet, but he'd drive west tonight and he was sure something would turn up. He paused at the French doors before going in for one last look at what he was leaving. He gave the old people, still sitting together, one last, private, tremulous half-wave.

The visions came over him again. Magdalena, how she must have looked then, stubborn girl walking north hundreds of miles through uncharted sand. In one hand holding her cameo, a gift from a young boarder, and in the other, the deeds to her oil land. Reclining on rose petals with her long-lost lover.

Sung Wing On, orphan, a gritty little con man keeping his mermaid happy with quarters as he walked the length of the State. With enough lust and more for two wives. Finally, a man of wealth and prosperity surrounded by descendants who would guarantee him immortality.

And Clifford Abercrombie Creighton, red-eyed, rye-swollen, riding his California train. Riding pell-mell into the hunt that was to bring him untold fortune. And riding, finally, eternally, on Black Barb, Victoria at his side on her Appaloosa, across the clean open land of the Arroyo.

The three out on the terrace didn't notice that their observer had left. Wordlessly, Clifford refilled their glasses. They toasted themselves, the past, the present, the future.

ACKNOWLEDGMENTS

THE author wishes to acknowledge Vivian Carothers and Antonia Turman for their historical and sociological expertise, which they so generously contributed to this book. Particular thanks are also extended to Frederico Casteneda for his detailed scholarship on the evolution of the *mariachi,* and to John Espey for permission to assimilate his earlier material on the development of Pasadena. Carolyn See has been gracious in sharing her knowledge of Sonoran folklore and Lisa See Kendall equally so with her research on the Chinese in early California. Joe Kanon and Nancy Perlman have been patient and meticulous editors. Without all these fine minds, *Lotus Land* could not have been written. Any distortions or inaccuracies are, of course, the sole responsibility of the author.

NOTES

Sometime in the last quarter of the nineteenth century, Fong See On made his way down the center of California, selling tickets for a look at his stuffed "mermaid." He was then about twelve years old. He lived to become one of the foremost Chinese citizens of Los Angeles.

Mary Austin, author of the California classic *The Land of Little Rain,* was afflicted with a periodic nervous disability—rumored to have been of a sexual nature—which, on occasion, drove her into public displays of hysteria.

The author has taken the liberty of moving the bar concession owned by the forebear of Senator Barry Goldwater of Arizona and his son, Congressman Barry Goldwater, Jr., of California, from the Bella Union Hotel to the Pico House.

Book I

The Valley Hunt Club was so named because many prominent members of early Pasadena society enjoyed riding to hounds. On one such hunt a coyote was brought to earth in the Post Office.

The Logan–Fisher family is loosely based on the Campbell–Johnstones, members of the British gentry, who played a leading role in Pasadena life; however, the details of Percy Logan–Fisher's death are entirely fictional.

Alessandro de Mariné's first name is used here in tribute to Helen Hunt Jackson's famous novel of California and land-grant life, *Ramona.* Mrs. Jackson felt that the Spanish "Alejandro" would confuse her readers.

Because they were at first forbidden to do business above ground, Chinese traders in Los Angeles conducted their affairs in a series of underground tunnels, some of which still exist.

Although the date has been changed, early Los Angeles did experience an epidemic of the plague. It was brought by a sailor to a boardinghouse on Clara Street. Seven people died there in two days. There was a human cordon, and serious attempts made to burn down Chinatown. A total of thirty-nine fatalities occurred. In the boardinghouse on Clara Street, the sole survivor was a toddler of Mexican descent.

Book II

On several occasions in California the Chinese were subjected to physical violence, ranging from simple expulsion to vigilante hangings.

Book III

Although Magdalena Ortiz would have grown up with the *norteño* tradition of Mexican folk music, the Señora and Raoul are equally enamored of the more sophisticated *mariachi,* which had its origins in Central Mexico. For the purist, it is worth noting that the horns of the *mariachi* were added much later, in 1934, to facilitate radio broadcasting.

"The dude, habitué of street corners in every land, is there called *lagartijo* (lizard), because he basks so lazily in the sunshine. But how much less disagreeable to be called a *lagartijo* than a dude." *(An American Girl in Mexico,* by Elizabeth Visère McGary [New York: Dodd, Mead, 1904], pp. 33–34).

Probably the most accessible, and certainly the most readable, account of Saint Joseph of Copertino's life constitutes Chapter X ("The Flying Monk") of Norman Douglas's *Old Calabria* (pp. 93–100 of the Modern Library Edition). That a Spanish-Californian land-grant family should have taken him as patron is probably explained by the fact that in 1645 the Lord High Admiral of Castile, at the time Ambassador of Spain to the Vatican, together with his lady, witnessed one of Saint Joseph's flights in Assisi and thus helped to spread the Italian's fame to Spain. No more appropriate protector could be imagined for the even longer "flight" from the Old to the New World. As late as World War II, devout aviators wore Saint Joseph of Copertino medals in the interest of their safety.

Book IV

Although the incident occurred in World War II rather than World War I, it is true that Air Force pilot William Bowers gave a flying lesson to a trainee, instructed him to "do a slow roll," and then fell out of the plane. Bowers lived to tell the tale and went on to write many successful Hollywood motion pictures, including the author's particular favorite, the cult film *The Last Time I Saw Archie*.

Book V

California laws against miscegenation applying to the marriage of Chinese and Caucasians remained in force through the first third of this century.

Although their immigration had been legalized, the indignities that the Chinese, particularly women and children, were forced to endure at Angel Island in San Francisco Bay led many Orientals to choose illegal entry as the wiser alternative.

Book VI

For the duration of World War II and after, the Vista del Arroyo Hotel was commandeered for use as a hospital. It is now being renovated to house Pasadena's Juvenile Court.

Catalog

If you are interested in a list of fine Paperback
books, covering a wide range of subjects
and interests, send your name and address,
requesting your free catalog, to:

McGraw-Hill Paperbacks
1221 Avenue of Americas
New York, N.Y. 10020